# 中国古代官制和英用語集

（職官組織図, 英和索引付き）

Japanese-English Glossary of the Bureaucratic System of
Ancient China -- with the Organization Chart and
English-Japanese Index

藤田敏正
*Fujita Toshimasa*

冨谷　至
*Tomiya Itaru*

編

昭和堂

# 序

冨谷 至

　2006年から2011年にわたる5年間，科学研究費基盤研究(S)を受けて国際共同研究「東アジアにおける儀礼と刑罰」を進めてきた。本書『中国古代官制和英用語集』は，その研究成果の一つである。

　共同研究の主たる目的は，東アジアにおける礼的秩序と法的秩序の有機的連関を明らかにし，そこから西洋社会とは異なる東洋的法環境，法秩序を浮かび上がらせることだったが，今ひとつの研究の目的もあった。それは，東洋学の国際化，アジアの東洋学から世界の Oriental studies を目指すことである。

　中国を中心として広がる漢字文化圏に関する歴史，文学，思想の研究は，我が日本においては，長い伝統と世界に誇る水準を有している。しかしながら，それが欧米で認知されているのかといえば，残念ながらそうではない。否，東洋学そのものが欧米の歴史学界でしかるべき地位を得ているとは言えず，東アジア史は周辺史の一部に過ぎず，研究者層も決して多くはない。

　かかる状況を招く原因は，やはり我々が欧米に向かって東洋学の成果を十分に発信してこなかったからであるが，それは漢字文化圏の制度，思想などの専門用語をどう英語に翻訳するのか，そこに困難な問題が横たわっているからにほかならない。論文の英文要旨を作成するにあたり専門学術用語，制度用語，官制用語の英文表記は必ずしも決まっているわけではなく，どの様に表記するかに我々は頭を悩ましてきたのである。

　我々の国際共同研究では，その成果の外部評価として，また成果の発信のために，積極的にヨーロッパの学術機関との協力のもと，シンポジウムをオランダライデン大学，スウェーデン王立アカデミー等で行ってきた。かかる東洋学の国際化をめざす成果の一端と

してここに本書を出版することにする。

　本書は，古代中国の特に西漢時代の官制体系，官職名の英文表記を内容とする。もとより，中国全時代の官職名の英文表記，さらには官制にかぎらず法制，税制，礼制などの領域に関する同様の英語表記に取り組むべきであることは，十分に承知している。今後，引き続き，法制用語の和英用語集も作成していかねばならないが，本書はそのまず第一歩としての成果報告として寛容していただければ幸甚である。

　また官制に関しても，漢だけでなく以後の時代の英語表記を考えていかねばならない。ただ，いうまでもなくそれぞれの官職が担う内容，つまり職掌は時代とともに変化していく。畢竟，同一官職名でも時代によって英語表記は異なり，異なった用語を準備せねばならない。しかし，中国の官僚制が始まった漢のそれを基準として以後の展開があるとするならば，まず漢の官職から始めるのが正攻法だと考える。以後の時代の英文表記は，この成果を参考，修正することで進めていけるのではないだろうか。

　本書は，翻訳家の藤田敏正氏との共編である。藤田氏と私は定期的に会合をもち，官職の職務内容，その序列を確認し，そこから欧米における官職のどれに相当するのか，また対応する英語名がないならば，そういった仕事は英語ではどのように言われているのかを，英文百科事典等から引き出して考究した。本書第2章「職官名対訳作成資料」はその考証過程を提示したものであり，決して適当な訳語を適当に当てはめるのではなく，かならずその根拠，英語における使用例を確認して，初めて用語を確定するという藤田氏のきわめて実証的な方法を示す一端である。氏はその翻訳の方法において，私が最も信頼を寄せる翻訳家なのである。

　また本書は Burton Watson 博士の『史記』，『漢書』の英文翻訳を大いに利用し，参照した。Watson 氏の翻訳がいかに優れているのかは，本書でも言及しているが，第4章「職官名関連和英表現集」は，Watson 氏の官職名の翻訳と日文を対照させ，また官職に関連した表現を示し，英文要約作成などに役立てばと考えて設けた一章である。採用した表現は一部であり，すべてを網羅しているわけでもない，もっと多く優れた表現，なるほど英語ではこう表現するのかといういくつもの例を取り上げたかったが，一部にとどまって

## 序

いること，これもご寛容いただきたい。

　もう三十数年前になるだろうか，私は京都大学文学部東洋史学科の学生であったとき，非常勤講師として中国文学を担当されていた博士の授業に列席していた。今は無き文学部旧館の中国文学研究室で『春秋左氏伝』の晋重耳に関する箇所を読んでいた。博士の日本語は実に堪能で，また吉川幸次郎先生に学んだ博士の日本の中国学に対する理解も並大抵のものではなかった。講読は中国語で読んでいたが，私が担当したある時に，曖昧な解釈を質された先生の言葉をいまでも記憶している。
「君，その部分をちょっと訓読してごらん」

　とまれ，本書が世界の Oriental studies 確立に少しでも貢献できることを願ってやまない。

2011 年初春

# 目次

序 　　　　　　　　　　　　　　　　　　　　　　　　　　　　　　　i

第1章　漢代職官組織図 Government Official Organization Chart of the Han Period 　　　1

第2章　職官名対訳作成資料 　　　　　　　　　　　　　　　　　　　　　9

第3章　各職位の職掌・属官（『漢書』百官公卿表，『續漢書』百官志） 　　　51

第4章　職官名関連和英表現集 Japanese-English Expressions Related to the Official Titles (An index to Watson translations of the *Han Shu* and *Shi ji*) 　　　69

付録
　　1.　職官名英訳参照英文集 　　　　　　　　　　　　　　　　　　　181
　　2.　Dubs ほかの研究者による職官名英訳比較表 　　　　　　　　　272
　　3.　職官名対訳確定作業の要約 　　　　　　　　　　　　　　　　315

職官名和英索引 　　　　　　　　　　　　　　　　　　　　　　　　　321
職官名英和索引 　　　　　　　　　　　　　　　　　　　　　　　　　326
職官名キーワード索引 　　　　　　　　　　　　　　　　　　　　　　331
職官名関連和英表現集英和索引 　　　　　　　　　　　　　　　　　　344

# 第 1 章　漢代職官組織図

## Government Official Organization Chart of the Han Period

石高色分け
- 中 2000
- 2000 石
- 比 2000 石
- 1000 石
- 比 1000 石
- 比 800
- 600
- 比 600
- 400
- 比 400
- 比 300
- 200
- 不明

## 三公 three highest ministers*

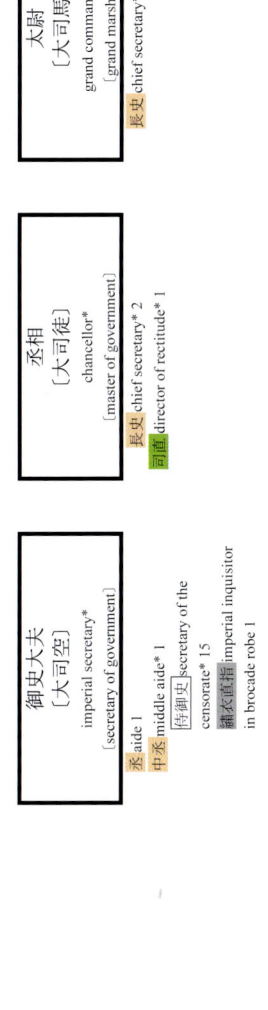

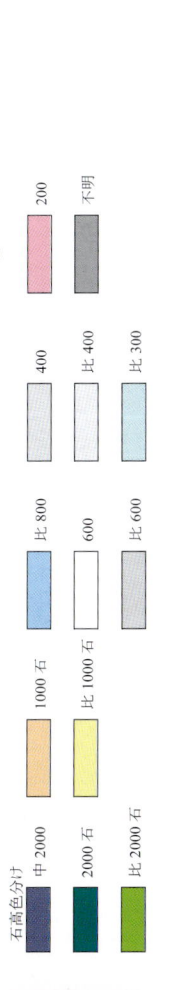

## 九卿 nine highest ministers*

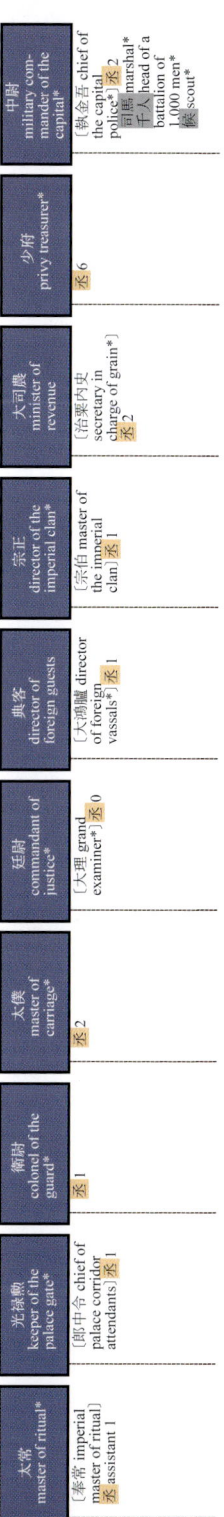

*印は Watson 訳変更なし。[ ] 内は別称

# Organizational Chart

## 太常 master of ritual*
[奉常 imperial master of ritual*] 丞 assistant 1

- 太樂令 grand musician
- 太祝令 grand invocator*
- 太宰令 grand servant
- 太史令 grand historian*

## 光祿勳 keeper of the palace gate*
[郎中令 chief of palace corridor attendants*] 丞 1

- 太中大夫 grand palace counselor
- 中大夫 palace counselor*
  - [光祿大夫 counselor to the keeper of the palace gate*]
- 諫大夫 admonisher*
- 五官中郎將 senior officer of palace corridor attendants at the "Five Bureaus"
  - 中郎 palace gentleman*
  - 侍郎 attendant in the inner palace*
  - 郎中 palace corridor attendant

## 衛尉 colonel of the guard*
丞 1

- 公車司馬令 chief marshal of the palace gates
- 衛士令 chief of the palace guard
- 旅賁令 chief of envoys
  - [屯司馬 marshal of the stationed unit
  - 衛司馬 marshal of the palace guard
  - 騎 scout*]

## 太僕 master of carriage*
丞 2

- 大廄令 chief of the imperial stables
- 未央令 chief of carriage and horses for the Eternal Palace
- 家馬令 chief of the imperial household's horses
  - [騶馬令 chief of the emperor's horses]
- 車府令 chief of the office of carriage

## 廷尉 commandant of justice*
[大理 grand examiner*] 丞 0

- 正監 superintendent of the center
- 左監 superintendent of the left
  - [左平 judge of the left]
- 右監 superintendent of the right
  - [右平 judge of the right]

## 典客 director of foreign guests
[大鴻臚 director of foreign vassals*] 丞 1

- 行人令 chief of messengers
  - [大行令 grand messenger*]
- 譯官令 chief of interpreters
- 別火令 chief of the maintenance of the sacred fire
- 都部長 head of the provincial offices in the capital

## 宗正 director of the imperial clan*
[宗伯 master of the imperial clan*] 丞 1

- 都司空令 chief of criminal affairs in the imperial family
- 內官長 head of the office of weights and measures
- 諸公主家令 steward in the household of the princess
- 諸公主門尉 commander of gatekeepers in the household of the princess

## 大司農 minister of revenue
[治粟內史 secretary in charge of grain*] 丞 2

- 太倉令 chief of the central granary
- 太行令 transport office for equalizing prices
- 平準令 chief of the office for the balanced standard
- 都內令 chief of granaries in the capital

## 少府 privy treasurer*
丞 6

- 尚書令 master of palace writers
- 符節令 chief of the imperial credentials
- 太醫令 grand physician for the imperial household
- 太官令 grand butler of the imperial household

## 中尉 military commander of the capital*
[執金吾 chief of the capital police*] 丞 2

- 司馬 marshal, head of a battalion of 1,000 men*
- 候 scout*
- 中壘令 commander of the security force
- 寺互令 chief of interoffice liaison
- 武庫令 chief of the arsenal*
- 都船令 chief of the water police

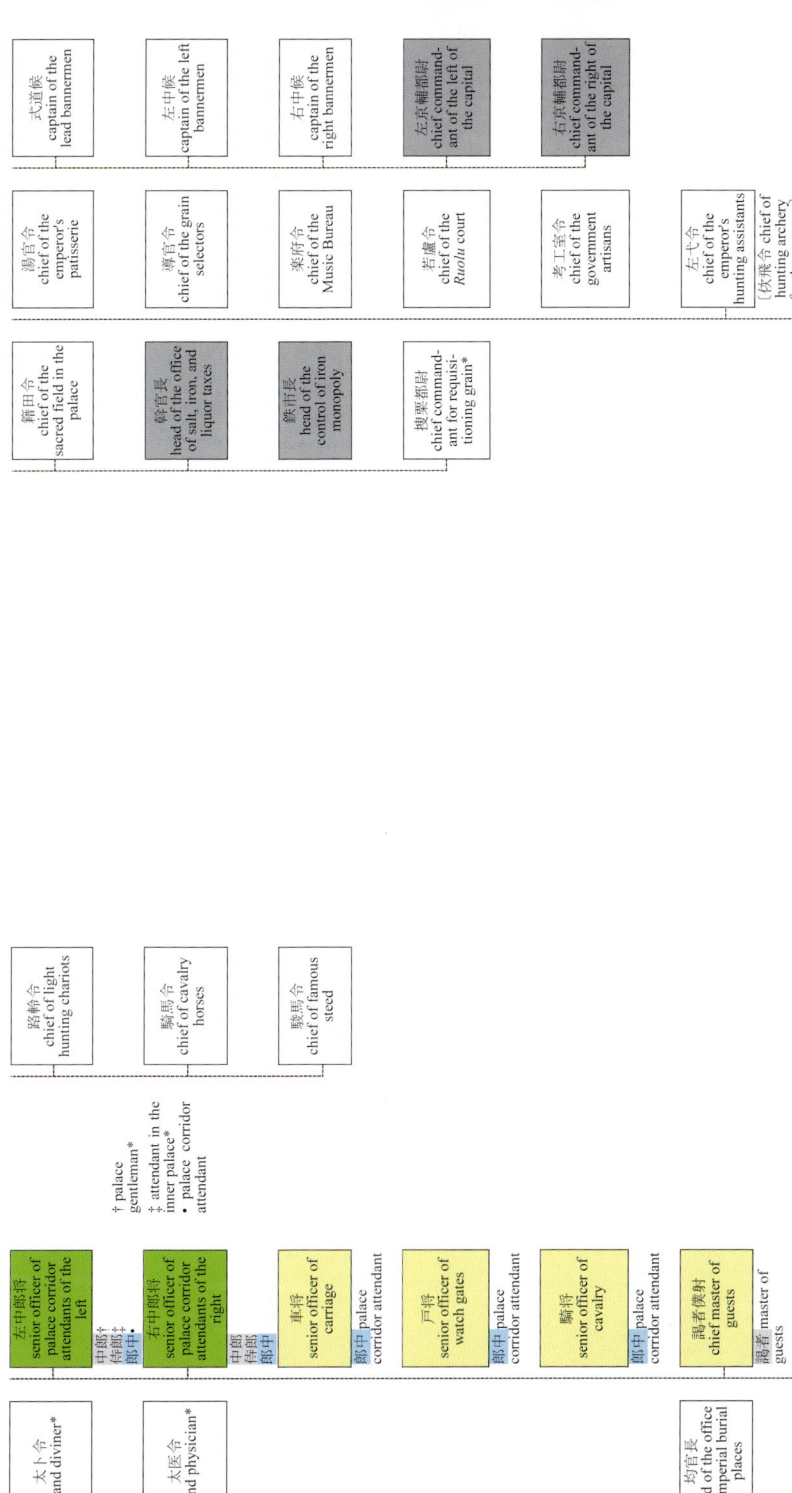

居室令 chief of the detention room in the palace

(保居令 supervisor of the detention room)

昆台令 chief of the *Kuntai* detention room

[甘泉居室令 chief of the detention room in the Palace of Sweet Springs]

左司空令 chief of compulsory labour of the left

右司空令 chief of compulsory labour of the right

東織令 chief of the eastern weaving room

西織令 chief of the western weaving room

東園匠令 chief of the craftsmen of the imperial tombs

‡ keeper of the Rendezvous Gate* (junior officer of the picked troops)

‡ chief commandant of cavalry for Feather and Forest Guard

† (senior officer of palace corridor attendants for the picked troops)

† senior officer of palace corridor attendants for the Feather and Forest Guard

期門僕射 archery captain at the Rendezvous Gate

(虎賁中郎將)† 期門 (虎賁郎)‡

羽林中郎將† 羽林騎都尉‡

羽林郎 horseman of the Feather and Forest Guard*

都水長 head of water control at the imperial parks

諸廟寢官令 chief of the inner chamber of the funerary temple

諸廟園官令 chief of the park of the funerary temple

諸廟食官令 chief of food offerings at the funerary temple

博士* erudit*

| 庖人長 head of cooks | 都水長 head of water control at the imperial parks | 均官長 head of the office of imperial burial places | 上林十池監 supervisor of the maintenance of ponds at the Imperial Forest Park | 中書謁者令 master of documents and guests [中書令 chief of palace writers*] | 黃門令 chief of the Yellow Gate | 鉤盾令 chief of the control of the imperial parks | 尚方令 chief of the royal craftsmen |

| 二千石の官 | | | | | | | | | | | |
|---|---|---|---|---|---|---|---|---|---|---|---|
| 太子大傅 grand tutor to the heir apparent* | 太子少傅 lesser tutor to the heir apparent* | 将作大匠 master of construction works | 詹事 chamberlain to the empress and the heir apparent | 大長秋 supervisor of the harem* | 典屬國 director of dependent states* | 水衡都尉 chief commandant of the palace gardens | 左馮翊 left prefect of the capital | 京兆尹 prefect of the capital | 右扶風 right prefect of the capital* | | |

司隸都尉へ →

| | | | | | | | | | |
|---|---|---|---|---|---|---|---|---|---|
| | | | | | | | | | 御府令 chief of royal garments |
| | | | | | | | | | 永巷令 chief of the Long Halls Palace |
| | | | | | | | | | [掖庭令 chief of the women's quarters] |
| | | | | | | | | | 內者令 chief of the palace interior |
| | | | | | | | | | 宦者令 chief of eunuchs |

太子門大夫 lord of the gate to the heir apparent | 太子門大夫 lord of the gate to the heir apparent | 石庫令 chief of stone materials | 太子率更令 chief of the night guard in the household of the heir apparent | | 九譯令 chief of foreign languages | 上林令 chief of the Imperial Forest Park | 廩犧令 chief of grain offerings and animal sacrifices | 長安東市令 chief of the Chang'an East Marketplace | 牧畜令 chief of animal husbandry

[主爵中尉 master of titles military commander** 主爵都尉 master of titles chief commandant*]

[右內史 prefect in charge of the western area of the capital*]

[左內史 prefect in charge of the eastern area of the capital*]

佽飛 assistant 1 騎 scout* 千人 head of a battalion of 1,000 men*

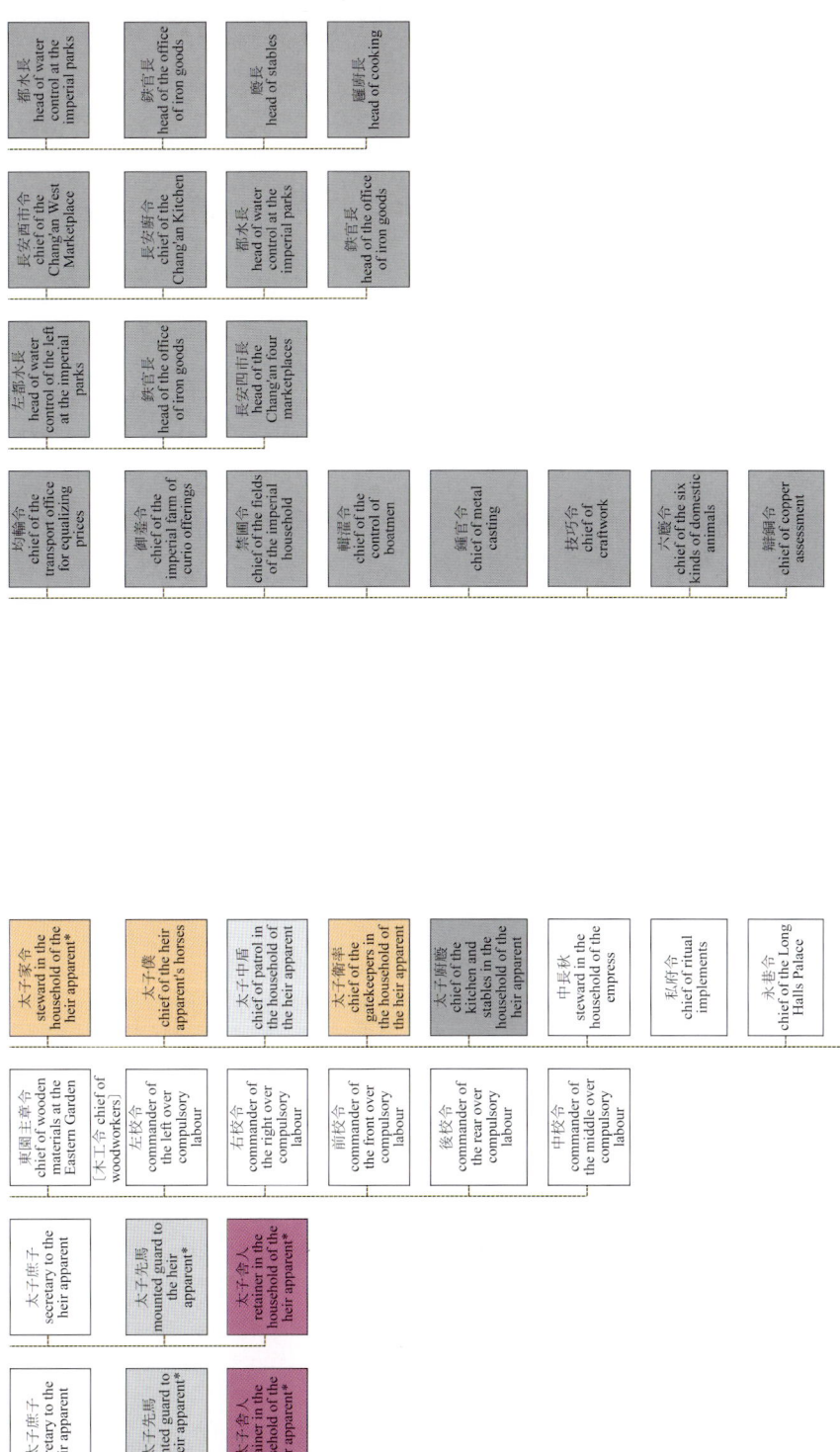

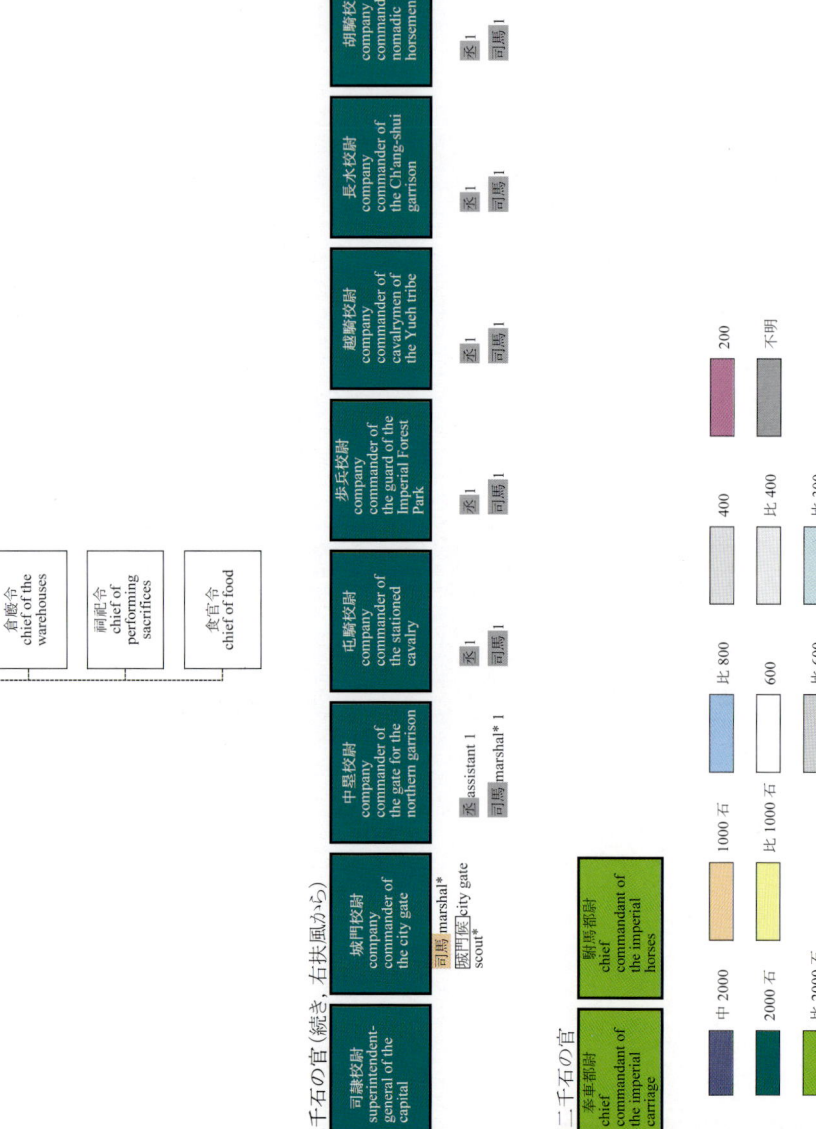

# 第2章　職官名対訳作成資料

凡例

| | |
|---|---|
| 〔　〕 | 職官名別称 |
| 【　】 | 原漢文 |
| [　] | 備考 |
| 〈　〉 | 出典名 |
| * | Watson 訳保存 |
| 太字網かけ 20% | 中二千石の官 |
| 太字網かけ 10% | 二千石の官 |
| 太字(参照表現中) | 英語対訳として採用または援用した語 |
| 下線(参照表現中) | 注意または注目すべき語 |
| Br | Encyclopædia Britannica 2006 Ultimate Reference Suite DVD |
| Gr | Grolier Encyclopedia |
| LDOCE | Longman Dictionary of Contemporary English |
| LgAm | Longman Advanced American Dictionary |
| NSOED | New Shorter Oxford English Dictionary |
| OAD | Oxford American Dictionary |
| OALD | Oxford Advanced Learner's Dictionary |
| RH | Random-House Webster's Unabridged |
| 三コ | 三省堂コンサイス和英または英和 |
| 法律用語対訳集 | 法務省刑事局外国法令研究会, 商事法務研究会, 1995 |
| JPT | 和英翻訳ハンドブック, ジャパンタイムズ, 1987 |
| JPD | 和英翻訳データ, ジャパンタイムズ, 2000 |
| CHJ | Cambridge History of Japan Volume 4, Early Modern Japan, Cambridge University Press, 1991。CHJ のあとの数字はページ数 |
| A ⇒ B | A については B を参照せよの意。特に指定がない限り、B は付録1「職官名英訳参照英文集」中の項目見出し。A が自明のときは省略 |
| (漢〇〇) | 漢書巻〇〇 |
| (史〇〇) | 史記巻〇〇 |

| 職官名 | 英語対訳 | 英訳用参照表現 |
|---|---|---|
| 三公 | three highest ministers* | three highest ministers（漢 63.74）｜three highest officials（漢 68）｜three highest posts in the government（漢 71）｜three highest ministries（漢 78） |
| 丞相〔大司徒〕 | chancellor*〔master of government〕 | chancellor 出現多数。minister of education（漢 67.92）chancellor ⇒ public administration |
| 　長史 | chief secretary* | clerk（漢 54）｜chief secretary（漢 54）｜head secretary（漢 63）｜chief clerk（漢 68.78.74）｜chief secretary（史 7.101.104.107.120.122）｜his clerk（史 109）｜three chief secretaries〔三長史〕（史 122）｜secretaries of the chancellor〔丞相長史〕（史 122） |
| 　司直 | director of rectitude* | director of rectitude（漢 65.92）｜director of rectitude under the chancellor〔丞相司直〕（漢 78）｜director of rectitude in the office of the chancellor〔丞相司直〕（漢 78）｜director of justice（史 104） |
| 太尉〔大司馬〕 | grand commandant*〔grand marshal*〕 | grand commandant（漢 54）｜grand commandant（史 10.108.124）〔grand marshal（漢 54.68.71.78.92.97）｜grand marshal（史 48.91.51.111.117）〕● commandant ⇒ public administration, Br |
| 　長史 | chief secretary* | 丞相下の長史参照。 |
| 御史大夫〔大司空〕 | imperial secretary*〔secretary of government〕 | 〔minister of works（漢 92）〕 |
| 　丞 | aide | served as his [高祖] aide（史 53）｜aide in the imperial stables〔大廐丞〕（史 122）｜aide in the city government of Chang'an〔長安丞〕（史 122）｜palace eunuchs and their assistants〔中官者丞〕（史 9）｜private secretary〔家丞〕（史 107）｜law officer of the city of Shouchun〔寿春の |

10

第2章 職官名対訳作成資料

| 職官名 | 英語対訳 | 英訳用参照表現 |
|---|---|---|
|  |  | 丞](史 118) ｜ the assistant to the imperial butler [大官の丞](漢 65) ｜ a clerk in charge of rites under the grand messenger [大行の治礼丞](漢 78) ｜ 大鴻臚丞 the assistant to the director of foreign vassals（漢 63）｜ as **aide** to the inspector of the garrisons guarding the capital [軍正の丞]（漢 67）｜ the assistant to the magistrate of Mou-ling [県丞]（漢 74） |
| 中丞―侍御史 | middle aide*―secretary of the censorate* | 中丞 **middle aide**（漢 67）｜ middle aide to the minister of agriculture［大司農中丞］（漢 78）｜ middle aide（漢 78）｜ aide to the imperial secretary（史 122）｜ aide of the imperial secretary［御史中丞］（史 122）―**secretary of the censorate**（漢 68.71） |
| 繡衣直指 | imperial inquisitor in brocade robe | 繡衣使者 special envoy in his **brocade robe**（漢 78）<br>直指 **imperial inquisitor**（史 30）｜ Swift and straight is their course（史 117）｜ imperial inquisitor（史 122）<br>直指使者 directly appointed envoy（漢 71） |
| 九卿 | **nine highest ministers*** | nine lower offices of government（漢 54）｜ nine high ministers（漢 67.68.78）｜ **nine highest ministers**（漢 68.史 10.30.122.123）｜ high ministers（漢 68）｜ high ministries（漢 92）｜ nine high officials（漢 74.92）｜ nine highest officers in the government（史 30）｜ nine highest officials（史 122）｜ nine highest ministerial posts（史 122）｜ nine highest offices（史 120）｜ highest officials（史 101）｜ highest ministerial posts（史 103）｜ high minister（史 103）｜ high ministerial posts（史 30）｜ nine lower offices of the government（史 109）｜ high |

11

| 職官名 | 英語対訳 | 英訳用参照表現 |
|---|---|---|
| | | officials(史 122) |
| 中二千石 | **officials of the middle two thousand picul class*** | full two thousand picul official(漢 54)｜two thousand picul class(漢 63)｜**middle two thousand picul class**(漢 68)｜**officials of the middle two thousand picul class**(漢 68)｜two thousand picul officials(漢 71)｜officials of the two thousand picul class(漢 71)｜officials of 2,000 picul rank(史 120)｜2,000 picul official(史 118) |
| 太常〔奉常〕 | **master of ritual*** 〔**imperial master of ritual**〕 | **master of ritual**(漢 65.68.78.史 11.111)〔director of ritual(史 11)〕<br>⇒ master<br>● imperial<br>奉車都尉 chief commandant of the **imperial** carriage(漢 068 霍光・097 外戚伝)<br>⇒ imperial |
| 太楽令 | grand musician | 楽府 Music Bureau(漢 68)<br>楽人 musician(漢 68)<br>楽人 experts of the Music Bureau(漢 97)<br>礼楽がすたれる rites and music fell into disuse(史 121)<br>礼楽を修め興す worked to revive rites and music(史 121)<br>⇒ music<br>⇒ musician<br>⇒ rite/ritual |
| 太祝令 | grand invocator* | **grand invocator**(漢 68)｜master of invocations[太祝](史 28)｜master of invocation[太祝](史 28)<br>● 史 028「封禅」中の太祝の役割<br>祠る sacrifice to smb が主で，酒などを用意して祝宴 feast を司る(幹事をする)ようには見えない。<br>⇒ 太祝<br>● invoke<br>[LgAm] to ask for help from someone |

## 第 2 章 職官名対訳作成資料

| 職官名 | 英語対訳 | 英訳用参照表現 |
|---|---|---|
|  |  | more powerful than you, especially God or a god: *Rev. Moran invoked a blessing.* 祝福を呼び求めた。<br>[RH] 1. to call for with earnest desire; make supplication or pray for: to invoke God's mercy. 2. to call on (a deity, Muse, etc.), as in prayer or supplication.<br>⇒ invoke |
| 太宰令 | grand servant（史 28） | 太宰 grand supervisor（史 28）｜chief steward（史 91）｜master of ceremonies は大行（史 099）<br>〈漢 019A, 師古注〉【太宰即是具食之官】<br>⇒ butler: Europe, history of: The growth of a permanent bureaucracy (the king's **servant**)<br>⇒ 太祝太宰ほか<br>⇒ priest<br>⇒ offer |
| 太史令 | grand historian*（漢 54） | grand historian（漢 54） |
| 太卜令 | grand diviner*（史 127） | 太卜 grand diviner（史 127）<br>日者 Diviners of the Lucky Days（史 127）<br>⇒ diviner |
| 太医令 | grand physician*（史 110） | grand physician（史 110） |
| 均官長 | head of the office of imperial burial places | ● 長<br>衛士長 chief of the palace guard（漢 63）<br>官職の長 **head** of this office（史 119）<br>食官長 chief steward（史 058）<br>亭長 illage head（史 053.122）<br>● office for か office of か<br>for＋機能・活動, of＋場所・人・物か。<br>平準 office for equalizing prices; 鉄官 offices for the control of iron goods<br>公車 office of public carriage; 宦者丞 clerk in the office of eunuchs（漢 97）<br>● 陵 |

| 職官名 | 英語対訳 | 英訳用参照表現 |
|---|---|---|
|  |  | 陵寝 imperial burial place; **mausoleum** (中英辞典)<br>● 寝<br>寝令 Prefects of the Funerary Chambers (Dubs)<br>● mausoleum<br>陵 imperial tomb ｜ **mausoleum** (Dubs)<br>〈NSOED〉 mausoleum, The magnificent tomb of Mausolus, King of Caria, erected in the 4th cent. BC at Halicarnassus by his queen Artemisia.　2 gen. A large and stately place of burial. ()<br>● funerary<br>詔武奉一太守謁武帝園廟 On instructions from the emperor he paid his respects at the **funerary park** and temple of Emperor Wu, where he offered a t'ai-lao sacrifice. (漢 54)<br>Two principal kinds of temple can be distinguished—cult temples and **funerary** or mortuary temples. (⇒ temple/shrine: art and architecture, Egyptian)<br>● mortuary temple<br>… in ancient Egypt, place of worship of a deceased king and the depository for food and objects offered to the dead monarch. (⇒temple/shrine: mortuary temple)<br>● mortuary<br>〈NSOED〉 2 A funeral.　3 A burial place, a sepulchre.　4 A place where dead bodies are kept for a time, either for purposes of examination or pending burial or cremation. |
| 都水長 | head of water control at the imperial parks | 如淳曰：「律，都水治渠隄水門。三輔黄圖雲三輔皆有都水也。」(漢 19A)<br>渠＝溝 canal; ditch; channel (中英)<br>隄＝堤<br>⇒ 水利 |

## 第 2 章 職官名対訳作成資料

| 職官名 | 英語対訳 | 英訳用参照表現 |
|---|---|---|
|  |  | ● water management<br>耕地にいつ水を入れたり出したりすれば収量が増えるかといった，水利用の運営面に力点ありか。<br>⇒ 水利: agricultural technology<br>● water control はもう少し意味が広い<br>Soil and **water control** engineering deals with soil drainage, irrigation, conservation, hydrology, and flood control.<br>⇒ 水利: agricultural science, the |
| 諸廟寝官令 | chief of the inner chamber of the funerary temple | 食官 supervisor of food（漢 68）<br>【立廟，因園為寝，以時薦享焉】A **funerary temple** should be built for him, utilizing the present **park** for the **inner chambers**, and seasonal offerings presented there.（漢 63）<br>● funerary temple ⇒ temple/shrine: art and architecture, Egyptian）<br>〈Dubs〉陵 imperial tomb｜mausoleum。<br>寝令 Prefects of the Funerary Chambers<br>〈中英〉陵寝 imperial burial place; mausoleum |
| 諸廟園官令 | chief of the park of the funerary temple | 【益奉園民満千六百家，以為奉明県】The number of households maintaining the **park** should be increased to a full 1,600 and the area made into the Feng-ming District（漢 63）<br>【尊戻夫人曰戻後，置園奉邑，及益戻園各満三百家】Lady Li should be honored with the title of Empress Li and a **park** and village set up for her with three hundred households. The park of the heir apparent Li should also be increased by three hundred households.（漢 63）<br>〈Dubs〉園令 Prefects of the Funerary Parks |
| 諸廟食官令 | chief of food offerings | 食官 supervisor of food（漢 68） |

15

| 職官名 | 英語対訳 | 英訳用参照表現 |
|---|---|---|
|  | at the funerary temple | 〈Dubs〉食官令 Prefect of the Offices for Offerings |
| 博士 | erudit* | erudit（漢 67） |
| 光禄勲<br>〔郎中令〕 | **keeper of the palace gate***（漢 68.71.78.97）<br>〔**chief of palace corridor attendants**（漢 54.63）〕 | keeper of the palace gate（漢 68.71.78.97）〔chief of palace attendants（漢 54.63）｜chief of palace attendants（史 10.103.107）｜palace secretary（史 9）｜郎中令賈壽 palace attendant Jia Shou（史 9）〕<br>corridor ⇒ Tokugawa Bakufu (The Great Corridor)<br>● 以下「令」⇒ chief |
| 太中大夫 | grand palace counselor | **palace counselor**（漢 54.65.68.71.97）｜palace counsellor（史 103.107.108.109.122） |
| 中大夫<br>〔光禄大夫〕 | palace counselor*（漢 63）<br>〔counselor to the keeper of the palace gate*（漢 63.68.71.74）〕 | **palace counselor**（漢 63）｜palace counsellor（史 101.103.107.108.109.120.122）｜general of palace attendants（史 102）<br>〔**counselor to the keeper of the palace gate**（漢 63）｜counselor to the keeper of the palace gate（漢 68.71.74.78）〕 |
| 諫大夫 | admonisher* | admonisher（漢 78） |
| 五官中郎将 | senior officer of palace corridor attendants at the "Five Bureaus" | 中郎将 general of palace attendants（漢 54.63.68.71.74.史 103.123） |
| 中郎 | palace gentleman*（漢 54） | **palace gentlemen**（漢 54）｜palace attendant（漢 65.67.78.92）｜palace attendant（史 109.122） |
| 侍郎 | attendant in the inner palace*（漢 65） | palace attendant（漢 65）<br>侍中 **attendant in the inner palace**（漢 54.63.68.71.78.97）｜attendant of the inner palace（漢 54.63.68.78.97）｜gentlemen（漢 65）｜inner palace attendant（漢 68）｜palace attendant（漢 92）enfeoffed her younger brother, the attendant of the inner palace and commandant of the imperial horses Chao Ch'in, as marquis of Hsin-ch'eng（漢 97） |

## 第2章 職官名対訳作成資料

| 職官名 | 英語対訳 | 英訳用参照表現 |
|---|---|---|
|  |  | 郎官 attendant in the inner palace（漢 54） |
| 郎中 | palace corridor attendant | corridor ⇒ Tokugawa Bakufu (The Great Corridor) |
| 左中郎将 | senior officer of palace corridor attendants of the left | 中郎将 general of palace attendants（漢 54.63.68.71.74.史 103.123）<br>左馮翊 left prefect of the capital（漢 68.78.97）<br>右内史 right prefect of the capital（史 120.122）<br>左校 colonels **of the left**（史 48）<br>左将軍 general **of the left**（漢 63.67.68.78.97） |
| 中郎<br>侍郎<br>郎中 | ［五官中郎将に同じ］ |  |
| 右中郎将 | senior officer of palace corridor attendants of the right | 右監 superintendent **of the right**（漢 74）<br>右校 colonels **of the right**（史 48）<br>右将軍 general **of the right**（漢 54.68.71.74.97） |
| 中郎<br>侍郎<br>郎中 | ［五官中郎将に同じ］ |  |
| 車将 | senior officer of carriage |  |
| 郎中 | 略 |  |
| 戸将 | senior officer of watch gates |  |
| 郎中 | 略 |  |
| 騎将 | senior officer of cavalry（史 7） | cavalry general（史 7.8.106） |
| 郎中 | 略 |  |
| 謁者僕射 | chief master of guests（史 101.102） | chief master of guests（史 101.102） |
| 謁者 | master of guests（漢 63.65.74.78） | **master of guests**（漢 63.65.74.78）｜**master of guests**（史 9.122）｜palace attendant（史 9） |
| 期門僕射 | archery captain at the | 期門 rendezvous gate（漢 65）｜ |

17

| 職官名 | 英語対訳 | 英訳用参照表現 |
|---|---|---|
| 〔虎賁中郎将〕 | Rendezvous Gate（漢 67.68）〔senior officer of palace corridor attendants for the picked troops（漢 54.63.68.71.74.史 103.123）〕 | **Rendezvous Gate**（漢 68）<br>僕射 **archery captain**（漢 67.68）｜謁者僕射 chief master of guests（史 101.102）<br>中郎将 **general of palace attendants**（漢 54.63.68.71.74.史 103.123）<br>虎賁令 magistrate of Hubi（史 57）<br>● magistrate<br>〈NSOED〉⇒ magistrate<br>〈CHJ 166〉江戸町奉行 Edo City Magistrate; 京都町奉行 Kyoto City Magistrate; 長崎奉行 Magistrate of Nagasaki<br>⇒ Tokugawa bakufu<br>⇒ **picked troop** |
| 期門〔虎賁郎〕 | keeper of the Rendezvous Gate*（漢 65）〔junior officer of the picked troops〕 | 期門 rendezvous gate（漢 65）｜**Rendezvous Gate**（漢 68）<br>期門郎 **keeper of the Rendezvous Gate**（漢 65）<br>虎賁令 magistrate of Hubi（史 57） |
| 羽林中郎将 | senior officer of palace corridor attendants for the Feather and Forest Guard | 羽林 **Feather and Forest Guard**（漢 63.68）<br>中郎将 **general of palace attendants**（漢 54.63.68.71.74.史 103.123） |
| 羽林騎都尉 | chief commandant of cavalry for Feather and Forest Guard | 羽林 **Feather and Forest Guard**（漢 63.68）<br>騎都尉 **chief commandant of cavalry**（漢 54）｜colonel of the cavalry（漢 68）｜chief commandant of regular cavalry（漢 68）｜chief commandant of cavalry（史 109）<br>⇒ commandant |
| 羽林郎 | horseman of the Feather and Forest Guard*（漢 68） | 羽林の騎士 **horsemen of the Feather and Forest Guard**（漢 68） |
| 衛尉 | colonel of the guard*（漢 | colonel of the guard（漢 |

## 第 2 章 職官名対訳作成資料

| 職官名 | 英語対訳 | 英訳用参照表現 |
|---|---|---|
|  | 54.63.65.68.74.78) | 54.63.65.68.74.78）| colonel of the palace guards（史 9.011.108.109) |
| 公車司馬令 | chief marshal of the palace gates | 公車 office of public carriage（漢 65.71）| chief of public carriage（漢 71）司馬 marshal（史 48.7.8.101.102.111）| marshal for the military commander［中司馬］（史 100）| grand marshal［人司馬］（史 91.51）| attacking marshal［鷹撃司馬］（史 111）〔**master of the public carriage**（史 102）〕⇒ marshal |
| 衛士令 | chief of the palace guard | 衛士 **palace guard**（漢 63) |
| 旅賁令 | chief of envoys | 旅賁令 |
| 屯司馬 | marshal of the stationed unit | 屯兵 garrison troop（漢 68）屯田していた漢兵 the Han garrison and farm in Ch'u'-shih（漢 74）屯戍［とんじゅ］の卒 **farming garrisons**（史 30）司馬 marshal（史 48.7.8.101.102.111）| marshal for the military commander［中司馬］（史 100）| grand marshal［大司馬］（史 91.51）| attacking marshal［鷹撃司馬］（史 111) |
| 衛司馬 | marshal of the palace guard | 司馬 marshal（史 48.7.8.101.102.111）| marshal for the military commander［中司馬］（史 100）| grand marshal［大司馬］（史 91.51）| attacking marshal［鷹撃司馬］（史 111) |
| 候司馬 | marshal of scouts | 候 lieutenant（史 007）| **scout**（史 123）| **scout**［斥候］【斥候】（史 109）司馬 **marshal**（史 48.7.8.101.102.111）| **marshal** for the military commander［中司馬］（史 100）| grand **marshal**［大司馬］（史 91.51）| attacking **marshal**［鷹撃司馬］（史 111) |
| 太僕 | **master of carriage\***（漢 65.68.74) | **master of carriage**（漢 65.68.74）| master of the carriage（漢 68）| master of |

19

| 職官名 | 英語対訳 | 英訳用参照表現 |
|---|---|---|
|  |  | carriage（史 9.111） |
| 大廏令 | chief of the imperial stables | 廏監, 移中〜 superintendent of the I-chung Stables（漢 54）<br>廏将 cavalry general（史 055）<br>廏置【屍郷〜】reached the carriage station at Shixiang（史 094）<br>大廏丞 aide in the imperial stables（史 122） |
| 未央令 | chief of carriage and horses for the Eternal Palace |  |
| 家馬令〔挏馬令〕 | chief of the imperial household's horses〔chief of the emperor's horses〕 | 家令 steward in the **household of the heir apparent**（史 101）<br>● of horses<br>駙馬都尉 commandant of the imperial horses（漢 68.97）<br>● 挏馬<br>【武帝太初元年更名家馬為挏馬,〔七〕初置路軨‥‥<br>〔七〕應劭曰：「主乳馬, 取其汁挏治之, 味酢可飲, 因以名官也。」如淳曰：「主乳馬, 以韋革為夾兜, 受數斗, 盛馬乳, 挏取其上(把)〔肥〕, 因名曰挏馬。礼楽志丞相孔光奏省楽官七十二人, 給大官挏馬酒。今梁州亦名馬酪為馬酒。」晉灼曰：「挏音挺挏之挏。」師古曰：「晉音是也。挏音徒孔反。」‥‥七三〇頁二行挏取其上(把)〔肥〕, 景祐, 殿本都作「肥」。】（漢 019A 卷十九上百官公卿表第七上）<br>【其七十二人給大官挏馬酒】（漢 022 巻二十二礼楽志第二）<br>● brood mare<br>〈OALD〉a female horse kept for breeding<br>〈LDOCE〉a mare (= female horse ) that is kept for breeding<br>groom ⇒ 本表「太子僕」 |
| 車府令 | chief of the office of | ● 〜 office の例 |

## 第 2 章　職官名対訳作成資料

| 職官名 | 英語対訳 | 英訳用参照表現 |
|---|---|---|
|  | carriage | 均輸 **transport offices** for equalizing prices（史 30）<br>塩鉄 **salt and iron offices**（史 30）<br>都官令　secretaries of the **law offices**（史 118）<br>carriage と office の組み合わせ<br>公車 **office of** public carriage（漢 65.71）<br>● 府　office<br>宗正府 **office** of the director of the imperial clan（漢 68）<br>府 **office**（漢 68.92） |
| 路軨令 | chief of light hunting chariots | 軨獵車【太僕以軨獵車】=The master of carriage went in a **light hunting chariot** to fetch（漢 68）<br>太僕 master of carriage（漢 65.68.74）<br>【太僕, 秦官,<br>〔一〕掌輿馬, 有兩丞。属官有大廄, 未央, 家馬三令, 各五丞一尉。<br>〔二〕又車府, 路軨[路軨], 騎馬, 駿馬四令丞;<br>〔三〕又龍馬, 閑駒, 橐泉, 騊駼, 承華五監長丞;<br>〔四〕又辺郡六牧師えん令[牧師苑令], 各三丞;<br>〔五〕又牧とう[牧橐], 昆蹄令丞<br>〔六〕皆属焉。中太僕掌皇太后輿馬, 不常置也。武帝太初元年更名家馬為挏馬,<br>〔七〕初置路軨。<br><br>〔一〕應劭曰:「周穆王所置也, 蓋大御眾僕之長, 中大夫也。」<br><br>〔二〕師古曰:「家馬者, 主供天子私用, 非大祀戎事軍国所須, 故謂之家馬也。」<br><br>〔三〕伏儼曰:「主乘輿路車, 又主凡小車。軨, 今之小馬車曲輿也。」師古曰: |

21

| 職官名 | 英語対訳 | 英訳用参照表現 |
|---|---|---|
| | | 「輅音零。」〕(漢 019A 卷十九上百官公卿表第七上)<br>【明年,以歲比登,詔有司增雍五時路車各一乘,駕被具】(漢 025A 卷二十五上郊祀志第五上) |
| 騎馬令 | chief of cavalry horses | |
| 駿馬令 | chief of famous steed | 駿馬 famous steed (史 7) |
| 廷尉<br>〔大理〕 | commandant of justice*<br>〔grand examiner*(史 11)〕 | commandant of justice (漢 54.63.68.71.74.92)<br>〔chief coordinator (漢 65) | grand examiner (史 11)〕<br>⇒ commandant |
| 正監 | superintendent of the center (史 30) | **assistant under the commandant of justice**〔廷尉正監〕(史 30)<br>監 supervision (史 48) | supervision over (史 93) | supervisor of the Jianzhang Palace〔建章監〕(史 109) | take charge of (史 48) | overseer (史 8.113) | overseer〔郡監〕(史 96) | overseeing (史 53) | in charge of (史 55) | secretary (史 122) | keeper of the imperial hunting dogs〔狗監〕(史 117)<br>● superintendent ⇒ 警察組織, 宮内庁 |
| 左監<br>〔左平〕 | superintendent of the left<br>〔judge of the left〕 | ⇒ 本表「右監」<br>【廷尉,秦官,<br>〔一〕掌刑辟,有正廷尉,秦官,<br>〔一〕掌刑辟,有正,左右監,秩皆千石。景帝中六年更名大理,武帝建元四年復為廷尉。宣帝地節三年初置左右平,秩皆六百石。哀帝元壽二年復為大理。王莽改曰作士。<br><br>〔一〕應劭曰:「聽獄必質諸朝廷,与眾共之,兵獄同制,故稱廷尉。」師古曰:「廷,平也。治獄貴平,故以為号。」〕(漢 019A 卷十九上百官公卿表第七上)<br>監兼侍中 made him **superintendent of** |

第 2 章　職官名対訳作成資料

| 職官名 | 英語対訳 | 英訳用参照表現 |
|---|---|---|
|  |  | **the guards** at the Jianzhang Palace（史 111）<br>● superintendent ⇒ 警察組織，宮内庁 |
| 右監<br>〔右平〕 | superintendent of the right（漢 74）<br>〔judge of the right〕 | **superintendent of the right**（漢 74）<br>● superintendent ⇒ 警察組織，宮内庁 |
| 典客<br>〔大鴻臚〕 | **director of foreign guests**（史 9.9.10.11.118）<br>〔**director of foreign vassals***（漢 63.68.78）〕 | director of guests（史 9.9.10.11.118）<br>〔director of foreign vassals（漢 63.68.78）〕 |
| 行人令<br>〔大行令〕 | chief of messengers〔grand messenger*（漢 78.史 11.49.108.111.114.116.118.120.123）〕 | 行人 **messenger**（史 11）<br>大行 **grand messenger**（漢 78.史 11.49.108.111.114.116.118.120.123）｜<br>master of ceremonies（史 99） |
| 訳官令 | chief of interpreters | 【重九訳，致殊俗】men of strange customs who would come **translating** and retranslating their languages（史 123）<br>【烏孫發導訳送驩還】the Wusun providing them with guides and **interpreters**（史 123） |
| 別火令 | chief of the maintenance of the sacred fire | ● sacred fire 聖火<br>- an Aztec priest centred on **the maintenance of the sacred fire**, making sure that it should burn perpetually ⇒ sacred fire: Xiuhtecuhtli<br>- all the village fires were then made anew from the **sacred fire** ⇒ sacred fire: Natchez<br>- The chief ceremony … is celebrated before the **sacred fire** …The **sacred fire** must be kept burning continually ⇒ sacred fire: Zoroastriaism<br>- Aztecs kindled a **sacred fire** to initiate each cycle of their calendar ⇒ sacred fire: Iztapalapa |
| 郡邸長 | head of the provincial | 郡邸 the Ch'u'n-ti, the lodge for official |

| 職官名 | 英語対訳 | 英訳用参照表現 |
|---|---|---|
| | offices in the capital | visitors from the provinces（漢 74）｜郡邸 a petty official in the Ch'u'n-ti, the lodge for official visitors from the provinces（漢 74）｜郡邸獄 was in the Ch'u'n-ti prison（漢 74）｜郡邸 Shui-ju, one of the officials in charge of the Ch'u'n-ti lodge（漢 74） |
| 宗正 〔宗伯〕 | **director of the imperial clan*** （漢 54.63.68.74） 〔**master of the imperial clan**〕 | director of the imperial clan（漢 54.63.68.74）｜heads the imperial clan（漢 65）｜director of the imperial clan（史 10.120） <br>● elder <br>〈RH〉an influential member of a tribe or community, often a chief or ruler; a superior. <br>〈Thesaurus〉leader, manager, overseer, administrator, supervisor, head, executive, foreman, overlord, captain. <br>● master［of 組織・集団（技能ではなく）］ <br>⇒ master <br>**master** of the market place（史 119）｜ **master** of the privy treasury（史 011）｜ **master** of public works（史 011） <br>● 謁者令＝master of guests（漢 74）は guests の頭ではなく，guests を扱う技能にたけた者。 <br>東宮大夫，東宮職＝Grand **Master of the** Crown Prince's **Household** <br>⇒ 宮内庁 |
| 都司空令 | chief of criminal affairs in the imperial family | 都司空 **head of criminal affairs for the imperial family**（史 107）｜prison officials of the legal offices in the capital and Shanglin Park【又偽為左右都司空上林中都官詔獄書，諸侯太子幸臣】（史 118） <br>司空 **Director** of Public Works（史 121） |
| 内官長 | head of the office of | 内官 **Inner Office**（漢 65）｜inner |

第 2 章 職官名対訳作成資料

| 職官名 | 英語対訳 | 英訳用参照表現 |
|---|---|---|
|  | weights and measures | treasury（史 11）<br>● 長<br>chief of the palace guard［衛士長］（漢 63）｜ **head of this office**［官職の長］（史 119）｜ chief steward［食官長］（史 058）｜ village head［亭長］（史 053.122） |
| 諸公主家令 | steward in the household of the princess | 公主　princess（漢 63.65.68.71）｜ Princess（漢 63.65.68.97.67）｜ imperial princess（漢 67）｜ young princess（漢 78）<br>家令　steward in the household of（史 101）<br>steward & chamberlain ⇒ 本表「詹事」<br>● steward が常に王室の要職を指すわけではない。単なる家令, 執事の意味も。ただし家僕の長的存在か。<br>- A man could work his way up from groom［馬丁］ to valet［従者・側用人］ and then on to butler or even **steward**.<br>⇒ steward: domestic service<br>- Penn's final years were unhappy. ... and his **steward**, Philip Ford, cheated him on such a staggering scale that Penn was forced to spend nine months in a debtors' prison.<br>⇒ steward: Penn, William［English Quaker leader］ |
| 諸公主門尉 | commander of gatekeepers in the household of the princess | 公主　princess（漢 63.65.68.71）｜ Princess（漢 63.65.68.97.67）｜ imperial princess（漢 67）｜ young princess（漢 78）<br>● keeper<br>光禄勲 keeper of the palace gate（漢 68.71.78.97）｜ 期門郎 keeper of the Rendezvous Gate（漢 65）<br>● 尉 & gate<br>衛尉 colonel of the guard（漢 54.63.65.68.74.78）｜ 城門校尉 subordinate commander of the city gate（漢 74）｜ 中塁校尉 commander of the |

25

| 職官名 | 英語対訳 | 英訳用参照表現 |
|---|---|---|
|  |  | gate for the northern garrison(漢 74) | 監門吏 keeper of the village gate(史 97) |
| 大司農<br>〔治粟内史〕 | **minister of revenue**<br>〔**secretary in charge of grain**\*(史 11.56)〕 | minister of agriculture(漢 54.68.74)<br>〔secretary in charge of grain(史 11.56)〕<br>- Similarly, financial matters were controlled by two permanent ministries: the Department of Agriculture and **Revenue** and the Privy Treasury. ⇒ privy: China: The civil service 〈CHJ 166〉 superintendent of finance 徳川勘定奉行 |
| 太倉令 | chief of the central granary | chief of the treasury(史 10)<br>太倉 great storehouse(史 8) | **central granary** of the government(史 30) | granary(史 30)<br>● granary<br>- remained in local and provincial **granaries** and treasuries ⇒ salt tax: China: Taxation<br>● land tax 年貢<br>- In place of previous land taxes (nengu) assessed in money as so many hundred or ten thousand kan of silver ⇒ land tax 年貢: Japan: Hideyoshi regime<br>● tax grain ⇒ salt tax: China: Taxation 〔Charles O. Hucker〕 |
| 均輸令 | chief of the transport office for equalizing prices | 均輸 equalization of goods through transportation(史 30) | equitable transport(史 30) | **transport offices for equalizing prices**(史 30) | transportation office(史 30) |
| 平準令 | chief of the office for the balanced standard | 平準書 The Treatise on the **Balanced Standard**(史 30) |
| 都内令 | chief of granaries in the capital | 都内 financial officers of the ministry of agriculture in the capital(史 30) |
| 籍田令 | chief of the sacred field in the palace | 籍田 **sacred field** that the emperor plows in person(漢 65) | Field of Tribute(史 10) |

## 第 2 章 職官名対訳作成資料

| 職官名 | 英語対訳 | 英訳用参照表現 |
|---|---|---|
| 斡官長 | head of the office of salt, iron, and liquor taxes | ● salt/wine tax<br>- others, such as **salt taxes**, **wine taxes**, and taxes on mercantile goods in transit, were based on consumption ⇒ salt tax: China: Taxation［Charles O. Hucker］ |
| 鉄市長 | head of the control of iron monopoly | |
| 捜粟都尉 | chief commandant for requisitioning grain*（漢 54.63.68） | chief commandant for requisitioning grain（漢 54.63.68）<br>● requisition 徴発<br>〈NSOED〉vt, 1 Require (a thing or person) to be supplied or lent for military purposes; demand the use of; acquire by requisition. M19.b Make demands for supplies etc. on (a place). L19.<br>2 gen. Take over the use of; press (a thing) into service; request to have (a thing). L19.　n, 3 The action or an act of requiring a certain amount or number of something to be supplied; esp. an official demand or order made on a town, district, etc., to supply or lend something required for military purposes; a thing taken by this means. L18. |
| 少府 | **privy treasurer*** | privy treasurer（漢 54）｜ privy treasurer（漢 67.71.78）｜ privy treasurer（史 11）⇒ privy |
| 尚書令 | master of palace writers | chief of **palace writers**（漢 68）<br>● chief ではなく master とした理由 1000 石であり地位もい。令=chief は原則ではあるが，「尚書令」は原則から離れるべき特殊な職掌を持つ。 |
| 符節令 | chief of the imperial credentials | 符節 in charge of the imperial credentials（史 9）｜ imperial credential（史 122）⇒ credential |
| 太医令 | grand physician for the imperial household | **grand physician**（史 110）｜ court physician（日本皇室） |

| 職官名 | 英語対訳 | 英訳用参照表現 |
|---|---|---|
| 太官令 | grand butler of the imperial household | 太官 **imperial butler**（漢 63.78）<br>● butler<br>〈OAD〉chief manservant of a household<br>〈NSOED〉1 A servant who has charge of a household's or other establishment's wine cellar and plate etc.; a principal manservant. ME.　2 *Hist.* An officer of high rank (nominally) in charge of wine for the royal table.<br>⇒ butler |
| 湯官令 | chief of the emperor's patisserie | ● 師古曰：「太官主膳食，湯官主餅餌，導官主擇米。‥‥」（漢 019A 卷十九上百官公卿表第七上）<br>〈中英〉餅餌 bbinger［cakes; pastry］｜餅 round flat cake: 月餅 moon cake［餌=饅頭］<br>● **patisserie**<br>〈NSOED〉1 *sing. & in pl.* Articles of food made by a pastry-cook, pastries collectively. |
| 導官令 | chief of the grain selectors | 導官　office of the grain selector（史 122）｜**grain selector's office**（史 122） |
| 楽府令 | chief of the Music Bureau | 楽府 **Music Bureau**（漢 68）｜楽人 musician（漢 68）｜楽人 experts of the Music Bureau（漢 97） |
| 若盧令 | chief of the *Ruolu* court | 服虔曰：「若盧，詔獄也。」鄧展曰：「舊洛陽兩獄，一名若盧，主受親戚婦女。」如淳曰：「若盧，官名也‥‥」（漢 019A 卷十九上百官公卿表第七上）<br>● 詔獄<br>had them taken off to the commandant of justice and the prison for persons under imperial indictment（漢 68）｜had the man sent to the prison for offenders who are under imperial indictment（漢 71）｜the prisons（漢 74）｜been summoned before the emperor's law officials and thrown into prison（史 118）｜the commandant of |

第 2 章 職官名対訳作成資料

| 職官名 | 英語対訳 | 英訳用参照表現 |
|---|---|---|
|  |  | justice and the other law officials〔中都官〕 of the capital had succeeded in arresting 60,000 or 70,000 persons on imperial order（史 122）<br>● indictment 起訴, 告発, 起訴状<br>〈Oxford Dic. of Law〉A formal document accusing one or more persons of committing a specified indictable offence or offences. It is read out to the accused at the trial.<br>〈Black's Law Dic.〉1. The formal written accusation of a crime, made by a grand jury and presented to a court for prosecution against the accused person.<br>2. The act or process of preparing or bringing forward such a formal written accusation. |
| 考工室令 | chief of the government artisans | 考工室 **government artisan**（史 107）<br>● artisan 職人<br>〈NSOED〉1 A skilled (esp. manual) worker; a mechanic; a craftsman.<br>2 A person who practises or cultivates an art. |
| 左弋令〔佽飛令〕 | chief of the emperor's hunting assistants〔chief of hunting archery for the emperor〕 | 【武帝太初元年更名考工室為考工, 左弋為佽飛, …佽飛掌弋射, …師古曰：「太官主膳食, 湯官主餅餌, 導官主擇米。若盧, 如說是也。左弋, 地名。…」】（漢 019A 卷十九上百官公卿表第七上）<br>● 弋 yì<br>〈中英〉a retrievable arrow with a string attached to it<br>〈Gr〉Hunting with the bow and arrow is still popular … Although archery is limited to hunting and target shooting today, romantic tales of such fabled archers as Robin Hood and William Tell continue to delight adventurers of all |

29

| 職官名 | 英語対訳 | 英訳用参照表現 |
|---|---|---|
| | | ages. (archery) |
| 居室令〔保宮令〕 | chief of the detention room in the palace〔supervisor of the detention room〕 | 居室 within the curtains of the chamber（史 28）｜ Inquiry Room（史 107）｜ prison at the Palace of Sweet Springs〔甘泉居室〕（史 111）<br>保宮 **Detention Room**（漢 54）<br>● detention<br>〈法律用語対訳集〉拘留，拘禁<br>● supervisor ⇒ 宮内庁 |
| 昆台令〔甘泉居室令〕 | chief of the *Kuntai* detention room〔chief of the detention room in the Palace of Sweet Springs〕 | 【〔六〕武帝太初元年更名考工室為考工，左弋為佽飛〔佽飛〕，居室為保宮，甘泉居室為昆台，永巷為掖廷。佽飛〔佽飛〕掌弋射，有九丞兩尉，太官七丞，昆台五丞，楽府三丞，掖廷八丞，宦者七丞，鉤盾五丞兩尉】（漢 019A 卷十九上百官公卿表第七上）<br>〈中英〉昆 kūn 1 elder brother.　2 <書> offspring.｜台 tái 1 platform; stage; terrace.<br>甘泉居室 prison at the Palace of Sweet Springs（史 111）<br>居室 ⇒ 本表「居室令」 |
| 左司空令 | chief of compulsory labour of the left | 司空 Director of Public Works（史 121） |
| 右司空令 | chief of compulsory labour of the right | 司空 Director of Public Works（史 121） |
| 東織令 | chief of the eastern weaving room | 東織室の令史張赦= the clerk of the **eastern weaving rooms** Chang She（漢 68） |
| 西織令 | chief of the western weaving room | |
| 東園匠令 | chief of the craftsmen of the imperial tombs | 東園 Eastern Garden Office（漢 68）<br>⇒ imperial tomb |
| 胞人長 | head of cooks | 胞人 **cook**（漢 65） |
| 都水長 | head of water control at the imperial parks | |
| 均官長 | head of the office of | ● 官=office |

30

第2章 職官名対訳作成資料

| 職官名 | 英語対訳 | 英訳用参照表現 |
|---|---|---|
|  | imperial burial places | 鉄官 **offices** for the control of iron goods（史 030） |
| 上林十池監 | supervisor of the maintenance of ponds at the Imperial Forest Park | 上林十池監<br>上林 Shanglin Park（史 30）<br>● supervisor ⇒ 宮内庁 |
| 中書謁者令〔中書令〕 | master of documents and guests〔chief of palace writers*（漢 67.68.78.92）〕 | 中書 office of palace writers（漢 78）<br>謁者令 master of guests（漢 74）<br>謁者 masters of guests（漢 63.65.74.78. 史 009.122）｜palace attendant（史 009）<br>尚書(令)・中書令 **chief of palace writers**（漢 67.68.78.92） |
| 黄門令 | chief the Yellow Gate | 黄門 Yellow Gate（漢 54.68）｜gentleman of the Yellow Gate（漢 63） |
| 鉤盾令 | chief of the control of the imperial parks | 【己亥，上耕於鉤盾弄田】（漢 007 巻七昭帝紀第七）<br>【上小女陳持弓聞大水至，走入横城門，闌入尚方掖門，至未央宮鉤盾中】（漢 010 巻十成帝紀第十）<br>【少府，秦官，…<br>〔三〕又上林中十池監，<br>〔四〕又中書謁者，黄門，鉤盾，尚方，…師古曰：「鉤盾主近苑囿…」】（漢 019A 巻十九上百官公卿表第七上）<br>【官属及諸中宮黄門，鉤盾，掖庭官吏，挙奏按論，畏諴，皆失気】（漢 066 巻六十六公孫劉田王楊蔡陳鄭伝第三十六）<br>【可休丞相，以御史大夫鄭弘代之，遷中書令置他官，以鉤盾令徐立代之，…】<br>（漢 075 巻七十五眭兩夏侯京翼李伝第四十五） |
| 尚方令 | chief of the royal craftsmen | 尚方 emperor's own（史 57）｜master of magical arts（史 28）｜physician（史 117）<br>〈NSOED〉craftwork<br>work in a handicraft, (the production of) items of handicraft.<br>〈NSOED〉craft<br>I 1 Strength, power, force. O　2 Skill, art; |

31

| 職官名 | 英語対訳 | 英訳用参照表現 |
|---|---|---|
|  |  | ability in planning or constructing; ingenuity, dexterity. Now chiefly as 2nd elem. of comb. OE.<unknown>　b spec. <u>Occult art, magic</u>. ME.<unknown>　c Human skill; art as opp. to nature. LME.<unknown>　3 An artifice, a device, a skilful contrivance; spec. <u>a magical device</u>. OE.　4 In a bad sense:<unknown>a A deceitful action; a trick, a fraud. OE.<br>● craftsman<br>〈NSOED〉1 A person who practises a handicraft; an artisan. LME.<br>● armoury<br>〈NSOED〉1 Arms or armour collectively (arch.); an array of weapons or (fig.) resources etc. ME.　2 A place where arms and armour are kept or (chiefly US) made; an arsenal; N. Amer. a drill hall. LME.<br>● royal<br>〈NSOED〉I 1 Originating or derived from a king, queen, <u>emperor</u>, or other monarch, or from a line of such monarchs. LME.　2 Pertaining to a monarch, or the dignity or office of a monarch; pertaining to a monarch as head of State or the armed forces. LME.　3 Of, belonging to, or used by a monarch; in the service of a monarch. LME.<br>⇒ royal: China<br>● monarch<br>〈NSOED〉1 Orig., a sole and absolute ruler of a State. Later also, any ruler bearing the title of king, queen, <u>emperor</u>, <u>empress</u>, or the equivalent. LME. |
| 御府令 | chief of royal garments | 御府 imperial treasury（漢 68）<br>【稟稟鄉改正服封禪矣】The time had |

第 2 章 職官名対訳作成資料

| 職官名 | 英語対訳 | 英訳用参照表現 |
|---|---|---|
|  |  | drawn near when he might appropriately have changed the beginning of the year, altered the **court vestment**, and performed the Feng nand Shan sacrifices. (史 010 孝文本紀)<br>● vestment<br>〈RH〉1. a garment, esp. an outer garment.　2. vestments, Chiefly Literary. attire; clothing.　3. an official or ceremonial robe. [attire = clothes or apparel, esp. rich or splendid garments.]<br>〈三コ〉礼装用のガウン, 法衣, 祭服［多分に宗教的］<br>⇒ dress<br>● garment<br>〈RH〉1. any article of clothing: dresses, suits, and other garments.　2. an outer covering or outward appearance.<br>〈三コ〉衣服［clothes を服, clothing を衣類としたとき, garment は衣服と, 日常生活語よりは改まった感覚での衣服全般］<br>⇒ dress |
| 永巷令〔掖庭令〕 | chief of the Long Halls Palace〔chief of the women's quarters〕 | 永巷 women's quarters of the grave keeper's house（漢 68）｜ Long Halls（史 9）｜ women's quarters of the palace（史 125）<br>〔supervisor of the women's quarters（漢 68.74.97）〕<br>supervisor ⇒ 本表「大長秋」 |
| 内者令 | chief of the palace interior（漢 97） | supervisor of the inner palace（漢 97）<br>● inner<br>〈NSOED〉<u>inner</u> Cabinet, a group of decisionmakers within a ministerial Cabinet etc; <u>inner</u> circle an exclusive group of friends or associates within a larger group |
| 宦者令 | chief of eunuchs（史 9） | 宦者令=chief eunuch（史 9）｜ palace eunuchs and their secretaries［中宦者令］ |

33

| 職官名 | 英語対訳 | 英訳用参照表現 |
|---|---|---|
|  |  | (史 9) ｜ 宦者 office of eunuchs (漢 97) 中宦者 palace eunuchs (史 9) |
| 中尉〔執金吾〕 | **military commander of the capital\***(史 122)〔**chief of the capital police\***(漢 63.68.78.97)〕 | military commander (漢 63.史 10.11.101.118.120.122) ｜ **military commander of the capital** (史 11.122) ｜ commander (漢 65)〔chief of the capital police (漢 63.68.78.97) ｜ chief of capital police (漢 65)〕 |
| 候 | scout\*(史 109.123) | lieutenant (史 007) ｜ **scout** (史 123) ｜ scout〔斥候〕【斥候】(史 109) |
| 司馬 | marshal\*(史 7.8.48.101.102.111) | **marshal** (史 7.8.48.101.102.111) ｜ marshal for the military commander〔中司馬〕(史 100) ｜ grand marshal〔大司馬〕(史 91.51) ｜ attacking marshal〔鷹撃司馬〕(史 111) |
| 千人 | head of a battalion of 1,000 men\*(史 107) | **head of a battalion of 1,000 men** (史 107) |
| 中塁令 | commander of the security force | ● 塁【穿北軍塁垣以為賈區】cutting a hole in the wall surrounding the northern garrison (漢 67)〈中英〉rampart ● rampart〈OAD〉a broad bank of earth built as a fortification, usually topped with a parapet and wide enough for troops etc. to walk on.〈三コ〉塁壁, 城壁 ● security force〈JPT〉警察庁警備局 Security Bureau 法務省刑事局公安課 Public Security Division 海上保安庁警備救難部警備第二課 Security Division 参議院警務部警備課 Security Division ただし警視庁警備部 Guard Division |

第 2 章 職官名対訳作成資料

| 職官名 | 英語対訳 | 英訳用参照表現 |
|---|---|---|
|  |  | 〈三コ〉機動隊 riot police; a riot squad ⇒ security force |
| 寺互令 | chief of interoffice liaison | ● interoffice<br>〈RH〉functioning or communicating between the offices of a company or organization; within a company: *an interoffice memo.* |
| 武庫令 | chief of the arsenal*（漢 74） | chief of the military arsenal（漢 74）｜**chief of the arsenal**（漢 74） |
| 都船令 | chief of the water police | 都船令<br>⇒ water police<br>⇒ water patrol<br>⇒ waterway watch |
| 式道候 | captain of the lead bannermen | 【宋萬為式道侯】Sung Wan makes certain that <u>the road has been cleared</u>（漢 65）<br>● lead<br>マラソンの先導車 ⇒ lead motorcycle<br>● bannerman<br>〈CHJ 152〉shogun's enfeoffed **bannerman** 旗本。<br>● banner<br>〈NSOED〉1 A piece of cloth attached by one side to the upper part of a pole, and used as the standard of a king, knight, army, etc.; a national flag, esp. as inspiring emotional attachment; Her. a flag displaying a person's arms. ME.<br>● **bannerman**<br>〈NSOED〉(a) Sc. arch. a standard-bearer; (b) Hist. a soldier of one of the banners of the Manchu army.<br>〈Sansom *A Short Cultural History of Japan* 290〉Bannerman (hatasashi) of a feudal warrior 旗差 ⇒ bannerman<br>● Dubs<br>式道侯Captains of the Standard Bearers<br>式道中侯 Captain of the Centre Standard Bearers |

35

| 職官名 | 英語対訳 | 英訳用参照表現 |
|---|---|---|
| | | 式道左候 Captain of the Left Standard Bearers<br>式道右候 Captain of the Right Standard Bearers<br>中候 Captain of the Central Parts of the Capital Region<br>［左中候，右中候という見出し語はない］<br>● Bielenstein<br>式道中候 Captain of the Centre of the Standard Bearers<br>式道左候 Captain of the Left of the Standard Bearers<br>式道右候 Captain of the Right of the Standard Bearers<br>captain ⇒ marshal; 軍組織 |
| 左中候 | captain of the left bannermen | 中候 master of guests（史 96） |
| 右中候 | captain of the right bannermen | 中候 master of guests（史 96） |
| 左京輔都尉 | chief commandant of the left of the capital | 京輔都尉 chief commandant of the capital area（漢 68） |
| 右京輔都尉 | chief commandant of the right of the capital | 京輔都尉 chief commandant of the capital area（漢 68） |
| 二千石 | **official of the two thousand picul rank*** | two thousand picul official（漢 54）｜ two thousand picul class（漢 54）｜ official of the two thousand picul class（漢 63.92）｜ **official of the two thousand picul rank**（漢 92）｜ official of the 2,000 picul rank（史 11.107）｜ two thousand picul official（漢 68.71.74.78）｜ two thousand picul level（漢 78）｜ two thousand picul class（漢 92） |
| 太子太傅 | **grand tutor to the heir apparent***（漢書 74.78） | **grand tutor to the heir apparent**（漢 74.78）｜ grand tutor to the heir apparent（史 30.57.99）<br>● 太子<br>crown prince（漢 54.71）｜ heir apparent（漢 54.63.67.68.74.97）｜ siring a son［sire |

第 2 章　職官名対訳作成資料

| 職官名 | 英語対訳 | 英訳用参照表現 |
|---|---|---|
|  |  | father または male ancestor になる］（漢 63）｜ prince（漢 63）｜ son（漢 63）｜ king's heir（漢 63）｜ heir（漢 63.68）｜ **heir apparent**（漢 63） |
| 太子門大夫 | lord of the gate to the heir apparent | 門大夫 **lord of the gate to the heir apparent**（史 121） |
| 太子庶子 | secretary to the heir apparent | ● secretary to 新安県の令史李寿 Li Shou, the **secretary to** the magistrate of Hsin-an（漢 63） |
| 太子先馬 | mounted guard to the heir apparent*（史 120） | **mounted guard to the heir apparent**（史 120） |
| 太子舎人 | retainer in the household of the heir apparent*（史 120） | **retainer in the household of the heir apparent**（史 120）<br>● 舎人 steward（漢 63）｜ retainer（漢 63.史 104） |
| 太子少傅 | **lesser tutor to the heir apparent***（漢書 67） | **lesser tutor to the heir apparent**（漢 67） |
| 太子門大夫<br>太子庶子<br>太子先馬<br>太子舎人 | ［太子太傅に同じ］ |  |
| 将作大匠 | **master of construction works** | master of public works（史 11） |
| 石庫令 | chief of stone materials |  |
| 東園主章令<br>〔木工令〕 | chief of wooden materials at the Eastern Garden<br>〔chief of woodworkers〕 | 東園 **Eastern Garden** Office（漢 68） |
| 左校令 | commander of the left over compulsory labour | 左校 colonels of the left（史 48）｜ commanders of the left（史 111）<br>● convict labour<br>International whalers made use of Hobart's superb harbour; it became a major port for whaling ships. **Convict labour** assisted in all this and in constructing public works and handsome |

| 職官名 | 英語対訳 | 英訳用参照表現 |
|---|---|---|
| | | buildings, both urban and rural.<br>⇒ labour 労役: Tasmania<br>● 令を commander とした理由<br>校令の「校」には軍人的要素が入っている可能性がある。<br>● commander<br>… in 1192 he [Minamoto Yoritomo] acquired the title of supreme **commander** (shogun) over the shugo and jitō. (⇒ steward: Minamoto Yoritomo) |
| 右校令 | commander of the right over compulsory labour | 右校 colonels of the right（史 48） |
| 前校令 | commander of the front over compulsory labour | |
| 後校令 | commander of the rear over compulsory labour | |
| 中校令 | commander of the middle over compulsory labour | |
| 詹事 | **chamberlain to the empress and the heir apparent**（史 107.120） | manages the heir apparent's household（漢 65）｜purveyor（史 11）｜steward of the household of the empress and the heir apparent（史 107.120）｜steward in the household of the empress dowager and the heir apparent（史 108）<br>家令 steward in the household of the heir apparent（史 101）<br>● steward = <u>公務要職性強い</u>。hall を司る。hall は宮殿, 法廷, 食堂。ゲストの席順を決め, 祝祭を指揮する。王の代行主幹。財政監査。摂政。<br>⇒ butler (Europe, history of: The royal household)<br>⇒ steward: domestic service<br>⇒ master (lord steward) |

第 2 章　職官名対訳作成資料

| 職官名 | 英語対訳 | 英訳用参照表現 |
|---|---|---|
|  |  | ● chamberlain = 王室私的執務性強い。王の寝室 chamber に仕える。特に歳入確保、王の要請に応じて出費調達。<br>⇒ butler (Europe, history of: The royal household)<br>● 日本皇室の侍従長は grand chamberlain、宮内庁長官は grand steward。上の西洋史での用法に適合する。<br>⇒ 宮内庁 |
| 太子率更令 | chief of the night guard in the household of the heir apparent | 太子 crown prince（漢 54.71） ｜ heir apparent（漢 54.63.67.68.74.97） ｜ siring a son［sire father または male ancestor になる］（漢 63） ｜ prince（漢 63） ｜ son（漢 63） ｜ king's heir（漢 63） ｜ heir（漢 63.68） ｜ heir apparent（漢 63））<br>率更令 |
| 太子家令 | steward in the household of the heir apparent*（史 101） | 家令 **steward in the household of the heir apparent**（史 101）<br>● 諸公主家令 steward in the household of the princess<br>steward & chamberlain ⇒ 本表「詹事」 |
| 太子僕 | chief of the heir apparent's horses | ● keeper<br>駙馬 keeper of the emperor's auxiliary horse（漢 54） ｜ keeper of the horse（漢 54）<br>● 馬丁<br>⇒ groom［馬丁］ |
| 太子中盾 | chief of patrol in the household of the heir apparent |  |
| 太子衛率 | chief of the gatekeepers in the household of the heir apparent |  |
| 太子廚廄 | chief of the kitchen and stables in the household of the heir |  |

39

| 職官名 | 英語対訳 | 英訳用参照表現 |
|---|---|---|
|  | apparent |  |
| 中長秋 | steward in the household of the empress | steward ⇒ 本表「詹事」 |
| 私府令 | chief of ritual implements |  |
| 永巷令 | chief of the Long Halls Palace |  |
| 倉廏令 | chief of the warehouses |  |
| 祠祀令 | chief of performing sacrifices | 【不能繼嗣奉宗廟祭祀】He is not fit to carry on the imperial line and **perform the sacrifices** in the ancestral temples, nor can he ... (史記 9 呂后本紀) |
| 食官令 | chief of food (漢 68) | 食官 supervisor of food (漢 68) |
| 大長秋 | **supervisor of the harem**\*(漢 65) | supervisor of your harem (漢 65) ｜ messenger of the long autumn (史 11) ● supervise [教育的意味合い] 〈NSOED〉2 Superintend the execution or performance of (a task, operation, etc.); oversee the actions or work of (a person); spec. act as an <u>academic</u> supervisor to. L16.2. W. S. CHURCHILL *He had <u>supervised</u> the day-to-day administration of the country.* ● supervisor ⇒ 宮内庁 |
| 典属国 | **director of dependent states**\*(漢 54.63.65.68.史 109) | **director of dependent states** (漢 54.63.65.68.史 109) |
| 丞 | Assistant |  |
| 候 | scout\*(史 123) | lieutenant (史 007) ｜ **scout** (史 123) ｜ **scout** [斥候]【斥候】(史 109) |
| 千人 | head of a battalion of 1,000 men\*(史 107) | **head of a battalion of 1,000 men** (史 107) |
| 九訳令 | chief of foreign languages | 九訳 translating and retranslating their languages (史 123) 令 |

40

## 第 2 章 職官名対訳作成資料

| 職官名 | 英語対訳 | 英訳用参照表現 |
|---|---|---|
|  |  | 訳官令 chief of interpreters |
| 水衡都尉 | chief commandant of the palace gardens | director of waterworks（漢 71.74）<br>東園 Eastern Garden Office（漢 68） |
| 上林令 | chief of the Imperial Forest Park | director of the Shanglin Park（史 102） |
| 均輸令 | chief of the transport office for equalizing prices | ⇒ 本表「大司農」下「均輸令」chief of the transport office for equalizing prices |
| 御羞令 | chief of the imperial farm of curio offerings | 御羞＝珍しい供え物を産出する。<br>● curio 珍品<br>〈RH〉any unusual article, object of art, etc., valued as a curiosity.<br>- workshops producing jewelry, giftware, religious articles, **curios**, and printed fabrics ⇒ curio<br>● vegetable offerings<br>**Vegetable offerings** have included not only the edible herbaceous plants but also grains, fruits, and flowers. ⇒ sacrifice<br>● material of the oblation ⇒ sacrifice<br>● rituals of oblation ⇒ rite/ritual<br>● farm<br>〈NSOED〉4 A tract of land held (orig. on lease) under one management for the purposes of <u>cultivation</u> or the rearing of certain <u>animals</u> (for food or fur etc.).<br>● oblation<br>〈RH〉1. the offering to God of the elements of bread and wine in the Eucharist. 2. the whole office of the Eucharist. 3. the act of making an offering, esp. to a deity. 4. any offering for religious or charitable uses.<br>● stuff<br>〈NSOED〉Stock or provision of food. Also, corn or grain as a growing crop or in its harvested state.<br>● stock |

41

| 職官名 | 英語対訳 | 英訳用参照表現 |
|---|---|---|
| | | 〈NSOED〉25 The equipment and animals used by a farm etc.; the raw materials, equipment, vehicles, etc., used by a firm, esp. an industrial concern; spec. (a) livestock; (b) rolling-stock.<br>C. G. SELIGMAN Cattle are..most valued..and the attainment of 1,000 head of stock is marked by a special ceremony. Farmers Weekly (Durban) Bush area is..suitable for small stock such as goats.<br>● supply<br>〈NSOED〉A thing supplied; a means of supplying something. |
| 禁圃令 | chief of the fields of the imperial household | 外構工事 external work and landscaping (和英建築用語辞典)<br>緑地 greens; green field<br>緑野 green fields<br>畑 fields<br>⇒ 外構・緑地 |
| 輯濯令 | chief of the control of boatmen | 【〔二〕如淳曰：「御羞, 地名也, 在藍田, 其土肥沃, 多出御物可進者, 揚雄傳謂之御宿。三輔黄圖御羞, 宜春皆苑名也。輯濯, 船官也。鍾官, 主鑄錢官也。辯銅, 主分別銅之種類也。」】(漢017 景武昭宣元成功臣表第五)<br>● 濯＝船を操る<br>【鄧通, 蜀郡南安人也, 以濯船為黄頭郎】Deng Tong was a native of Nan'an in the province of Shu. Because he knew how to **pole a boat** he was made a yellow-capped **boatman** in the grounds of the imperial palace.(史125 佞幸列伝) [濯を竿で船を操るの意に解釈している]<br>● pole<br>〈RH〉vi, to push, strike, or propel with a pole: to pole a raft.[竿を差す]<br>〈Gr〉The punt is a shallow draft boat with blunt ends that is usually propelled by |

## 第 2 章 職官名対訳作成資料

| 職官名 | 英語対訳 | 英訳用参照表現 |
|---|---|---|
|  |  | poling. (boat and boating)<br>● boating<br>〈Gr〉Professional basketball and football franchises are located in Phoenix. **Boating**, water skiing, and fishing on the state's many lakes and streams abound. (Arizona) ｜ many freshwater ponds and lakes, where **boating**, sailing, and fishing dominate (Rhode Island)など多数。<br>［**boating** は船を出して遊ぶに近い］<br>●輯＝集める<br>「輯」で史記検索も，船関連の用例なし。<br>【使韓信等輯河北趙地, 連燕齊】... and in the meantime send Han Xin and others to **gather** forces in Hebei and the region of Zhao and to form an alliance with Yan and Qi. (史 8 高祖本紀) |
| 鍾官令 | chief of metal casting | 鍾官 officials in the capital who were in charge of casting metal（史 30） |
| 技巧令 | chief of craftwork | 技巧 craft industries（史 129） |
| 六廏令 | chief of the six kinds of domestic animals | 掌畜令 chief of animal husbandry<br>【沂, 泗水以北, 宜五穀桑麻六畜, ･･･】The region north of the Zhe and Si rivers is suitale for growing the five types of grain, mulberries, and hemp, and for raising the **six kinds of domestic animals**, ...（史 129 貨殖列伝）<br>● 六畜<br>Horses, cattle, pigs, goats, dogs, and chickens. Dogs were raised to be eaten. (Watson *Shi ji* Han Dynasty II p. 446 footnote) |
| 辯銅令 | chief of copper assessment |  |
| 左馮翊<br>〔左内史〕 | **left prefect of the capital\***（漢 68.97）〔**prefect in charge of the eastern area of the** | **left prefect of the capital**（漢 68.78.97）｜ left prefect of the capital area（漢 78）〔**prefect in charge of the eastern area of the capital**（漢 65）｜ left prefect of the |

43

| 職官名 | 英語対訳 | 英訳用参照表現 |
|---|---|---|
|  | capital*（漢 65）〕 | capital（史 111.122）〕<br>⇒ prefect |
| 廩犧令 | chief of grain offerings and animal sacrifices | ● grain offerings<br>- The sickle for harvesting plants, a winnowing basket for preparing **grain offering**s, a reed broom for cleaning the sacrificial area, …⇒ ceremonial object: Objects used in sacrifices and in sacred meals<br>- The goodwill of the ancestors, and of certain river and mountain powers, was sought through prayer and **offerings of grain**, millet wine, and a**nimal and human sacrifice**. ⇒ China: Late Shang divination and religion: State and society<br>- One form of thank **offering** is the **offering** of the first fruits in agricultural societies. Until the first fruits of the harvest have been presented with homage and thanks (and often with animal **sacrifices**) to the deity of the harvest (sometimes regarded as embodied in the crop), the whole crop is considered sacred and thus taboo and may not be used as food. ⇒ sacrifice |
| 左都水長 | head of water control of the left at the imperial parks | 左都水長<br>⇒ 本表「太常」下「都水長」head of water control at the imperial parks |
| 鉄官長 | head of the office of iron goods | 鉄官 offices for the control of iron goods（史 030）｜iron official（史 122）<br>小鉄官 suboffices for the control of iron goods（史 30） |
| 長安四市長 | head of the Chang'an four marketplaces |  |
| 京兆尹〔右内史〕 | **prefect of the capital*** （漢 54.67.71.74.78.92）〔**prefect in charge of the western area of the** | **prefect of the capital** Chang Ch'ang（漢 54.78）｜prefect of the capital（漢 67.71.74.92）<br>〔**prefect in charge of the western area** |

44

第 2 章 職官名対訳作成資料

| 職官名 | 英語対訳 | 英訳用参照表現 |
|---|---|---|
| | capital*(漢 65)〕 | of the capital(漢 65)｜prefect in charge of the western area(漢 65)｜right prefect of the capital(史 120.122)｜right prefect (史 120)〕<br>⇒ prefect |
| 長安東市令 | chief of the Chang'an East Marketplace | 市令 master of the market place(史 119)｜master of the market(史 119)<br>長安廚 Ch'ang-an Kitchen(漢 68) |
| 長安西市令 | chief of the Chang'an West Marketplace | 市令 master of the market place(史 119)｜master of the market(史 119) |
| 長安廚令 | chief of the Chang'an Kitchen | 長安廚 Ch'ang-an Kitchen(漢 68) |
| 都水長 | head of water control at the imperial parks | |
| 鉄官長 | head of the office of iron goods | 小鉄官 suboffices for the control of iron goods(史 30)<br>鉄官 iron official(史 122) |
| 右扶風<br>〔主爵中尉・主爵都尉〕 | **right prefect of the capital***(漢 54.68)<br>〔**master of titles military commander***(史 11)/ **master of titles chief commandant***(史 11.107.111.113.120.122)〕 | **right prefect of the capital**(漢 54.68)｜oversees the western reaches of the capital(漢 65)｜Fu-feng official(漢 92)｜commanded the Fufeng district of the capital area(漢 97)｜**supervisor of the right district of the capital**(史 122)<br>〔**master of titles military commander**(史 11)・**master of titles chief commandant**(史 11.107.111.113.120.122)〕 |
| 掌畜令 | chief of animal husbandry | 六畜 the six kinds of domestic **animal**s(史 129 貨殖列伝) ⇒ 本表「六廄令」 |
| 都水長 | head of water control at the imperial parks | |
| 鉄官長 | head of the office of iron goods(史 30) | 小鉄官 suboffices for the control of iron goods(史 30)<br>鉄官 iron official(史 122) |
| 廄長 | head of stables | |
| 龐廚長 | head of cooking | |
| 司隷校尉 | **superintendent-general of the capital** | subordinate commander in charge of convicts(漢 68.74) |

45

| 職官名 | 英語対訳 | 英訳用参照表現 |
|---|---|---|
|  |  | 校尉 company commander（漢 54.68.92）｜ commander（漢 54.71.74）｜ colonel（漢 92）｜ colonel（史 89.113）⇒ 本表「左校令・右校令」｜ commander（史 7.101.109）｜ subordinate commander（漢 68.74.史 107.111）<br>城門校尉 subordinate commander of the city gate（漢 74）<br>中塁・屯騎・長水校尉は単に commander<br>警察庁長官 Commissioner-General for the National Police Agency (JPT)<br>警視総監 **Superintendent-General**<br>県警察本部長 Chief of the Osaka Prefectural Police Headquarters など。<br>● superintendent ⇒ 警察組織, 宮内庁 |
| 城門校尉 | **company commander of the city gate** | subordinate commander of the city gate（漢 74）<br>● Watson 訳 subordinate の意図不明<br>● company は中隊。上から旅団, 連隊, 中隊, 分隊, 小隊 ⇒ 軍組織 |
| 司馬 | marshal*（史 48.7.8.101.102. 111） | **marshal**（史 48.7.8.101.102.111）｜ marshal for the military commander［中司馬］（史 100）｜ grand marshal［大司馬］（史 91.51）｜ attacking marshal［鷹撃司馬］（史 111） |
| 城門候 | city gate scout | 城門 city gate（漢 63）｜ inner wall gate（漢 63）｜ gate of the inner wall（漢 63）｜ city gate（史 8）｜ gate of the city（史 104） |
| 中塁校尉 | **company commander of the gate for the northern garrison** | commander of the gate for the northern garrison（漢 74）<br>company ⇒ 軍組織 |
| 屯騎校尉 | **company commander of the stationed cavalry** | 屯兵 **garrison** troop（漢 68）<br>屯田していた漢兵 the Han garrison and farm in Ch'u'-shih（漢 74）<br>屯戌［とんじゅ］の卒 farming **garrisons**（史 30）<br>校尉 company commander（漢 54.68.92） |

## 第 2 章　職官名対訳作成資料

| 職官名 | 英語対訳 | 英訳用参照表現 |
|---|---|---|
|  |  | ｜ commander（漢 54.71.74）｜ colonel（漢 92）｜ colonel（史 89.113. *see* 左校・右校）｜ commander（史 7.101.109）｜ subordinate commander（史 107.111） |
| 歩兵校尉 | company commander of the guard of the Imperial Forest Park | 歩兵校尉 |
| 越騎校尉 | company commander of cavalrymen of the Yueh tribe | 越騎 cavalrymen of the Yueh tribe（漢 68） |
| 長水校尉 | company commander of the Ch'ang-shui garrison | **commander of the Ch'ang-shui garrison**（漢 71） |
| 胡騎校尉 | company commander of nomadic horsemen | 胡騎 barbarian horsemen（漢 54）｜ **The cavalrymen of the Hu tribe**（漢 68） |
| 射声校尉 | company commander of archers |  |
| 虎賁校尉 | company commander of the picked troops | 虎賁令 magistrate of Hubi（史 57）〈三コ〉精鋭部隊 picked troops |
| 比二千石 | official of the two thousand picul or over rank | 比二百石 those who have a rank of 200 piculs **or over**（史 121）二千石 **two thousand picul** official（漢 54）｜ **two thousand picul** class（漢 54）｜ official of the **two thousand picul** class（漢 63.92）｜ official of the **two thousand picul rank**（漢 92）｜ official of the 2,000 picul rank（史 11.107）｜ **two thousand picul official**（漢 68.71.74.78）｜ **two thousand picul** level（漢 78）｜ **two thousand picul** class（漢 92） |
| 奉車都尉 | chief commandant of the imperial carriage | chief commandant in charge of carriage（漢 54）｜ in charge of the imperial carriage（漢 54）｜ chief commandant in charge of the imperial carriage（漢 68.97）｜ carriage server（史 28） |
| 駙馬都尉 | chief commandant of the imperial horses | **commandant of the imperial horses**（漢 68.97） |

| 職官名 | 英語対訳 | 英訳用参照表現 |
|---|---|---|
| | | 駙馬 keeper of the emperor's auxiliary horse（漢 54）｜ keeper of the horse（漢 54） |

## 九卿および中二千石以外

| 名称 | 英語対訳 | 英訳用参照表現 |
|---|---|---|
| 太師 | grand commandant*（漢 67） | **grand commandant**（漢 67） |
| 太傅 | grand tutor*（漢 54.63.65.71.74） | **grand tutor**（漢 **54.63.65.71.74**）｜ grand tutor to the heir apparent（史 103）｜ grand tutor to the heir apparent［太子太傅］（史 99.30）｜ grand tutor（史 121）｜ tutor to the heir apparent（史 103）｜ the boy's tutor（史 103） |
| 太保 | grand fosterer | ● foster 〈LDOCE〉to help a skill, feeling, idea etc develop over a period of time ⇒ foster |
| 大将軍 | general in chief*（漢 54.67.68.71.74.97） | **general in chief**（漢 **54.67.68.71.74.97**）｜ commander in chief（史 10 ほか多数） |
| 票騎将軍 | general of swift cavalry*（漢 54.68.97） | **general of swift cavalry**（漢 **54.68.97**）｜ general of light cavalry（漢 54）｜ General of Swift Cavalry（史 49.111）｜ general of swift cavalry（史 109.110.111）｜ general of light cavalry（史 109）｜ swift cavalry general（史 111） |
| 車騎将軍 | general of carriage and cavalry*（漢 54.63.68.71.74.78.97） | **general of carriage and cavalry**（漢 **54.63.68.71.74.78.97**）｜ carriage and cavalry general（漢 67.97） |
| 衛将軍 | general of the guard*（漢 54.92） | **general of the guard**（漢 **54.92**）｜ general of the guards（史 10） |
| 前将軍 | general of the vanguard*（漢 54.67） | **general of the vanguard**（漢 **54.67**）｜ general of the vanguard（漢 68）｜ general of the vanguard（史 109） |
| 後将軍 | general of the rear*（漢 54.68） | **general of the rear**（漢 **54.68**）｜ general of the rear（史 111）｜ general of rear（史 111） |
| 左将軍 | general of the left*（漢 | **general of the left**（漢 **63.67.68.78.97**） |

第 2 章 職官名対訳作成資料

| 名称 | 英語対訳 | 英訳用参照表現 |
|---|---|---|
| 右将軍 | 63.67.68.78.97)<br>general of the right*（漢 54.68.71.74.97) | **general of the right**（漢 **54.68.71.74.97**）｜ general of the right（史 111）｜ general of right（史 111） |
| 騎郎将 | general of palace horsemen*（漢 54） | **general of palace horsemen**（漢 **54**）｜ general of palace horsemen（史 109） |
| 驍騎将軍 | cavalry general*（漢 54） | **cavalry general**（漢 **54**）｜ cavalry general（史 109）｜ commanded the cavalry（史 108） |
| 軽車将軍 | general of light carriage*（漢 54） | **general of light carriage**（漢 **54**）｜ general of light carriage（史 109.111） |
| 弐師将軍 | Sutrishna general*（漢 54.97） | **Sutrishna general**（漢 **54.97**） |

# 第3章　各職位の職掌・属官
（『漢書』百官公卿表,『續漢書』百官志）

| 職官名 | 職掌・属官 |
|---|---|
| 相國・丞相 | 相國・丞相, 應劭曰「丞者, 承也。相者, 助也」。皆秦官, 金印紫綬, 掌丞天子助理萬機。秦有左右, 荀悅曰「秦本次國, 命卿二人, 是以置左右丞相, 無三公官」。高帝即位, 置一丞相, 十一年更名相國, 綠綬。孝惠・高后置左右丞相, 文帝二年復置一丞相。有兩長史, 秩千石。哀帝元壽二年更名大司徒。武帝元狩五年初置司直, 秩比二千石, 掌佐丞相擧不法。(『漢書』百官公卿表)<br><br>司徒, 公一人。本注曰, 掌人民事。凡教民孝悌・遜順・謙儉・養生送死之事, 則議其制, 建其度。凡四方民事功課, 歲盡則奏其殿最而行賞罰。凡郊祀之事, 掌省牲視濯, 大喪則掌奉安梓宮。凡國有大疑大事, 與太尉同。世祖即位, 為大司徒, 建武二十七年, 去大。長史一人, 千石。掾屬三十一人。令史及御屬三十六人。本注曰, 世祖即位, 以武帝故事, 置司直, 居丞相府, 助督錄諸州, 建武十八年省也。(『續漢書』百官志) |
| 太尉 | 太尉, 秦官, 應劭曰「自上安下曰尉, 武官悉以為稱」。金印紫綬, 掌武事。武帝建元二年省。元狩四年初置大司馬, 應劭曰「司馬, 主武也, 諸武官亦以為號」。以冠將軍之號。宣帝地節三年置大司馬, 不冠將軍, 亦無印綬官屬。成帝綏和元年賜大司馬金印紫綬, 置官屬, 祿比丞相, 去將軍。哀帝建平二年復去大司馬印綬, 官屬, 冠將軍如故。元壽二年復賜大司馬印綬, 置官屬, 去將軍, 位在司徒上。有長史, 秩千石。(『漢書』百官公卿表)<br><br>太尉, 公一人。本注曰, 掌四方兵事功課, 歲盡即奏其殿最而行賞罰。凡郊祀之事, 掌亞獻, 大喪則告謚南郊, 凡國有大造大疑, 則與司徒, 司空通而論之。國有過事, 則與二公通諫爭之。世祖即位, 為大司馬。建武二十七年, 改為太尉。長史一人, 千石。本注曰, 署諸曹事。掾史屬二十四人。本注曰, 漢舊注東西曹掾比四百石, 餘掾比三百石, 屬比二百石, 故曰公府掾, 比古元士三命者也。或曰, 漢初掾史辟, 皆上言之, 故有秩比命士。其所不言, 則為百石屬。其後皆自辟除, 故通為百石云。西曹主府史署用。東曹主二千石長吏遷除及軍吏。戶曹主民戶, 祠祀, 農桑。奏曹主奏議事。辭曹主辭訟事。法曹主郵驛科程事。尉曹主卒徒轉運事。賊曹主盜賊事。決曹主罪法事。兵曹主兵事。金曹主貨幣・鹽・鐵事。倉曹主倉穀事。黃閣主簿錄省眾事。令史及御屬二十三人。本注曰, 漢舊注公令史百石, 自中興以後, 注不說石數。御屬主為公御。閣下令史主閣 |

| 職官名 | 職掌・属官 |
|---|---|
| | 下威儀事。記室令史主上章表報書記。門令史主府門。其餘令史,各典曹文書。(『續漢書』百官志) |
| 御史大夫(司空) | 御史大夫,秦官,應劭曰「侍御史之率,故稱大夫云。」臣瓚曰「茂陵書御史大夫秩中二千石」。位上卿,銀印青綬,掌副丞相。有兩丞,秩千石。一曰中丞,在殿中蘭臺,掌圖籍祕書,外督部刺史,內領侍御史員十五人,受公卿奏事,舉劾按章。成帝綏和元年更名大司空,金印紫綬,祿比丞相,置長史如中丞,官職如故。哀帝建平二年復為御史大夫,元壽二年復為大司空,御史中丞更名御史長史。侍御史有繡衣直指,服虔曰,「指事而行,無阿私也。」師古曰「衣以繡者,尊寵之也。」出討姦猾,治大獄,武帝所制,不常置(『漢書』百官公卿表) |
| | 司空,公一人。本注曰,掌水土事。凡營城起邑,浚溝洫,修墳防之事,則議其利,建其功。凡四方水土功課,歲盡則奏其殿最而行賞罰。凡郊祀之事,掌掃除樂器,大喪則掌將校復土。凡國有大造大疑,諫爭,與太尉同。世祖即位,為大司空,建武二十七年,去大。屬長史一人,千石。掾屬二十九人。令史及御屬四十二人。(『續漢書』百官志) |
| 太傅 | 古官,高后元年初置,金印紫綬。後省,八年復置。後省,哀帝元壽二年復置。位在三公上。(『漢書』百官公卿表) |
| | 太傅,上公一人。本注曰,掌以善導,無常職。世祖以卓茂為太傅,薨,因省。其後每帝初即位,輒置太傅錄尚書事,薨,輒省。(『續漢書』百官志) |
| 太師・太保 | 皆古官,平帝元始元年皆初置,金印紫綬。太師位在太傅上,太保次太傅。(『漢書』百官公卿表) |
| 前後左右將軍 | 皆周末官,秦因之,位上卿,金印紫綬。漢不常置,或有前後,或有左右,皆掌兵及四夷。有長史,秩千石。(『漢書』百官公卿表) |
| | 將軍,不常置。本注曰,掌征伐背叛。比公者四,第一大將軍,次驃騎將軍,次車騎將軍,次衛將軍。又有前・後・左・右將軍。初,武帝以衛青數征伐有功,以為大將軍,欲尊寵之。以古尊官唯有三公,皆將軍始自秦,晉,以為卿號,故置大司馬官號以冠之。其後霍光・王鳳等皆然。成帝綏和元年,賜大司馬印綬,罷將軍官。世祖中興,吳漢以大將軍為大司馬,景丹為驃騎大將軍,位在公下,及前・後・左・右雜號將軍眾多,皆主征伐,事訖皆罷。帝初即位,以弟東平王蒼有賢才,以為驃騎將軍,以王故,位在公上,數年後罷。章帝即位,西羌反,故以舅馬防行車騎將軍征之,還後罷。和帝即位,以舅竇憲為車騎將軍,征匈奴,位在公下,還復有功,遷大將軍,位在公上,復征西羌,還免官,罷。安帝即位,西羌寇亂,復以舅鄧騭為車騎將軍征之,還遷大將軍,位如憲,數年復罷。自安 |

52

第3章 各職位の職掌・属官

| 職官名 | 職掌・属官 |
|---|---|
|  | 帝政治衰缺,始以嫡舅耿寶為**大將軍**,常在京都。順帝即位,又以皇后父・兄・弟相繼為**大將軍**,如三公焉。(『續漢書』百官志) |
| 奉常 | 秦官,掌宗廟禮儀,有丞。秩中二千石,丞千石。景帝中六年更名太常。應劭曰「常,典也,掌典三禮也。」師古曰「太常,王者旌旗也,畫日月焉,王有大事則建以行,禮官主奉持之,故曰奉常也。後改曰太常,尊大之義也。」屬官有太樂・太祝・太宰・太史・太卜・太醫六令丞,又均官,都水兩長丞,服虔曰「均官,主山陵上稾輸入之官也。」如淳曰「律,都水治渠隄水門。三輔黃圖云三輔皆有都水也。」又**諸廟寢園食官令長丞**,有**雍太宰・太祝令丞**,文穎曰「雍,主熟食官。」如淳曰「五時在雍,故特置太宰以下諸官。」師古曰「如説是也。雍,右扶風之縣也。太宰即是具食之官,不當復置饔人也。」五時各一尉。又博士及諸陵縣皆屬焉。景帝中六年更名太祝為**祠祀**,武帝太初元年更曰**廟祀**,初置太卜。**博士**,秦官,掌通古今,秩比六百石,員多至數十人。武帝建元五年初置五經博士,宣帝黃龍元年稍增員十二人。元帝永光元年分諸陵邑屬三輔。王莽改太常曰秩宗。(『漢書』百官公卿表)

**太常**,卿一人,中二千石。本注曰,掌禮儀祭祀,每祭祀,先奏其禮儀,及行事,常贊天子。每選試博士,奏其能否。大射・養老・大喪,皆奏其禮儀。每月前晦,察行陵廟。丞一人,比千石。本注曰,掌凡行禮及祭祀小事,總署曹事。其署曹掾史,隨事為員,諸卿皆然。**太史令**一人,六百石。本注曰,掌天時,星曆。凡歲將終,奏新年曆。凡國祭祀,喪,娶之事,掌奏良日及時節禁忌。凡國有瑞應,災異,掌記之。丞一人。**明堂及靈臺丞**一人,二百石。本注曰,二丞,掌守明堂・靈臺。靈臺掌候日月星氣,皆屬太史。**博士祭酒**一人,六百石。本僕射,中興轉為祭酒。博士十四人,比六百石。本注曰,易四,施・孟・梁丘・京氏。尚書三,歐陽・大小夏侯氏。詩三,魯・齊・韓氏。禮二,大小戴氏。春秋二,公羊嚴・顏氏。掌教弟子。國有疑事,掌承問對。本四百石,宣帝增秩。**太祝令**一人,六百石。本注曰,凡國祭祀,掌讀祝,及迎送神。丞一人。本注曰,掌祝小神事。**太宰令**一人,六百石。本注曰,掌宰工鼎俎饌具之物。凡國祭祀,掌陳饌具。丞一人。**大予樂令**一人,六百石。本注曰,掌伎樂。凡國祭祀,掌請奏樂,及大饗用樂,掌其陳序。丞一人。**高廟令**一人,六百石。本注曰,守廟,掌案行掃除。無丞。**世祖廟令**一人,六百石。本注曰,如高廟。先帝陵,每陵園令各一人,六百石。本注曰,掌守陵園,案行掃除。丞及**校長**各一人。本注曰,校長,主兵戎盗賊事。先帝陵,**每陵食官令**各一人,六百石。本注曰,掌望晦時節祭祀。右屬太常。本注曰,有祠祀令一人,後轉屬少府。有太卜令,六百石,後省并太史。中興以來,省前凡十官。(『續漢書』百官志) |

| 職官名 | 職掌・属官 |
|---|---|
| 郎中令<br>(光祿勳) | 秦官,臣瓚曰「主郎內諸官,故曰郎中令。」掌宮殿掖門戶,有丞。秩中二千石,丞千石。武帝太初元年更名光祿勳。應劭曰「光者,明也。祿者,爵也。勳,功也。」如淳曰「胡公曰勳之言閽也。閽者,古主門官也。光祿主宮門。」師古曰「應說是也。」屬官有大夫・郎・謁者,皆秦官。又期門,羽林皆屬焉。服虔曰「與期門下以微行,後遂以名官。」師古曰「羽林,亦宿衞之官,言其如羽之疾,如林之多也。一說羽所以為王者羽翼也。」(『漢書』百官公卿表)<br><br>光祿勳,卿一人,中二千石。本注曰,掌宿衞宮殿門戶,典謁署郎更直執戟,宿衞門戶,考其德行而進退之。郊祀之事,掌三獻。丞一人,比千石。右屬光祿勳。本注曰,職屬光祿者,自五官將至羽林右監,凡七署。自奉車都尉至謁者,以文屬焉。舊有左右曹,秩以二千石,上殿中,主受尚書奏事,平省之。世祖省,使小黃門郎受事,車駕出,給黃門郎兼。有請室令,車駕出,在前請所幸,徼車迎白,示重慎。中興但以郎兼,事訖罷,又省車・戶・騎凡三將,及羽林令。(『續漢書』百官志) |
| 大夫 | 掌論議,有太中大夫・中大夫・諫大夫,皆無員,多至數十人。武帝元狩五年初置諫大夫,秩比八百石,太初元年更名中大夫為光祿大夫,秩比二千石,太中大夫秩比千石如故。(『漢書』百官公卿表)<br><br>光祿大夫,比二千石。本注曰,無員。凡大夫,議郎皆掌顧問應對,無常事,唯詔令所使。凡諸國嗣之喪,則光祿大夫掌弔。太中大夫,千石。本注曰,無員。中散大夫,六百石。本注曰,無員。諫議大夫,六百石。本注曰,無員。(『續漢書』百官志) |
| 郎 | 掌守門戶,出充車騎,有議郎・中郎・侍郎・郎中,皆無員,多至千人。議郎・中郎秩比六百石,侍郎比四百石,郎中比三百石。中郎有五官・左・右三將,秩皆比二千石。郎中有車・戶・騎三將,如淳曰「主車曰車郎,主戶衞曰戶郎。漢儀注郎中令主郎中,左右車將主左右車郎,左右戶將主左右戶郎也。」秩皆比千石。(『漢書』百官公卿表)<br><br>五官中郎將一人,比二千石。本注曰,主五官郎。五官中郎,比六百石。本注曰,無員。五官侍郎,比四百石。本注曰,無員。五官郎中,比三百石。本注曰,無員。凡郎官皆主更直執戟,宿衞諸殿門,出充車騎。唯議郎不在直中。左中郎將,比二千石。本注曰,主左署郎。中郎,比六百石。侍郎,比四百石。郎中,比三百石。本注曰,皆無員。右中郎將,比二千石。本注曰,主右署郎。中郎,比六百石。侍郎,比四百石。郎中,比三百石。本注曰,皆無員。議郎,六百石。本注曰,無員。(『續漢書』百官志) |
| 謁者 | 掌賓讚受事,員七十人,秩比六百石,有僕射,應劭曰「謁,請也,白也。 |

第3章 各職位の職掌・属官

| 職官名 | 職掌・属官 |
|---|---|
|  | 僕,主也。」秩比千石。(『漢書』百官公卿表)<br><br>**謁者僕射**一人,比千石。本注曰,為謁者臺率,主謁者,天子出,奉引。古重習武,有主射以督録之,故曰僕射。**常侍謁者**五人,比六百石。本注曰,主殿上時節威儀。**謁者**三十人。其**給事謁者**,四百石。其**灌謁者郎中**,比三百石。本注曰,掌賓贊受事,及上章報問。將・大夫以下之喪,掌使弔。本員七十人,中興但三十人。初為**灌謁者**,滿歲為**給事謁者**。(『續漢書』百官志) |
| 期門 | 掌執兵送從,武帝建元三年初置,比郎,無員,多至千人,有僕射,秩比千石。平帝元始元年更名**虎賁郎**,師古曰「賁讀與奔同,言如猛獸之奔。」置中郎將,秩比二千石。(『漢書』百官公卿表)<br><br>**虎賁中郎將**,比二千石。本注曰,主虎賁宿衞。**左右僕射・左右陛長**各一人,比六百石。本注曰,僕射,主虎賁郎習射。陛長,主直虎賁,朝會在殿中。**虎賁中郎**,比六百石。**虎賁侍郎**,比四百石。**虎賁郎中**,比三百石。**節從虎賁**,比二百石。本注曰,皆無員。掌宿衞侍從。自節從虎賁久者轉遷,才能差高至中郎。(『續漢書』百官志) |
| 僕射 | 秦官,自侍中・尚書・博士・郎皆有。古者重武官,有主射以督課之,軍屯吏・騶・宰・永巷宮人皆有,取其領事之號。孟康曰「皆有僕射,隨所領之事以為號也。若軍屯吏則曰**軍屯僕射**,永巷則曰**永巷僕射**。」(『漢書』百官公卿表) |
| 羽林 | 掌送從,次期門,武帝太初元年初置,名曰**建章營騎**,後更名**羽林騎**。又取從軍死事之子孫養羽林,官教以五兵,號曰**羽林孤兒**。師古曰「五兵謂弓矢・殳・矛・戈・戟也。」羽林有令丞。宣帝令中郎將・騎都尉監羽林,秩比二千石。(『漢書』百官公卿表)<br><br>**羽林中郎將**,比二千石。本注曰,主**羽林郎**。**羽林郎**,此三百石。本注曰,無員。掌宿衞侍從。常選漢陽・隴西・安定・北地・上郡・西河凡六郡良家補。本武帝以便馬從獵,還宿殿陛巖下室中,故號巖郎。**羽林左監**一人,六百石。本注曰,主羽林左騎。丞一人。**羽林右監**一人,六百石。本注曰,主羽林右騎。丞一人。<br>**奉車都尉**,比二千石。本注曰,無員。掌御乘輿車。**駙馬都尉**,比二千石。本注曰,無員。掌駙馬。**騎都尉**,比二千石。本注曰,無員。本監羽林騎。(『續漢書』百官志) |
| 衞尉 | 秦官,掌宮門衞屯兵,師古曰「漢舊儀云衞尉寺在宮内。胡廣云主宮闕之門内衞士,於周垣下為區廬。區廬者,若今之仗宿屋矣。」有丞。秩中二千石,丞千石。景帝初更名中大夫令,後元年復為衞尉。屬官有公車 |

55

| 職官名 | 職掌・属官 |
|---|---|
|  | 司馬・衞士・旅賁三令丞。師古曰「漢官儀云公車司馬掌殿司馬門，夜徼宮中，天下上事及闕下凡所徵召皆總領之，令秩六百石。旅，衆也。賁與奔同，言為奔走之任也。」衞士三丞。又諸屯衞候，司馬二十二官皆屬焉。長樂・建章・甘泉衞尉皆掌其宮，師古曰「各隨所掌之宮以名官。」職略同，不常置。(『漢書』百官公卿表)<br><br>衞尉，卿一人，中二千石。本注曰，掌宮門衞士，宮中徼循事。丞一人，比千石。公車司馬令一人，六百石。本注曰掌宮南闕門，凡吏民上章，四方貢獻，及徵詣公車者。丞・尉各一人。本注曰，丞選曉諱，掌知非法。尉主闕門兵禁，戒非常。南宮衞士令一人，六百石。本注曰，掌南宮衞士。丞一人。北宮衞士令一人，六百石，本注曰，掌北宮衞士。丞一人。左右都候各一人，六百石。本注曰，主劍戟士，徼循宮，及天子有所收考。丞各一人。宮掖門，每門司馬一人，比千石。本注曰，南宮南屯司馬，主平城門。宮門蒼龍司馬，主東門。玄武司馬，主玄武門。北屯司馬，主北門。北宮朱爵司馬，主南掖門。東明司馬，主東門。朔平司馬，主北門。凡七門。凡居宮中者，皆有口籍於門之所屬。宮名兩字，為鐵印文符，案省符乃內之。若外人以事當入，本官長史為封棨傳。其有官位，出入令御者言其官。右屬衞尉。本注曰，中興省旅賁令，衞士一人丞。(『續漢書』百官志) |
| 太僕 | 秦官，應劭曰「周穆王所置也，蓋大御衆僕之長，中大夫也。」掌輿馬，有兩丞。秩中二千石，丞千石。屬官有大廏・未央・家馬三令，各五丞一尉。師古曰「家馬者，主供天子私用，非大祀戎事軍國所須，故謂之家馬也。」又車府・路軨・騎馬・駿馬四令丞。伏儼曰「主乘輿路車，又主凡小車。軨，今之小馬車曲輿也。」師古曰「軨音零。」又龍馬・閑駒・橐泉・騊駼・承華五監長丞。如淳曰「橐泉殿在橐泉宮下。騊駼，野馬也。」師古曰「閑，闌，養馬之所也，故曰閑駒。騊駼出北海中，其狀如馬，非野馬也。駒音徒高反。駼音塗。」又邊郡六牧師苑令，各三丞。師古曰「漢官儀云牧師諸苑三十六所，分置北邊，西邊，分養馬三十萬頭。」又牧橐・昆蹏令丞，應劭曰「橐，橐佗。昆蹏，好馬名也。蹏音啼。」如淳曰「爾雅曰『昆蹏研，善升甗』者也，因以為廐名。」師古曰「牧橐，言牧養橐佗也。昆，獸名也。蹏研者，謂其蹏下平也。善升甗者，謂山形如甑，而能升之也。蹏即古蹄字耳。研音五見反。甗音言，又音牛偃反。」皆屬焉。中太僕掌皇太后輿馬，不常置也。武帝太初元年更名家馬為挏馬，應劭曰「主乳馬，取其汁挏治之，味酢可飲，因以名官也。」如淳曰「主乳馬，以韋革為夾兜，受數斗，盛馬乳，挏取其上肥，因名曰挏馬。禮樂志丞相孔光奏省樂官七十二人，給大官挏馬酒。今梁州亦名馬酪為馬酒。」晉灼曰「挏音挺挏之挏。」師古曰「晉音是也。挏音徒孔反。」初置路軨。(『漢書』百官公卿表) |

第3章 各職位の職掌・属官

| 職官名 | 職掌・属官 |
|---|---|
|  | 太僕, 卿一人, 中二千石。本注曰, 掌車馬。天子毎出, 奏駕上鹵簿用, 大駕則執馭。丞一人, 比千石。考工令一人, 六百石。本注曰, 主作兵器弓弩刀鎧之屬, 成則傳執金吾入武庫, 及主織綬諸雜工。左右丞各一人。車府令一人, 六百石。本注曰, 主乘輿諸車。丞一人。未央廄令一人, 六百石。本注曰, 主乘輿及廄中諸馬。長樂廄丞一人。右屬太僕。本注曰, 舊有六廄, 皆六百石令, 中興省約, 但置一廄。後置左駿令・廄, 別主乘輿御馬, 後或并省。又有牧師苑, 皆令官, 主養馬, 分在河西六郡界中, 中興皆省, 唯漢陽有流馬苑, 但以羽林郎監領。(『續漢書』百官志) |
| 廷尉 | 秦官, 應劭曰「聽獄必質諸朝廷, 與衆共之, 兵獄同制, 故稱廷尉。」師古曰「廷, 平也。治獄貴平, 故以爲號。」掌刑辟。秩中二千石。有正・左右監, 秩皆千石。景帝中六年更名大理, 武帝建元四年復爲廷尉。宣帝地節三年初置左右平, 秩皆六百石。哀帝元壽二年復爲大理。王莽改曰作士。(『漢書』百官公卿表)<br><br>廷尉, 卿一人, 中二千石。本注曰, 掌平獄, 奏當所應。凡郡國讞疑罪, 皆處當以報。正・左監各一人。左平一人, 六百石。本注曰, 掌平決詔獄。右屬廷尉。本注曰, 孝武帝以下, 置中都官獄二十六所, 各令長名世祖中興皆省, 唯廷尉及雒陽有詔獄。(『續漢書』百官志) |
| 典客<br>(大鴻臚) | 秦官, 掌諸歸義蠻夷, 有丞。秩中二千石, 丞千石。景帝中六年更名大行令, 武帝太初元年更名大鴻臚。應劭曰「郊廟行禮讚九賓, 鴻聲臚傳之也。」屬官有行人・譯官・別火三令丞, 如淳曰「漢儀注別火, 獄令官, 主治改火之事。」及郡邸長丞。師古曰「主諸郡之邸在京師者也。」武帝太初元年更名行人爲大行令, 初置別火。王莽改大鴻臚曰典樂。初, 置郡國邸屬少府, 中屬中尉, 後屬大鴻臚。(『漢書』百官公卿表)<br><br>大鴻臚, 卿一人, 中二千石。本注曰, 掌諸侯及四方歸義蠻夷。其郊廟行禮, 贊導, 請行事, 既可, 以命羣司。諸王入朝, 當郊迎, 典其禮儀。及郡國上計, 匡四方來, 亦屬焉。皇子拜王, 贊授印綬。及拜諸侯, 諸侯嗣子及四方夷狄封者, 臺下鴻臚召拜之。王薨則使弔之, 及拜王嗣。丞一人, 比千石。大行令一人, 六百石。本注曰, 主諸郎。丞一人。治禮郎四十七人。右屬大鴻臚。本注曰, 承秦有典屬國, 別主四方夷狄朝貢侍子, 成帝時省并大鴻臚。中興省驛官・別火二令・丞, 及郡邸長・丞, 但令郎治郡邸。(『續漢書』百官志) |
| 宗正 | 秦官, 應劭曰「周成王之時彤伯入爲宗正也。」師古曰「彤伯爲宗伯, 不謂之宗正。」掌親屬, 有丞。秩中二千石, 丞千石。平帝元始四年更名宗伯。屬官有都司空令丞, 如淳曰「律, 司空主水及罪人。賈誼曰『輸之司 |

57

| 職官名 | 職掌・屬官 |
|---|---|
|  | 空,編之徒官』。」內官長丞。師古曰「律曆志主分寸尺丈也。」又諸公主家令・門尉皆屬焉。王莽并其官於秩宗。初,內官屬少府,中屬主爵,後屬宗正。(『漢書』百官公卿表) |
|  | 宗正,卿一人,中二千石。本注曰,掌序錄王國嫡庶之次,及諸宗室親屬遠近,郡國歲因計上宗室名籍。若有犯法當髡以上,先上諸宗正,宗正以聞,乃報決。丞一人,比千石。諸公主,每主家令一人,六百石。丞一人,三百石。本注曰,其餘屬吏增減無常。右屬宗正。本注曰,中興省都司空令・丞。(『續漢書』百官志) |
| 治粟內史<br>(大司農) | 秦官,掌穀貨,有兩丞。秩中二千石,丞千石。景帝後元年更名大農令,武帝太初元年更名大司農。屬官有太倉・均輸・平準・都內・籍田五令丞,孟康曰「均輸,謂諸當所有輸於官者,皆令輸其地土所饒,平其所在時賈,官更於佗處賣之,輸者既便,而官有利也。」斡官・鐵市兩長丞。如淳曰「斡音筦,或作幹。幹,主也,主均輸之事,所謂斡鹽鐵而榷酒酤也。」晉灼曰「此竹箭幹之官長也。均輸自有令。」師古曰「如說近是也。縱作斡讀,當以斡持財貨之事耳,非謂箭幹也。」又郡國諸倉農監・都水六十五長丞皆屬焉。騪粟都尉,服虔曰「騪音搜狩之搜。搜,索也。」武帝軍官,不常置。王莽改大司農曰羲和,後更為納言。初,斡官屬少府,中屬主爵,後屬大司農。(『漢書』百官公卿表) |
|  | 大司農,卿一人,中二千石。本注曰,掌諸錢穀金帛諸貨幣。郡國四時上月旦見錢穀簿,其逋未畢,各具別之。邊郡諸官請調度者,皆為報給,損多益寡,取相給足。丞一人,比千石。部丞一人,六百石。本注曰,部丞主帑藏。太倉令一人,六百石。本注曰,主受郡國傳漕穀。丞一人。平準令一人,六百石。本注曰,掌知物賈,主練染,作采色。丞一人。導官令六百石。本注曰,主舂御米,及作乾糒。導,擇也。丞一人。右屬大司農。本注曰,郡國鹽官・鐵官本屬司農,中興皆屬郡縣。又有廩犧令,六百石,掌祭祀犧牲鴈鶩之屬。及雒陽市長・滎陽敖倉官,中興皆屬河南尹。餘均輸等皆省。(『續漢書』百官志) |
| 少府 | 秦官,掌山海池澤之稅,以給共養,應劭曰「名曰禁錢,以給私養,自別為藏。少者,小也,故稱少府。」師古曰「大司農供軍國之用,少府以養天子也。共音居用反。養音弋亮反。」有六丞。秩中二千石,丞千石。屬官有尚書・符節・太醫・太官・湯官・導官・樂府・若盧・考工室・左弋・居室・甘泉居室・左右司空・東織・西織・東園匠十六官令丞,服虔曰「若盧,詔獄也。」鄧展曰「舊洛陽兩獄,一名若盧,主受親戚婦女。」如淳曰「若盧,官名也,藏兵器。品令曰若盧郎中二十人,主弩射。漢儀注有若盧獄令,主治庫兵將相大臣。」臣瓚曰「冬官為考工,主作器械也。」師古曰「太官主膳食,湯官主餅餌,導官主擇米。若盧,如說是也。左弋,地名。東園 |

58

第3章 各職位の職掌・属官

| 職官名 | 職掌・属官 |
|---|---|
| | 匠, 主作陵内器物者也。」又胞人・都水・均官三長丞, 師古曰「胞人, 主掌宰割者也。胞與庖同。」又上林中十池監, 師古曰「三輔黄圖云上林中池上籞五所, 而此云十池監, 未詳其數。」又**中書謁者・黄門・鉤盾・尚方・御府・永巷・内者・宦者**八官令丞。師古曰「鉤盾主近苑囿, 尚方主作禁器物, 御府主天子衣服也。」諸僕射・署長・中黄門皆屬焉。師古曰「**中黄門**, 奄人居禁中在黄門之内給事者也。」武帝太初元年更名考工室為考工, 左弋為佽飛, 居室為保宮, 甘泉居室為昆臺, 永巷為掖庭。佽飛掌弋射, 有九丞兩尉, 太官七丞, **昆臺**五丞, 樂府三丞, 掖庭八丞, 宦者七丞, 鉤盾五丞兩尉。成帝建始四年更名中書謁者令為中謁者令, 初置尚書, 員五人, 有四丞。河平元年省**東織**, 更名**西織**為織室。綏和二年, 哀帝省樂府。王莽改少府曰共工。(『漢書』百官公卿表) |
| | **少府**, 卿一人, 中二千石。本注曰, 掌中服御諸物, 衣服寶貨珍膳之屬。丞一人, 比千石。**太醫令**一人, 六百石。本注曰, 掌諸醫。**藥丞・方丞**各一人。本注曰, 藥丞主藥。方丞主藥方。**太官令**一人, 六百石。本注曰, 掌御飲食。**左丞・甘丞・湯官丞・果丞**各一人。本注曰, 左丞主飲食。甘丞主膳具。湯官丞主酒。果丞主果。**守宮令**一人, 六百石。本注曰, 主御紙筆墨, 及尚書財用諸物及封泥。丞一人。**上林苑令**一人, 六百石。本注曰, 主苑中禽獸。頗有民居, 皆主之。捕得其獸送太官。丞・尉各一人。**侍中**, 比二千石。本注曰, 無員。掌侍左右, 贊導眾事, 顧問應對。法駕出, 則多識者一人參乘, 餘皆騎在乘輿車後。本有僕射一人, 中興轉為**祭酒**, 或置或否。**中常侍**, 千石。本注曰, 宦者, 無員。後增秩比二千石。掌侍左右, 從入内宮, 贊導内眾事, 顧問應對給事。**黄門侍郎**, 六百石。本注曰, 無員。掌侍從左右, 給事中, 關通中外。及諸王朝見於殿上, 引王就坐。 |
| | **小黄門**, 六百石。本注曰, 宦者, 無員。掌侍左右, 受尚書事。上在内宮, 關通中外, 及中宮已下眾事。諸公主及王太妃等有疾苦, 則使問之。**黄門令**一人, 六百石。本注曰, 宦者。主省中諸宦者。丞・從丞各一人。本注曰, 宦者。從丞主出入從。**黄門署長・畫室署長・玉堂署長**各一人。丙署長七人, 皆四百石, 黄綬。本注曰, 宦者。各主中宮別處。**中黄門冗從僕射**一人, 六百石。本注曰, 宦者。主中黄門冗從。居則宿衛, 直守門戶。出則騎從, 夾乘輿車。**中黄門**, 比百石。本注曰, 宦者, 無員。後增比三百石。掌給事禁中。**掖庭令**一人, 六百石。本注曰, 宦者。掌後宮貴人采女事。**左右丞・暴室丞**各一人。本注曰, 宦者。暴室丞主中婦人疾病者, 就此室治。其皇后・貴人有罪, 亦就此室。**永巷令**一人, 六百石。本注曰, 宦者。典官婢侍使。丞一人。本注曰, 宦者。**御府令**一人, 六百石。本注曰, 宦者。典官婢作中衣服及補浣之屬。丞・**織室丞**各一人。本注曰, 宦者。 |

59

| 職官名 | 職掌・属官 |
|---|---|
|  | 祠祀令一人，六百石。本注曰，典中諸小祠祀。丞一人。本注曰，宦者。鉤盾令一人，六百石。本注曰，宦者。典諸近池苑囿遊觀之處。丞・永安丞各一人，三百石。本注曰，宦者。永安，北宮東北別小宮名，有園觀。苑中丞・果丞・鴻池丞・南園丞各一人，二百石。本注曰，苑中丞主苑中離宮。果丞主果園。鴻池，池名，在雒陽東二十里。南園在雒水南。**濯龍監・直里監**各一人，四百石。本注曰，濯龍亦園名，近北宮。直里亦園名也，在雒陽城西南角。**中藏府令**一人，六百石。本注曰，掌中幣帛金銀諸貨物。丞一人。**內者令**一人，六百石。本注曰，掌宮中布張諸藝物。左右丞各一人。**尚方令**一人，六百石。本注曰，掌上手工作御刀劍諸好器物。丞一人。**尚書令**一人，千石。本注曰，承秦所置，武帝用宦者，更為中書謁者令，成帝用士人，復故。掌凡選署及奏下尚書曹文書眾事。**尚書僕射**一人，六百石。本注曰，署尚書事，令不在則奏下眾事。**尚書**六人，六百石。本注曰，成帝初置尚書四人，分為四曹。常侍曹尚書主公卿事。二千石曹尚書主郡國二千石事。民曹尚書主凡吏上書事。客曹尚書主外國夷狄事。世祖承遵，後分二千石曹，又分客曹為南主客曹・北主客曹，凡六曹。**左右丞**各一人，四百石。本注曰，掌錄文書期會。左丞主吏民章報及騶伯史。右丞假署印綬，及紙筆墨諸財用庫藏。**侍郎**三十六人，四百石。本注曰，一曹有六人，主作文書起草。**令史**十八人，二百石。本注曰，曹有三，主書。後增劇曹三人，合二十一人。**符節令**一人，六百石。本注曰，為符節臺率，主符節事。凡遣使掌授節。**尚符璽郎中**四人。本注曰，舊二人在中，主璽及虎符・竹符之半者。**符節令史**，二百石。本注曰，掌書。**御史中丞**一人，千石。本注曰，御史大夫之丞也。舊別監御史在殿中，密舉非法。及御史大夫轉為司空，因別留中，為御史臺率，後又屬少府。**治書侍御史**二人，六百石。本注曰，掌選明法律者為之。凡天下諸讞疑事，掌以法律當其是非。**侍御史**十五人，六百石。本注曰，掌察舉非法，受公卿羣吏奏事，有違失舉劾之。凡郊廟之祠及大朝會・大封拜，則二人監威儀，有違失則劾奏。**蘭臺令史**，六百石。本注曰，掌奏及印工文書。右屬少府。本注曰，職屬少府者，自太醫・上林凡四官。自侍中至御史，皆以文屬焉。承秦，凡山澤陂池之稅，名曰禁錢，屬少府。世祖改屬司農，考工轉屬太僕，都水屬郡國。孝武帝初置水衡都尉，秩比二千石，別主上林苑有離宮燕休之處，世祖省之，并其職於少府。每立秋貙劉之日，輒暫置水衡都尉，事訖乃罷之。少府本六丞，省五。又省湯官・織室令，置丞。又省上林十池監・胞人長丞，宦者・昆臺・佽飛三令，二十一丞。又省水衡屬官令・長・丞・尉二十餘人。章和以下，中官稍廣，加嘗藥・太官・御者・鉤盾・尚方・考工・別作監，皆六百石，宦者為之，轉為兼副，或省，故錄本官。(『續漢書』百官志) |
| 中尉<br>(執金吾) | 秦官，掌徼循京師，如淳曰「所謂遊徼，徼循禁備盜賊也。」師古曰「徼謂遮繞也。徼音工釣反。」有兩丞・候・司馬・千人。秩中二千石，丞千石。 |

第 3 章 各職位の職掌・属官

| 職官名 | 職掌・属官 |
|---|---|
|  | 師古曰「候及司馬及千人皆官名也。屬國都尉云有丞・候・千人。西域都護云司馬・候・千人各二人。凡此千人, 皆官名也。」武帝太初元年更名執金吾, 應劭曰「吾者, 禦也, 掌執金革以禦非常。」師古曰「金吾, 鳥名也, 主辟不祥。天子出行, 職主先導, 以禦非常, 故執此鳥之象, 因以名官。」屬官有中壘・寺互・武庫・都船四令丞。如淳曰「漢儀注有寺互。都船獄令, 治水官也。」都船・武庫有三丞, 中壘兩尉。又式道左右中候・候丞及左右京輔都尉・尉丞兵卒皆屬焉。應劭曰「式道凡三候, 車駕出還, 式道候持麾至宮門, 門乃開。」師古曰「式, 表也。」初, 寺互屬少府, 中屬主爵, 後屬中尉。(『漢書』百官公卿表) <br><br> 執金吾一人, 中二千石。本注曰, 掌宮外戒司非常水火之事。月三繞行宮外, 及主兵器。吾猶禦也。丞一人, 比千石。緹騎二百人。本注曰, 無秩, 比吏食奉。武庫令一人, 六百石。本注曰, 主兵器。丞一人。右屬執金吾。本注曰, 本有式道, 左右中候三人, 六百石。車駕出, 掌在前清道, 還持麾至宮門, 宮門乃開。中興但一人, 又不常置, 每出, 以郎兼式道候, 事已罷, 不復屬執金吾。又省中壘・寺互・都船令・丞・尉及左右京輔都尉。(『續漢書』百官志) |
| 太子太傅 | 少傅, 古官。秩二千石。屬官有太子門大夫, 應劭曰「員五人, 秩六百石。」庶子, 應劭曰「員五人, 秩六百石。」先馬, 張晏曰「先馬, 員十六人, 秩比謁者。」如淳曰「前驅也。國語曰句踐親為夫差先馬。先或作洗也。」舍人。(『漢書』百官公卿表) <br><br> 太子太傅一人, 中二千石。本注曰, 職掌輔導太子。禮如師, 不領官屬。(『續漢書』百官志) |
| 將作少府 | 秦官, 掌治宮室, 有兩丞・左右中候。秩二千石, 丞六百石。景帝中六年更名將作大匠。屬官有石庫・東園主章・左右前後中校七令丞, 如淳曰「章謂大材也。舊將作大匠主材吏名章曹掾。」師古曰「今所謂木鍾者, 蓋章聲之轉耳。東園主章掌大材, 以供東園大匠也。」又主章長丞。師古曰「掌凡大木也。」武帝太初元年更名東園主章為木工。成帝陽朔三年省中候及左右前後中校五丞。(『漢書』百官公卿表) <br><br> 將作大匠一人, 二千石。本注曰, 承秦, 曰將作少府, 景帝改為將作大匠。掌修作宗廟・路寢・宮室・陵園木土之功, 并樹桐梓之類列于道側。丞一人, 六百石。<br>左校令一人, 六百石。本注曰, 掌左工徒。丞一人。右校令一人, 六百石。本注曰, 掌右工徒。丞一人。(『續漢書』百官志) |
| 詹事 | 秦官, 應劭曰「詹, 省也, 給也。」臣瓚曰「茂陵書詹事秩真二千石。」掌皇后・太子家, 有丞。秩二千石, 丞六百石。師古曰「皇后, 太子各置詹 |

| 職官名 | 職掌・属官 |
|---|---|
|  | 事,隨其所在以名官。」屬官有太子率更・家令丞・僕・中盾・衞率・廚廄長丞。張晏曰「太子稱家,故曰家令。」臣瓚曰「茂陵中書太子家令秩八百石。」應劭曰「中盾主周衞徼道,秩四百石。」如淳曰「漢儀注衞率主門衞,秩千石。」師古曰「掌知漏刻,故曰率更。自此以上,太子之官也。更音工衡反。」又中長秋・私府・永巷・倉・廄・祠祀・食官令長丞。諸宦官皆屬焉。師古曰「自此以上,皆皇后之官。」成帝鴻嘉三年省詹事官,并屬大長秋。師古曰「省皇后詹事,總屬長秋也。」長信詹事掌皇太后宮,景帝中六年更名長信少府,張晏曰「以太后所居宮為名也。居長信宮則曰長信少府,居長樂宮則曰長樂少府也。」平帝元始四年更名長樂少府。(『漢書』百官公卿表) |
| 將行<br>(大長秋) | 秦官,應劭曰「皇后卿也。」秩二千石。景帝中六年更名大長秋,師古曰「秋者收成之時,長者恆久之義,故以為皇后官名。」或用中人,或用士人。師古曰「中人,奄人也。」(『漢書』百官公卿表)<br><br>大長秋一人,二千石。本注曰,承秦將行,宦者。景帝更為大長秋,或用士人。中興常用宦者,職掌奉宣中宮命。凡給賜宗親,及宗親當謁見者關通之,中宮出則從。丞一人,六百石。本注曰,宦者。中宮僕一人,千石。本注曰,宦者。主馭。本注曰,太僕,秩二千石,中興省「太」,減秩千石,以屬長秋。中宮謁者令一人,六百石。本注曰,宦者。中宮謁者三人,四百石。本注曰:宦者。主報中章。中宮尚書五人,六百石。本注曰,宦者。主中文書。中宮私府令一人,六百石。本注曰,宦者。主中藏幣帛諸物,裁衣被補浣者皆主之。丞一人,六百石。本注曰,宦者。中宮永巷令一人,六百石。本注曰,宦者。主宮人。丞一人,六百石。本注曰,宦者。中宮黃門冗從僕射一人,六百石。本注曰,宦者。主中黃門冗從。中宮署令一人,六百石。本注曰,宦者。主中宮清署天子數。女騎六人,丞・復道丞各一人。本注曰,宦者。復道丞主中閣道。中宮藥長一人,四百石。本注曰,宦者。右屬大長秋。本注曰,承秦,有詹事一人,位在長秋上,亦宦者,主中諸官。成帝省之,以其職并長秋。是後皇后當法駕出,則中謁・中宦者職吏權兼詹事奉引,訖罷。宦者誅後,尚書選兼職吏一人奉引云。其中長信・長樂宮者,置少府一人,職如長秋,及餘吏皆以宮名為號,員數秩次如中宮。本注曰,帝祖母稱長信宮,故有長信少府,長樂少府,位在長秋上,及職吏皆宦者,秩次如中宮。長樂又有衞尉,僕為太僕,皆二千石,在少府上。其崩則省,不常置。(『續漢書』百官志) |
| 典屬國 | 秦官,掌蠻夷降者。武帝元狩三年昆邪王降,師古曰「昆音下門反。」復增屬國,置都尉・丞・候・千人。秩二千石,丞六百石。屬官,九譯令。成帝河平元年省并大鴻臚。(『漢書』百官公卿表) |
| 水衡都尉 | 應劭曰「古山林之官曰衡。掌諸池苑,故稱水衡。」張晏曰「主都水及上林苑,故曰水衡。主諸官,故曰都。有卒徒武事,故曰尉。」師古曰「衡, |

第3章 各職位の職掌・属官

| 職官名 | 職掌・属官 |
|---|---|
| | 平也, 主平其税入。」武帝元鼎二年初置, 掌上林苑, 有五丞。秩二千石, 丞六百石。屬官有上林・均輸・御羞・禁圃・輯濯・鍾官・技巧・六廐・辯銅九官令丞。如淳曰「御羞, 地名也, 在藍田, 其土肥沃, 多出御物可進者, 揚雄傳謂之御宿。三輔黃圖御羞, 宜春皆苑名也。輯濯, 船官也。鍾官, 主鑄錢官也。辯銅, 主分別銅之種類也。」師古曰「御宿, 則今長安城南御宿川也, 不在藍田。羞・宿聲相近, 故或云御羞, 或云御宿耳。羞者, 珍羞所出。宿者, 止宿之義。輯讀與楫同, 音集, 濯音直孝反。皆所以行船也。漢舊儀云天子六廐, 未央・承華・駒駼・騎馬・輅軨・大廐也, 馬皆萬匹。據此表, 大僕屬官已有大廐・未央・輅軨・騎馬・駒駼・承華, 而水衡又云六廐技巧官, 是則技巧之徒供六廐者, 其官別屬水衡也。」又衡官・水司空・都水・農倉, 又甘泉上林・都水七官長丞皆屬焉。上林有八丞十二尉, 均輸四丞, 御羞兩丞, 都水三丞, 禁圃兩尉, 甘泉上林四丞。成帝建始二年省技巧・六廐官。王莽改水衡都尉曰予虞。初, 御羞・上林・衡官及鑄錢皆屬少府。(『漢書』百官公卿表) |
| 內史<br>(京兆尹・左馮翊)<br>河南尹 | 周官, 秦因之, 掌治京師。秩二千石。景帝二年分置左右內史。師古曰「地理志云武帝建元六年置左右內史, 而此表云景帝二年分置, 表志不同。又據史記, 知志誤矣。」右內史武帝太初元年更名京兆尹, 張晏曰「地絕高曰京。左傳曰『莫之與京』。十億曰兆。尹, 正也。」師古曰「京, 大也。兆者, 衆數。言大衆所在, 故云京兆也。」屬官有長安市・廚兩令丞, 又都水・鐵官兩長丞。左內史更名左馮翊, 張晏曰「馮, 輔也。翊, 佐也。」屬官有廩犧令丞尉。師古曰「廩主藏穀, 犧主養牲, 皆所以供祭祀也。」又左都水・鐵官・雲壘・長安四市四長丞皆屬焉。(『漢書』百官公卿表)<br><br>河南尹一人, 主京都, 特奉朝請。其京兆尹・左馮翊・右扶風三人, 漢初都長安, 皆秩中二千石, 謂之三輔。中興都雒陽, 更以河南郡為尹, 以三輔陵廟所在, 不改其號, 但減其秩。其餘弘農・河內・河東三郡。其置尹・馮翊・扶風及太守丞奉之本位, 在地理志。(『續漢書』百官志) |
| 主爵中尉<br>(右扶風) | 秦官, 掌列侯。景帝中六年更名都尉, 武帝太初元年更名右扶風, 張晏曰「扶, 助也。風, 化也。」治內史右地。秩二千石, 丞六百石。屬官有掌畜令丞。如淳曰「尹翁歸傳『豪強有論罪, 輸掌畜官, 使斫莝』。東方朔曰『益為右扶風』, 畜牧之所在也。」又都水・鐵官・廐・廱廚四長丞皆屬焉。如淳曰「五時在廱, 故有廚。」與左馮翊・京兆尹是為三輔, 服虔曰「皆治在長安城中。」師古曰「三輔黃圖云京兆在尚冠前街東入, 故中尉府, 馮翊在太上皇廟西入, 右扶風在夕陰街北入, 故主爵府。長安以東為京兆, 長陵以北為左馮翊, 渭城以西為右扶風也。」皆有兩丞。列侯更屬大鴻臚。元鼎四年更置三輔都尉・都尉丞各一人。(『漢書』百官公卿表) |

| 職官名 | 職掌・属官 |
|---|---|
| 護軍都尉 | 秦官。武帝元狩四年屬大司馬，成帝綏和元年居大司馬府比司直，哀帝元壽元年更名司寇，平帝元始元年更名護軍。(『漢書』百官公卿表) |
| 司隷校尉 | 周官，師古曰「以掌徒隷而巡察，故云司隷。」武帝征和四年初置。持節，從中都官徒千二百人，師古曰「中都官，京師諸官府也。」捕巫蠱，督大姦猾。師古曰「督謂察視也。」後罷其兵。察三輔・三河・弘農。元帝初元四年去節。成帝元延四年省。綏和二年，哀帝復置，但為司隷，冠進賢冠，屬大司空，比司直。(『漢書』百官公卿表)<br><br>司隷校尉一人，比二千石。本注曰，孝武帝初置，持節，掌察舉百官以下，及京師近郡犯法者。元帝去節，成帝省，建武中復置，并領一州。從事史十二人。本注曰，都官從事，主察舉百官犯法者。功曹從事，主州選署及眾事。別駕從事，校尉行部則奉引，錄眾事。簿曹從事，主財穀簿書。其有軍事，則置兵曹從事，主兵事。其餘部郡國從事，每郡國各一人，主督促文書，察舉非法，皆州自辟除，故通為百石云。假佐二十五人。本注曰，主簿錄閣下事，省文書。門亭長主州正。門功曹書佐主選用。孝經師主監試經。月令師主時節祠祀。律令師主平法律。簿曹書佐主簿書。其餘都官書佐及每郡國，各有典郡書佐一人，各主一郡文書，以郡吏補，歲滿一更。司隷所部郡七。(『續漢書』百官志) |
| 城門校尉 | 掌京師城門屯兵，有司馬，師古曰「八屯各有司馬也。」十二城門候。師古曰「門各有候，蕭望之署小苑東門候，亦其比也。」中壘校尉掌北軍壘門內，外掌西域。師古曰「掌北軍壘門之內，而又外掌西域。」屯騎校尉掌騎士。步兵校尉掌上林苑門屯兵。越騎校尉掌越騎。如淳曰「越人內附，以為騎也。」晉灼曰「取其材力超越也。」師古曰「宣紀言佽飛射士・胡越騎，又此有胡騎校尉。如說是。」長水校尉掌長水宣曲胡騎。師古曰「長水，胡名也。宣曲，觀名，胡騎之屯於宣曲者。」又有胡騎校尉，掌池陽胡騎，不常置。師古曰「胡騎之屯池陽者也。」射聲校尉掌待詔射聲士。服虔曰「工射者也。冥冥中聞聲則中之，因以名也。」應劭曰「須詔所命而射，故曰待詔射也。」虎賁校尉掌輕車。凡八校尉，皆武帝初置，有丞・司馬。師古曰「自中壘以下凡八校尉。城門不在此數中。」自司隷至虎賁校尉，秩皆二千石。西域都護加官，宣帝地節二年初置，以騎都尉・諫大夫使護西域三十六國，有副校尉，秩比二千石，丞一人，司馬・候・千人各二人。戊己校尉，元帝初元元年置，師古曰「甲乙丙丁庚辛壬癸皆有正位，唯戊己寄治耳。今所置校尉亦無常居，故取戊己為名也。有戊校尉，有己校尉。一說戊己居中，鎮覆四方，今所置校尉亦處西域之中撫諸國也。」有丞・司馬各一人，候五人，秩比六百石。(『漢書』百官公卿表)<br><br>城門校尉一人，比二千石。本注曰，掌雒陽城門十二所。司馬一人，千 |

第3章 各職位の職掌・属官

| 職官名 | 職掌・属官 |
|---|---|
|  | 石。本注曰,主兵。**城門每門候一人**,本注曰,雒陽城十二門,其正南一門曰平城門,北宮門,屬衛尉。其餘上西門,雍門,廣陽門,津門,小苑門,開陽門,秏門,中東門,上東門,穀門,夏門,凡十二門。右屬**城門校尉**。**北軍中候一人**,六百石。本注曰,掌監五營。**屯騎校尉一人**,比二千石。本注曰,掌宿衛兵。司馬一人,千石。**越騎校尉一人**,比二千石。本注曰,掌宿衛兵。司馬一人,千石。**步兵校尉一人**,比二千石。本注曰,掌宿衛兵。司馬一人,千石。**長水校尉一人**,比二千石。本注曰,掌宿衛兵。司馬・胡騎司馬各一人,千石。本注曰,掌宿衛,主烏桓騎。**射聲校尉一人**,比二千石。本注曰,掌宿衛兵。司馬一人,千石。右屬**北軍中候**。本注曰,舊有中壘校尉,領北軍營壘之事。有胡騎・虎賁校尉,皆武帝置。中興省中壘,但置中候,以監五營。胡騎并長水。虎賁主輕車并射聲。(『續漢書』百官志) |
| **奉車都尉・駙馬都尉** | **奉車都尉**掌御乘輿車,**駙馬都尉**掌駙馬,師古曰「駙,副馬也。非正駕車,皆為副馬。一曰駙,近也,疾也。」皆武帝初置,秩比二千石。**侍中・左右曹・諸吏・散騎・中常侍**,皆加官,應劭曰「入侍天子,故曰侍中。」晉灼曰「漢儀注諸吏,給事中日上朝謁,平尚書奏事,分為左右曹。魏文帝合散騎,中常侍為散騎常侍也。」所加或列侯・將軍・卿大夫・將・都尉・尚書・太醫・太官令至郎中,亡員,如淳曰「將謂郎將以下也。自列侯下至郎中,皆得有散騎及中常侍加官。是時散騎及常侍各自一官,亡員也。」多至數十人。侍中・中常侍得入禁中,諸曹受尚書事,諸吏得舉法,**散騎**騎並乘輿車。師古曰「並音步浪反。騎而散從,無常職也。」給事中亦加官,師古曰「漢官解詁云掌侍從左右,無員,常侍中。」所加或大夫・博士・議郎,掌顧問應對,位次中常侍。中黃門有給事黃門,位從將大夫。皆秦制。(『漢書』百官公卿表) <br><br> (**光祿勳**)本注曰,職屬光祿者,自五官將至羽林右監,凡七署。自奉車都尉至謁者,以文屬焉。舊有左右曹,秩以二千石,上殿中,主受尚書奏事,平省之。世祖省,使小黃門郎受事,車駕出,給黃門郎兼。有請室令,車駕出,在前請所幸,徼車迎白,示重慎。中興但以郎兼,事訖罷,又省車・戶・騎凡三將,及羽林令。(『續漢書』百官志) |
| **諸侯王** | **高帝初置**,師古曰「蔡邕云漢制皇子封為王,其實諸侯也。周末諸侯或稱王,漢天子自以皇帝為稱,故以王號加之,總名諸侯王也。」**金璽盭綬**,如淳曰「盭音戾。盭,綠也,以綠為質。」晉灼曰「盭,草名也,出琅邪平昌縣,似艾,可染綠,因以為綬名也。」師古曰「晉說是也。璽之言信也。古者印璽通名,今則尊卑有別。漢舊儀云諸侯王黃金璽,橐佗鈕,文曰璽,謂刻云某王之璽。」**掌治其國**。有**太傅輔王,內史治國民,中尉掌武職,丞相統衆官,羣卿大夫都官如漢朝**。景帝中五年令諸侯王不得復 |

65

| 職官名 | 職掌・属官 |
|---|---|
| | 治國、天子為置吏、改丞相曰相、省御史大夫・廷尉・少府・宗正・博士官、大夫・謁者・郎諸官長丞皆損其員。武帝改漢內史為京兆尹、中尉為執金吾、郎中令為光祿勳、故王國如故。損其郎中令、秩千石。改太僕曰僕、秩亦千石。成帝綏和元年省內史、更令相治民、如郡太守、中尉如郡都尉。(『漢書』百官公卿表) |
| | 皇子封王、其郡為國、每置傅一人、相一人、皆二千石。本注曰、傅主導王以善、禮如師、不臣也。相如太守。有長史、如郡丞。漢初立諸王、因項羽所立諸王之制、地既廣大、且至千里。又其官職傅為太傅、相為丞相、又有御史大夫及諸卿、皆秩二千石、石官皆如朝廷。國家唯為置丞相、其御史大夫以下皆自置之。至景帝時、吳・楚七國恃其國大、遂以作亂、幾危漢室。及其誅滅、景帝懲之、遂令諸王不得治民、令內史主治民、改丞相曰相、省御史大夫・廷尉・少府・宗正・博士官。武帝改漢內史・中尉。郎中令之名、而王國如故、員職皆朝廷為署、不得自置。至成帝省內史治民、更令相治民、太傅但曰傅。中尉一人、比二千石。本注曰、職如郡都尉、主盜賊。郎中令一人、僕一人、皆千石。本注曰、郎中令掌王大夫・郎中宿衛、官如光祿勳。自省少府、職皆并焉。僕主車及馭、如太僕。本注曰太僕、比二千石、武帝改、但曰僕、又皆減其秩。治書、比六百石。本注曰、治書本尚書更名。大夫、比六百石。本注曰、無員。掌奉王使至京都、奉璧賀正月、及使諸國。本皆持節、後去節。謁者、比四百石。本注曰、掌冠長冠。本員十六人、後減。禮樂長。本注曰、主樂人。衛士長。本注曰、主衛士。醫工長。本注曰、主醫藥。永巷長。本注曰、宦者、主宮中婢使。祠祀長。本注曰、主祠祀。皆比四百石。郎中、二百石。本注曰、無員。(『續漢書』百官志) |
| 監御史(刺史) | 秦官、掌監郡。漢省、丞相遣史分刺州、不常置。武帝元封五年初置部刺史、掌奉詔條察州、師古曰「漢官典職儀云刺史班宣、周行郡國、省察治狀、黜陟能否、斷治冤獄、以六條問事、非條所問、即不省。一條、強宗豪右田宅踰制、以強淩弱、以眾暴寡。二條、二千石不奉詔書遵承典制、倍公向私、旁詔守利、侵漁百姓、聚斂為姦。三條、二千石不卹疑獄、風厲殺人、怒則任刑、喜則淫賞、煩擾刻暴、剝截黎元、為百姓所疾、山崩石裂、祅祥訛言。四條、二千石選署不平、苟阿所愛、蔽賢寵頑。五條、二千石子弟恃怙榮勢、請託所監。六條、二千石違公下比、阿附豪強、通行貨賂、割損正令也。」秩六百石、員十三人。成帝綏和元年更名牧、秩二千石。哀帝建平二年復為刺史、元壽二年復為牧。(『漢書』百官公卿表)<br><br>外十二州、每州刺史一人、六百石。本注曰、秦有監御史、監諸郡、漢興 |

第3章 各職位の職掌・属官

| 職官名 | 職掌・属官 |
|---|---|
|  | 省之、但遣丞相史分刺諸州、無常官。孝武帝初置刺史十三人、秩六百石。諸書不同也。成帝更為牧、秩二千石。建武十八年、復為刺史、十二人各主一州、其一州屬司隸校尉。諸州常以八月巡行所部郡國、錄囚徒、考殿最。初歲盡詣京都奏事、中興但因計吏。凡州所監都為京都、置尹一人、二千石、丞一人。(『續漢書』百官志) |
| 郡守<br>(太守) | 秦官、掌治其郡、秩二千石。有丞、邊郡又有長史、掌兵馬、秩皆六百石。景帝中二年更名太守。(『漢書』百官公卿表)<br><br>每郡置太守一人、二千石、丞一人。郡當邊戍者、丞為長史。王國之相亦如之。(『續漢書』百官志) |
| 郡尉<br>(都尉) | 秦官、掌佐守典武職甲卒、秩比二千石。有丞、秩皆六百石。景帝中二年更名都尉。(『漢書』百官公卿表)<br><br>每屬國置都尉一人、比二千石、丞一人。本注曰、凡郡國皆掌治民、進賢勸功、決訟檢姦。常以春行所主縣、勸民農桑、振救乏絕。秋冬遣無害吏案訊諸囚、平其罪法、論課殿最。歲盡遣吏上計。并舉孝廉、郡口二十萬舉一人。尉一人、典兵禁、備盜賊、景帝更名都尉。(『續漢書』百官志) |
| 關都尉 | 秦官。農都尉・屬國都尉、皆武帝初置。(『漢書』百官公卿表)<br><br>武帝又置三輔都尉各一人、譏出入。邊郡置農都尉、主屯田殖穀。又置屬國都尉、主蠻夷降者。中興建武六年、省諸郡都尉、并職太守、無都試之役。省關都尉、唯邊郡往往置都尉及屬國都尉、稍有分縣、治民比郡。安帝以羌犯法、三輔有陵園之守、乃復置右扶風都尉、京兆虎牙都尉。皆置諸曹掾史。本注曰、諸曹略如公府曹、無東西曹。有功曹史、主選署功勞。有五官掾、署功曹及諸曹事。其監屬縣、有五部督郵、曹掾一人。正門有亭長一人。主記室史、主錄記書、催期會。無令史、閤下及諸曹各有書佐、幹主文書。(『續漢書』百官志) |
| 縣令・長 | 皆秦官、掌治其縣。萬戶以上為令、秩千石至六百石。減萬戶為長、秩五百石至三百石。皆有丞・尉、秩四百石至二百石、是為長吏。師古曰「吏、理也、主理其縣內也。」百石以下有斗食・佐史之秩、師古曰「漢官名秩簿云斗食月奉十一斛、佐史月奉八斛也。一說、斗食者、歲奉不滿百石、計日而食一斗二升、故云斗食也。」是為少吏。大率十里一亭、亭有長。十亭一鄉、鄉有三老・有秩・嗇夫・游徼。三老掌教化。嗇夫職聽訟、收賦稅。游徼徼循禁賊盜。縣大率方百里、其民稠則減、稀則曠、鄉・亭亦如之、皆秦制也。列侯所食縣曰國、皇太后・皇后・公主所食曰邑、有蠻夷曰道。縣・道・國・邑千五百八十七、鄉六千六百二十二、亭二萬九千六百三十五。(『漢書』百官公卿表) |

67

| 職官名 | 職掌・属官 |
|---|---|
|  | 每縣・邑・道，大者置令一人，千石。其次置長，四百石。小者置長，三百石。侯國之相，秩次亦如之。本注曰，皆掌治民，顯善勸義，禁姦罰惡，理訟平賊，恤民時務，秋冬集課，上計於所屬郡國。凡縣主蠻夷曰道。公主所食湯沐曰邑。縣萬戶以上為令，不滿為長。侯國為相。皆秦制也。**丞**各一人。**尉**大縣二人，小縣一人。本注曰，丞署文書，典知倉獄。尉主盜賊。凡有賊發，主名不立，則推索行尋，案察姦宄，以起端緒。各署諸**曹掾史**。本注曰，諸曹略如郡員，五官為廷掾，監鄉五部，春夏為勸農掾，秋冬為制度掾。鄉置**有秩・三老・游徼**。本注曰，有秩，郡所署，秩百石，掌一鄉人。其鄉小者，縣置嗇夫一人。皆主知民善惡，為役先後，知民貧富，為賦多少，平其差品。三老掌教化。凡有孝子順孫，貞女義婦，讓財救患，及學士為民法式者，皆扁表其門，以興善行。游徼掌徼循，禁司姦盜。又有**鄉佐**，屬鄉，主民收賦稅。亭有亭長，以禁盜賊。本注曰，亭長，主求捕盜賊，承望都尉。（『續漢書』百官志） |

# 第4章　職官名関連和英表現集

## Japanese-English Expressions Related to the Official Titles
### (An index to Watson translations of the *Han Shu* and *Shi ji*)

凡例
1. 本章タイトルにある an index とは，本表現集が漢書 Watson 訳 *Courtier and Commoner in Ancient China* に現われる官職名およびそれに関する表現用例の<u>部分的索引</u>でしかないことをいう。すなわち英語対訳は Watson 訳からの切り出しそのままであって，一般辞書のように品詞対応にはなっていないし，和英両語間の語句も完全には一致していない。あくまでも英文作成時の<u>一ヒントとして</u>利用されることを想定している。したがって本表現集はわれわれ**著者の見解ではない**。われわれの見解は第1章「組織表」に集約されている。本表現集は「こういう表現を Watson はどう言っているか」といった関心を持たれる読者にのみ，多少の便を供することができるであろう。
2. 抽出した英訳の範囲は単数複数，冠詞の用法がわかる程度に広くした。
3. 見出し語に同じ語句や類似表現が反復して現われることがあるが，それらは Watson 訳の一貫性や，それら語句・表現の出現頻度を見る調査の跡である。整理編集せず無加工で掲載する。バリエーションの参考などに資するかもしれない。

| 記号 | 意味 |
|---|---|
| :: | 語順の逆転。B::A の場合，元来はABという語順であったものを，Bを見出し語語頭に持ち出すために逆転させている。B の元の位置がわかりにくいときは「〜」を置いた(例，B::A〜C では，元来の語順は ABC)。「〜」が語尾に来る場合，それがなくても語順が明白と思われる場合は省略した。(例，B:A の，B:A を) |
| B⟨A〜⟩C | 語順の逆転。本来の語順が ABC であることを示す。 |
| [　]内 | 編者からの備考。<br>　1. 漢字の読み。<br>　2. 日本語欄の語句に対応しないが，文脈理解を助けるために追加した原英文。<br>　3. 英訳解釈上の注意点。 |
| 太字 | 日本語見出し語と，それに対応する英訳部分。 |
| (漢○○) | 漢書巻○○の略。 |
| 【　】 | 原漢文。 |
| 英語対応部分の範囲 | 典型例のみ。<br>1代名詞—**勇を好む** his love of daring ｜ **引見** called her into his presence |

| 記号 | 意味 |
|---|---|
| | これらにおける his や her は用途に応じて変化させなければならない。 |

2　冠詞―漢室 the throne of the Han
この場合 throne には常に the が付くと判断されるので, the を保存している。通常, 名詞は冠詞なしで掲載している（emperor など）。また単数複数, 大文字小文字の区別は原文から抽出したまま未加工である。

3　前置詞―令史 secretary to the magistrate of
of を温存したのは, magistrate がだれか既定の一人ではないということを示唆するためである。ここでは「どこそこの magistrate」と, 何か後ろに続くものがあると了解されたい。

4　その他―処せられ was cut
「刑に処す」は sentence や punish ばかりでなく, こうした簡単な単語でも表現できることを示す。もちろんどう cut するかが要であるので, 英訳欄に前後を収載してある。

＊並び順はひらがな→漢字の音読み

| | |
|---|---|
| あえて::太官が〜具えない | The imperial butler did not **dare** comply（漢 68） |
| あばきたて::大将軍の過失を【発揚大將軍過失】 | **expose** the failures and shortcomings of the general in chief（漢 68） |
| いつわりのあること::〜を察知 | realized there was **deception afoot**（漢 63） |
| いないのを見て【苟見丞相不在】 | you see that the chancellor **is no longer around** to protest（漢 74） |
| いにしえ | men **of antiquity**（漢 74） |
| うるわしくする::風俗を【美風俗】 | **beautifying** his ways and customs（漢 65） |
| おのが意に従ごうて過つことなく【帥意亡諐】 | **give all your thoughts to** the avoidance of error（漢 78） |
| およそ［…で］::〜校尉以下で | were **mere** company commanders or even lower（漢 54） |
| かかわり::尚書に〜ないようにし【不関尚書】 | without first **clearing them with the office of** palace writers（漢 68） |
| かかわる::食監に〜な【無関食監】 | not to **send them by way of** the supervisor of food（漢 68） |
| かけ離れて::凡人と〜いる【有絕異之姿】 | we recognize in them qualities that are **far removed from** the ordinary（漢 92） |
| からかい〈ばかにして〜〉::相手かまわず【敖弄】 | would **bait and banter with** everyone（漢 65） |
| きわまりなく::滑稽〜 | for his **never-ending fund of** waggery（漢 65） |

## 第4章 職官名関連和英表現集

| | |
|---|---|
| くじき::その力は公侯を～しのいだ【力折公侯】 | Their strength **humbled** dukes and marquises（漢 92） |
| これによる::「期門」という官名は | the term *ch'i-men* or "rendezvous gate" **first came into use**（漢 65） |
| ご恩::陛下の～をこうむって【蒙恩】 | have received **great blessing** from Your Majesty（漢 92） |
| させない::西域を擾乱～【使不敢復擾西域】 | **intimidating** them **from** making further trouble for the region west of China（漢 74） |
| さとすべからざる::何とも～やつ | You **never understand anything I say**（漢 97B） |
| さらし首::ついに渉を斬って、長安の市に～にした【遂斬渉, 縣之長安市】 | Yüan She was in the end executed and **his head hung** in the market place of Ch'ang-an（漢 92） |
| されんことを | **I only hope that**（漢 97B） |
| さわぎ::群衆は～立って怪しんでいる【群衆讙譁怪之】 | among the populace there is **a buzz of** suspicion and speculation（漢 97B） |
| しようとしない::太守は聴き入れようとせず【太守不聴】 | the governor **refused to** listen to him（漢 71） |
| しようとしない::役人は［租税を］免除～【吏不肯除】 | the officials are **unwilling to** grant them exemptions from taxes（漢 71） |
| しようとする::丞相・御史大夫・中二千石たちは誰一人発言しようとしなかった【丞相御史中二千石至者並莫敢発言】 | The chancellor, the imperial secretary, and the two thousand picul officials all arrived on the spot but none **dared to** speak up.（漢 71） |
| しりぞけ::文書を～奏上しない【屏不奏其書】 | I used to **put** such letters **aside** and not allow them to be submitted to the throne（漢 68） |
| すぎない::位は執戟に～【位不過執戟】 | your post is **no more than** that of lance-bearer（漢 65） |
| すぎない::官は侍郎に～すぎず【官不過侍郎】 | your rank does **not exceed** palace attendant（漢 65） |
| すみやかに［…しない］::役人は～追わない【吏不亟追】 | the officials **make no haste to** pursue them（漢 71） |
| せい::君のみの【何必顓焉】 | you alone be held **responsible**（漢 71） |
| そしり::上を【訕上】 | **slandering** his superiors（漢 67） |
| その後 | **Sometime later**（漢 78） |
| たまたま | **It so happened that**（漢 63） |
| たまたま | **As it happened, …**（漢 68） |
| たまたま天佑をもって【適有天幸】 | **met with** extraordinary luck（漢 92） |

| | |
|---|---|
| ついにこれを斬った | **summarily** executed the superintendent（漢67） |
| つかさどらせる | **gave him supervision over**（漢74） |
| つかわし::中郎将蘇武を匈奴に | **dispatched** Su Wu, a general of palace attendants, as his envoy to the Hsiung-nu（漢63） |
| つかわし::廷尉と大鴻臚を | **dispatched** the commandant of justice and the director of foreign vassals to go to Kuang-ling（漢63） |
| であった::太子〜 | **had originally been** the heir apparent of the Hsiung-nu Hsiu-t'u king（漢68） |
| できなくなる::制止【不制】 | **reach the point where it cannot** be checked（漢74） |
| とある::司馬法に〜… | The Rules of the Marshal **states**（漢67） |
| ともに::反乱〜発し | rebellion broke out **both within the state and abroad**（漢63） |
| と述べられ | **reads as follows:**（漢74） |
| なる::移 中廐監になった | **reached the position of** superintendent of the I-chung Stables（漢54） |
| なる::典属国にしかなれなかった【乃爲典属国】 | was only **given the post of** director of dependent states（漢54） |
| なる::郎となり | being **made** palace attendants（漢54） |
| なる〈廷尉と〜〉::張釈之が〜 | Chang Shih-chih **was commandant of justice**（漢71） |
| にまでなり::九卿・封侯〜【至九卿封侯】 | **rose to become** one of the nine high ministers and to be enfeoffed as a marquis（漢68） |
| にわかに::皇帝が〜崩御された【皇帝暴崩】 | His Imperial Majesty has passed away **with great suddenness**（漢97B） |
| はかりしれない | are **beyond estimation**（漢74） |
| はかる::陰謀を | **plotted** to（漢74） |
| はじめとして::公卿を〜位にある者すべて【自公卿在位】 | **From** the highest nobles and office-holders **on down**（漢65） |
| ばかにしてからかい::相手かまわず【敖弄】 | would **bait and banter with** everyone（漢65） |
| ひきい用いて::義を〜その身を正し【引義以正其身】 | **enlisting** righteousness to help him rectify himself（漢65） |
| ひそかに | **personally**（漢74） |
| ほしいままに::権勢を〜しようとしている【専擅権勢】 | their desire to **gather all power and authority into their own hands**（漢78） |
| ほしいままにし::末流を〜【放縦於末流】 | **allowed themselves to drift into** a shabby and inferior way of life（漢92） |
| ほしいままにして::一姓が勢いを〜【一姓擅勢】 | one clan has **arrogated** all authority to itself alone（漢78） |

## 第4章 職官名関連和英表現集

| | |
|---|---|
| ほしいままに使役する【擅使】 | order his subordinates about **on any errands he pleases**（漢78） |
| まっとうした：：天寿を【以寿終】 | **lived to a ripe old age**（漢71） |
| みだりにほめあげているのは，邪心があるように疑われる【妄相称挙，疑有姦心】 | Behind such **wild** praise and recommendation I fear there may be sinister designs that should not be left to flourish unchecked（漢67） |
| みだりに一胡児を得る【妄得一胡児】 | **by some quirk of circumstance** gets himself a barbarian boy（漢68） |
| むすっとして【不快】 | **sullen**（漢92） |
| もっとも：：九卿が私を責めるのは～だ【九卿責光是也】 | is **right** for the high ministers to berate me（漢68） |
| もっともである | **it's only right that**（漢68） |
| もっぱらにし：：権力を～朝廷をほしいままにする【専権擅朝】 | **arrogate to himself** all the power of the court（漢78） |
| もとの丞相吉 | The **late** chancellor Ping Chi（漢74） |
| もとの太子の舎人であった | was a retainer of the **late** crown prince Li（漢71） |
| やめさせる【斥之】 | **have the man discharged**（漢74） |
| やめる：：副封を【去副封】 | the system of submitting duplicate copies be **abolished**（漢74） |
| ゆだねられず：：政は大夫に～【政不在大夫】 | government will **not be in the hands of** the high officials（漢92） |
| よいではないか【不亦可乎】 | **is there any great harm?**（漢71） |
| よいではないか【不亦善乎】 | **wouldn't that be best?**（漢71） |
| よりて〈これに～〉姦をなす | see 因りて |
| よろしく…する【宜】 | **It would be best to**（漢74） |
| りっぱな：：何と～大夫【賢哉二大夫】 | What **fine** gentlemen these two are!（漢71） |
| わけがわからない：：驚愕し何がなんだか～【愕驚不知所以】 | were **thrown into a state of complete bewilderment**（漢67） |
| 悪む | **criticizing**（漢74） |
| 悪を懲らし義を崇ぶ【懲悪崇誼示四方也】 | in censuring **evil** and displaying respect for right（漢97B） |
| 悪を誅して：：武を立てて衆に威を示し，～もって邪を禁ず【立武以威衆，誅悪以禁邪】 | make a display of military force in order to inspire awe, and one should **punish evildoers** in order to prevent malefaction（漢67） |
| 悪んで淫乱を～【悪其淫乱】 | **disgusted** by his licentious and unruly ways（漢68） |
| 悪人の一味とみなし【為悪人黨】 | looking upon them as the followers of an **evildoer**（漢67） |

| | |
|---|---|
| 悪吏 | **Evil officials**（漢 71） |
| 悪吏が法を無視し | **villainous officials** ignore the law（漢 63） |
| 安んじ::社稷を～た【安社稷】 | **insured the safety of** the altars of the soil and grain（漢 68） |
| 安んじる::天下を【安天下】 | **bringing peace to** the world（漢 74） |
| 安楽::君～にして【君安虞】 | the ruler will enjoy **safety and contentment**（漢 74） |
| 安治::天下を | **bring peace and good government to** the world（漢 74） |
| 安撫する::海内を～【撫海内】 | **bringing solace to** all within the four seas（漢 74） |
| 暗く::道理に【闇於大理】 | was **blind to** fundamental principles（漢 68） |
| 暗誦 | **recite**（漢 92） |
| 暗誦::経書を～し【諷誦経書】 | sit **mumbling over** your Classics and other texts（漢 92） |
| 案験::有司に下して～し，善悪を明らかにする【下有司案験以明好惡】 | to **refer the matter** to the authorities **for investigation** so that they may determine the right and wrong of it（漢 67） |
| 案内::謁者に命じて董君を宣室の中に～させた【引内】 | instructing the master of guests to have Lord Tung **conducted into** the hall（漢 65） |
| 以下::百官～が | everyone **from** the hundred officials **on down**（漢 68） |
| 位::みな尊貴の～におり【皆在尊貴之位】 | are all allowed to occupy **position**s of eminence（漢 97B） |
| 位にある者::公卿をはじめとして～すべて【自公卿在位】 | From the highest nobles and **office-holders** on down（漢 65） |
| 位におり | **hold office**（漢 78） |
| 位に列なって::諸侯・宗室で～いる者【諸侯宗室在列位】 | anyone **among the marquises and other titled members** of the imperial family（漢 74） |
| 位は執戟にすぎない【位不過執戟】 | your **post** is no more than that of lance-bearer（漢 65） |
| 夷狄の人::金日磾は【夷狄】 | Chin Mi-ti was a **barbarian**（漢 68） |
| 委任して::公卿に～ | have **entrusted** its direction to the high ministers（漢 63） |
| 威を示し::武を立てて衆に～，悪を誅してもって邪を禁ず【立武以威衆，誅悪以禁邪】 | make a display of military force in order to **inspire awe**, and one should punish evildoers in order to prevent malefaction（漢 67） |
| 威厳をつくろう【為威嚴】 | be as **stern and exacting**（漢 74） |
| 威名::久しく暴公子の～を聞く | have long heard the **awesome name** of Pao Kung-tzu（漢 71） |
| 威力を具え【有卞莊之威】 | inspire as much **awe** as Chuang of Pien（漢 78） |

## 第4章　職官名関連和英表現集

| | |
|---|---|
| 意見が合わず::扶風と〜【與扶風相失】 | having **failed to get along with** the other Fu-feng officials（漢92） |
| 意志::自分の〜に従う【従其志】 | does **what he thinks** is right（漢78） |
| 易 | the ***Book of Changes***（漢74） |
| 易経 | the ***Book of Changes***（漢74） |
| 為す::太守と【為平原太守】 | been **appointed** governor of P'ing-yüan（漢78） |
| 畏れた::百僚はこれを【百僚畏之】 | All the men who held public office **stood in awe of him**（漢67） |
| 異聞 | any **unusual happenings**（漢74） |
| 衣::天子の〜を賜い【賜御衣】 | present him with **robes** from the imperial treasury（漢68） |
| 衣冠の士が渉を慕うて【衣冠慕之】 | **Men of position** admired him（漢92） |
| 衣服::天子の | the **vestments** of the Son of Heaven（漢74） |
| 衣服の制 | what **vestments** it is **proper** for the Son of Heaven **to wear**（漢74） |
| 遺詔 | a **testamentary edict**（漢68） |
| 遺詔 | **instructions left** by Emperor Wu **at his death**（漢74） |
| 遺詔 | **testamentary edicts**（漢78） |
| 遺漏のない【亡有闕遺】 | be **guilty of no lack or oversight**（漢78） |
| 医::侍〜 | the palace **physician**（漢63） |
| 幃幄に側近している【迫近幃幄】 | to approach the **imperial curtains of state**（漢97B） |
| 一族が天誅に伏するのは当然【家属當伏天誅】 | her **family and associates** deserve to suffer the punishment of Heaven（漢97B） |
| 一味::悪人の〜とみなし【為悪人黨】 | looking upon them as the **followers** of an evildoer（漢67） |
| 印綬::度遼将軍の | the **seal and seal cord** that had been given him when he was made general who crosses the Liao（漢68） |
| 因りて〈これに〜〉姦をなす | **make use of** it for his own evil ends（漢63） |
| 因杆将軍 | **Yin-yü general**（漢54） |
| 引見 | **called her into his presence**（漢74） |
| 引見した | **summoned** the chancellor and the imperial secretary **to a private interview**（漢71） |
| 淫楽を聴いて楽しむ::鄭・衛の【聴鄭衛之楽】 | listens to the **lascivious music** of the states of Cheng and Wei（漢71） |
| 淫乱を憎んで【悪其淫乱】 | disgusted by his **licentious and unruly ways**（漢68） |
| 陰徳が多く【多陰徳】 | have done many **unknown kindnesses**（漢71） |
| 陰謀を打ち砕く【破散陰謀】 | block its **secret schemes**（漢74） |

| | |
|---|---|
| 陰陽の調和をつかさどり【典調和陰陽】 | are charged with the task of **harmonizing the yin and yang**(漢 74) |
| 右に出ようとする::九卿の【超九卿之右】 | **promote him over the heads of** the nine high ministers(漢 67) |
| 右監::廷尉～になった | reached the post of **superintendent of the right** under the commandant of justice(漢 74) |
| 右校王 | **right company king**(漢 54) |
| 右将軍 | the **general of the right**(漢 54) |
| 右将軍 | the **general of the right**(漢 54) |
| 右将軍 | the **general of the right**(漢 71) |
| 右将軍::その子禹を～とし | appointed his son Ho Yü **general of the right**(漢 74) |
| 右将軍::守備警衛を掌る～の官職を罷免し【罷其右將軍屯兵官屬】 | relieved him of the garrison troops and officials that had been under his command as **general of the right**(漢 68) |
| 右将軍とした | was appointed **general of the right**(漢 68) |
| 右将軍光禄勲となり | held the posts of **general of the right** and keeper of the palace gate(漢 97B) |
| 右内史[⇒左右内史] | **prefect in charge of the western area of the capital**(漢 65) |
| 右内史より下民をつかわして | had the **prefect in charge of the western area** muster a force of commoners(漢 65) |
| 右扶風 | the **right prefect of the capital** Yin Weng-kuei(漢 54) |
| 右扶風::益を～とし | Yi **oversees the western reaches of the capital**(漢 65) |
| 右扶風に二百戸の園邑を置く::詔して【詔右扶風置園邑二百家】 | commanded the **Fufeng district of the capital area**, in which his grave was situated, to set up a funerary park and village of two hundred households(漢 97A) |
| 右扶風は面会を請う【扶風謁請】 | the **Fu-feng officials** visited him(漢 92) |
| 右扶風臣周徳 | the **right prefect of the capital** Chou Te(漢 68) |
| 右輔都尉に命じて・・・を巡回警備させ | instructed the **chief commandant in charge of the western area of the capital** to inspect and alert the area(漢 65) |
| 右方の地【右地】 | **the western portion of** their territory(漢 74) |
| 羽林 | **Feather and Forest Guard**(漢 68) |
| 羽林::郎・～の閲兵を行う【光出都肄郎羽林】 | hold an inspection and drill of the palace attendants and the **Feather and Forest Guard**(漢 68) |
| 羽林::郎・～の属を総検閲した | called out the palace attendants and the **Feather and** |

76

第 4 章 職官名関連和英表現集

|  |  |
|---|---|
|  | **Forest Guard** for inspection（漢 63） |
| 羽林の騎士を率いて【車騎将軍安世将羽林騎】 | leading the horsemen of the **Feather and Forest Guard**（漢 68） |
| 羽林監::諸吏中郎将〜任勝 | who held the titles of official in charge, general of palace attendants, and **superintendent of the Feather and Forest Guard**（漢 68） |
| 永巷::天子の車の通る道［輦閣］を・〜に通じ【輦閣通属永巷】 | built a covered road for hand-drawn carriages connecting it with the **women's quarters of the grave keeper's house**（漢 68） |
| 英明な王 | **enlightened** king（漢 74） |
| 衛尉 | a **colonel of the guard**（漢 54） |
| 衛尉 | your **colonel of the guard**（漢 65） |
| 衛尉::侍中〜 | The attendant of the inner palace and **colonel of the guard** Chin An-shang（漢 63） |
| 衛尉::侍中建章〜金安上 | the attendant in the inner palace and **colonel of the guard** of the Chien-chang Palace Chin An-shang（漢 78） |
| 衛尉::長楽〜鄧広漢を選任して | shifted Teng Kuang-han, …, who had been **colonel of the guard** in the Palace of Lasting Joy, to（漢 68） |
| 衛尉::長楽宮の | the **colonel of the guard of** the Palace of Lasting Joy（漢 54） |
| 衛尉::度遼将軍未央〜平陵侯范明友 | who held the titles of general who crosses the Liao and marquis of P'iug-ling and who was a **colonel of the guard** in the Eternal Palace（漢 68） |
| 衛尉::東宮・西宮の〜となり | were **colonels of the guard** in the western and eastern palaces respectively（漢 68） |
| 衛尉であった王莽 | the **colonel of the guard** Wang Mang（漢 68） |
| 衛尉として | because of his services as **colonel of the guard**（漢 54） |
| 衛尉太僕に至った::官職は | In public office he rose as high as the post of **colonel of the guard** and master of carriage（漢 74） |
| 衛士の長に引き渡し法を執行させた | handed him over to **the chief of the palace guard** for the law to deal with（漢 63） |
| 衛将軍 | **General of the guard**（漢 54） |
| 衛将軍::大司馬〜となる | became grand marshal and **general of the guard**（漢 92） |
| 衛将軍張安世 | the **general of the guard** Chang An-shih（漢 54） |
| 衛兵::長楽宮の〜を発し | called out the **guard** from the Palace of Lasting Joy |

| | |
|---|---|
| | （漢 63） |
| 掖庭::今は〜におる | later in the **women's quarters of the palace**（漢 74） |
| 掖庭::曾孫を〜より迎えさせた【迎曾孫於掖庭】 | escort him to the **women's quarters of the palace**（漢 74） |
| 掖庭【遊戯掖庭中】 | **women's quarters**（漢 68） |
| 掖庭からお輿をめぐらし【従中〜回輿】 | emerge from your **private apartments**, turn aside your carriage（漢 65） |
| 掖庭で養育され | be raised in the **women's quarters of the palace**（漢 68） |
| 掖庭で養育され【養於掖庭】 | was being brought up in the **women's quarters of the palace**（漢 97A） |
| 掖庭に送られ【輸掖庭】 | was assigned to the **women's quarters of the palace**（漢 97A） |
| 掖庭の牛官舎【掖庭牛官令舎】 | the lodge of the supervisor of cattle for the **women's quarters**（漢 97B） |
| 掖庭の府庫を掌る嗇夫【少内嗇夫】 | the keeper of stores for the **women's quarters**（漢 74） |
| 掖庭の婢の則という者【掖庭宮婢則】 | a woman named Tse who was a maid in the **women's quarters of the palace**（漢 74） |
| 掖庭戸衛であった | was a guard of the gate of the **women's quarters**（漢 97A） |
| 掖庭令 | the **supervisor of the women's quarters**（漢 68） |
| 掖庭令に下げ渡し【下掖庭令】 | was referred to the **supervisor of the women's quarters**（漢 74） |
| 掖庭令吾丘遵 | the former **supervisor of the women's quarters** Wu-ch'iu Tsun（漢 97B） |
| 掖庭令輔らは | the **supervisor of the women's quarters** and his assistants（漢 97B） |
| 謁す::館陶公主の胞人臣偃,昧死再拝して〜【館陶公主胞人臣偃昧死再拝謁】 | Your servant Yen, cook to the Kuan-t'ao Princess, braving death, bows twice and **presents himself for an interview**.（漢 65） |
| 謁見 | **a gathering of the court**（漢 78） |
| 謁見したくない | have no desire for an **interview**（漢 78） |
| 謁見しようとする | came to him [霍光 Ho Kuang] for an **interview**（漢 78） |
| 謁見を賜り | be granted an **audience** with the emperor（漢 78） |
| 謁見を賜る | had occasion to **meet with him**（漢 78） |
| 謁者::侍中〜良 | the attendant in the inner palace and **master of guests** |

78

## 第4章 職官名関連和英表現集

| | Liang（漢78） |
|---|---|
| 謁者::大〜襄章 | The grand **master of guests** Hsiang Chang（漢74） |
| 謁者::中〜趙堯 | The middle **master of guests** Chao Yao（漢74） |
| 謁者::郎〜五十余人 | fifty or more of the king's palace attendants and **masters of guests**（漢63） |
| 謁者に命じて董君を宣室の中に案内させた【引内】 | instructing the **master of guests** to have Lord Tung conducted into the hall（漢65） |
| 謁者令::内〜郭穣 | The **master of guests** in the inner palace Kuo Jang（漢74） |
| 越えず::礼に率いて〜【率禮不越】 | Obeying ritual, **never overstepping**（漢78） |
| 閲兵::郎・羽林の〜を行う | hold **an inspection and drill of** the palace attendants and the Feather and Forest Guard（漢68） |
| 園邑::右扶風に二百戸の〜を置く【詔右扶風置園邑二百家】 | commanded the Fufeng district of the capital area, in which his grave was situated, to set up a **funerary park and village** of two hundred households（漢97A） |
| 怨みなく::上下に〜【上下亡怨】 | superior and inferior will **bear no grudge against** one another（漢74） |
| 怨みの::衆人の【衆人之怨】 | riches incite the **envy** of the common crowd（漢71） |
| 遠くは・・・近くは・・・ | **sometimes ..., sometimes ...**（漢74） |
| 遠回しに殺人を扇動した | having **indirectly** incited one of his officials to commit murder（漢67） |
| 遠見の明::賢聖の〜に違い【失賢聖遠見之明】 | completely failing to understand his sacred and **far-sighted wisdom**（漢97B） |
| 冤獄を平し【平冤獄】 | redressing **cases of injustice** in the courts（漢74） |
| 冤罪::天下に〜の民なく【天下無冤民】 | there were in fact no people in the empire who suffered **injustice**（漢71） |
| 冤罪::民は〜に陥るおそれがない | people assume as a matter of course that there will be no **injustice**（漢71） |
| 掾::県の門下〜となり | was a minor **official** in the district office（漢92） |
| 掾::従事〜業 | dispatched my **attendant clerk** Yeh（漢97B） |
| 掾::西曹の諸〜 | the **chief clerk**（漢92） |
| 掾::大司徒の〜であった | was a **clerk in the office of** the minister of education（漢67） |
| 掾に命じて後を追わせ【使掾追】 | sent some of his **clerks** to pursue the man（漢74） |
| 掾史 | the **clerks and secretaries** in his office（漢74） |
| 掾史::九卿の府の〜になることを求め【求為卿府掾史】 | attempted to secure a post as a **clerk** in one of the high ministries（漢92） |

| | |
|---|---|
| 掾史::公府の【公府掾史】 | The **clerks** of the ministry(漢92) |
| 掾史::属僚の〜に対しては【官屬掾史】 | the **clerks, secretaries, and other officials** under him(漢74) |
| 掾史たち | Ping Chi's **clerks and secretaries**(漢74) |
| 掾史たちがいぶかり | much to the surprise of his **clerks and attendants**(漢74) |
| 掾史たちは・・・と思い | The **clerks** concluded that(漢74) |
| 掾史ら | the **clerks and secretaries** in his office(漢74) |
| 汚名を負わせ::天下に背いて主上殺しの〜なくてはならない【令我負天下, 有殺主名】 | would be guilty of betraying the empire and would be **branded as** a regicide!(漢68) |
| 汚穢【汙濊】 | **disreputable conduct**(漢78) |
| 往来の頻繁な::使者の〜【冠蓋交道】 | an **endless stream of such officials pouring forth** from the capital(漢74) |
| 応兵 | a **campaign of response**(漢74) |
| 王たり::戦争の義しきは【兵義者王】 | such a campaign **is the mark of a true king**(漢74) |
| 王侯 | the **kings and marquises**(漢74) |
| 王室 | the **imperial household**(漢74) |
| 王道【王事】 | the **ways appropriate to a true king**(漢78) |
| 黄金二十斤を賜い【賜黃金二十斤】 | presenting them with a gift of **twenty catties of gold**(漢71) |
| 黄帝李法 | **the Yellow Emperor's Rules of the Adjudicator**† (漢67)［†adjudication 1 司法的判断；裁判；判決；決定；裁決 2(英)破産宣告―田中英夫編「BASIC 英米法辞典」］ |
| 黄門に送られて馬を養うた【輸黃門養馬】 | was assigned as a keeper of the horses of the **Yellow Gate**(漢68) |
| 黄門の画工【黃門畫者】 | one of the painters of the **Yellow Gate**(漢68) |
| 黄門蘇文 | the **gentleman of the Yellow Gate** Su Wen(漢63) |
| 黄門郎となり | had been made an **attendant of the Yellow Gate**(漢68) |
| 黄門郎揚雄は「酒箴」を作って【揚雄作酒箴】 | the **attendant of the Yellow Gate** Yang Hsiung had written a "Remonstrance on Wine"(漢92) |
| 恩恵を天下に施し【施恩惠於天下】 | the government performed **acts of charity and kindness** toward the empire(漢74) |
| 恩赦にあたる【遇赦】 | was pardoned by a **general amnesty**(漢92) |
| 温柔::人となり〜で【爲人】 | was by nature **a warm, gentle person**(漢65) |
| 下, 人倫を奪わない【不奪人倫】 | nor **on the lower [plane]** rob men of their proper |

80

第4章　職官名関連和英表現集

| | |
|---|---|
| | relationships（漢65） |
| 下して::有司に〜案験し,善悪を明らかにする【下有司案験以明好悪】 | to **refer the matter to** the authorities for investigation so that they may determine the right and wrong of it（漢67） |
| 下す | **came from the ruler**（漢78） |
| 下す::御史中丞に下される | the matter **be referred to** the middle aide to the imperial secretary（漢67） |
| 下の者が高爵のものを軽んじ【下軽其上爵】 | **inferiors** look lightly on those of high rank（漢67） |
| 下る::処理が廷尉に〜【事下廷尉】 | the matter was **turned over to** the commandant of justice for investigation（漢68） |
| 下僚 | the **officials under him**（漢74） |
| 何と不幸な【非不幸也】 | **what a pity**（漢92） |
| 可 | **met with** the latter's **approval**（漢78） |
| 家属とともに | Along with their **families and followers**（漢97B） |
| 家令::太子〜として | acting as **overseer** of the heir apparent's household（漢74） |
| 家婢王業・任嬺・公孫習 | the **government slave women** Wang Yeh, Jen Li, and Kung-sun His（漢97B） |
| 箇条書き::昌邑王を諌めた者を〜にして【條奏羣臣諌昌邑王者】 | **compiled a list of** the various officials who had reprimanded the king of Ch'ang-i（漢71） |
| 箇条書きにして職務上の責任を問う【條責以職事】 | berating them **item by item** for deficiencies in their performance of duty（漢71） |
| 課す::賦を〜【加賦】 | **imposing** any additional taxes **upon** the common people（漢78） |
| 課税::賦や〜を興す【興賦斂】 | imposing a lot of irresponsible taxes and **levies**（漢78） |
| 過つことなく::おのが意に従おうて〜【帥意亡僣】 | give all your thoughts to the **avoidance of error**（漢78） |
| 過ちを益す::愚にして財多ければ〜【愚而多財,則益其過】 | a fool with much wealth **finds his faults magnified**（漢71） |
| 過失::大将軍の〜をあばきたて【発揚大將軍過失】 | expose the **failures and shortcomings** of the general in chief（漢68） |
| 過失が多かった【多過失】 | was guilty of many **indiscretions**（漢71） |
| 過失は全くなく【未嘗有過失】 | was never guilty of **error or oversight**（漢68） |
| 画工::黄門の【黄門畫者】 | one of the **painters** of the Yellow Gate（漢68） |
| 回::笞二五〇〜 | two hundred and fifty **blows** of the stick（漢78） |
| 怪しんで::群衆はさわぎ立って | among the populace there is a buzz of **suspicion and** |

| | |
|---|---|
| 〜いる【群衆讙譁怪之】 | **speculation**（漢 97B） |
| 戒め::鬼神の〜であるかのように【若鬼神之戒】 | as though it were a **warning** from the ghosts and spirits（漢 67） |
| 海内 | all the people **within the four seas**（漢 74） |
| 海内に誰ひとり聞き知らぬ者はない【海内莫不聞知】 | there is no one within **the four seas** who does not know of his reputation（漢 67） |
| 海内を安撫する【撫海内】 | bringing solace to all **within the four seas**（漢 74） |
| 海浜に伏し【竊伏海瀕】 | live at **the faraway border of the sea**（漢 71） |
| 劾せられる::不敬と〜 | had been **indicted on charges of** irreverence（漢 65） |
| 外家::淮陽王の〜左氏 | the Tso family, who were **related by marriage to** the late king of Huai-yang（漢 92） |
| 外出し::微行して〜【微行出】 | had left the palace on one of his incognito **outings**（漢 97B） |
| 外戚 | the **emperor's relatives** of the Hsü and Shih families（漢 78） |
| 外戚::貴人〜の家に出入り【出入貴戚】 | coming and going in the houses of the nobles and **relatives of the emperor**（漢 92） |
| 外戚として大臣であった魏其侯・・・のともがら【外戚大臣魏其, 武安之属】 | Men like the great ministers Ton Ying, the marquis of Wei-ch'i, and T'ien Fen, the marquis of Wu-an, who were **related to the imperial family by marriage**（漢 92） |
| 外戚の | **paternal** grandmother's nephew（漢 78） |
| 外戚の許氏だけを親しくさせる【独親外家許氏】 | associate only with his **maternal relatives** of the Hsü family（漢 71） |
| 外戚家 | his **grandmother's relatives**（漢 74） |
| 外戚家を捜し【求外家】 | to search for the **members of his mother's family**（漢 97A） |
| 外戚伝 | **Accounts of the Families Related to the Emperors by Marriage**（漢 97A） |
| 外祖父::太子の | The **maternal grandfather** of the heir apparent（漢 71） |
| 街里【街閭】 | each **street and lane**（漢 92） |
| 骸骨を乞う【乞骸骨】 | begging that he be **released from public service**（漢 71） |
| 骸骨を乞う【乞骸骨】 | requesting **release from government service**（漢 71） |
| 格別の::その行義には〜ものがない【其行義未有以異】 | there is still nothing **particularly distinguished about** his conduct（漢 67） |
| 郭門::城門と〜は同じ | The gate of the inner wall is no different from **the gate** |

## 第4章 職官名関連和英表現集

| | |
|---|---|
| | of the outer wall（漢 63） |
| 郭門::長安の東の〜である | is the eastern **gate of the outer wall** of Ch'ang-an（漢 63） |
| 学識がなく，策もなく【不学亡術】 | lacked **learning** and over-all **strategy**（漢 68） |
| 楽府 | the **Music Bureau**（漢 68） |
| 滑稽きわまりなく | for his never-ending fund of **waggery**（漢 65） |
| 瓦解し::輔弼の臣は【補弼之臣瓦解】 | ministers who might aid and assist you **fall away like broken tiles**（漢 65） |
| 冠::大夫は〜をつけよ【大夫冠】 | Put on your **cap**, sir!（漢 71） |
| 冠を脱ぎ::左将軍辛慶忌が【免冠】 | the general of the left Hsin Ch'ing-chi **doffed his cap**（漢 67） |
| 寒心して::群臣は〜いる【群下寒心】 | As one of the lesser officials, may I say that it is enough to **make the heart turn cold with fear**（漢 97B） |
| 寒心に堪えない | **my heart turns cold to think** what may happen!（漢 74） |
| 姦をなす::此れに因りて | make use of it **for his own evil ends**（漢 63） |
| 姦詐がある | something irregular was **afoot**（漢 74） |
| 姦吏が私利を遂げて【姦吏成其私】 | **evil officials** work for their own private gain（漢 74） |
| 姦邪 | **evil and lawlessness**（漢 74） |
| 姦臣の変を監察 | keep watch on the doings of **villainous ministers**（漢 63） |
| 姦人::これを〜といい | be regarded as an **offender**（漢 67） |
| 官::御史の〜は宰相の副【御史之官,宰相之副】 | The **man who occupies the post of** imperial secretary acts as assistant to the chancellor（漢 67） |
| 官に没収され【没入官】 | all became **government** slaves（漢 68） |
| 官は侍郎にすぎず【官不過侍郎】 | your **rank** does not exceed palace attendant（漢 65） |
| 官を失い【失官】 | **removed from office**（漢 74） |
| 官を免ぜられ | retired from **office**（漢 92） |
| 官を免ぜられ【免官】 | retired from **office**（漢 92） |
| 官爵功名は子より劣ることなく【官爵功名,不減於子】 | In **position, title, accomplishment, and fame**, I am in no way inferior to you（漢 92） |
| 官署::諸〜に詔して… | delivering commands to the various **officials and bureaus** to summon（漢 68） |
| 官署にいる::皇曾孫は郡邸の〜べきでない【皇孫不當在官】 | it was improper for the imperial great-grandson to **be quartered in** such a place（漢 74） |

| | |
|---|---|
| 官女【宮女】 | **palace ladies in waiting**（漢 68） |
| 官職はよく修まり【衆職修理】 | all **official duties** tended to with exactitude（漢 74） |
| 官属 | his **attendants**（漢 92） |
| 官属が具備され【官属已備】 | all the **posts in his household** are already filled（漢 71） |
| 官二千石 | the **two thousand picul level**（漢 78） |
| 官名∷ただ大司馬の〜だけを | leaving him with only the **title and office** of grand marshal（漢 68） |
| 官吏 | an **official**（漢 78） |
| 官吏十人を呼び出し∷書を善くする〜【召善書吏十人於前】 | sent for ten **clerks** who were good at writing（漢 92） |
| 寛やか[ゆるやか]で和やかな気色【寛和之色】 | had been granted ... a **benign** and sympathetic glance |
| 寛容 | **easygoing**（漢 74） |
| 感知する∷鬼神が〜ものなら【使鬼神有知】 | If the gods **have understanding**（漢 97B） |
| 漢室の嫡嗣として | is the rightful heir to **the throne of the Han**（漢 63） |
| 監∷栘中廐〜になった | reached the position of **superintendent** of the I-chung Stables（漢 54） |
| 監∷安池〜の職を求めてもらいたい【為我求安池監】 | Ask her if I may have the post of **overseer** of the salt ponds of An-i（漢 97A） |
| 監∷建章宮〜となった | being appointed **supervisor** of the Chien-chang Palace（漢 54） |
| 監∷廷尉〜として | as **superintendent** under the commandant of justice（漢 74） |
| 監軍御史が悪事をはたらき【時監軍御史為奸】 | the **clerk of the censorate** ... was engaged in underhanded activities（漢 67） |
| 監軍御史が悪事をはたらき【時監軍御史為奸】 | the clerk of the **censorate** ... was engaged in underhanded activities（漢 67） |
| 監軍御史が公然と兵営の壁垣に穴を穿って【監御史公穿軍垣】 | the **clerk of the censorate superintending the garrison** has brazenly cut a hole in the garrison wall（漢 67） |
| 監軍御史を指差して【指監御史】 | pointed to the **superintendent of the garrison**（漢 67） |
| 監御史と護軍の諸部校が堂皇に列座した | the **superintendent of the garrison** took his seat on the reviewing platform along with the various company commanders attached to the garrison（漢 67） |
| 監察∷姦臣の変を | **keep watch on** the doings of villainous ministers（漢 63） |

## 第4章 職官名関連和英表現集

| | |
|---|---|
| 監察する::勉めて【勉察】 | **examining**（漢71） |
| 監督保護::太子家を | to **supervise and look after** the household of the heir apparent（漢71） |
| 管尚書事【領尚書事】 | was given **the supervision of** matters pertaining to the office of palace writers（漢68） |
| 観る | **looking over**（漢74） |
| 観る | **reading**（漢74） |
| 観る | **examine**（漢74） |
| 旱魃::洪水～が時節をはずれ発生【水旱不時】 | flood and **drought** visit us without respite（漢74） |
| 諫めた::昌邑王を～者を箇条書きにして【條奏羣臣諫昌邑王者】 | compiled a list of the various officials who had **reprimanded** the king of Ch'ang-i（漢71） |
| 諫めて::進み出て～言った | stepped forward with the following **remonstrance**（漢65） |
| 諫める | **admonished** Liu Tan（漢63） |
| 諫める | **opposing** such a plan of action（漢74） |
| 諫官 | **audacious ministers**（漢78） |
| 諫言の官【諫官】 | **admonishers**（漢78） |
| 諫言を納れ【納諫】 | is willing to listen to **admonition**（漢78） |
| 諫争::直言～した【直言諫争】 | did not hesitate to speak out boldly in **reprimand**（漢71） |
| 諫大夫 | the post of **admonisher**（漢78） |
| 諫大夫・博士をつかわし | dispatched the **admonishers** and erudits（漢74） |
| 諫大夫::推薦して中郎～とした | recommending him as a palace attendant and **admonisher**（漢67） |
| 諫大夫となる | to become an **admonisher**（漢74） |
| 諫大夫に為る | was given a post as an **admonisher**（漢92） |
| 諫大夫に遷り | was promoted to the post of **admonisher**（漢71） |
| 鑑みる::先聖に～【観於先聖】 | be carried out **in the light of the practices of** the former sages（漢74） |
| 間に::三年の | **in the course of** three years（漢78） |
| 関都尉::弟をもって～とし【以丞相弟為関都尉】 | have appointed the younger brother of the late chancellor as **colonel of the Han-ku Pass**（漢74） |
| 関内侯 | the rank of **marquis within the Pass**（漢74） |
| 関吏 | the **officials guarding the pass**（漢74） |
| 宦者署 | the **office of the eunuchs**（漢54） |
| 宦者丞 | was made a clerk in the **office of eunuchs**（漢97A） |
| 願う::争うて力を致し将軍の高 | vying with one another in **volunteering their services** |

| | |
|---|---|
| い明知を輔けたい【爭願自効，以輔高明】と | to assist in this lofty and enlightened undertaking（漢78） |
| 危うい::宗室が | **endanger** the ruling house（漢78） |
| 危うい【殆矣】 | **face trouble**（漢74） |
| 危うく::国家を乱し〜する【危乱国家】 | **danger** and disorder to the state resulted in both cases（漢74） |
| 危うくし::社稷を〜【危社稷】 | the altars of the soil and grain will be **imperiled**（漢97B） |
| 器の大きい士である【大度士】 | is a gentleman **of great capability**（漢92） |
| 器量をかくす【臧器于身】 | keep your **talents** hidden from sight（漢74） |
| 基づいて::進退がかならず礼に〜いた【進退必以禮】 | in all his comings and goings he invariably **abided by the dictates of** ritual（漢71） |
| 期門::「〜」という官名はこれによる | the term *ch'i-men* or "**rendezvous gate**" first came into use（漢65） |
| 期門の武士 | The warriors of the **Rendezvous Gate**（漢68） |
| 期門董忠に語り | giving word of it to Tung Chung of the **Rendezvous Gate**（漢68） |
| 期門郎::王子慶忌を〜とし | Prince Ch'ing-chi is **keeper of the Rendezvous Gate**（漢65） |
| 機微があり謀慮の士【幾微謀慮之士】 | men of **subtle understanding** who are skilled at laying plans（漢78） |
| 機敏で話がじょうず【敏而有辭】 | was **alert** and well-spoken（漢71） |
| 帰す::美徳をもっぱら・・・に〜【專歸美於組，徵卿】 | **gave all** the credit **to** Hu Tsu and Kuo Cheng-ch'ing（漢74） |
| 気::宮中に巫蠱の〜がある | there were "**airs** of sorcery in the palace" and entered the palace（漢63） |
| 気色::寛やか[ゆるやか]で和やかな〜【寛和之色】 | had been granted ... a benign and sympathetic **glance** |
| 気色が見られ::飢え寒さの〜【飢寒之色】 | there are those who wear the **look** of hunger and poverty（漢74） |
| 気節を好む士 | a man who **placed honor above all else**（漢78） |
| 気脈を通じる::昭儀と【与昭儀合通】 | are all **in league with** the Bright Companion（漢97B） |
| 貴ぶ::中国の仁義を【中国之仁義】 | **esteem** China for its benevolence and righteousness（漢78） |
| 貴幸::少府五鹿充宗が天子に〜され | the privy treasurer Wu-lu Ch'ung-tsung **enjoyed great favor with** the emperor（漢67） |
| 貴人 | **powerful people**（漢74） |

## 第4章 職官名関連和英表現集

| | |
|---|---|
| 貴人::公主や～で礼制を踰える【踰礼制】 | the princesses and **nobles** took to overstepping the rites and regulations（漢 65） |
| 貴人::左右の～や傅昭儀【左右貴人傅昭儀】 | The Bright Companion Fu and the other **ladies in attendance**（漢 97B） |
| 貴人外戚の家に出入り【出入貴戚】 | coming and going in the houses of the **nobles** and relatives of the emperor（漢 92） |
| 騎士::羽林の～を率いて | leading the **horsemen** of the Feather and Forest Guard（漢 68） |
| 騎士に命じ | sent one of his **riders** to ask how many miles（漢 74） |
| 騎常侍::郎官となり～を授かる【為郎, 騎常侍】 | was rewarded with the position of **cavalry attendant** in the inner palace（漢 54） |
| 騎都尉 | a **chief commandant of cavalry**（漢 54） |
| 騎都尉::諸官署の大夫・～・給事中になった【為諸曹大夫, 騎都尉, 給事中】 | being clerks, counselors, **colonels of the cavalry**, or stewards of the palace（漢 68） |
| 騎都尉::拝せられて～となる | was appointed a **chief commandant of cavalry**（漢 54） |
| 騎都尉の印綬 | the seal and seal cord of **chief commandant of regular cavalry**（漢 68） |
| 騎郎将となった | was made **general of palace horsemen**（漢 54） |
| 鬼の言は帰であり【鬼之為言歸】 | the spirits of the dead are called *gui*, which is to say that they have 'returned' (*gui*)（漢 67） |
| 鬼神が感知するものなら【使鬼神有知】 | If the **gods** have understanding（漢 97B） |
| 鬼神の戒めであるかのように【若鬼神之戒】 | as though it were a warning from the **ghosts and spirits**（漢 67） |
| 鬼薪の刑を論告され【論為鬼薪】 | was condemned to **become a provider of "firewood for the spirits."**（漢 97A） |
| 譏る | **condemns**（漢 74） |
| 戯れる::宮女と～【與宮人戯】 | **amuse himself with** the emperor's ladies in waiting（漢 68） |
| 欺::天子の従官を詆～ | to **hoodwink** and humiliate an attendant of the Son of Heaven（漢 65） |
| 疑われる::みだりにほめあげているのは, 邪心があるように～【妄相稱舉, 疑有姦心】 | Behind such wild praise and recommendation **I fear** there may be sinister designs that should not be left to flourish unchecked（漢 67） |
| 義::悪を懲らし～を崇ぶ【懲悪崇誼示四方也】 | in censuring evil and displaying respect for **right**（漢 97B） |

| | |
|---|---|
| 義::聖人の〜を敬慕し【慕聖人之義】 | pursue the **ideals** of the sages（漢 65） |
| 義をひきい用いてその身を正し【引義以正其身】 | enlisting **righteousness** to help him rectify himself（漢 65） |
| 義を好み利を欲する心があり【好義欲利之心】 | possess hearts moved both by concerns of **benevolence and righteousness** and by the longing for personal profit（漢 78） |
| 羲和の官【羲和之官】 | the **office of astronomer**（漢 74） |
| 義俠を行う::好んで〜【喜為俠】 | delight in **daring and chivalrous actions**（漢 92） |
| 義兵 | a **campaign of righteousness**（漢 74） |
| 義務::天子の【天子之義】 | The **actions** of the Son of Heaven（漢 74） |
| 議::文吏の〜を用いれば【用文吏議】 | were turned over to the civil officials for **trial**（漢 67） |
| 議す::正法を〜【議正法】 | **deliberate** as to the correct way to apply the law（漢 97B） |
| 議曹とし | invited him to become an **advisory clerk**（漢 92） |
| 議郎::ときの〜耿育が上疏して言った【時議郎耿育上疏言】 | the **palace attendant in charge of deliberations** Keng Yu submitted a memorial which read（漢 97B） |
| 客::趙平の〜石夏【趙平客石夏】 | Shih Hsia who was a **retainer** to Ho Kuang's son-in-law Chao P'ing（漢 68） |
| 逆らい::先帝憂国の意に〜【逆負先帝憂国之意】 | **frustrating all his plans** to save the nation from distress（漢 97B） |
| 逆賊 | **rebels or bandits**（漢 74） |
| 久しくして::その後〜【久之】 | **After a considerable time had passed**, …（漢 68） |
| 久しく暴公子の威名を聞く | have **long** heard the awesome name of Pao Kung-tzu（漢 71） |
| 宮刑に処せられ【坐法宮刑】 | condemned to suffer **castration**（漢 97A） |
| 宮女と戯れる【與宮人戯】 | amuse himself with the **emperor's ladies in waiting**（漢 68） |
| 宮人::もと長安の〜で【本長安宮人】 | was originally a **government slave** of Ch'ang-an（漢 97B） |
| 宮中に繋がれた虜であった【羇虜漢庭】 | came to the Han **court** as a prisoner in bonds（漢 68） |
| 宮門内に入れない【無入霍氏禁闥】 | be barred from entering the **inner palace**（漢 68） |
| 急[うなが]す::下が上を【下急上】 | those below **take thought for the urgent needs of** those above（漢 78） |
| 救う::県官の穀物では〜に足り | the government does not have enough supplies of |

88

## 第4章　職官名関連和英表現集

| | |
|---|---|
| ない【県官穀度不足以振之】 | grain on hand to **provide relief**(漢78) |
| 救う::災患を〜【救其災患】 | helping him to **surmount** this disaster(漢78) |
| 救う〈乱を〜〉【救乱】 | **rectify disorder**(漢74) |
| 給事中 | the **position of steward** (漢74) |
| 給事中::光は延年を招いて〜とし【光乃引延年給事中】 | [Ho Kuang] recommended T'ien Yen-nien for the honorary rank of **steward of the palace**(漢68) |
| 給事中::光禄大夫 | became a counselor to the keeper of the palace gate and a **steward of the palace**(漢74) |
| 給事中::朔を太中大夫〜に拝し | honored Shuo by making him a palace counselor, with the additional title of **steward of the palace**(漢65) |
| 給事中::大夫・騎都尉・〜になった, 諸官署の【為諸曹大夫, 騎都尉, 給事中】 | being clerks, counselors, colonels of the cavalry, or **stewards of the palace**(漢68) |
| 給事中光禄大夫張朔 | who held the titles of **steward of the palace** and counselor to the keeper of the palace gate(漢68) |
| 廄監〈移中〜〉になった | reached the position of **superintendent of the I-chung Stables**(漢54) |
| 去る::禄[さいわい]が【禄去】 | fortune **deserted**(漢74) |
| 挙げられ::賢良の科に【以賢良挙】 | **was selected as** a man of worth and goodness(漢71) |
| 挙げられ::方正の科に【挙方正】 | **was chosen as** a man of honesty and uprightness(漢67) |
| 京師 | the **metropolitan area**(漢74) |
| 京師::中大夫を〜につかわし | sent his palace counselor to the **capital**(漢63) |
| 京師に | in the **capital area**(漢92) |
| 京兆::伯夷を〜とし | Po-i serves as **prefect of the capital**(漢65) |
| 京兆の史となった【為京兆史】 | became clerks in the office of the **prefect of the capital**(漢92) |
| 京兆仟と称す::民がその道を【謂其道為京兆仟】 | the people all referred to the road which led to his tomb as "The **Prefect's Road**."(漢92) |
| 京兆尹 | the **prefect of the capital** Chang Ch'ang(漢54) |
| 京兆尹 | the **prefect of the capital**(漢74) |
| 京兆尹 | the **prefect of the capital**(漢74) |
| 京兆尹 | The **prefect of the capital**(漢78) |
| 京兆尹::徴して〜とし【徴遂為京兆尹】 | Sui was summoned to be **prefect of the capital**(漢92) |
| 京兆尹となり | was selected to become **prefect of the capital**(漢71) |
| 京兆尹となり | became **prefect of the capital**(漢71) |

| | |
|---|---|
| 京兆尹になる | became **prefect of the capital**(漢 92) |
| 京兆尹の門下督 | supervisor of retainers to the **prefect of the capital**(漢 92) |
| 京兆尹の吏になる | became an official in the office of the **prefect of the capital**(漢 92) |
| 京兆尹曹氏 | a man named Ts'ao who had held the post of **prefect of the capital**(漢 92) |
| 京兆尹不疑が遅れて来【京兆尹不疑後到】 | The **prefect of the capital** Ch'üan Pu-i, arriving late,(漢 71) |
| 京兆尹樊福を怨み | bearing a grudge against the former **prefect of the capital** Fan Fu(漢 67) |
| 京輔都尉臣趙広漢 | the **chief commandant of the capital area** Chao Kuang-han(漢 68) |
| 匡し::国家を【匡国家】 | **brought rectitude to** the nation(漢 68) |
| 匡す::いま朝廷の大臣がたは主上を〜ことができず【今朝廷大臣上不能匡主】 | The chief officials in the court today are incapable of **correcting the faults of** the sovereign above(漢 67) |
| 匡正::国家を【匡正国家】 | **restore order and propriety** to the state(漢 78) |
| 匡正しようとするところが多かった【多所欲匡正】 | **effect various reforms and improvements**(漢 78) |
| 卿::君〜 | **you**(漢 92) |
| 卿の身分を世々にすること【世卿】 | hereditary **office for ministers**(漢 74) |
| 卿大夫より以下庶人に【卿大夫以至于庶人】 | from the **great ministers and high officials** down to the common people(漢 92) |
| 強弩将軍孫建 | the **general of strong bowmen** Sun Chien(漢 92) |
| 彊弩都尉 | the **chief commandant of strong crossbowmen**(漢 54) |
| 恐れ憚り | **enraged at** Wei Hsiang **and fearful of** him as well(漢 74) |
| 恭謹::謙遜〜 | was modest and **unassuming**(漢 71) |
| 恭謙で::礼を好み〜【好礼恭謹】 | paid the strictest attention to ritual and **good manners**(漢 71) |
| 教えさとすのに,はなはだ節度があり【教誨兩子,甚有法度】 | had **trained her two sons very carefully** so that their behavior was without reproach(漢 68) |
| 矯[いつわり]::太后の詔と【矯太后詔】 | **forge** an imperial order from the empress dowager(漢 74) |
| 驕盛::女主が〜であれば【女主 | When a woman in a position of authority finds she can |

## 第4章 職官名関連和英表現集

| | |
|---|---|
| 驕盛】 | **do as she pleases**（漢 97B） |
| 驕兵 | a **campaign of arrogance**（漢 74） |
| 驕慢::日ましに〜になり | grew more **overbearing** each day（漢 65） |
| 驕慢放恣 | very **arrogant and unruly**（漢 67） |
| 驕奢放縦 | such **favoritism and affluence**, such **flagrant and unruly behavior**（漢 74） |
| 仰ぎみるところ::万民の【万姓所瞻仰】 | men whom the myriad commoners **look up to with awe**（漢 67） |
| 暁す［さとす］ | **trying to persuade** others（漢 71） |
| 驍騎将軍として | was appointed as **cavalry general**（漢 54） |
| 驍騎都尉となり | served as a **cavalry commander**（漢 54） |
| 斤::黄金百〜 | a hundred **catties** of gold（漢 65） |
| 禁止 | **put a stop to**（漢 74） |
| 禁令法網は疎略【禁網疏闊】 | **the net of the law** was widely spread and full of holes（漢 92） |
| 禁錮の刑に当てた【當禁錮】 | placed them all **under a ban**（漢 67） |
| 謹み::天を尊ぶことを〜 | **diligent** in paying honor to Heaven（漢 74） |
| 謹む:::事を〜【慎事】 | **cautious** in your handling of affairs（漢 74） |
| 謹んで::臣〜考えますに | I **would venture to** point out that（漢 67） |
| 謹んで::臣は〜法によって斬った【謹以斬】 | I have **respectfully** executed the offender（漢 67） |
| 謹んで思いますに::臣，〜【臣謹案】 | It is my **considered opinion** that（漢 74） |
| 近くは | **Turning to recent centuries**（漢 74） |
| 近づきに::諸公たちとも〜なり | was **accepted by** the members of the nobility（漢 65） |
| 近古 | in **recent centuries**（漢 78） |
| 近習が乱を起こす | **those close to the ruler** turned against him（漢 63） |
| 九卿 | the **nine lower offices of government**（漢 54） |
| 九卿 | the **nine high ministers**（漢 78） |
| 九卿・封侯にまでなり【至九卿封侯】 | rose to become one of the **nine high ministers** and to be enfeoffed as a marquis（漢 68） |
| 九卿::三公・〜・大夫を率いて | leading the three highest officials, the **nine high ministers**, and the counselors（漢 68） |
| 九卿が私を責めるのはもっともだ【九卿責光是也】 | is right for the **high ministers** to berate me（漢 68） |
| 九卿として十余年仕え【為九卿十餘年】 | held a position among the **nine high officials** for over ten years（漢 74） |
| 九卿となり | occupied a post among the **nine highest ministers**（漢 |

91

| | 68） |
|---|---|
| 九卿に列ねられ【列於九卿】 | ranked among the **nine high officials**（漢 92） |
| 九卿の右に出ようとする【超九卿之右】 | promote him over the heads of the **nine high ministers**（漢 67） |
| 九卿の中でも上位にある【九卿之右】 | superior to the **nine high ministers**（漢 67） |
| 九卿の府の掾史になることを求め【求為卿府掾史】 | attempted to secure a post as a clerk in one of the **high ministries**（漢 92） |
| 九市之宮::作〜 | built its **'palace the size of nine market places,'**（漢 65） |
| 咎[とが]::災いや〜が起こる【災咎之発】 | **portents** and disasters appear（漢 71） |
| 咎は臣らにある【咎在臣等】 | for which I and the other ministers **are to blame**（漢 74） |
| 苦楽を共にする::百姓と【与百姓同憂】 | join with the common people in **sharing their sorrows and joys**（漢 71） |
| 具え::太官があえて〜ない | The imperial butler did not dare **comply**（漢 68） |
| 具備され::官属が〜【官属已備】 | all the posts in his household are already **filled**（漢 71） |
| 愚かにも::臣は【臣愚】 | **Ignorant** as I am（漢 74） |
| 愚臣などにはわからない【愚臣無所能識】 | **I am not competent to** reply to such a question（漢 74） |
| 愚臣は | **these stupid officials**（漢 97B） |
| 空名 | **empty claim to virtue**（漢 74） |
| 遇する::その子を〜 | **treat** the son **with proper respect**（漢 74） |
| 君、君たらずば、臣、臣たらず | if the **ruler** is not a ruler, the minister will not be a minister（漢 63） |
| 君は尊ばれる | the **ruler** will be honored（漢 74） |
| 君安楽にして【君安虞】 | the **ruler** will enjoy safety and contentment（漢 74） |
| 君侯は漢の丞相 | **My lord, you** are chancellor of the Han（漢 74） |
| 君臣 | **ruler and minister**（漢 74） |
| 群衆はさわぎ立って怪しんでいる【群衆讙譁怪之】 | among the **populace** there is a buzz of suspicion and speculation（漢 97B） |
| 群臣 | his **courtiers**（漢 63） |
| 群臣 | the **various officials**（漢 68） |
| 群臣 | **all the officials**（漢 68） |
| 群臣 | the other **officials**（漢 68） |
| 群臣 | the **various officials**（漢 74） |

## 第4章 職官名関連和英表現集

| | |
|---|---|
| 群臣::賓客・〜 | his guests and **courtiers**（漢63） |
| 群臣がみな免冠して | The **courtiers** all removed their hats（漢63） |
| 群臣は寒心している【群下寒心】 | As one of the **lesser officials**, may I say that it is enough to make the heart turn cold with fear（漢97B） |
| 群臣や従官 | my old **followers** and attendants（漢68） |
| 群臣ら | the **courtiers**（漢63） |
| 群臣をえらび分ける【練羣臣】 | carefully selecting **men** for official posts（漢74） |
| 軍市令::車騎将軍の | the **commissary** under the general of carriage and cavalry（漢74） |
| 軍法には… | according to the **rules of the army**（漢67） |
| 郡 | the **provincial government**（漢74） |
| 郡県 | the **prefectures and provinces**（漢92） |
| 郡国には処々に | everywhere in the **provinces and feudal kingdoms**（漢92） |
| 郡国に使いした | sent out into the **provinces and feudal states**（漢92） |
| 郡国の太守・宰相に補任する | fill posts that had come vacant as governors of provinces or prime ministers of the **feudal states**（漢78） |
| 郡治が厳格【治郡厳】 | strict **rule in the province**（漢74） |
| 郡守::爵列侯として〜に備わり【遵爵列侯, 備郡守】 | has been ennobled as a feudal lord and appointed **governor of a province**（漢92） |
| 郡守に任ぜられ | been appointed **governor** of P'ing-yüan（漢78） |
| 郡臣が朝見した | the **various ministers** were attending audience in the palace（漢67） |
| 郡邸獄 | in the prison attached to the Chun-ti, the **lodge for official visitors from the provinces**（漢74） |
| 郡府::ふたたび…〜の吏となり【為府吏】 | go back to being a clerk in the **office**（漢92） |
| 傾け::聖朝を〜混乱させ【傾乱聖朝】 | has **brought danger** and chaos to our sacred dynasty（漢97B） |
| 傾け混乱させる::天下を〜【傾乱天下】 | the empire will be **in danger of chaos and subversion**（漢97B） |
| 刑余の人::広漢は【広漢刑人】 | Hsü Kuang-han **had in the past been condemned to corporal punishment**（漢97A） |
| 形骸は地の所有【形骸者地之有】 | the **bodily form** belongs to earth（漢67） |
| 恵む::上が下を【上恵下】 | those above **extend mercy to** those below（漢78） |
| 敬われ::親しみ〜【見親而敬】 | he was **treated with special** care and respect（漢92） |

| | |
|---|---|
| 敬んで::お指図に~従います【敬奉教】 | I am **only too happy to** follow your instructions.(漢 65) |
| 敬重した | **treated him with gravity and respect**(漢 71) |
| 敬慕し::聖人の義を【慕聖人之義】 | **pursue** the ideals of the sages(漢 65) |
| 経術 | the **teachings of the Classics**(漢 74) |
| 経術に通明し【經術通明】 | thoroughly versed in **the teachings of the Classics**(漢 67) |
| 経術の士を重んじ【重經術士】 | showed the highest respect for **scholars of classical learning**(漢 71) |
| 経術をもって【用經術】 | have mastered the **lessons of the Classics**(漢 71) |
| 経書 | the **Classics**(漢 74) |
| 経書::身に~を執り【身執經】 | holding **the copy of the text**(漢 71) |
| 経書を暗誦し【諷誦經書】 | sit mumbling over your **Classics and other texts**(漢 92) |
| 経典を論じる【論道經書】 | discuss the **Classics and other literary works**(漢 92) |
| 経伝 | the **Classics and commentaries**(漢 92) |
| 経伝に・・・ | An **old text** says,(漢 67) |
| 継いだ::太子が尊号を~【太子襲尊号】 | his heir **succeeded to** the position of highest honor(漢 68) |
| 繋がれた::宮中に~虜奴隷であった | came to the Han court as a **prisoner in bonds**(漢 68) |
| 繋がれている者 | **inmates**(漢 74) |
| 軽んじ::下の者が高爵のものを【下軽其上爵】 | inferiors **look lightly on** those of high rank(漢 67) |
| 軽視::丞相を【軽丞相】 | **belittle** the chancellor(漢 78) |
| 軽車 | attended by **war chariots**(漢 68) |
| 軽車将軍 | was appointed a **general of light carriage**(漢 54) |
| 軽重::罪の~にかかわらず | regardless of whether the charges against them were **serious or light**(漢 74) |
| 軽薄 | **frivolous and corrupt**(漢 74) |
| 軽薄な任侠の徒【軽侠之徒】 | this class of **worthless** knights(漢 92) |
| 決裁::政事は一切光によって~された【政事壹決於光】 | all affairs of government were left to the sole **decision** of Ho Kuang(漢 68) |
| 決曹::郡の | a **judge of criminal cases** for the province(漢 71) |
| 建て::天子が国を~【天子建国】 | the Son of Heaven **founded** the state(漢 92) |
| 建章衛尉::侍中~金安上 | the attendant in the inner palace and **colonel of the** |

## 第4章 職官名関連和英表現集

| | |
|---|---|
| | **guard of the Chien-chang Palace** Chin An-shang（漢78） |
| 権をもっぱらにする::季孫氏の〜【季孫之専権】 | **censuring the dictatorial power** of the Chi-sun family of Lu（漢74） |
| 権勢に依拠する【據権勢】 | occupy **positions of power**（漢74） |
| 権勢をほしいままにしようとしている【専擅権勢】 | their desire to gather all **power and authority** into their own hands（漢78） |
| 権柄の臣::賤人が〜を図む【賤人図柄臣】 | mean men lay schemes to control **the positions of power**（漢67） |
| 権力::私家の〜は廃れ【私権廃】 | an end to the exercise of private **authority**（漢78） |
| 権力::大夫が世々〜を握り【大夫世権】 | the high officials exercised **power** generation after generation（漢92） |
| 権力をもって敵を制し【因権制敵】 | **exercising the power vested in him**, curbing the enemies of the state（漢68） |
| 権力をもっぱらにし朝廷をほしいままにする【専権擅朝】 | arrogate to himself all the **power of the court**（漢78） |
| 権力をもっぱらにする【専権】 | had complete **control of the government**（漢78） |
| 権力を減らし奪う【損奪其権】 | strip the family of its **power**（漢74） |
| 献策 | **suggestions**（漢74） |
| 県::郡〜 | the prefectures and **provinces**（漢92） |
| 県の〈郁夷〜〉令に補任した | was assigned to the post of magistrate **of Yu-i**（漢92） |
| 県の〈谷口〜〉令となる | was appointed magistrate **of Ku-k'ou**（漢92） |
| 県官に衣食を得ているだけで十分【幸得以庶人衣食県官, 足矣】 | has been lucky enough to be made a commoner and to receive an allotment of food and clothing from the **government**, but that's all he deserves（漢97A） |
| 県官の穀物では救うに足りない【県官穀度不足以振之】 | the **government** does not have enough supplies of grain on hand to provide relief（漢78） |
| 県令::鄠・杜の〜に訴えた | reported the matter to the **magistrate** of Hu-tu（漢65） |
| 県令::杜陵の〜に遷り【遷杜陵令】 | was transferred to the post of **magistrate** of Tu-ling（漢67） |
| 県令::槐里〜となった | was made **magistrate** of Huai-li（漢67） |
| 県令::渭城〜建 | Hu Chien, the **magistrate of the district of** Wei-ch'eng（漢67） |
| 県令となり::渭城の | was appointed **magistrate of the district of** Wei-ch'eng（漢67） |
| 県掾 | A **district official** named Yang（漢92） |
| 見初めて【上見飛燕而説之】 | **took a liking to** her（漢97B） |

| | |
|---|---|
| 謙譲の心がなく【不遜撰】 | a total lack of **humility**(漢 78) |
| 謙遜して伐[ほこ]らない【謙退不伐】 | behaving **in a modest and retiring fashion** and not boasting of their deeds(漢 92) |
| 謙遜恭謹 | was **modest and unassuming**(漢 71) |
| 賢 | a **worthy man**(漢 92) |
| 賢にして財多ければ志を損ない【賢而多財，則損其志】 | A **worthy man** with much wealth finds his high ideals tarnished(漢 71) |
| 賢材を挙げ用い【挙賢材】 | promoting **men of worth and talent** to be his confidants(漢 78) |
| 賢士に手厚い【優礼賢士】 | was a patron of **men of worth**(漢 92) |
| 賢者::支宗の子孫のうち～を択んで【択支子孫賢者為嗣】 | select a **worthy person** from among the sons and grandsons of the collateral lines(漢 68) |
| 賢人::天下の～を得られ | attracting to your service the most **worthy gentlemen** of the world(漢 65) |
| 賢聖::古来 | The **worthies and sages** from ancient times(漢 74) |
| 賢聖の遠見の明に違い【失賢聖遠見之明】 | completely failing to understand his **sacred** and far-sighted wisdom(漢 97B) |
| 賢大夫 | the **virtuous men**(漢 92) |
| 賢輔下にあり【賢輔在下】 | worthy ministers **act as his assistants below**(漢 74) |
| 賢良 | **men of worth and good character**(漢 78) |
| 賢良の科に挙げられ【以賢良挙】 | was selected as a **man of worth and goodness**(漢 71) |
| 賢良の科に挙げられ【挙賢良】 | chosen as **a man of worth and goodness**(漢 74) |
| 賢良を挙げ【挙賢良】 | selecting **men of worth and goodness**(漢 74) |
| 遣わし::役人を【遣吏】 | **dispatched** one of his clerks(漢 71) |
| 譴責され | **scolded**(漢 74) |
| 元々を慰安する【慰安元元】 | bring comfort and relief to the **masses**(漢 74) |
| 元康中 | **During the *yüan-k'ang* era** (65-62 B.C.)(漢 74) |
| 元服する【以結髪內侍】 | bound up his hair and **entered manhood**(漢 68) |
| 厳格で剛毅【厳毅】 | Wei Hsiang was by nature **stern** and inflexible(漢 74) |
| 厳格ながらも残酷でない【厳而不残】 | was **stern** but never heartless(漢 71) |
| 厳刑峻法【厳刑峻法】 | **the most severe punishments of the law**(漢 74) |
| 減じて::死罪を | were **spared** the death penalty(漢 67) |
| 言う::その文に | **which read**(漢 74) |
| 言う::左右の者が・・・と言った | The attendants of the princess **remarked** on how good looking he was(漢 65) |
| 言は::鬼の～帰であり【鬼之為】 | the spirits of the dead are called *gui*, which **is to say** |

96

## 第4章 職官名関連和英表現集

| | |
|---|---|
| 言歸】 | **that** they have 'returned' (*gui*)（漢 67） |
| 言上 | **asked that**（漢 74） |
| 古えの制度【古制】 | the institutions **of antiquity**（漢 78） |
| 古の通義【古之通義】 | the accepted practice **of antiquity**（漢 78） |
| 古今の常道【古今常道】 | a constant rule **of past and present**（漢 74） |
| 古来かつて例のない【自古未之有也】 | Such a thing has **never happened before**（漢 78） |
| 呼び出し∷書を善くする官吏十人を〜【召善書吏十人於前】 | **sent for** ten clerks who were good at writing（漢 92） |
| 呼び戻す【呼之】 | **invite him back**（漢 74） |
| 呼号して∷昼夜【昼夜呼号】 | went about day and night **bellowing and shouting**（漢 92） |
| 固め【京師之固】 | the **key to the defense** of（漢 74） |
| 固辞 | **adamantly declining to accept** the marquisate（漢 74） |
| 戸∷右扶風に詔して二百〜の園邑を置く【詔右扶風置園邑二百家】 | commanded the Fufeng district of the capital area, in which his grave was situated, to set up a funerary park and village of two hundred **households**（漢 97A） |
| 戸衛∷掖庭〜であった | was **a guard of the gate of** the women's quarters（漢 97A） |
| 故旧∷宗族や〜【宗族故人】 | his relatives and **old friends**（漢 92） |
| 故事 | it **had been the custom up to this time**（漢 74） |
| 故事 | **actions taken in previous times**（漢 74） |
| 故事 | the **practice in times past**（漢 78） |
| 故事∷漢の【漢故事】 | **old regulations and precedents** of the Han court（漢 74） |
| 故事∷西曹が〜によって【西曹以故事】 | The chief clerk, following the **customary practice**,（漢 92） |
| 故事先例∷国の〜に通じる【曉国家故事】 | understands the **precedents** that govern the nation（漢 74） |
| 股肱 | **"arms and legs"**（漢 74） |
| 股肱∷大臣は国家の【大臣者,国家之股肱】 | The chief officials are **the arms and legs of the nation**（漢 67） |
| 胡児∷みだりに一〜を得る【妄得一胡兒】 | by some quirk of circumstance gets himself a **barbarian boy**（漢 68） |
| 胡人 | a **barbarian**（漢 54） |
| 後を嗣ぐ | **succeeded to** the marquisate（漢 74） |
| 後宮 | the **women of the palace**（漢 97B） |
| 後宮∷召されて〜に入る【召入 | was summoned to the **palace**（漢 97B） |

| | |
|---|---|
| 宮】 | |
| 後宮に入った::選ばれて | was selected to enter the **women's quarters**(漢 97B) |
| 後宮に入った【入後宮】 | was selected to enter the **women's quarters**(漢 97B) |
| 後宮に納れようとする【欲內其女後宮】 | to enter his daughter among the **ladies of the palace**(漢 68) |
| 後宮のものを祝詛し【祝詛後宮】 | attempting to put a curse on the other **women of the palace**(漢 97B) |
| 後宮の女たちが側らにあふれ【後宮滿側】 | The **ladies of the palace** were grouped about him in large numbers(漢 68) |
| 後宮を姦乱した罪に坐し【坐姦乱後宮】 | were tried on charges of immoral behavior with the **women of the palace**(漢 97A) |
| 後将軍 | **General of the rear**(漢 54) |
| 後将軍臣趙充国 | the **general of the rear** Chao Gh'ung-kuo(漢 68) |
| 後将軍趙充国ら | the **general of the rear** Chao Ch'ung-kuo and others(漢 74) |
| 後世に::名を〜顕わし【名顕後世】 | their names are well known to **later ages**(漢 65) |
| 後庭で遊ぶ | was amusing himself in the **women's quarters**(漢 97B) |
| 御意にかなう【稱上意】 | performed his duties in a way that **pleased the emperor greatly**(漢 74) |
| 御史・丞相・廷尉を交え | cooperate with the **clerks of the censorate**, the chancellor, and the commandant of justice(漢 97B) |
| 御史::監軍〜が悪事をはたらき【時監軍御史為奸】 | the **clerk** of the censorate ... was engaged in underhanded activities(漢 67) |
| 御史::丞相〜 | the chancellor and the **imperial secretary**(漢 63) |
| 御史に言う | remarking to his **secretary**(漢 78) |
| 御史はそのまま雲をつれ去った【御史遂將雲去】 | the **clerks of the censorate** had removed Chu Yün from the hall(漢 67) |
| 御史章贛 | the **imperial secretary** Chang Kung(漢 63) |
| 御史大夫に試守して | try him out temporarily in the post of **imperial secretary**(漢 67) |
| 御史大夫に遷った | was transferred to the post of **imperial secretary**(漢 71) |
| 御史大夫に遷った | and later promoted to **imperial secretary**(漢 74) |
| 御史大夫黄霸を丞相とし | transferred the **imperial secretary** Huang Pa to the post of chancellor(漢 74) |
| 御史中丞に下される | the matter be referred to the **middle aide to the** |

## 第4章 職官名関連和英表現集

| | |
|---|---|
| | imperial secretary（漢 67） |
| 御史中丞に下される | the matter be referred to the middle aide to the **imperial secretary**（漢 67） |
| 御史中丞に遷任され | advanced to the post of **middle aide to the imperial secretary**（漢 71） |
| 御史中丞に遷任され | advanced to the post of middle aide to the **imperial secretary**（漢 71） |
| 御史中丞の印で封印して【封以御史中丞印】 | were sealed with the seal of the **middle aide to the imperial secretary**（漢 97B） |
| 御史中丞の印で封印して【封御史中丞印】 | sealed with the seal of the **middle aide to the imperial secretary**（漢 97B） |
| 御史中丞王忠 | the middle aide to the **imperial secretary** Wang Chung（漢 78） |
| 御史中丞従事となり | to serve under the **middle aide to the imperial secretary**（漢 71） |
| 御史中丞従事となり | to serve under the middle aide to the **imperial secretary**（漢 71） |
| 御史中丞陳咸 | Ch'en Hsien, the **middle aide to the imperial secretary**（漢 67） |
| 御史中丞陳咸 | Ch'en Hsien, the middle aide to the **imperial secretary**（漢 67） |
| 御史府::則を連れて〜に行き | escorted her to the **office of the imperial secretary**（漢 74） |
| 御史府に入り | entered the **office of the imperial secretary** Wei Hsiang（漢 68） |
| 御者::故の趙昭儀の〜于客子・王偏・臧兼【故趙昭儀御者于客子,王偏,臧兼等】 | the former **coachmen** of the Bright Companion Chao, Yu K'o-tzu, Wang P'ien, and Tsang Chien（漢 97B） |
| 御者::従僕寿成を〜とし | ordered his own master of carriage Shou Ch'eng to act as **driver**（漢 63） |
| 御府の金銭・・・を出させて【発御府金銭】 | had gold, cash, swords, jade vessels, and colored silks brought from the **imperial treasury**（漢 68） |
| 護軍::監御史と〜の諸部校が堂皇に列座した | the superintendent of the garrison took his seat on the reviewing platform along with the various company commanders attached to the **garrison**（漢 67） |
| 護軍::大司馬〜となり | Ch'en Tsun for the post of grand marshal of the **supporting army**（漢 92） |
| 交わって::長者と〜【交長者】 | in his **friendships with** prominent people（漢 92） |

| | |
|---|---|
| 交われば::士大夫と〜【結士大夫】 | the gentlemen and great officials **with whom he associated**(漢 92) |
| 交渉を絶つ | broke off **relations**(漢 78) |
| 侯::淑徳〜に封ぜられる | was enfeoffed as **marquis** of Shu-te(漢 92) |
| 侯::中郎将雲を封じて…〜とする | let the general of palace attendants Ho Yün … be enfeoffed as **marquis** of Kuan-yang(漢 68) |
| 光輝の少ない【少輝】 | **fail to shine brightly**(漢 78) |
| 光禄::宗正, 大鴻臚, 〜をつかわし | dispatched the director of the imperial clan, the director of foreign vassals, and the **counselor to the keeper of the palace gate**(漢 68) |
| 光禄::仲山甫を〜とし | Chung-shan Fu your **censor**(漢 65) |
| 光禄勲::右将軍〜となり | held the posts of general of the right and **keeper of the palace gate**(漢 97B) |
| 光禄勲::散騎〜となり | was made **keeper of the palace gate** in charge of supplementary cavalry(漢 71) |
| 光禄勲とし | had him made **keeper of the palace gate**(漢 68) |
| 光禄勲となり | was made **keeper of the palace gate**(漢 68) |
| 光禄勲楊惲 | the **keeper of the palace gate** Yang Yün(漢 78) |
| 光禄大夫::給事中〜張朔 | who held the titles of steward of the palace and **counselor to the keeper of the palace gate**(漢 68) |
| 光禄大夫::侍中駙馬都尉〜に遷した | he advanced to the posts of attendant in the inner palace, commandant of the imperial horses, and **counselor to the keeper of the palace gate**(漢 68) |
| 光禄大夫::諸吏文学〜臣王遷… | the various officers, doctors of learning, and **counselors to the keeper of the palace gate** Wang Ch'ien …(漢 68) |
| 光禄大夫::文学〜夏侯勝ら | The doctors of learning and **counselors to the keeper of the palace gate** such as Hsia-hou Sheng and others(漢 68) |
| 光禄大夫::奉車都尉, 〜となり | became chief commandant in charge of the imperial carriage and **counselor to the keeper of the palace gate**(漢 68) |
| 光禄大夫となって | was made **counselor to the keeper of the palace gate**(漢 71) |
| 光禄大夫となる | be made a **counselor to the keeper of the palace gate**(漢 68) |
| 光禄大夫となる | was a **counselor to the keeper of the palace gate**(漢 74) |

## 第４章　職官名関連和英表現集

| 光禄大夫吉 | the **counselor to the keeper of the palace gate** Ping Chi（漢 63） |
|---|---|
| 光禄大夫吉 | the **counselor to the keeper of the palace gate** Ping Chi（漢 68） |
| 光禄大夫給事中 | became a **counselor to the keeper of the palace gate** and a steward of the palace（漢 74） |
| 光禄大夫張猛 | the **counselor to the keeper of the palace gate** Chang Meng（漢 71） |
| 公卿 | the **high ministers**（漢 74） |
| 公卿 | the **high officials**（漢 78） |
| 公卿 | the **high ministers**（漢 78） |
| 公卿・大臣を用いる | appointing **high ministers** and major officials（漢 71） |
| 公卿・大夫 | **high ministers** and officials（漢 71） |
| 公卿::詔して〜, 将軍, 中二千石らに識別させ【詔使公卿將軍中二千石雜識視】 | sent down an order for the **high ministers**, generals, and officials of the two thousand picul class to go in a group（漢 71） |
| 公卿が・・・を請う | The **high ministers** requested that（漢 63） |
| 公卿たちが前にいて | stood in the presence of the ruler and the **high ministers**（漢 67） |
| 公卿たちに諮問した | referred the matter to his **ministers**, asking for their advice（漢 67） |
| 公卿たちは皇后の冊立を論議し【公卿議更立皇后】 | the **ministers and high officials** were instructed to discuss who should be made empress（漢 97A） |
| 公卿に委任して | have entrusted its direction to the **high ministers**（漢 63） |
| 公卿に至った【至公卿】 | assigned to **important posts at court**（漢 65） |
| 公卿は未然の［禍い］を防ぐ【公卿有可以防其未然】 | You, the **high officials**, are supposed to be able to take steps to prevent future disasters（漢 71） |
| 公卿や位はすべて適任の者を得て【公卿在位咸得其人矣】 | **Every high post** has been filled with exactly the right man（漢 65） |
| 公卿をはじめとして位にある者すべて【自公卿在位】 | From the **highest nobles** and office-holders on down（漢 65） |
| 公卿宰相の地位におり【卿相之位】 | won the position of **highest ministers**（漢 65） |
| 公卿大臣 | the **high officials** and great ministers（漢 78） |
| 公侯::爵位を与えて〜とし【爵為公侯】 | are ennobled as **dukes and marquises**（漢 65） |
| 公侯をくじきしのいだ::その力は | Their strength humbled **dukes and marquises**（漢 92） |

101

| | |
|---|---|
| 【力折公侯】 | |
| 公子::張〜 | **Young gentleman** Chang（漢 97B） |
| 公車::詔を〜で待たせた【待詔】 | ordered him to await the imperial command in the **office of public carriage**（漢 65） |
| 公車::徴されて〜に出頭する【徴詣公車】 | was summoned to the **office of public carriage**（漢 71） |
| 公車が上聞する【公車以聞】 | The **chief of public carriage** reported the matter to the emperor（漢 71） |
| 公主 | The **princess**（漢 68） |
| 公主 | **princesses**（漢 68） |
| 公主::ひそかに〜に侍っており | has been carrying on a secret alliance with a **princess** of the imperial family（漢 65） |
| 公主::館陶〜施を尚る【尚館陶公主施】 | was married to the Kuan-t'ao **princess**, Liu Shih（漢 71） |
| 公主::長〜 | **Princess** Kai（漢 68） |
| 公主::長〜を侵害侮辱し【侵辱長主】 | insulting and mistreating an **imperial princess**, the eldest daughter of Emperor Wu（漢 67） |
| 公主::帝のおばの館陶〜 | the emperor's aunt **Princess** Kuan-t'ao（漢 65） |
| 公主::陽石・諸邑の二〜 | the **princesses** of Yang-shih and Chu-i,[3]（漢 63） |
| 公主::隆慮〜の子 | the son of **Princess** Lung-lu（漢 65） |
| 公主::鄂邑蓋長〜 | **Princess** Kai of O-i（漢 63） |
| 公主〔夷安〕::帝女〜を尚[めと]った | married a daughter of the emperor, **Princess I-an**（漢 65） |
| 公主〈蓋〜〉 | **Princess Kai**（漢 67） |
| 公主の家に属して::陽阿〜【属陽阿主家】 | was attached to the household of Emperor Ch'eng's elder sister **Princess** Yang-a（漢 97B） |
| 公主の子である | was the son of a **princess**（漢 65） |
| 公主はそこでお許しを得て | the **princess** requested that（漢 65） |
| 公主は自ら食物を捧げ | The **princess** in person served the food（漢 65） |
| 公主や貴人で礼制を超える | the **princesses** and nobles took to overstepping the rites and regulations（漢 65） |
| 公府に入り | they took positions in one of the **three highest ministries of the government**（漢 92） |
| 公府の掾史【公府掾史】 | The clerks of the **ministry**（漢 92） |
| 功 | **merit**（漢 74） |
| 功臣の世系を全うさせてやる【全功臣之世】 | the descendants of a **meritorious minister** may be spared the consequences of their own folly（漢 74） |
| 功遂りて[なりて]身退くは天の道 | When **deeds have been accomplished**, one should |

102

## 第 4 章　職官名関連和英表現集

| | |
|---|---|
| なり【功遂身退, 天之道】 | retire -- that is the Way of Heaven（漢 71） |
| 功徳 | The **merit and virtue** he displayed（漢 74） |
| 功徳 | **merit and virtue**（漢 78） |
| 功徳を思い【思其功徳】 | In memory of the **great services which he had performed**（漢 74） |
| 厚い::聖徳仁恩の〜ことを観みますに【観先帝聖徳仁恩之厚】 | in **the wealth of** their sacred virtue, their benevolence and mercy（漢 74） |
| 好み::もともと勇を | was originally noted for **his love of** daring（漢 67） |
| 好み::義を〜利を欲する心があり【好義欲利之心】 | **possess hearts moved** both by concerns of benevolence and righteousness and by the longing for personal profit（漢 78） |
| 好み::礼を〜恭謙で【好礼恭謹】 | **paid the strictest attention to** ritual and good manners（漢 71） |
| 孝行で | with **true filial piety**（漢 74） |
| 孝行をもって知られた【孝行聞】 | gained a name for **filial conduct**（漢 71） |
| 孝昭皇帝 | **Emperor Chao the Filial**（漢 68） |
| 孝弟・力田の者 | those who had behaved **in a filial or brotherly fashion** or had worked hard in the fields（漢 74） |
| 孝武皇帝 | **Emperor Wu the Filial**（漢 68） |
| 巷間これを歌って【閭里歌之曰】 | **In the lanes and alleys** they sang a jingle that went（漢 92） |
| 幸いに::臣相は | I have **graciously been permitted to**（漢 74） |
| 幸甚 | **enjoy great blessing**（漢 74） |
| 幸甚::天下〜 | the whole empire **enjoy the blessings** thereof（漢 74） |
| 幸倡::天子に寵幸されていた〜の郭舎人 | an **actor** named Courtier Kuo who enjoyed great favor with the emperor（漢 65） |
| 拘束::内官に〜される | **held in confinement** in the Inner Office（漢 65） |
| 更生する | the region **was granted a new lease on life**（漢 74） |
| 校尉 | **company commander**（漢 54） |
| 校尉::侍中・中郎将・長水〜となった | was made attendant in the inner palace, general of palace attendants, and **commander** of the Ch'ang-shui garrison（漢 71） |
| 校尉::守復士〜 | was temporarily appointed as a **colonel** in charge of the construction of the grave mound（漢 92） |
| 校尉::大将軍幕府の〜を選考して増し【調益莫府校尉】 | increased the number of **company commanders** in his staff（漢 68） |
| 校尉::末子高は中塁〜となった | his youngest son Ping Kao became **commander** of the gate for the northern garrison（漢 74） |

| | |
|---|---|
| 校尉たち | my **commanders**（漢 54） |
| 校尉として | served as a **commander**（漢 54） |
| 校尉として従軍 | accompanying Li Ling as a **company commander**（漢 54） |
| 校尉となる | was made a **company commander**（漢 92） |
| 校尉に侮辱され | humiliated by his **company commander**（漢 54） |
| 校尉を選考して【調校尉】 | transferred the **company commanders** to your staff（漢 68） |
| 校王::右〜 | right **company king**（漢 54） |
| 洪水旱魃が時節をはずれ発生【水旱不時】 | **flood** and drought visit us without respite（漢 74） |
| 皇位を陛下に譲る【致位陛下】 | to make certain that the **throne** would pass to Your Majesty（漢 97B） |
| 皇曾孫と号ばれ【号皇曾孫】 | known as the **imperial great-grandson**（漢 97A） |
| 皇太子 | the **crown prince**（漢 63） |
| 皇太子が立てられ | the **heir apparent** to Emperor Hsüan was designated（漢 71） |
| 皇太子が立てられ【立皇太子】 | the **heir apparent** of Emperor Hsüan was officially designated（漢 74） |
| 皇太子となり | was appointed **heir to the emperor**（漢 63） |
| 皇太子に立てられ | had been made **imperial heir**（漢 68） |
| 皇帝がにわかに崩御された【皇帝暴崩】 | **His Imperial Majesty** has passed away with great suddenness（漢 97B） |
| 綱紀・法度を一にし | unifying his **laws and precedents**（漢 65） |
| 綱紀を執り【執綱紀】 | to hold firm to the **reins of good rule**（漢 71） |
| 考えもしない::常侍郎の職につきたいと〜【安敢望常侍郎乎】 | they would never even get to be a clerk …, much less **could they ever dare hope to** become a palace attendant（漢 65） |
| 考査する【考案】 | a **review** was held of（漢 74） |
| 行いを修め【修行】 | began to be more careful in his **conduct**（漢 71） |
| 行う〈〜のことを〉::大鴻臚のことを | is also **acting for** the director of foreign vassals（漢 63） |
| 行義::その〜には格別のものがない【其行義未有以異】 | there is still nothing particularly distinguished about his **conduct**（漢 67） |
| 行幸::甘泉宮への〜に従う【從幸甘泉】 | accompanied the emperor on a **visit** to the Palace of Sweet Springs（漢 97A） |
| 行幸::太子宮に | **visited** the heir apparent's palace（漢 71） |
| 行幸して | **visited** the so-called tiger pens（漢 97B） |

## 第4章 職官名関連和英表現集

| | |
|---|---|
| 行事 | actions（漢74） |
| 高蓋::四頭立て〜の馬車が通れる【容駟馬高蓋車】 | to admit a team of four horses and a **high topped carriage**（漢71） |
| 高爵のもの::下の者が〜を軽んじ【下軽其上爵】 | inferiors look lightly on **those of high rank**（漢67） |
| 高廟 | the **ancestral temple** of Kao-tsu（漢74） |
| 鴻臚::契を〜とし | Hsieh is **director of vassals**（漢65） |
| 鉤弋::寵姫の〜趙倢伃 | reserved all his favor for Lady Chao, the Beautiful Companion of the **Hook and Dart Palace**（漢68） |
| 鉤弋宮にいて【居鉤弋宮】 | took up residence in the **Hook and Dart Palace**（漢97A） |
| 薨じる | **passed away**（漢74） |
| 剛::およそ役人たるものは〜に過ぎれば【凡為吏太剛則折】 | if an official is too **unbending**（漢71） |
| 剛毅 | of an **unbending nature**（漢78） |
| 剛毅::厳格で〜【厳毅】 | Wei Hsiang was by nature stern and **inflexible**（漢74） |
| 号される::聖王と【号聖王】 | will **earn the epithet of** sage king（漢65） |
| 号する::侍中と〜 | were all **referred to as** "attendants in the inner palace."（漢63） |
| 豪::長安の名〜【長安名豪】 | were famous as **"strong men"** of Ch'ang-an（漢92） |
| 豪俠 | **"strong men" and knights**（漢92） |
| 豪強 | the **powerful and influential families** of the area（漢74） |
| 豪傑 | **"strong men" and heroes**（漢92） |
| 豪傑::四人の | The Four **Strong Men**（漢92） |
| 傲慢で【踞慢】 | behaving with **swaggering insolence**（漢78） |
| 傲慢不遜になり | will become **rebellious**（漢68） |
| 刻::昼の漏の十〜に崩御した【晝漏上十刻而崩】 | By the time the water clock pointed to the tenth **notch** [8:30 A.M.], he had passed away（漢97B） |
| 刻::漏の五〜に【漏上五刻】 | Tonight at the fifth **notch** of the water clock around [7 P.M.]（漢97B） |
| 告令::百官に〜して | **Issuing an announcement** to the various officials that（漢63） |
| 国益 | **benefit to the government**（漢78） |
| 国家の大綱に明らかでなく【不明国家大体】 | failed to comprehend the **basic principles of the nation**（漢74） |
| 国君にふさわしくない【不宜君国】 | was not qualified to become the **lord of a fief**（漢97A） |

105

| | |
|---|---|
| 国君の後継者【国儲】 | is **the future hope of the nation**（漢 71） |
| 国内では諸種の制度を実行にうつし【内興制度】 | **at home** he was putting into effect his **new laws and statutes**（漢 65） |
| 国容［平時の儀礼］には軍を入れず | The **procedures of civil government** shall not be applied to the army（漢 67） |
| 穀物：：県官の～では救うに足りない【県官穀度不足以振之】 | the government does not have enough **supplies of grain** on hand to provide relief（漢 78） |
| 獄に下す：：廷尉の～【下相廷尉獄】 | had Wei Hsiang **sent to prison**†  for prosecution（漢 74）［†prison は court と訳すべきであろう］ |
| 獄を治めて【治獄】 | deciding **criminal cases**（漢 71） |
| 獄を治める：：反逆者の【治反者獄】 | to **investigate** persons charged with treason（漢 71） |
| 獄丞：：掖庭～籍武 | The **keeper of the jail** in the women's quarters Chi Wu（漢 97B） |
| 獄吏：：県の | had been **district prison official**†（漢 71）［†prison official は interrogator と訳すべきであろう］ interrogator ⇒ Europe, history of |
| 獄吏となった | became a **prison official**†（漢 74）［†prison official は interrogator と訳すべきであろう］ |
| 腰斬 | have the supervisor **cut in two at the waist**（漢 68） |
| 腰斬の刑に処せられ | ［was］... **cut in two at the waist**（漢 67） |
| 腰斬の刑に処せられ | was **cut in two at the waist**（漢 71） |
| 骨肉：：天子の | are **flesh and blood relations of** the emperor（漢 68） |
| 今年の統計【今年計】 | the statistics for **the past year**（漢 74） |
| 困って：：刺史は大変に～【刺史大窮】 | The circuit inspector, much **upset** at being unable to leave（漢 92） |
| 困苦欠乏し | are beset by **poverty and want**（漢 74） |
| 混乱させ：：聖朝を傾け～【傾乱聖朝】 | has **brought** danger and **chaos** to our sacred dynasty（漢 97B） |
| 些細ではない：：その憂患は【其憂不細】 | the damage will be **far from slight**（漢 71） |
| 左右 | **those about him**（漢 78） |
| 左右に：：常に～侍る | was constantly in attendance **at the ruler's side**（漢 65） |
| 左右にいて：：枚皋・郭舎人らとともに主上の～ | **waiting on the emperor** along with Mei Kao and the courtier Kuo（漢 65） |
| 左右に侍った【入侍左右】 | was **constantly in attendance**（漢 68） |
| 左右に侍って【在左右】 | served **at the emperor's side**（漢 68） |

## 第4章 職官名関連和英表現集

| | |
|---|---|
| 左右のものをしりぞけ【辟左右】 | sending the **servants** out of the room（漢97A） |
| 左右の貴人や傅昭儀【左右貴人傅昭儀】 | The Bright Companion Fu and the other ladies **in attendance**（漢97B） |
| 左右の者 | **everyone around him**（漢63） |
| 左右の者 | **others who were in attendance**（漢68） |
| 左右の者 | the **guards in attendance**（漢97B） |
| 左右の者が・・・と言った | The **attendants** of the princess remarked on how good looking he was（漢65） |
| 左右の者が刃を抜いて【左右拔】 | **attendants** drew their swords（漢68） |
| 左右の者に言った | said to **those about him**（漢68） |
| 左右の人々 | Various people **close to the emperor**（漢65） |
| 左右内史::中尉と～に詔して | ordered the commanders and **prefects in charge of the eastern and western areas of the capital**（漢65） |
| 左将軍がすでに死んで | The **general of the left** is already dead（漢63） |
| 左将軍に | to the position of **general of the left**（漢68） |
| 左将軍孔光を拝して丞相に任じる【拜左將軍孔光為丞相】 | to bestow upon the **general of the left** K'ung Kuang the position of chancellor（漢97B） |
| 左将軍上官桀 | the **general of the left** Shang-kuan Chieh（漢63） |
| 左将軍辛慶忌が冠を脱ぎ【免冠】 | the **general of the left** Hsin Ch'ing-chi doffed his cap（漢67） |
| 左将軍桀 | the **general of the left** Shang-kuan Chieh（漢68） |
| 左遷 | being **demoted**（漢78） |
| 左遷 | **demoting** you to the post of grand tutor（漢78） |
| 左遷され【貶】 | were **demoted**（漢74） |
| 左曹楊惲に告げ | reported it to the **clerk of the left** Yang Yun（漢68） |
| 左内史［⇒左右内史］ | **prefect in charge of the eastern area of the capital**（漢65） |
| 左馮翊となって | was serving as **left prefect of the capital**（漢97B） |
| 左馮翊臣田広明 | the **left prefect of the capital** T'ien Kuang-ming（漢68） |
| 左馮翊賈勝胡 | the **left prefect of the capital** Chia Sheng-hu（漢68） |
| 蹉跌［つまず］こうとしない【不敢差跌】 | not daring to commit the tiniest **misstep**（漢92） |
| 坐した::大逆の咎に～【坐大逆】 | **was accused of** major treason（漢97B） |
| 宰相::もと済南国の～で | formerly **prime minister** to the king of Chinan（漢54） |
| 宰相::郡国の太守・～ | the various provincial governors and **prime ministers** |

107

| | |
|---|---|
| | of the feudal states（漢 74） |
| 宰相::郡国の太守・〜に補任する | fill posts that had come vacant as governors of provinces or **prime ministers** of the feudal states（漢 78） |
| 宰相::代の〜陳豨 | Ch'en Hsi, the **prime minister** of Tai（漢 92） |
| 宰相::趙の〜虞卿 | Yu Ch'ing, the **prime minister** of Chao（漢 92） |
| 宰相安楽を責めた | berated the king's **prime minister** An Lo（漢 63） |
| 宰相二千石らに謝し | apologized to the **prime minister** and other officials of the two thousand picul class（漢 63） |
| 宰相平 | his **prime minister** P'ing（漢 63） |
| 宰相平に相談すると | discussed his plans with P'ing, his **prime minister**,（漢 63） |
| 災いや咎［とが］が起こる【災咎之発】 | portents and **disasters** appear（漢 71） |
| 災患を救う【救其災患】 | helping him to surmount this **disaster**（漢 78） |
| 災変 | **natural disasters**（漢 74） |
| 祭服 | the **robes to be worn at the sacrifice**（漢 74） |
| 裁判が公平であった【決獄平】 | was very fair in his **administration of justice**（漢 71） |
| 際限がなく::欲望に〜【耆欲無極】 | there is **no end to** her cravings and desires（漢 97B） |
| 摧き［くじき］::燕王を【摧燕王】 | **foiled** the evil ambitions of the king of Yen（漢 68） |
| 罪, 万死に当たり【罪當萬死】 | Truly my **blame** is such that I deserve ten thousand deaths（漢 74） |
| 罪::万方〜あらば【万方有罪】 | If there is **blame** in any of the people of the ten thousand quarters（漢 71） |
| 罪に陥る【獲罪】 | **be accused of some fault**（漢 74） |
| 罪に坐し::誣妄不道の〜【坐誣罔不道】 | **was accused of** malicious falsehood and unprincipled behavior（漢 71） |
| 罪に当てる::大逆無道の〜 | **be condemned as a** treasonable and unprincipled **criminal**（漢 92） |
| 罪に伏した | **admitted their guilt**（漢 68） |
| 罪の軽重にかかわらず | regardless of whether the **charges** against them were serious or light（漢 74） |
| 罪を得た::このことで【坐之】 | **charges were brought against** Chia for his part in the affair（漢 67） |
| 罪を得る | was **accused of** a crime（漢 74） |
| 罪を趙昭儀に帰し【帰罪趙昭儀】 | **placing the blame** for his demise **on the Bright Companion Chao**（漢 97B） |

## 第4章 職官名関連和英表現集

| | |
|---|---|
| 罪朕が躬にあらん【罪在朕躬】 | there must be **blame** in me, the ruler（漢 71） |
| 罪不道に至るとして【罪至不道】 | accusing him of **the most serious kind of wrongdoing**（漢 74） |
| 財を散じて士と交際させ | urged him to **dole out money** in order to attract friends（漢 65） |
| 財多ければ::賢にして〜志を損ない【賢而多財, 則損其志】 | A worthy man **with much wealth** finds his high ideals tarnished（漢 71） |
| 削られ | was **reduced to**（漢 74） |
| 策::学識がなく, 〜もなく【不学亡術】 | lacked learning and **overall strategy**（漢 68） |
| 察す:天変を【察於天変】 | had **been careful to observe** the portents sent by Heaven（漢 78） |
| 察知::いつわりのあることを | **realized** there was deception afoot（漢 63） |
| 殺戮::聖賢が追放されたり〜されたりする【放戮聖賢】 | To banish and **slaughter** worthy ministers（漢 65） |
| 三光 | the **three luminaries of the heavens**, the sun, the moon, and the stars（漢 78） |
| 三公 | the **three highest ministers** of the state（漢 63） |
| 三公 | one of the **three highest posts in the government**（漢 71） |
| 三公 | The **three highest ministers**（漢 74） |
| 三公 | the **three highest ministries**（漢 78） |
| 三公・九卿・大夫を率いて | leading the **three highest officials**, the nine high ministers, and the counselors（漢 68） |
| 三公の府【三公之府】 | the **three highest offices** in the nation（漢 74） |
| 三年::地節〜 | In the **third year** of *ti-chieh* (67 B.C.)（漢 74） |
| 三輔の治めにくい県を治める【治三輔劇県】 | govern one of the more troublesome districts of the **capital area**（漢 92） |
| 三輔を鎮定したい【鎮三輔】 | could guard the **three areas adjacent to the capital**（漢 92） |
| 参朝させ | shall be permitted to **attend audiences**（漢 78） |
| 参与させ::政謀に〜【与政謀】 | **consulting with** them on government policy（漢 78） |
| 散騎光禄勲となり | was made **keeper of the palace gate in charge of supplementary cavalry**（漢 71） |
| 散騎光禄勲となり | was made **keeper of the palace gate in charge of supplementary cavalry**（漢 71） |
| 散騎都尉 | **chief commandant of supplementary cavalry**（漢 |

109

| | 68) |
|---|---|
| 賛に言う【賛曰】 | **In appraisal we say**(漢 74) |
| 賛文を書いていた::拝命の【書賛】 | had prepared the **text of the pronouncement** he would make at the time of the presentation(漢 97B) |
| 簒奪::莽が帝位を | Wang Mang **usurped** the throne(漢 67) |
| 斬して::充を〜もって徇う[したがう] | they proceeded to have Ch'ung **cut in two** to serve as a warning(漢 63) |
| 斬った::ついにこれを | summarily **executed** the superintendent(漢 67) |
| 斬った::臣は謹んで法によって【謹以斬】 | I have respectfully **executed** the offender(漢 67) |
| 斬って::佞臣一人を【斷佞臣一人】 | **strike down** one of these mealymouthed ministers(漢 67) |
| 残酷::厳格ながらも〜でない【厳而不残】 | was stern but never **heartless**(漢 71) |
| 讒言する::媚道をうちにもっていると〜【譖告許皇后, 班倢伃挾媚道】 | **slanderously accused** Empress Hsü and Lady Pan of resorting to sorcery to win favor(漢 97B) |
| 讒言する者さえいた【或以譏吉】 | one of them ventured to **criticize him to his face**(漢 74) |
| 讒言する者を親近させ【親近讒夫】 | [To banish and slaughter worthy ministers] and instead surround oneself with **slanderers**(漢 65) |
| 仕官::ふたたび〜せず【不復仕】 | no longer **held office**(漢 67) |
| 仕官して秩禄二千石に至り | have advanced **in public service** to the two thousand picul rank(漢 71) |
| 仕官しようとして学ぶ【宦学】 | study **for public office**(漢 92) |
| 仕官できないようにした【不得仕宦】 | would not permit them to **hold public office**(漢 67) |
| 使者::莽の州牧・〜 | the provincial governors and **envoys** appointed by Wang Mang(漢 92) |
| 使者をつかわし | dispatched **messengers** to(漢 74) |
| 刺客を養う【養刺客】 | gave support to **professional killers**(漢 92) |
| 刺史::青州〜を殺そうとした | he planned to kill Ch'üan Pu-i, the **provincial director** of Ch'ing-chon(漢 71) |
| 刺史::青州〜を拝命 | appointed **provincial director** of Ch'ing-chou(漢 71) |
| 刺史::青州の | the **provincial director** of Ch'ing-chou(漢 63) |
| 刺史::揚州〜柯 | K'o, the **provincial director** of Yang-chou,(漢 63) |
| 刺史::揚州の〜に遷った | was promoted to **provincial director** of Yang-chou |

110

## 第4章 職官名関連和英表現集

| | （漢 74） |
|---|---|
| 刺史が事を奏するため∷部の【部刺史奏事】 | a **circuit inspector** who had to make a report to the throne（漢 92） |
| 刺史は大変に困って【刺史大窮】 | The **circuit inspector**, much upset at being unable to leave（漢 92） |
| 司直∷史魚を～とし | Shih Yu your **director of rectitude**（漢 65） |
| 司直∷丞相～ | **director of rectitude** under the chancellor（漢 78） |
| 司直〈丞相～〉 | P'o Yen-shou, the **director of rectitude** in the office of the chancellor（漢 78） |
| 司直の陳崇 | the **director of rectitude** Ch'en Ch'ung（漢 92） |
| 司農 | your **minister of agriculture**（漢 65） |
| 司馬法に…とある | The **Rules of the Marshal** states（漢 67） |
| 司隷解光が奏上して【司隷解光奏言】 | the **commander of convicts** Chieh Kuang submitted a report（漢 97B） |
| 司隷校尉昌はこれを取り調べ弾劾し【司隷校尉昌案劾】 | The **subordinate commander in charge of convicts**, a man named Ch'ang, investigated the matter and brought charges against Ping Hsien（漢 74） |
| 司隷校尉臣辟兵 | the **subordinate commander in charge of convicts** P'i-ping（漢 68） |
| 史∷尉の | the **military officials** of the district（漢 92） |
| 史∷京兆の～となった【為京兆史】 | became **clerks** in the office of the prefect of the capital（漢 92） |
| 史∷廷尉の～に補任され | was appointed a **clerk** under the commandant of justice（漢 71） |
| 史∷東織室の令～張赦 | the **clerk** of the eastern weaving rooms Chang She（漢 68） |
| 史に補せられ∷大将軍の | made **clerks** in the staff of the general in chief（漢 78） |
| 史望 | my **secretary** Wang（漢 97B） |
| 四夷 | **foreign tribes**（漢 78） |
| 四国を乱す | bring confusion to the lands of the **four quarters**（漢 65） |
| 四頭立て高蓋の馬車が通れる【容駟馬高蓋車】 | to admit **a team of four horses and a high topped carriage**（漢 71） |
| 四方 | in the **four quarters of the empire**（漢 74） |
| 士 | the **man**（漢 74） |
| 士∷謁見しようとする～ | **gentlemen** are to be granted an interview with you（漢 78） |
| 士∷器の大きい～である【大度 | is a **gentleman** of great capability（漢 92） |

| | |
|---|---|
| 士】 | |
| 士∷機微があり謀慮の【幾微謀慮之士】 | **men** of subtle understanding who are skilled at laying plans（漢 78） |
| 士∷寿命を大切にする～は【養寿命之士】 | those **gentlemen** who are intent upon nourishing life and longevity（漢 65） |
| 士∷天下の | the **gentlemen** of the empire（漢 78） |
| 士∷法度をまもる～を難詰する【難法度士】 | criticizes a strait-laced **gentleman**（漢 92） |
| 士〈経術の〉∷～を重んじ【重経術士】 | showed the highest respect for **scholars of classical learning**（漢 71） |
| 士としてもっとも高い位∷まことに【誠士之高致也】 | truly the highest eminence that any **man** could hope to attain!（漢 78） |
| 士と交際させ∷財を散じて | urged him to dole out money in order to **attract friends**（漢 65） |
| 士など…ない | **No man**（漢 74） |
| 士人を置く【更置士人】 | the office be staffed once more with **ordinary officials**（漢 78） |
| 士卒は風雨にさらされ【士卒暴露】 | your **officers and soldiers** are exposed to the dew of the field（漢 71） |
| 士大夫 | **gentlemen and officials**（漢 54） |
| 士大夫と交われば【結士大夫】 | the **gentlemen and great officials** with whom he associated（漢 92） |
| 士大夫に率先しない【亡以帥先士大夫】 | lacks the qualities that would entitle him to be a leader of **officers and gentlemen**（漢 67） |
| 子∷官爵功名は～より劣ることなく【官爵功名，不減於子】 | In position, title, accomplishment, and fame, I am in no way inferior to **you**（漢 92） |
| 子はもともと吏二千石の大官の子孫で【子本吏二千石之世】 | **You** started out as the heir of an official of the two thousand picul class（漢 92） |
| 子孫∷国を～に伝え【伝国子孫】 | their states pass down to their **sons and grandsons**（漢 65） |
| 子孫∷子はもともと吏二千石の大官の～で【子本吏二千石之世】 | You started out as the **heir** of an official of the two thousand picul class（漢 92） |
| 子孫∷支宗の～のうち賢者を択んで【択支子孫賢者為嗣】 | select a worthy person from among the **sons and grandsons** of the collateral lines（漢 68） |
| 子大夫たちに思慮の至らない | **you, my lords**, have not given sufficient thought to the matter（漢 63） |
| 子大夫たちよ，おのおの心を尽 | **My lords**, let each of you endeavor with all his heart |

112

第4章　職官名関連和英表現集

| | |
|---|---|
| くして | to find an answer（漢63） |
| 屍体::東市門に〜を磔せられた【磔尸東市門】 | his **corpse** was displayed at the gate to the eastern market（漢67） |
| 師事した::呉章に | **studied under** Wu Chang（漢67） |
| 師法が正しく【有師法】 | expounded the **text just as he had learned it from his teacher**（漢74） |
| 師旅 | the **armies**（漢74） |
| 師傅::ともに〜となり | both serving as his **mentors**（漢71） |
| 師傅::朝廷で〜を辱めた【廷辱師傅】 | insulting the **imperial tutor** in the presence of the court（漢67） |
| 師傅として | as **tutor**（漢63） |
| 志を損ない::賢にして財多ければ【賢而多財, 則損其志】 | A worthy man with much wealth **finds his high ideals tarnished**（漢71） |
| 志士・仁人としてなすに忍びない【志士仁人不忍為】 | no **gentleman of principle** or benevolent man could ever bring himself to act in this way（漢65） |
| 思い::政を〜【思政】 | **turning all your thoughts to** rule（漢78） |
| 支宗の子孫のうち賢者を択んで【択支子孫賢者為嗣】 | select a worthy person from among the sons and grandsons of the **collateral lines**（漢68） |
| 死罪::頓首〜 | I bow my head, confessing that **my fault deserves death.**（漢65） |
| 死罪に当る | I deserve to **die**（漢65） |
| 死傷者 | **The dead and injured**（漢74） |
| 死生命あり, 富貴, 天にあり【死生有命, 富貴在天】 | **life and death** are decreed by Fate, and wealth and eminence are decided by Heaven（漢97B） |
| 氏::霍〜が | The **members of** the Ho **family**（漢74） |
| 私家が盛ん【私家盛】 | **private families** flourish to excess（漢78） |
| 至った::公卿に【至公卿】 | **assigned to** important posts at court（漢65） |
| 至尊 | you are a man of **the highest position**（漢92） |
| 詩経 | the *Book of Odes*（漢74） |
| 試守して::御史大夫に | **try him out temporarily** in the post of imperial secretary（漢67） |
| 諮問::公卿たちに〜した | **referred the matter to** his ministers, asking for their advice（漢67） |
| 資格がなく【不逮】 | I am **unworthy of such honor**（漢78） |
| 資質を取り守り【秉公綽之質】 | possess the **wholesome nature** of Meng Kung-ch'o（漢78） |
| 賜い::黄金二十斤を〜【賜黄金二十斤】 | **presenting them with a gift of** twenty catties of gold（漢71） |

113

| | |
|---|---|
| 賜い::天子の衣を〜【賜御衣】 | **present him with** robes from the imperial treasury（漢 68） |
| 賜る::謁見を〜 | **had occasion** to meet with him（漢 78） |
| 賜与::百万銭を〜された【賜銭百万】 | was **awarded a gift** of a million cash（漢 71） |
| 厠の豚が群がり出て | The pigs broke out of the **privy** in a herd（漢 63） |
| 嗜む::票騎将軍は銭を貪り〜【票騎將軍貪者錢】 | the general of swift cavalry Wang Ken is **only interested in** squeezing money out of people（漢 97B） |
| 諡された::憲侯と〜【諡曰憲侯】 | was **given the posthumous title of** Hsien, the "Model Marquis."（漢 74） |
| 諡されて | was **given the posthumous title of** Ting（漢 74） |
| 事を謹む【慎事】 | **cautious** in your handling of affairs（漢 74） |
| 事案が有司に下げ渡され【事下有司】 | the **case** was handed over to the authorities for investigation（漢 74） |
| 事件::巫蠱の〜が起こった | the black magic **affair** occurred（漢 63） |
| 似ている | **took after** Kuo Hsieh（漢 92） |
| 侍して::主上に〜いた | was **attending** the emperor（漢 97A） |
| 侍った〈左右に〜〉【入侍左右】 | **was constantly in attendance**（漢 68） |
| 侍って::左右に〜【在左右】 | **served at** the emperor's side（漢 68） |
| 侍り::宮中に【内侍】 | **served** within the palace（漢 68） |
| 侍る::常に左右に〜 | was constantly **in attendance** at the ruler's side（漢 65） |
| 侍医 | the **palace physician**（漢 63） |
| 侍御史に推挙され | was appointed as one of the **secretaries of the censorate**（漢 71） |
| 侍御史五人とともに | along with five **secretaries of the censorate**（漢 68） |
| 侍御数百人がみな武器を執り | with several hundred **attendants** about her, all bearing weapons（漢 68） |
| 侍者::自分の〜李平を進め【進侍者李平】 | recommended to him an **attendant** of hers named Li P'ing（漢 97B） |
| 侍従::郎中の〜する者 | The palace attendants who **accompanied** him（漢 63） |
| 侍従の官は労れ倦んで【從官労倦】 | your **attendant officials** weary and exhausted（漢 71） |
| 侍詔の隴西郡・北地郡の良家子 | the sons of good families from Lung-hsi and Pei-ti who had been **assigned to await his command**（漢 65） |
| 侍曹::部下の | one of the **attendant clerks**（漢 92） |
| 侍中 | **attendants of the inner palace**（漢 54） |

## 第4章　職官名関連和英表現集

| | |
|---|---|
| 侍中 | an **attendant in the inner palace**（漢 68） |
| 侍中 | an **attendant in the inner palace**（漢 97B） |
| 侍中駙馬都尉光禄大夫に遷した | he advanced to the posts of **attendant in the inner palace**, commandant of the imperial horses, and counselor to the keeper of the palace gate（漢 68） |
| 侍中・中郎将・長水校尉となった | was made **attendant in the inner palace**, general of palace attendants, and commander of the Ch'ang-shui garrison（漢 71） |
| 侍中::〜駙馬都尉欽を封じて新成侯とした | enfeoffed her younger brother, the **attendant of the inner palace** and commandant of the imperial horses Chao Ch'in, as marquis of Hsin-ch'eng（漢 97B） |
| 侍中::奉車都尉〜となって | was chief commandant in charge of the imperial carriage and an **attendant in the inner palace**（漢 68） |
| 侍中となった | was made an **attendant in the inner palace**（漢 54） |
| 侍中となり | became **attendants in the inner palace**（漢 68） |
| 侍中と号する | were all referred to as "**attendants in the inner palace**."（漢 63） |
| 侍中衛尉 | The **attendant of the inner palace** and colonel of the guard Chin An-shang（漢 63） |
| 侍中謁者良 | the **attendant in the inner palace** and master of guests Liang（漢 78） |
| 侍中楽陵侯史高 | the **attendant of the inner palace** and marquis of Lo-ling Shih Kao（漢 78） |
| 侍中金安上に告げ | reported it to the **attendant in the inner palace** Chin An-shang（漢 68） |
| 侍中君卿 | my **attendant of the inner palace** Chun-ch'ing（漢 68） |
| 侍中建章衛尉金安上 | the **attendant in the inner palace** and colonel of the guard of the Chien-chang Palace Chin An-shang（漢 78） |
| 侍中史高と金安上 | The **attendants in the inner palace** Shih Kao and Chin Anshang（漢 68） |
| 侍中諸侯貴人 | The **palace attendants**, feudal lords, and men of eminence（漢 92） |
| 侍中常侍武騎 | was accompanied by the **gentlemen** in constant attendance and armed riders（漢 65） |
| 侍中僕射莽何羅 | the archery captain of the **inner palace attendants** Ma$^2$ Ho-lo（漢 68） |

| | |
|---|---|
| 侍中傅嘉 | the **attendant in the inner palace** Fu Chia (漢 68) |
| 侍郎::官は～にすぎず【官不過侍郎】 | your rank does not exceed **palace attendant** (漢 65) |
| 侍郎に任じ::常～ | appointed Shuo a **gentleman** in constant attendance (漢 65) |
| 字は長孫執金吾厳延年 | Yen Yen-nien, whose **polite name** is Ch'ang-sun and who is chief of the capital police (漢 63) |
| 時の宜しきに明らか【時用之宜】 | perceive what measures are **appropriate for the times** (漢 74) |
| 時節をはずれ::洪水旱魃が～発生【水旱不時】 | flood and drought visit us **without respite** (漢 74) |
| 治まった::大いに～【大治】 | was **a model of good order** (漢 74) |
| 治績 | **record as a model administrator** (漢 74) |
| 治道::成王と康王の～ | **an age of peace and prosperity** such as prevailed under kings Ch'eng and K'ang of the Chou dynasty (漢 78) |
| 治平を致す【致於治平】 | bring about a **state of harmony and peace** (漢 78) |
| 治乱 | the **principles of government** (漢 78) |
| 璽〈符～〉::尚～郎を召し | summoned the palace attendant who had charge of the **imperial credentials and seals** (漢 68) |
| 璽書を賜り | **letters bearing the imperial seal** (漢 63) |
| 自ら::公主は～食物を捧げ | The princess **in person** served the food (漢 65) |
| 自重する | **Proceed with circumspection** (漢 74) |
| 自然の勢い【自然之勢】 | a **natural state of affairs** (漢 74) |
| 式道候::宋万を～とし | Sung Wan **makes certain that the road has been cleared** (漢 65) |
| 執り::身に経書を【身執経】 | **hold**ing the copy of the text (漢 71) |
| 執り〈武器を～〉::侍御数百人がみな～ | with several hundred attendants about her, all **bearing weapons** (漢 68) |
| 執金吾::字は長孫～厳延年 | Yen Yen-nien, whose polite name is Ch'ang-sun and who is **chief of the capital police** (漢 63) |
| 執金吾::李路を～とし | Tzu-lu is **chief of capital police** (漢 65) |
| 執金吾が･･･捕らえた【執金吾捕】 | The **chief of the capital police** arrested (漢 68) |
| 執金吾であった | held the post of **chief of the capital police** (漢 97B) |
| 執金吾郭広意 | Kuo Kuang-i, the **chief of the capital police**, (漢 63) |
| 執金吾臣李延寿 | the **chief of the capital police** Li Yen-shou (漢 68) |
| 執戟::位は～にすぎない【位不 | your post is no more than that of **lance-bearer** (漢 65) |

116

第 4 章　職官名関連和英表現集

| | |
|---|---|
| 過執戟】 | |
| 執行〈法を〉::衛士の長に引き渡し法を〜させた | handed him over to the chief of the palace guard **for the law to deal with**（漢 63） |
| 執法::宿衛〜の臣咸は | Ch'en Hsien, a member of the palace guard and an official **charged with the administration of the law**（漢 67） |
| 実::名と〜を正す【核名実】 | making certain that the title they held was in conformity with their **actual performance**（漢 74） |
| 実行にうつし::国内では諸種の制度を〜【内興制度】 | at home he was **putting into effect** his new laws and statutes（漢 65） |
| 実情::巫蠱の〜【蠱情】 | the **true facts** of the black magic affair（漢 63） |
| 舎人 | **retainers**（漢 63） |
| 舎人::もとの太子の〜であった | was a **retainer** of the late crown prince Li（漢 71） |
| 舎人::天子に寵幸されていた幸倡の郭〜 | an actor named **Courtier** Kuo who enjoyed great favor with the emperor（漢 65） |
| 舎人無且 | his **steward** Wu Chü（漢 63） |
| 赦し::太子建を | **pardoned** the king's heir, Liu Chien,（漢 63） |
| 赦令に会う【会赦】 | a **general amnesty** was declared（漢 74） |
| 赦令をこうむった【蒙赦令】 | was granted **pardon**（漢 97B） |
| 社稷::重大な任務に耐え、〜を任せられる【任大重,可属社稷】 | could be entrusted with such a grave responsibility and counted on to protect **the altars of the soil and grain**（漢 68） |
| 社稷の臣 | one of the true protectors of the **altars of the soil and grain**（漢 78） |
| 社稷を安んじた【安社稷】 | insured the safety of **the altars of the soil and grain**（漢 68） |
| 社稷を危うくし【危社稷】 | the **altars of the soil and grain** will be imperiled（漢 97B） |
| 社稷を尊ぶ【尊社稷】 | bring honor to **the altars of the soil and grain**（漢 67） |
| 謝す::叩頭して〜【叩頭謝】 | struck his head on the floor **in apology**（漢 65） |
| 車騎将軍 | **General of carriage and cavalry**（漢 54） |
| 車騎将軍 | his son An, the **general of carriage and cavalry**,（漢 63） |
| 車騎将軍::金日磾を〜となし | appointed Chin Mi-ti **general of carriage and cavalry**（漢 68） |
| 車騎将軍::大司馬〜として | appointed Hsü Yen-shou as grand marshall and **general of carriage and cavalry**（漢 97A） |
| 車騎将軍::大司馬〜となった | was also appointed grand marshal and **general of** |

117

| | |
|---|---|
| | **carriage and cavalry**(漢 97A) |
| 車騎将軍::大司馬〜となり | became grand marshal and **carriage and cavalry general**(漢 97A) |
| 車騎将軍::大司馬〜史高 | the grand marshal **general of carriage and cavalry** Shih Kao(漢 71) |
| 車騎将軍の軍市令 | the commissary under the **general of carriage and cavalry**(漢 74) |
| 車騎将軍安世 | the **general of carriage and cavalry** Chang An-shih(漢 68) |
| 車騎将軍王舜 | The **carriage and cavalry general** Wang Shun(漢 67) |
| 車騎将軍韓増 | the **general of carriage and cavalry** Han Tseng(漢 54) |
| 車騎将軍臣張安世 | the **general of carriage and cavalry** Chang An-shib(漢 68) |
| 車騎将軍張安世 | the **general of carriage and cavalry** Chang An-shib(漢 68) |
| 車騎将軍張安世 | the **general of carriage and cavalry** Chang An-shih(漢 68) |
| 車騎将軍張安世 | the **general of carriage and cavalry** Chang An-shih(漢 74) |
| 車騎勒す | called out his **carriage and horsemen**(漢 63) |
| 遮る::行く路を | **gathered en masse to block** the general in chief's path(漢 74) |
| 奢侈であった | was living in **extravagance and luxury**(漢 68) |
| 奢侈で乱脈【奢淫】 | given to **extravagant** and disorderly ways(漢 78) |
| 舎人::枚皋・郭〜らとともに主上の左右にいて | waiting on the emperor along with Mei Kao and the **courtier** Kuo(漢 65) |
| 邪::武を立てて衆に威を示し,悪を誅してもって〜を禁ず【立武以威衆,誅悪以禁邪】 | make a display of military force in order to inspire awe, and one should punish evildoers in order to prevent **malefaction**(漢 67) |
| 邪を禁ず::武を立てて衆に威を示し,悪を誅してもって〜【立武以威衆,誅悪以禁邪】 | make a display of military force in order to inspire awe, and one should punish evildoers in order to **prevent malefaction**(漢 67) |
| 邪心::みだりにほめあげているのは,〜があるように疑われる【妄相稱擧,疑有姦心】 | Behind such wild praise and recommendation I fear there may be **sinister designs** that should not be left to flourish unchecked(漢 67) |
| 邪諂の輩が並び進んで【邪諂之 | **vicious and sycophantic** men crowd forward side by |

## 第4章 職官名関連和英表現集

| | |
|---|---|
| 人並進】 | side（漢65） |
| 尺牘を与える::人に【與人尺牘】 | wrote **letters** to people（漢92） |
| 爵位を軽んじ辱め【軽辱爵位】 | holds his **title and position** in contempt（漢92） |
| 爵位を与えて公侯とし【爵為公侯】 | are **ennobled as** dukes and marquises（漢65） |
| 若舎::召されて飾室中の〜に入り【飾室中若舎】 | was often summoned to the Decorated Chamber or to **such-and-such a lodge** of the palace（漢97B） |
| 主〈蓋〜〉 | **Princess Kai**（漢63） |
| 主が聖なれば, 臣は直なり【主聖臣直】 | if the **ruler** is a sage, his ministers will speak frankly（漢71） |
| 主上 | **The emperor**（漢74） |
| 主上::枚皋・郭舎人らとともに〜の左右にいて | waiting on the **emperor** along with Mei Kao and the courtier Kuo（漢65） |
| 主上は春秋が高い | the **emperor** was well along in years（漢63） |
| 主上殺し::天下に背いて〜の汚名を負わなくてはならない【令我負天下, 有殺主名】 | would be guilty of betraying the empire and would be branded as a **regicide**!（漢68） |
| 主簿 | his **secretary**（漢92） |
| 主簿::建の〜となり | was at this time **secretary** to Shen-t'u Chien（漢92） |
| 主簿を殺す【刺殺主簿】 | murder the **secretary**（漢92） |
| 主吏::丞相府の西曹〜 | The **clerk** in charge of personnel（漢74） |
| 取りなす | **intercede for** the boy（漢74） |
| 取り調べた::有司は・・・の疑いで | the authorities began **investigating** Chu Yün on the suspicion of（漢67） |
| 守::県の〜令として | In your capacity as **acting** magistrate（漢92） |
| 守::茂陵県の〜令尹公 | the **acting** magistrate of Mou-ling Lord Yin（漢92） |
| 守丞::華陰県の | acting as **aide to the magistrate** of Hua-yin（漢67） |
| 守丞::郡邸の〜 | Shui-ju, one of the **officials in charge of** the Chün-ti lodge（漢74） |
| 守相::郡国の〜もろものの牧官【郡國守相群牧】 | the provincial governors and administrators and the **prime ministers** of the feudal states, making sure that（漢71） |
| 守復土校尉 | was temporarily appointed as a colonel **in charge of** the construction of the grave mound（漢92） |
| 守令::県の〜として | In your capacity as **acting magistrate**（漢92） |
| 守令::茂陵県の〜尹公 | the **acting magistrate** of Mou-ling Lord Yin（漢92） |
| 手をかけ::郎は剣に〜【按剣】 | The attendant, **his hand on** his sword（漢68） |
| 手厚い::賢士に〜【優礼賢士】 | **was a patron of** men of worth（漢92） |

| | |
|---|---|
| 手書::詔記の背面に〜して【手書對牘背】 | to **write** the answer on the back of the message board **in his own hand**(漢 97B) |
| 珠襦::盛装して〜を着 | wearing a **pearl-sewn coat and splendid robes**(漢 68) |
| 酒宴を催し::宣室で | **setting out wine** in the Proclamation Chamber of the palace(漢 65) |
| 酒肉の宴がうち続いた【酒肉相属】 | there was a never-ending **flow of wine and meat**(漢 92) |
| 儒術 | the **policies of Confucianism**(漢 78) |
| 儒生 | **Confucian scholars**(漢 78) |
| 儒生::一〜 | a certain **Confucian scholar**(漢 92) |
| 寿命を大切にする士は【養寿命之士】 | those gentlemen who are intent upon nourishing **life and longevity**(漢 65) |
| 授かる::郎官となり騎常侍を【為郎, 騎常侍】 | was **rewarded with** the position of cavalry attendant in the inner palace(漢 54) |
| 宗室が危うい【公室危】 | endanger the **ruling house**(漢 78) |
| 宗正 | **Director of the imperial clan**(漢 54) |
| 宗正, 大鴻臚, 光禄をつかわし | dispatched the **director of the imperial clan**, the director of foreign vassals, and the counselor to the keeper of the palace gate(漢 68) |
| 宗正::龍逢を〜とし | Kuan Lung-feng **heads the imperial clan**(漢 65) |
| 宗正臣徳 | the **director of the imperial clan** Liu Te(漢 68) |
| 宗正臣劉徳 | the **Director of the imperial clan** Liu Te(漢 68) |
| 宗正徳 | the **director of the imperial clan** Liu Te(漢 63) |
| 宗正徳 | the **director of the imperial clan** Lin Te(漢 68) |
| 宗正府に迎え | was taken to the office of the **director of the imperial clan**(漢 68) |
| 宗正劉徳 | the **director of the imperial clan** Liu Te to go to(漢 68) |
| 宗正劉徳 | the **director of the imperial clan** Liu Te(漢 74) |
| 宗族や故旧【宗族故人】 | his **relatives** and old friends(漢 92) |
| 宗廟 | The **ancestral temples**(漢 74) |
| 宗廟に奉祀【奉宗廟】 | attending the **ancestral temples**(漢 74) |
| 宗廟を安んじようと | the safety of the **ancestral temples** would be assured(漢 97B) |
| 州牧::莽の〜・使者 | the **provincial governors** and envoys appointed by Wang Mang(漢 92) |
| 修める::自らを〜【自修】 | **discipline** himself(漢 78) |

## 第4章　職官名関連和英表現集

| | |
|---|---|
| 繡衣::～使者をつかわし【繡衣使者】 | ordering his special envoys in their **brocade robes**（漢78） |
| 繡衣を着【衣繡衣】 | donned **embroidered robes**（漢71） |
| 習熟し::法律に～【明習文法】 | **highly practiced in the handling of** documents and the application of the law（漢78） |
| 衆人の怨みの【衆人之怨】 | riches incite the envy of the **common crowd**（漢71） |
| 襲す::尊号を【襲尊号】 | **succeeded to the position of** highest honor（漢78） |
| 羞[はず]かしめ::印綬を～汚す【羞汙印韍】 | **defiles** his seal and cord of office（漢92） |
| 十死一生の大事::お産は婦人にとって【婦人免乳大故, 十死一生】 | It is a very serious thing for a woman to give birth," said Ho Hsien. "**Hardly one woman out of ten survives**（漢97A） |
| 従います::お指図に敬んで【敬奉教】 | I am only too happy to **follow** your instructions.（漢65） |
| 従う::相の議に | **listened to** his advice（漢74） |
| 従う【上従】 | **heeded his advice**（漢74） |
| 従え::相や中尉以下を | **led** the prime minister, the military commander, and the other officials of the state（漢63） |
| 従官 | his **attendants**（漢68） |
| 従官::群臣や～ | my old followers and **attendants**（漢68） |
| 従官::天子の～を詆欺 | to hoodwink and humiliate an **attendant** of the Son of Heaven（漢65） |
| 従官たち | his **attendants**（漢65） |
| 従官たち | **officers in attendance**（漢65） |
| 従官に・・・を買いにやらせ | sending his own **followers** out to buy（漢68） |
| 従軍::校尉として～ | **accompanying** Li Ling as a company commander（漢54） |
| 従史を叱って捕縛させる【叱従吏収縛】 | shouted to his **attendants** to seize and arrest the young man（漢71） |
| 従史を西につかわす【遣従史西】 | send a **messenger** west to the capital（漢92） |
| 従事::御史中丞～となり | to **serve under** the middle aide to the imperial secretary（漢71） |
| 従僕寿成を御者とし | ordered his own **master of carriage** Shou Ch'eng to act as driver（漢63） |
| 重んじ::経術の士を【重経術士】 | **showed the highest respect for** scholars of classical learning（漢71） |
| 重んじる | The emperor **treated** them both **with great respect** |

| | |
|---|---|
| | (漢74) |
| 重大な任務に耐え,社稷を任せられる【任大重,可属社稷】 | could be entrusted with such a **grave** responsibility and counted on to protect the altars of the soil and grain(漢68) |
| 重用される::ますます【浸益任用】 | **entrusted with** even greater **responsibility** than before(漢78) |
| 宿衛::宮中に〜【宿衛内侍】 | **served** in the palace(漢78) |
| 宿衛し | be admitted as a member of the guard **quartered** in the palace(漢63) |
| 宿衛執法の臣咸は | Ch'en Hsien, a member of the **palace guard** and an official charged with the administration of the law(漢67) |
| 出頭する::徴されて公車に〜【徴詣公車】 | was **summoned to the office of** public carriage(漢71) |
| 出兵 | **sending a force of men**(漢74) |
| 出兵 | **an expedition against**(漢74) |
| 術::子は大夫として先王の〜を修め【修先王之術】 | you, sir, study the **arts** of the former kings(漢65) |
| 春になれば【至春】 | when the **lean months of spring** come(漢74) |
| 春秋 | The *Spring and Autumn Annals*(漢74) |
| 春秋 | the *Spring and Autumn Annals*(漢78) |
| 春秋が高い::主上は〜 | the emperor was **well along in years**(漢63) |
| 『春秋』に通暁し【明春秋】 | was an expert on the *Spring and Autumn Annals*(漢71) |
| 徇う[したがう]::充を斬してもって | they proceeded to have Ch'ung cut in two to **serve as a warning**(漢63) |
| 巡行::天下を | **travel about** the empire(漢74) |
| 巡狩して | on a **tour of inspection**(漢97A) |
| 処せられ::宮刑に〜【坐法宮刑】 | **condemned to** suffer castration(漢97A) |
| 処せられ::腰斬の刑に〜 | **was cut** in two at the waist(漢71) |
| 処士::今の世の | Nowadays our **gentlemen in retirement**(漢65) |
| 処断する::君を〜【致君于理】 | see you **subjected to punishment**(漢78) |
| 所服::天子〜 | the **vestments** of the Son of Heaven(漢74) |
| 所有::形骸は地の【形骸者地之有】 | the bodily form **belongs to** earth(漢67) |
| 所有::精神は天の〜【精神者天之有】 | the spirit **belongs to** Heaven(漢67) |

## 第4章 職官名関連和英表現集

| | |
|---|---|
| 庶人 | a **commoner**（漢 74） |
| 庶民 | the **common people**（漢 74） |
| 署名 | to add a **notation**, as though by the emperor（漢 97A） |
| 書を善くする官吏十人を呼び出し::【召善書吏十人於前】 | sent for ten clerks who were **good at writing**（漢 92） |
| 書経 | The ***Book of Documents***（漢 78） |
| 書嚢::緑色の～を許美人に渡す【綠囊書予許美人】 | to deliver to Lady Hsü a green **letter pouch**（漢 97B） |
| 書嚢で::緑色の～返書を厳に与え【綠囊報書】 | gave it to Chin Yen **along with the green letter pouch** in which she had deposited her reply（漢 97B） |
| 書付け【書】 | the **letter**（漢 97B） |
| 書類袋::緑色の厚絹の～に入れ【盛綠綈方底】 | contained in a **message pouch** tied with a heavy green cord（漢 97B） |
| 諸官署に詔して… | delivering commands to the **various officials and bureaus** to summon（漢 68） |
| 諸公たちとも近づきになり | was accepted by the **members of the nobility**（漢 65） |
| 諸公の間では | among the **various gentlemen**（漢 92） |
| 諸儒 | The **Confucian scholars**（漢 78） |
| 諸曹【始顯少為諸曹】::若年で～となり | was young and serving as a **clerk in charge of handling memorials**（漢 74） |
| 諸吏中郎将羽林監任勝 | who held the titles of **official in charge**, general of palace attendants, and superintendent of the Feather and Forest Guard（漢 68） |
| 女主が驕盛であれば【女主驕盛】 | When a **woman in a position of authority** finds she can do as she pleases（漢 97B） |
| 召されて謁見【召見】 | **summoned to court**（漢 78） |
| 召されて飾室中の若舎に入り【飾室中若舎】 | was often **summoned** to the Decorated Chamber or to such-and-such a lodge of the palace（漢 97B） |
| 召し::尚符璽郎を | **summoned** the palace attendant who had charge of the imperial credentials and seals（漢 68） |
| 召し::太子覇を | **summoning** the heir apparent Pa（漢 63） |
| 商利を求め【以求買利】 | to seek **commercial gain**（漢 67） |
| 妾::妃～ | his consort and **concubines**（漢 63） |
| 将軍臣陵 | the **general of the army** Wang Ling（漢 74） |
| 将作::魯般を～とし | Lu Pan is your **master carpenter**（漢 65） |
| 将相の位 | the post of **general and high minister**（漢 78） |
| 小故 | **petty wrangling and spite**（漢 74） |
| 小臣 | A **petty official** at the bottom of the ranks（漢 67） |

| | |
|---|---|
| 小変事ではない【此非小変】 | an **'unusual occurrence' of far from petty proportions**（漢 74） |
| 小役人::郡邸の〜であり【郡邸小吏】 | served as a **petty official** in the Chün-ti, the lodge for official visitors from the provinces（漢 74） |
| 小役人から立身【起獄法小吏】 | started out as a **petty clerk**（漢 74） |
| 少使であった | held the rank of **Young Attendant**（漢 97B） |
| 少史も法冠をかぶり【少史冠法冠】 | has his **petty clerks** dressed up in their official caps（漢 78） |
| 少主が幼弱であれば【少主幼弱】 | when a **ruler** is still a mere child（漢 97B） |
| 少主を輔佐する【以輔少主】 | to assist his **youthful successor**（漢 68） |
| 少府 | **Privy treasurer**（漢 54） |
| 少府 | the post of **privy treasurer** of the Palace of Lasting Trust（漢 68） |
| 少府::長信〜臣嘉 | the **privy treasurer** of the Palace of Lasting Trust Chia（漢 68） |
| 少府となる::貢禹に代って長信〜【代貢禹為長信少府】 | replaced Kung Yu, first as **privy treasurer** of the Palace of Lasting Trust（漢 71） |
| 少府楽成 | the **privy treasurer** Shih Lo-ch'eng（漢 68） |
| 少府五鹿充宗が天子に貴幸され | the **privy treasurer** Wu-lu Ch'ung-tsung enjoyed great favor with the emperor（漢 67） |
| 少府徐仁 | the **privy treasurer** Hsü Jen（漢 68） |
| 少府臣史楽成 | the **privy treasurer** Shih Lo-ch'eng（漢 68） |
| 少傅::太傅・〜がおり | has his own grand tutor and **lesser tutor**（漢 71） |
| 少傅::太傅を前に〜を後に従えた【太傅在前，少傅在後】 | the grand tutor Shu Kuang preceding him, the **lesser tutor** Shu Shou following behind（漢 71） |
| 少傅となり | Shu Kuang as **lesser tutor**（漢 71） |
| 少傅に任ぜられ | was appointed **lesser tutor** to the heir apparent（漢 71） |
| 少傅石徳 | his **lesser tutor** Shih Te（漢 63） |
| 尚書 | the **chief of palace writers**（漢 68） |
| 尚書 | the **office of palace writers**（漢 74） |
| 尚書 | the **office of palace writers**（漢 74） |
| 尚書::平〜事【平尚書事】 | was put in charge of the **office of palace writers**（漢 71） |
| 尚書::領〜【領尚書】 | was still in charge of the **office of palace writers**（漢 68） |
| 尚書::領〜事【領尚書事】 | was given the supervision of matters pertaining to the **office of palace writers**（漢 68） |

## 第4章 職官名関連和英表現集

| | |
|---|---|
| 尚書::領〜事【領尚書事】 | was in charge of the **office of palace writers**（漢 71） |
| 尚書にかかわりないようにし【不関尚書】 | without first clearing them with the **office of palace writers**（漢 68） |
| 尚書に申さず【不関尚書】 | without clearing it with the **office of palace writers**（漢 68） |
| 尚書に対[こた]えなくてはならない【当対尚書】 | had to go to the **office of palace writers** to keep an appointment（漢 92） |
| 尚書のことを省た【省尚書事】 | was also given charge of the **office of palace writers**（漢 74） |
| 尚書令 | The **chief of palace writers**（漢 68） |
| 尚書令が奏文を読み上げて言った | The **chief of palace writers** read the memorial aloud（漢 68） |
| 承服 | **admitted the wisdom of** this answer（漢 74） |
| 招致::遊士を〜した | **gathered about him** a number of wandering scholars（漢 63） |
| 掌握::政事を〜する【用事】 | **rose to a position of** power（漢 63） |
| 掌故の職を得る | get to be a **clerk in charge of precedents**（漢 65） |
| 昭儀::左右の貴人や傅〜【左右貴人傅昭儀】 | The **Bright Companion** Fu and the other ladies in attendance（漢 97B） |
| 昭儀となった | was promoted to the rank of **Bright Companion**（漢 97B） |
| 省察する | will **give the matter close examination**（漢 97B） |
| 祥::善〜 | felicitous **portents**（漢 78） |
| 称う | **fitted for**（漢 74） |
| 称賛する::口々に【稱述】 | all **spoke highly of** him（漢 78） |
| 章奏 | **memorials that had been submitted**（漢 74） |
| 詔して::右扶風に〜二百戸の園邑を置く【詔右扶風置園邑二百家】 | **commanded** the Fufeng district of the capital area, in which his grave was situated, to set up a funerary park and village of two hundred households（漢 97A） |
| 詔によって | by **imperial command**（漢 74） |
| 詔を公車で待たせた【待詔】 | ordered him to await the **imperial command** in the office of public carriage（漢 65） |
| 詔を受け【受詔】 | received an **imperial command**（漢 74） |
| 詔記を奉持し | with a **written message from the emperor**（漢 97B） |
| 詔記を奉持し【持詔記】 | with a **message from the emperor**（漢 97B） |
| 詔獄に送った【送詔獄】 | had the man sent to the prison† for offenders who are under **imperial indictment**（漢 71）［†prison は court と訳すべきであろう］ |

125

| 詔書 | **edicts and memorials**（漢 74） |
|---|---|
| 象徴により【繇象類】 | chose a name that would be **symbolic of** the thing itself（漢 74） |
| 賞賜は千金を累ね【賞賜累千金】 | **presenting** him **with** a thousand catties of gold（漢 68） |
| 鐘をつき::亡国秦の【撞亡秦之鐘】 | **strikes the bells** of the fallen Ch'in dynasty（漢 71） |
| 倢伃::寵姫の鉤弋趙〜 | reserved all his favor for Lady Chao, the **Beautiful Companion** of the Hook and Dart Palace（漢 68） |
| 倢伃::班〜 | The **Beautiful Companion** Pan（漢 97B） |
| 倢伃::平君は〜となった | His wife Hsü P'ing-chun was advanced to the rank of **Beautiful Companion**（漢 97A） |
| 倢伃となり | was advanced to the rank of **Beautiful Companion**（漢 97B） |
| 倢伃となり | were assigned the **rank of Beautiful Companion**（漢 97B） |
| 倢伃になった | was honored with the **rank of Beautiful Companion**（漢 97B） |
| 倢伃に立てられ | was promoted to the rank of **Beautiful Companion**（漢 97B） |
| 倢伃を立てて皇后とした | recommended that the **Beautiful Companion** Hsü be made empress. The recommendation was adopted（漢 97A） |
| 上, 天性を変えず【不変天性】 | **on the higher plane** he does not pervert the nature of Heaven（漢 65） |
| 上にあり【在上】 | **reigns above**（漢 74） |
| 上をそしり【訕上】 | slandering his **superiors**（漢 67） |
| 上下に怨みなく【上下亡怨】 | **superior and inferior** will bear no grudge against one another（漢 74） |
| 上書 | submit **petitions** to the throne（漢 74） |
| 上書 | submitted a **letter to the throne**（漢 74） |
| 上書する | **submitting a letter to the throne**（漢 74） |
| 上申する【所白処】 | **brought to the emperor's attention**（漢 78） |
| 上疏して言った | **submitted a memorial saying:**（漢 78） |
| 上奏::吉を弾劾する〜をした【劾奏吉】 | **drawing up** an indictment against Ping Chi（漢 74） |
| 上奏::大官が〜した | The imperial butler **reported him to the emperor**（漢 65） |

## 第4章 職官名関連和英表現集

| | |
|---|---|
| 上聞 | **duly reported**（漢74） |
| 上聞::昧死〜いたし | Braving death, I **make this report**（漢67） |
| 上林苑 | the **Shang-lin Park**（漢65） |
| 丞::軍正の〜【守軍正丞】 | was appointed as **aide** to the inspector of the garrisons（漢67） |
| 丞::郡邸の守〜 | Shui-ju, one of the **officials** in charge of the Chün-ti lodge（漢74） |
| 丞::県〜 | the **assistant** to the magistrate of Mou-ling（漢74） |
| 丞::大官の | the **assistant** to the imperial butler（漢65） |
| 丞::大鴻臚〜 | the **assistant** to the director of foreign vassals（漢63） |
| 丞::宦者〜 | was made a **clerk** in the office of eunuchs（漢97A） |
| 丞相::黄霸に代って〜となり | replaced Huang Pa as **chancellor**（漢71） |
| 丞相::御史大夫黄霸を〜とし | transferred the imperial secretary Huang Pa to the post of **chancellor**（漢74） |
| 丞相::公孫弘に代わって〜となった | replaced Kung-sun Hung as **chancellor** of the central court（漢54） |
| 丞相::車〜の女婿 | the husband of **chancellor** Chu Ch'ien-ch'iu's daughter（漢68） |
| 丞相となり | was at this time made **chancellor**（漢68） |
| 丞相御史 | the **chancellor** and the imperial secretary（漢63） |
| 丞相御史::【鴻嘉元年制詔丞相御史】 | an imperial edict was issued to the **imperial secretary** in the first year of *hung-chia* (20 B.C.)（漢74） |
| 丞相車千秋が死んだ | the **chancellor** Chü Ch'ien-ch'iu died（漢74） |
| 丞相韋玄成が地位を維持せんとして保身をはかる【丞相韋玄成容身保位】 | the **chancellor** Wei Hsuan-ch'eng was concerned only in looking out for himself（漢67） |
| 丞吏以下のもの::掖庭の | The **clerks and officials** under me（漢97B） |
| 乗じる::衰勢に【因匈奴衰弱】 | **take advantage of** the apparent weakness of the Hsiung-nu（漢74） |
| 城旦の刑とした | were sentenced to **convict labour building and repairing walls**（漢67） |
| 城門::天火によって〜が焼かれ | … could not be opened; fire from the sky burned up the **city gate**（漢63） |
| 城門と郭門は同じ | The **gate of the inner wall** is no different from the gate of the outer wall（漢63） |
| 城門に来た | reached the **inner wall gate**（漢63） |
| 城門校尉::後に至ってまた〜とした【後復以為城門校尉】 | later he once more held office, this time as **subordinate commander of the city gate**（漢74） |

| | |
|---|---|
| 常侍::侍中〜武騎 | was accompanied by the gentlemen **in constant attendance** and armed riders（漢 65） |
| 常侍郎に任じ | appointed Shuo a **gentleman in constant attendance**（漢 65） |
| 常侍郎の職につきたいと考えもしない【安敢望常侍郎乎】 | could they ever dare hope to become a **palace attendant**（漢 65） |
| 常道::古今の【古今常道】 | a **constant rule** of past and present（漢 74） |
| 擾乱::西域を〜させない【使不敢復擾西域】 | intimidating them from making further **trouble** for the region west of China（漢 74） |
| 職を辞す【自免去】 | **resigned his post**（漢 74） |
| 職掌 | **duties**（漢 74） |
| 職責::多くが〜に任えない【在位多不任職】 | there are many men in office who are not competent to fulfill their **duties**（漢 71） |
| 職責を果たすことができる臣【任職臣】 | were men who were well fitted for their **tasks**（漢 71） |
| 職責を思う | paid close attention to the **duties of his office**（漢 74） |
| 食監 | the **supervisor of food**（漢 68） |
| 食監にかかわるな【無関食監】 | not to send them by way of the **supervisor of food**（漢 68） |
| 食客 | The **retainer**（漢 92） |
| 食客::奴僕や〜など大勢 | a large body of slaves and **retainers**（漢 67） |
| 嗇夫::暴室の〜となった【暴室嗇夫】 | was later made an **orderly**† in charge of the women's sickroom（漢 97A）[†当番兵（三コ）] |
| 嗇夫::掖庭の府庫を掌る〜【少内嗇夫】 | the **keeper** of stores for the women's quarters（漢 74） |
| 贖う::罪を【贖太守罪】 | **atone** for the crime charged against their governor（漢 74） |
| 辱め::爵位を軽んじ〜【軽辱爵位】 | **holds** his title and position **in contempt**（漢 92） |
| 辱め::朝廷で師傅を〜 | **insulting** the imperial tutor in the presence of the court（漢 67） |
| 信愛し | **loved and trusted** him greatly（漢 68） |
| 信任され::はなはだ【甚見任用】 | **being entrusted with** a position of grave responsibility（漢 71） |
| 侵害侮辱::長公主を〜し【侵辱長主】 | **insulting and mistreating** an imperial princess, the eldest daughter of Emperor Wu（漢 67） |
| 心が解け::主上の【上意解】 | the emperor's **anger subsided**（漢 67） |
| 心ばせの区別があった::親疎そ | whether addressed to close or casual friends, each one |

## 第4章 職官名関連和英表現集

| | |
|---|---|
| れぞれに〜【親疏各有意】 | expressed just the **proper sentiment**（漢92） |
| 心をつかんで::彼らの〜いた | were **intensely loyal to** him（漢67） |
| 心を去る::利を欲する【去民欲利之心】 | **remove from the hearts** of the people their longing for personal profit（漢78） |
| 心を合わせて政事を輔佐【同心輔政】 | **worked in accord to** assist the government（漢74） |
| 心を合わせて相談議論し【同心謀議】 | **worked in close accord** to further their plans and proposals（漢78） |
| 心を尽くして::子大夫たちよ、おのおの〜 | My lords, let each of you **endeavor with all his heart** to find an answer（漢63） |
| 心を留めたまう【留神元元】 | **condescend to take thought for**（漢74） |
| 慎み深さ::彼の篤実と〜は【篤慎】 | how devoted and **circumspect** he was（漢68） |
| 深厚::人がらが【為人深厚】 | by nature **very warm and generous**（漢74） |
| 申す::尚書に申さず【不関尚書】 | without **clearing it with the office of** palace writers（漢68） |
| 真令が赴任してくれば【真令至】 | the **permanent magistrate** will come to take over（漢92） |
| 臣 | his **ministers**（漢74） |
| 臣,謹んで思いますに【臣謹案】 | It is **my** considered opinion that（漢74） |
| 臣::姦〜の変を監察 | keep watch on the doings of villainous **ministers**（漢63） |
| 臣::賢聖の君はみな名〜がその側にいる【賢聖之君,皆有名臣在側】 | one always sees the sage rulers with eminent **ministers** by their side（漢97B） |
| 臣::社稷の〜 | one of the **true protectors** of the altars of the soil and grain（漢78） |
| 臣::宿衛執法の〜咸は | Ch'en Hsien, a **member** of the palace guard and an official charged with the administration of the law（漢67） |
| 臣::推薦して輔弼の〜とする【輔職】 | recommended Yün Ch'ang as a **man** who was capable of assisting the government（漢67） |
| 臣::朝廷の内〜として | appoint them **ministers** of the court（漢78） |
| 臣::不〜の愬え[うったえ]を受けつけるわけがない【不受不臣之愬】 | will not listen to the pleas of a disloyal **subject**（漢97B） |
| 臣::輔弼の〜は瓦解し | **ministers** who might aid and assist you fall away like broken tiles（漢65） |

| | |
|---|---|
| 臣〔偃〕::館陶公主の胞人〜昧死再拝して謁す【館陶公主〜臣偃昧死再拝謁】 | **Your servant Yen**, cook to the Kuan-t'ao Princess, braving death, bows twice and presents himself for an interview.(漢 65) |
| 臣〈群〜〉 | his **courtiers**(漢 63) |
| 臣〈群〜〉がみな免冠して | The **courtiers** all removed their hats(漢 63) |
| 臣〈群〜〉ら | the **courtiers**(漢 63) |
| 臣と称する【称臣】 | acknowledge **allegiance to** the Han(漢 78) |
| 臣は謹んで法によって斬った【謹以斬】 | I have respectfully executed the offender(漢 67) |
| 臣直なり::主聖なれば | if the ruler is a sage, his **ministers** will speak frankly(漢 71) |
| 親しくさせる::外戚の許氏だけを〜【独親外家許氏】 | **associate** only **with** his maternal relatives of the Hsü family(漢 71) |
| 親しみ敬われ【見親而敬】 | he was **treated with special care** and respect(漢 92) |
| 親に忍びない::人情としてその【縁人情不忍其親】 | human nature will **not allow a man simply to cast his parents aside when they die**(漢 67) |
| 親近::讒言する者を〜させ【親近讒夫】 | instead **surround** oneself with slanderers(漢 65) |
| 親政::万機を【親万機】 | **took personal command** of the affairs of government(漢 74) |
| 親戚関係::皇太后と〜があった【与皇太后有親】 | was **on very close terms with** the empress dowager(漢 97A) |
| 親疎それぞれに心ばせの区別があった【親疎各有意】 | **whether addressed to close or casual friends**, each one expressed just the **proper sentiment**(漢 92) |
| 親臨【自臨問】 | **came in person** to inquire how he was(漢 74) |
| 身を正し::義をひきい用いてその〜【引義以正其身】 | enlisting righteousness to help him **rectify himself**(漢 65) |
| 身を全う::その〜した【全其身】 | to **save their skins**(漢 65) |
| 進み出て諫めて言った | **stepped forward** with the following remonstrance(漢 65) |
| 進退がかならず礼に基づいていた【進退必以禮】 | in all his **comings and goings** he invariably abided by the dictates of ritual(漢 71) |
| 人がらが深厚【為人深厚】 | **by nature** very warm and generous(漢 74) |
| 人となり温柔で【爲人】 | was **by nature** a warm, gentle person(漢 65) |
| 人事 | **something contrived by men**(漢 74) |
| 人情::驚き懼れるのが【人情驚懼】 | It is only **human nature** to be terrified in such a situation(漢 97B) |
| 人情としてその親に忍びない【縁 | **human nature** will not allow a man simply to cast his |

130

第 4 章 職官名関連和英表現集

| | |
|---|---|
| 人情不忍其親】 | parents aside when they die（漢 67） |
| 人選が十分ではない【郡國守相多不實選】 | many men … who are not **fitted for their jobs**（漢 74） |
| 人倫::下, 〜を奪わない【不奪人倫】 | nor on the lower [plane] rob men of their **proper relationships**（漢 65） |
| 仁恩が心の中に凝結していた【仁恩內結於心】 | the innate **benevolence and kindness** that welled up within his heart（漢 74） |
| 仁義::中国の〜を貴ぶ【中国之仁義】 | esteem China for its **benevolence and righteousness**（漢 78） |
| 仁義を失わない【不失仁義】 | never violated the principles of **benevolence and righteousness**（漢 92） |
| 仁人::志士・〜としてなすに忍びない | no gentleman of principle or **benevolent man** could ever bring himself to act in this way（漢 65） |
| 尽くして〈心を〜〉::子大夫たちよ, おのおの | My lords, let each of you **endeavor with all his heart** to find an answer（漢 63） |
| 図む::大臣の位を【図大臣之位】 | is **scheming to** control the post of a high official（漢 67） |
| 図む::賤人が権柄の臣を【賤人図柄臣】 | mean men **lay schemes to** control the positions of power（漢 67） |
| 推挙::方正の科に【挙護方正】 | **recommended** Lou Hu as a man of honesty and uprightness（漢 92） |
| 水衡::延陵の季子を〜とし | Chi Tzu of Yen-ling your **director of water** works（漢 65） |
| 水衡都尉::吉の中子禹は〜となり | Ping Chi's second son Ping Yü served as **director of waterworks**（漢 74） |
| 水衡都尉に遷り | was shifted to the post of **director of waterworks**（漢 71） |
| 崇ぶ::悪を懲らし義を〜【懲悪崇誼示四方也】 | in censuring evil and **displaying respect for** right（漢 97B） |
| 枢機をつかさどり【典枢機】 | deciding on **the most secret and crucial affairs of state**（漢 78） |
| 枢機を握る【秉枢機】 | wields crucial authority in the **inner councils of state**（漢 74） |
| 世嗣::大宗に〜がない【大宗亡嗣】, | there is no **heir** in the direct line（漢 68） |
| 制::古今はその〜を異にする | past and present might differ in **form and procedure**（漢 74） |
| 制し〈敵を〜〉::権力をもって〜 | exercising the power vested in him, **curbing the** |

| | |
|---|---|
| 【因権制敵】 | **enemies of the state**(漢 68) |
| 制止できなくなる【不制】 | reach the point where it cannot **be checked**(漢 74) |
| 制詔して〈御史に〉 | **commanded the imperial secretary** to(漢 97A) |
| 制詔して言った | **issued a command** to the chancellor saying:(漢 74) |
| 制定::礼を〜した【制禮】 | **devised** certain rules and rituals for their [a man's parents] burial(漢 67) |
| 制度::漢の〜を乱し【乱漢制度】 | throwing into confusion the **statutes and regulations** of the Han(漢 68) |
| 制度::国内では諸種の〜を実行にうつし【内興制度】 | at home he was putting into effect his new **laws and statutes**(漢 65) |
| 制曰可 | the emperor **gave his approval**(漢 74) |
| 勢い::一姓が〜をほしいままにして【一姓擅勢】 | one clan has **arrogated all authority to itself alone**(漢 78) |
| 姓::一〜が勢いをほしいままにして【一姓擅勢】 | one **clan** has arrogated all authority to itself alone(漢 78) |
| 成長して::太子[=拠]は | the prince **grew older**(漢 63) |
| 政を思い【思政】 | turning all your thoughts to **rule**(漢 78) |
| 政を施す | exercise **governmental control** over(漢 78) |
| 政を扶け【扶政】 | assisting the **government**(漢 78) |
| 政を輔け【輔政】 | assist the heir apparent in the conduct of the **government**(漢 78) |
| 政を輔け【輔政】 | took part in **affairs of government**(漢 78) |
| 政事 | **matters of government**(漢 78) |
| 政事::心を合わせて〜を輔佐【同心輔政】 | worked in accord to assist the **government**(漢 74) |
| 政事::大将軍霍光が〜をとり【大將軍霍光秉政】 | the general in chief Ho Kuang was handling **affairs of government**(漢 78) |
| 政事::中書令石顕が〜を執り【中書令石顯用事】 | the eunuch Shih Hsien, who was chief of palace writers, exercised great **influence in the government**(漢 67) |
| 政事に精通した【明習政事】 | was well versed in the handling of **government affairs**(漢 71) |
| 政事に通じている【通政事】 | were versed in **government affairs**(漢 78) |
| 政事は一切光によって決裁された【政事壹決於光】 | all **affairs of government** were left to the sole decision of Ho Kuang(漢 68) |
| 政事は冢宰の手により行われ【政繇冢宰】 | and **government** proceeded instead from the hands of its high minister(漢 74) |
| 政事を視ること九年【視事九歳】 | fulfilling the **duties of chancellor** for nine years(漢 |

第4章　職官名関連和英表現集

| | 74） |
|---|---|
| 政事を掌握する【用事】 | rose to a **position of power**（漢63） |
| 政事を輔佐させた | making use of his services in the **government**（漢97A） |
| 政事を憂え【憂政】 | is deeply concerned about the **problems of government**（漢78） |
| 政事を与り聞く【与聞政事】 | take part in **affairs of government**（漢78） |
| 政治::大臣に〜を委ね【大臣委政】 | the high ministers are exercising the **power of government**（漢78） |
| 政謀に参与させ【与参政謀】 | consulting with them on **government policy**（漢78） |
| 政務をとり | administer the **affairs of government**（漢74） |
| 政務万端をみずから行い【明主躬万機】 | exercise control of the **ten thousand matters** in person（漢78） |
| 正し::義をひきい用いてその身を〜【引義以正其身】 | enlisting righteousness to help him **rectify** himself（漢65） |
| 正視しない【目不忤視】 | never **questioned** the emperor's authority **by so much as a defiant glance**（漢68） |
| 正直これ与にし【正直是與】 | **truth and uprightness** be your companion（漢78） |
| 正道::民は禁を知り〜にかえる【知禁而反正】 | the people come to understand the prohibitions and return to **what is correct** -- that is, to the correct laws of ancient times（漢92） |
| 正法を議す【議正法】 | deliberate as to the **correct way to apply the law**（漢97B） |
| 清廉 | a man of **integrity**（漢78） |
| 清廉潔白 | is **a man of impeccable principles and absolute honesty**（漢67） |
| 生殺の大権をぬすむ【竊殺生之權】 | arrogate to themselves the **authority to take human life**（漢92） |
| 盛ん::私家が〜【私家盛】 | private families **flourish to excess**（漢78） |
| 盛大::外戚王氏の賓客が〜 | the guests and retainers of the Wang families were especially **numerous**（漢92） |
| 盛大で::賓客はいよいよ〜【賓客愈盛】 | Guests **flocked** about him in even greater numbers（漢92） |
| 盛徳::先帝の | the **splendid virtue** of the former emperors（漢74） |
| 精神は天の所有【精神者天之有】 | the **spirit** belongs to Heaven（漢67） |
| 精通した::政事に〜【明習政事】 | was **well versed in** the handling of government affairs（漢71） |

133

| | |
|---|---|
| 精兵 | **the finest troops**（漢 74） |
| 精励::政治に【厲精為治】 | **devoting all his energy to** the achievement of orderly rule（漢 74） |
| 聖意の存するところ::先帝の【先帝聖意所起】 | what the **sacred intentions** of the former emperor actually were（漢 97B） |
| 聖王 | **sage king**（漢 74） |
| 聖王::明王・〜でないかぎり | If one is not a truly enlightened and **sage-like ruler**（漢 65） |
| 聖王と号される【号聖王】 | will earn the epithet of **sage king**（漢 65） |
| 聖賢が追放されたり殺戮されたりする【放戮聖賢】 | To banish and slaughter **worthy ministers**（漢 65） |
| 聖主::明王・〜に遭遇させる | had met up with an enlightened king, a **sage ruler**（漢 65） |
| 聖人::誤り無きは〜のみ【能毋過者，其唯聖人】 | only a **sage** can be wholly free of error（漢 71） |
| 聖人の義を敬慕し【慕聖人之義】 | pursue the ideals of the **sages**（漢 65） |
| 聖朝を傾け混乱させ【傾乱聖朝】 | has brought danger and chaos to our **sacred dynasty**（漢 97B） |
| 聖徳仁恩の厚いことを観みますに【観先帝聖徳仁恩之厚】 | in the wealth of **their sacred virtue, their benevolence and mercy**（漢 74） |
| 声誉 | **highest praise**（漢 74） |
| 西域を擾乱させない【使不敢復擾西域】 | intimidating them from making further trouble for the **region west of China**（漢 74） |
| 西曹が故事によって【西曹以故事】 | The **chief clerk**, following the customary practice,（漢 92） |
| 西曹が申告して【西曹白請】 | the **chief clerk** requested that（漢 92） |
| 西曹主吏::丞相府の〜 | The **clerk in charge of personnel**（漢 74） |
| 西羌 | **Western Ch'iang tribes**（漢 74） |
| 籍田がある | the **sacred field that the emperor plows in person**（漢 65） |
| 責めた::宰相安楽を | **berated** the king's prime minister An Lo（漢 63） |
| 責める::九卿が私を〜のはもっともだ【九卿責光是也】 | is right for the high ministers to **berate** me（漢 68） |
| 責め過め【責過】 | **berate**（漢 74） |
| 責任を問う::箇条書きにして職務上の〜【條責以職事】 | **berating** them item by item for deficiencies in their performance of duty（漢 71） |
| 摂位::王莽は〜にいて【王莽居摂】 | Wang Mang was acting as **regent**（漢 92） |

## 第4章 職官名関連和英表現集

| | |
|---|---|
| 摂政としての輔佐がなくては | unless there is someone suitable to act as **regent**（漢97B） |
| 節〈忠孝の〉【忠孝節】 | **loyalty and devotion**（漢68） |
| 節を改め【折節】 | reformed his **ways**（漢71） |
| 節操を改めた | were careful to **behave correctly**（漢92） |
| 先に設ける::太官を | **sent** the imperial butler **ahead** to prepare his quarters（漢63） |
| 先王の術::子は大夫として〜を修め【修先王之術】 | you, sir, study **the arts of the former kings**（漢65） |
| 先聖に鑑みる【観於先聖】 | be carried out in the light of the practices of the **former sages**（漢74） |
| 先帝 | the **former emperors**（漢74） |
| 先例〈故事〜〉::国の〜に通じる【曉国家故事】 | understands the **precedents** that govern the nation（漢74） |
| 千金::賞賜は〜を累ね【賞賜累千金】 | presenting him with **a thousand catties of gold**（漢68） |
| 宣室[の中に案内]::謁者に命じて董君を〜させた【引内】 | instructing the master of guests to have Lord Tung **conducted into the hall**（漢65） |
| 宣室で酒宴を催し | setting out wine in the **Proclamation Chamber** of the palace（漢65） |
| 専権 | **had complete control of** the government（漢78） |
| 戦国時代 | **the age of the Warring States**（漢92） |
| 扇動した::遠回しに殺人を | having indirectly **incited** one of his officials to commit murder（漢67） |
| 浅薄::何と〜なこと【何淺薄也】 | a **very mean and shallow** act indeed!（漢74） |
| 選挙::二千石の〜が不実である【二千石選挙不実】 | The process of **selecting** the two thousand picul officials has not been carried out judiciously（漢71） |
| 選任::鄧広漢を少府へ〜して | **shifted** Teng Kuang-han, …, **to** the post of privy treasurer（漢68） |
| 遷し::侍中駙馬都尉光禄大夫に〜た | he **advanced to** the posts of attendant in the inner palace, commandant of the imperial horses, and counselor to the keeper of the palace gate（漢68） |
| 遷った::御史大夫に | was **transferred to the post of** imperial secretary（漢71） |
| 遷り::杜陵の県令に | was **transferred to** the post of magistrate of Tu-ling（漢67） |
| 遷任::御史中丞に〜され | **advanced to the post of** middle aide to the imperial secretary（漢71） |

135

| | |
|---|---|
| 遷任して | **moved up**（漢74） |
| 踐更 | **military service**（漢92） |
| 詹事::孔父を～とし | K'ung Fu **manages the heir apparent's household**（漢65） |
| 銭を貪り::票騎将軍は～嗜む【票騎將軍貪耆錢】 | the general of swift cavalry Wang Ken is only interested in **squeezing money out of people**（漢97B） |
| 前後をとりちがえている【前後失問】 | had **lost all sense of when it was appropriate to ask questions and when it was not**（漢74） |
| 前向きに受け入れる【鄉納之】 | **paid much heed to**（漢78） |
| 前将軍 | **general of the vanguard**（漢54） |
| 前将軍臣韓増 | the **general of the vanguard** Tseng（漢68） |
| 前将軍蕭望之に仕えて | studied with the **general of the vanguard** Hsiao Wang-chih（漢67） |
| 善しとする【善之】 | **approved** this suggestion（漢74） |
| 善悪を明らかにする::有司に下して案験し、～【下有司案驗以明好惡】 | to refer the matter to the authorities for investigation so that they may **determine the right and wrong of** it（漢67） |
| 善行 | **good deeds**（漢74） |
| 善祥 | **felicitous portents**（漢78） |
| 疎略::禁令法網は～【禁網疏闊】 | the net of the law was **widely spread and full of holes**（漢92） |
| 訴えた::役人に～ | **reported to** the officials that（漢71） |
| 訴訟を裁き【哲獄】 | were astute in judging **criminal cases**（漢71） |
| 愬え[うったえ]::不臣の～を受けつけるわけがない【不受不臣之愬】 | will not listen to the **pleas** of a disloyal subject（漢97B） |
| 奏する::刺史が事を～ため::部の【部刺史奏事】 | a circuit inspector who had to **make a report to** the throne（漢92） |
| 奏上 | **allow the matter to come before the emperor**（漢74） |
| 奏上 | **submitted a memorial saying:**（漢78） |
| 奏上 | a **memorial was submitted to the emperor** concerning the case（漢97A） |
| 奏上::上書をしりぞけ～しない【屏不奏其書】 | I used to put such letters aside and not allow them to be **submitted to the throne**（漢68） |
| 奏上::封書を【奏封事】 | **submitted** a sealed memorial to the throne（漢74） |
| 奏上した::弾劾して～【劾奏】 | **submitted a memorial to** the throne accusing the brothers（漢92） |

## 第4章 職官名関連和英表現集

| | |
|---|---|
| 捜粟都尉とし | was appointed **chief commandant for requisitioning grain**（漢68） |
| 捜粟都尉となり | was appointed **chief commandant for requisitioning grain**（漢54） |
| 捜粟都尉となり | has been appointed **chief commandant for requisitioning grain**（漢63） |
| 捜粟都尉桑弘羊を御史大夫に | promoted the **chief commandant for requisitioning grain**, Sang hung-yang, to the position of imperial secretary（漢68） |
| 争うて力を致し将軍の高い明知を輔けたいと願う【争願自効，以輔高明】 | **vying with one another** in volunteering their services to assist in this lofty and enlightened undertaking（漢78） |
| 相::諸侯国の〜となり | employed as governors of provinces or **prime ministers** of feudal states（漢65） |
| 相国臣何 | The **prime minister** Hsiao Ho（漢74） |
| 相待って成り立つ | **each must have the other before there can be completion**（漢74） |
| 相談::宰相平に〜すると | **discussed** his plans **with** P'ing, his prime minister（漢63） |
| 総検閲::郎・羽林の属を〜した | called out the palace attendants and the Feather and Forest Guard for inspection（漢63） |
| 総領::衆職を【総領衆職】 | **supervised** the various offices of government（漢74） |
| 聡明を尽くすことに務め【務悉聡明】 | strive for the utmost **astuteness and perspicacity**（漢71） |
| 走卒と起居を共にし【與走卒起居】 | living like a **common soldier of the lowest rank**（漢67） |
| 遭遇::明王・聖主に〜させる | had **met up with** an enlightened king, a sage ruler（漢65） |
| 蔵し::民間に〜【蔵於民】 | goods **were left stored** among the people（漢78） |
| 側らに::後宮の女たちが〜あふれ【後宮満側】 | The ladies of the palace were grouped **about him** in large numbers（漢68） |
| 側近::陛下の【左右】 | **those who attend** Your Majesty（漢74） |
| 側近している::幃幄に【迫近幃幄】 | to **approach** the imperial curtains of state（漢97B） |
| 側近の人々 | the **courtiers**（漢63） |
| 則る::天地に【法天地】 | **abide by** the pattern of heaven and earth（漢74） |
| 即位 | **became ruler**（漢78） |
| 即位::新たに〜され【幼主新 | has newly **ascended the throne**（漢74） |

| | |
|---|---|
| 立】 | |
| 即位し::哀帝は | Emperor Ai **ascended the throne**(漢 97B) |
| 即位したばかり【時上初即位】 | had newly **come to the throne**(漢 78) |
| 足りない::県官の穀物では救う に～【県官穀度不足以振之】 | the government does **not have enough** supplies of grain **on hand** to provide relief(漢 78) |
| 速やかに::太官に詔して～… | sent another command to the imperial butler to **hurry up** with the meals(漢 68) |
| 属して::中宮に～【属中宮】 | was formerly **attached to** the empress's palace(漢 97B) |
| 属官::太中大夫任宣に命じ丞相・御史の～をまじえ【令太中大夫任宣與丞相御史属雑考問】 | ordered the palace counselor Jen Hsüan, along with various **officials attached to the offices of** the chancellor and the imperial secretary(漢 97A) |
| 属官とする | be made a **clerk in the general's office**(漢 67) |
| 属官となり | to be one of his **subordinates**(漢 71) |
| 属官にする | selected him to become one of his **subordinate officials**(漢 78) |
| 属官の地位::郡の | an **acting aide** to a magistrate(漢 67) |
| 賊殺::無実の者を～した【賊殺不辜】 | having **persecuted and put to death** an innocent man(漢 74) |
| 卒史 | **clerk**(漢 74) |
| 存じます::愚…と～【愚以為】 | if **I may venture to say** so,(漢 68) |
| 尊ばれる::君は～ | the ruler will **be honored**(漢 74) |
| 尊ぶ::天を～ことを謹み | diligent in **paying honor to** Heaven(漢 74) |
| 尊ぶ::巫鬼を | is much given to shamanism and spirit **worship**(漢 63) |
| 尊官は帝のお心にあります【尊官在帝】 | It is up to Your Majesty to assign **offices** as you please(漢 97A) |
| 尊官を与えよう::兄弟に【予兄弟尊官】 | assign your brothers to **high office**(漢 97A) |
| 尊貴の::みな～位におり【皆在尊貴之位】 | are all allowed to occupy positions **of eminence**(漢 97B) |
| 尊号::孝武皇后といった～を追号して【追上尊號曰孝武皇后】 | **posthumously honoring** her with the title "Empress of Emperor Wu the Filial(漢 97A)" |
| 尊号::太子が～を継いだ【太子襲尊号】 | his heir succeeded to **the position of highest honor**(漢 68) |
| 尊号を襲す【襲尊号】 | succeeded to the position of **highest honor**(漢 78) |
| 尊重する【貴重之】 | **treat him with honor and respect**(漢 68) |
| 太尉周亜夫に従って | under the **grand commandant** Chou Ya-fu(漢 54) |

138

## 第4章　職官名関連和英表現集

| | |
|---|---|
| 太官があえて具えない | The **imperial butler** did not dare comply（漢68） |
| 太官がまっ先に供し | [Ho Kuang] sent the **imperial butler** ahead to prepare his quarters（漢68） |
| 太官に詔して… | commanded the **imperial butler**　漢68） |
| 太官に詔して速やかに… | sent another command to the **imperial butler** to hurry up with the meals（漢68） |
| 太官を先に設ける | sent the **imperial butler** ahead to prepare his quarters（漢63） |
| 太史令司馬遷に問うた | questioned the **grand historian** Ssu-ma Ch'ien（漢54） |
| 太子 | the **prince**（漢63） |
| 太子 | The **prince**（漢63） |
| 太子::もとの〜の舎人であった | was a retainer of the late **crown prince** Li（漢71） |
| 太子::衛〜 | the **heir apparent** Li（漢68） |
| 太子::衛〜 | the **heir apparent** Li（漢74） |
| 太子::衛〜が敗れ | the **heir apparent**, the emperor's son by Empress Wei, was driven to his downfall（漢68） |
| 太子::衛〜と名乗り | claiming that he was **crown prince** Li（漢71） |
| 太子::衛〜を案ずる【患於衛太子】 | worried about the **crown prince**（漢71） |
| 太子::燕 | the **crown prince** of Yen（漢54） |
| 太子::故の〜建を立てた | enfeoffed the son of Liu Tan's **heir**, Liu Chien, who had died（漢63） |
| 太子::初めて〜が生まれ | first succeeded in **siring a son**（漢63） |
| 太子::戻〜 | the **heir apparent** Li（漢63） |
| 太子::戻〜拠 | The **heir apparent** Li, whose name was Liu Chü,（漢63） |
| 太子[=拠]は成長して | the **prince** grew older（漢63） |
| 太子が尊号を継いだ【太子襲尊号】 | his **heir** succeeded to the position of highest honor（漢68） |
| 太子が立った | this **son** succeeded to the throne（漢63） |
| 太子であった | had originally been the **heir apparent** of the Hsiung-nu Hsiu-t'u king（漢68） |
| 太子になった | became **heir apparent**（漢97B） |
| 太子の孫 | a grandson of the **heir apparent** Li（漢63） |
| 太子家令として | acting as **overseer of the heir apparent's household**（漢74） |
| 太子家令となった | appointed **overseer of the heir apparent's household**（漢71） |

| | |
|---|---|
| 太子宮 | the **heir apparent's palace**（漢 63） |
| 太子建を赦し | pardoned the **king's heir**, Liu Chien,（漢 63） |
| 太子少傅匡衡 | **lesser tutor to the heir apparent** K'uang Heng（漢 67） |
| 太子太傅臣通 | the **grand tutor to the heir apparent** Shu-sun Tung（漢 74） |
| 太子中人となり | became a lady in waiting to the **heir apparent**（漢 54） |
| 太子霸を召し | summoning the **heir apparent** Pa（漢 63） |
| 太師になる | Wang Shun was made **grand commandant**（漢 67） |
| 太主::寶～とも呼ばれ | known as the **Elder Princess** Tou（漢 65） |
| 太守・宰相::郡国の | the various **provincial governors** and prime ministers of the feudal states（漢 74） |
| 太守::河南～が | you are acting as **governor** of Ho-nan（漢 74） |
| 太守::河南郡の | **governor** of Honan（漢 74） |
| 太守::河南郡の～となる | to become **governor** of Ho-nan（漢 74） |
| 太守::上谷郡の | **governor** of Shang-ku Province（漢 54） |
| 太守::西河郡の～杜延年 | Tu Yen-nien, the **governor** of Hsi-ho（漢 74） |
| 太守::登用され…太原の～になった【稍遷至太原太守】 | advanced him to the post of **governor** of T'ai-yuan（漢 92） |
| 太守となった::河南郡の | become **governor** of Ho-nan（漢 92） |
| 太守となった::抜擢されて天水郡の【擢為天水太守】 | the emperor was pleased and promoted him to the post of **governor** of T'ien-shui（漢 92） |
| 太祝とともに | along with the **grand invocator**（漢 68） |
| 太常とし | is **master of ritual**（漢 65） |
| 太常臣昌 | the **master of ritual** Su Ch'ang（漢 68） |
| 太常臣蘇昌 | the **master of ritual** Su Ch'ang（漢 68） |
| 太中大夫 | the position of **palace counselor**（漢 54） |
| 太中大夫::朔を～給事中に拝し | honored Shuo by making him a **palace counselor**, with the additional title of steward of the palace（漢 65） |
| 太中大夫となった | had once risen as high as **palace counselor**（漢 65） |
| 太中大夫となった::博士・～ | was chosen to become an erudit and **palace counselor**（漢 71） |
| 太中大夫吾丘寿王をつかわし | ordered the **palace counselor** Wu-ch'iu Shou-wang（漢 65） |
| 太中大夫臣德・臣印 | the **palace counselors** Te and Chao Ang（漢 68） |
| 太中大夫任宣 | the **palace counselor** Jen Hsüan（漢 68） |
| 太中大夫任宣に命じ丞相・御史 | ordered the **palace counselor** Jen Hsüan, along with |

140

## 第4章　職官名関連和英表現集

| | |
|---|---|
| の属官をまじえ【令太中大夫任宣與丞相御史屬雜考問】 | various officials attached to the offices of the chancellor and the imperial secretary（漢97A） |
| 太僕::官職は衛尉〜に至った | In public office he rose as high as the post of colonel of the guard and **master of carriage**（漢74） |
| 太僕::賞は〜となり | appointed Chin Shang as **master of carriage**（漢68） |
| 太僕::申伯を | Shen Po your **master of carriage**（漢65） |
| 太僕か奉車都尉に当たり | correspond to the **master of carriage** or the chief commandant in charge of the imperial carriage（漢68） |
| 太僕たること十余年に及び【為太僕十餘年】 | had held the post of **master of carriage** for over ten years（漢74） |
| 太僕は・・・軽車をもって | The **master of carriage** went in a light hunting chariot（漢68） |
| 太僕上官桀 | the **master of the carriage**, Shang-kuan Chieh（漢68） |
| 太僕臣杜延年 | the **master of carriage** Tu Yen-mien（漢68） |
| 太僕陳万年は継母に仕えて【太僕陳萬年事後母】 | The **master of carriage** Ch'en Wan-nien has served his stepmother（漢74） |
| 太牢::長安廚の三〜を出し | had the Ch'ang-an Kitchen supply the animals for three **t'ai-lao sacrifices**（漢68） |
| 太傅・少傅がおり | has his own **grand tutor** and lesser tutor（漢71） |
| 太傅::蘧伯玉を | Ch'ü Po-yü your **grand tutor**（漢65） |
| 太傅::太子 | **Grand tutor** to the heir apparent（漢54） |
| 太傅::太子〜となり | was appointed as his **grand tutor**（漢74） |
| 太傅::太子〜夏侯勝 | the **grand tutor** to the heir apparent Hsia-hou Sheng（漢74） |
| 太傅::太子〜臣通 | the **grand tutor** to the heir apparent Shu-sun Tung（漢74） |
| 太傅となった | was made **grand tutor**（漢71） |
| 太傅となり | was chosen to act as **grand tutor**（漢71） |
| 太傅を前に少傅を後に従えた【太傅在前, 少傅在後】 | the **grand tutor** Shu Kuang preceding him, the lesser tutor Shu Shou following behind（漢71） |
| 太傅豹ら | the **grand tutor** Pao and others（漢63） |
| 対応する::既然の禍に【救其已然者】 | to **remedy** those which have already occurred（漢71） |
| 待詔の算術の上手な二人とともに【能用算者二人】 | along with two men **in the imperial service** who were good at calculations（漢65） |
| 怠ることがない【不怠】 | is **pursued with diligence**（漢78） |
| 退けて:他の仕事にかこつけて【以他職事】 | **had the secretary dismissed** on some other pretext（漢92） |

141

| | |
|---|---|
| 退けられる【退】 | **removed from office**（漢74） |
| 退出::朝廷から〜【罷朝】 | **left** the court（漢92） |
| 逮捕収監した【収捕】 | **arrested** the conspirators（漢71） |
| 代わって・・・となる【代為】 | **was replaced by** Wei Hsiang（漢74） |
| 代わって::・・・に〜御史大夫となり【代定国為御史大夫】 | to **replace him as** imperial secretary（漢74） |
| 代わって::公孫弘に〜丞相となった | **replaced** Kung-sun Hung as chancellor of the central court（漢54） |
| 大医大丸 | the big pill prepared by the **chief doctor**（漢97A） |
| 大謁者臣章 | The **grand master of guests** Hsiang Chang（漢74） |
| 大謁者襄章 | The **grand master of guests** Hsiang Chang（漢74） |
| 大吏::子はもともと吏二千石の〜の子孫で【子本吏二千石之世】 | You started out as the heir of an **official** of the two thousand picul class（漢92） |
| 大官が上奏した | The **imperial butler** reported him to the emperor（漢65） |
| 大官の丞 | the assistant to the **imperial butler**（漢65） |
| 大官を得られないでいる | had failed to attain any **important office**（漢65） |
| 大義に通暁【通大義】 | mastered their **principles**（漢74） |
| 大義に明らか【明於大義】 | understand **basic principles**（漢71） |
| 大逆の咎に坐した【坐大逆】 | was accused of **major treason**（漢97B） |
| 大逆無道の罪に当てる | be condemned as a **treasonable and unprincipled criminal**（漢92） |
| 大局を知っていると思った | based on a comprehension of the **true basic principles underlying the matter**（漢74） |
| 大綱::国家の〜に明らかでなく【不明国家大体】 | failed to comprehend the **basic principles** of the nation（漢74） |
| 大行 | the **coffin of the deceased emperor**（漢68） |
| 大行の治礼丞となった【為大行治禮丞】 | had him made a clerk in charge of rites under the **grand messenger**（漢78） |
| 大鴻臚 | the **director of foreign vassals**（漢63） |
| 大鴻臚 | was acting for the **director of foreign vassals**（漢68） |
| 大鴻臚::宗正，〜，光禄をつかわし | dispatched the director of the imperial clan, the **director of foreign vassals**, and the counselor to the keeper of the palace gate（漢68） |
| 大鴻臚::廷尉と〜をつかわし | dispatched the commandant of justice and the **director of foreign vassals** to go to Kuang-ling（漢63） |
| 大鴻臚のことを行う | is also acting for the **director of foreign vassals**（漢 |

## 第4章 職官名関連和英表現集

| | |
|---|---|
| | 63) |
| 大鴻臚丞 | the assistant to the **director of foreign vassals**（漢 63） |
| 大策::国家の～を深く考えず【不深惟國家大策】 | fail to give careful consideration to the **over-all welfare of the nation**（漢 74） |
| 大司空とする::商の子邑を | appointed Wang Yi, the son of Wang Shang, the marquis of Ch'eng-tu, as **minister of works**（漢 92） |
| 大司徒 | the **minister of education**（漢 92） |
| 大司徒の掾であった | was a clerk in the office of the **minister of education**（漢 67） |
| 大司徒馬人は大儒者であって【大司徒馬宮大儒優士】 | The **minister of education** Ma Kung, a prominent Confucian,（漢 92） |
| 大司農 | the **minister of agriculture** Chu Yi（漢 54） |
| 大司農となり::宮中に入って | was recalled to the capital, appointed **minister of agriculture**（漢 74） |
| 大司農中丞 | Keng Shou-ch'ang, the middle aide to the **minister of agriculture**（漢 78） |
| 大司農田延年 | the **minister of agriculture** T'ien Yen-nien（漢 68） |
| 大司馬::ただ～の官名だけを | leaving him with only the title and office of **grand marshal**（漢 68） |
| 大司馬とし | appointed Ho Yü as **grand marshal**（漢 68） |
| 大司馬になった | had been made **grand marshal**（漢 68） |
| 大司馬衛将軍となる | became **grand marshal** and general of the guard（漢 92） |
| 大司馬護軍となり | Ch'en Tsun for the post of **grand marshal** of the supporting army（漢 92） |
| 大司馬車騎将軍として | appointed Hsü Yen-shou as **grand marshal and general of carriage and cavalry**（漢 97A） |
| 大司馬車騎将軍となった | was also appointed **grand marshal and general of carriage and cavalry**（漢 97A） |
| 大司馬車騎将軍となり | became **grand marshal** and carriage and cavalry general（漢 97A） |
| 大司馬車騎将軍史高 | the **grand marshal general of carriage and cavalry** Shih Kao（漢 71） |
| 大司馬車騎将軍史高 | the **grand marshal** general of carriage and cavalry Shih Kao（漢 71） |
| 大司馬大将軍 | the post of **grand marshal** general in chief（漢 97A） |
| 大司馬大将軍::光を～となし | appointed Ho Kuang **grand marshal general in chief**（漢 68） |

| | |
|---|---|
| 大司馬大将軍光 | The **grand marshal general in chief** Ho Kuang（漢68） |
| 大司馬大将軍臣霍光 | the **grand marshal general in chief** Ho Kuang（漢68） |
| 大司馬博陸侯禹 | the **grand marshal** Ho Yü, marquis of Po-lu（漢68） |
| 大司馬莽・丞相・大司空に詔して | issued an edict to the **grand marshal** Wang Mang and the chancellor and minister of works（漢97B） |
| 大赦に遭うたのち【遭大赦】 | after a **general amnesty** had been issued（漢74） |
| 大宗に世嗣がない【大宗亡嗣】, | there is no heir in the **direct line**（漢68） |
| 大衆 | the **populace** as a whole（漢63） |
| 大将軍 | **general in chief**（漢54） |
| 大将軍 | the **general in chief**（漢54） |
| 大将軍 | the **general in chief**（漢54） |
| 大将軍 | **general in chief**（漢54） |
| 大将軍 | the **general in chief** Ho Kuang（漢74） |
| 大将軍：：光を大司馬〜となし | appointed Ho Kuang grand marshal **general in chief**（漢68） |
| 大将軍：：大司馬〜 | the post of grand marshal **general in chief**（漢97A） |
| 大将軍：：大司馬〜光 | The grand marshal **general in chief** Ho Kuang（漢68） |
| 大将軍：：大司馬〜臣霍光 | the grand marshal **general in chief** Ho Kuang（漢68） |
| 大将軍の長史に遷り | was promoted to the post of chief clerk to the **general in chief** Ho Kuang（漢74） |
| 大将軍光がそえのりした【大將軍光從驂乘】 | the **general in chief** rode by his side in the carriage（漢68） |
| 大将軍長史敞 | Yang Ch'ang, head secretary to the **general in chief** Ho Kuang（漢68） |
| 大将軍霍光 | The **general in chief** Ho Kuang（漢67） |
| 大将軍霍光 | the **general in chief** Ho Kuang（漢71） |
| 大将軍霍光が政事をとり【大將軍霍光秉政】 | the **general in chief** Ho Kuang was handling affairs of government（漢78） |
| 大将軍霍光は主上の雅意にそうて【大將軍霍光緣上雅意】 | the **general in chief** Ho Kuang, following what he knew to have been the emperor's wishes（漢97A） |
| 大臣 | a **high official**（漢78） |
| 大臣 | the **high ministers**（漢78） |
| 大臣：：いま朝廷の〜がたは主上を匡すことができず【今朝廷大臣上不能匡主】 | The **chief officials** in the court today are incapable of correcting the faults of the sovereign above（漢67） |
| 大臣：：このことを〜に言う【言之 | to report the situation to one of the **high ministers**（漢 |

144

# 第4章　職官名関連和英表現集

| | |
|---|---|
| 大臣】 | 97B) |
| 大臣::外戚として～であった魏其侯···のともがら【外戚大臣魏其,武安之属】 | Men like the **great ministers** Ton Ying, the marquis of Wei-ch'i, and T'ien Fen, the marquis of Wu-an, who were related to the imperial family by marriage（漢92） |
| 大臣::公卿・～を用いる | appointing high ministers and **major officials**（漢71） |
| 大臣::公卿～ | the high officials and **great ministers**（漢78） |
| 大臣::天子の～たるにふさわしい | I am fit to become a **great minister** to the Son of Heaven（漢65） |
| 大臣が命令に従わない【大臣不使】 | the **high ministers** will not obey him（漢97B） |
| 大臣たちは意向を知り【大臣知指】 | the **high ministers**, perceiving his meaning（漢97A） |
| 大臣に命じて輔佐させる【命大臣輔之】 | intending to appoint one of the **high ministers** to assist the boy in governing（漢68） |
| 大臣の推薦によって | the **high ministers** recommended（漢92） |
| 大臣は国家の股肱【大臣者,国家之股肱】 | The **chief officials** are the arms and legs of the nation（漢67） |
| 大勢::奴僕や食客など～ | **a large body of** slaves and retainers（漢67） |
| 大切にする::寿命を～士【養寿命之士】 | those gentlemen who are **intent upon** nourishing life and longevity（漢65） |
| 大節〈偶儻～〉を好み | liked to behave in a very **lofty and imperturbable** manner, caring only for the larger concerns of honor（漢67） |
| 大長秋::柳下恵を～とし | Hui of Liu-hsia the **supervisor of your harem**（漢65） |
| 大夫 | the **counselors**（漢68） |
| 大夫::何とりっぱな【賢哉二大夫】 | What fine **gentlemen** these two are!（漢71） |
| 大夫::公卿・～ | high ministers and **officials**（漢71） |
| 大夫::三公・九卿・～を率いて | leading the three highest officials, the nine high ministers, and the **counselors**（漢68） |
| 大夫::三世にわたる～の存在したことを【三世為大夫】 | allowing a **ministerial family** to hold sway for three generations in a row（漢74） |
| 大夫::政は～にゆだねられず【政不在大夫】 | government will not be in the hands of the **high officials**（漢92） |
| 大夫が世々権力を握り【大夫世権】 | the **high officials** exercised power generation after generation（漢92） |
| 大夫として::子は～先王の術を | you, **sir**, study the arts of the former kings（漢65） |

| | |
|---|---|
| 修め【修先王之術】 | |
| 大夫は冠をつけよ【大夫冠】 | Put on your cap, **sir**!（漢71） |
| 大夫家の門を踏みつけようと【欲躙大夫門】 | threatened to kick open the gate to the **secretary's quarters**（漢68） |
| 大理 | your **chief coordinator**（漢65） |
| 大礼 | the **basic ritual principle to be observed**（漢74） |
| 大尹::鎮戎～に任じる【拜鎮戎大尹】 | made him **governor** of Chen-jung, formerly called T'ien-shui（漢92） |
| 大尹::魯郡の～となる | was chosen to become **governor** of Lu（漢67） |
| 頽廃::風俗教化が～し【俗化陵夷】 | its customs have **fallen into sad decline**（漢71） |
| 磔せられた::東市門に屍体を～【磔尸東市門】 | his corpse was **displayed** at the gate to the eastern market（漢67） |
| 濁りがない::刑罰は～【刑罰清】 | his punishments and fines are **just**（漢74） |
| 濁世を避けて【避濁世】 | fled from a **muddy age**（漢65） |
| 叩頭して謝す【叩頭謝】 | **struck his head on the floor** in apology（漢65） |
| 叩頭して詫び | to **knock his head on the ground** and apologize（漢68） |
| 脱ぎ::左将軍辛慶忌が冠を【免冠】 | the general of the left Hsin Ch'ing-chi **doffed** his cap（漢67） |
| 探知して【発覚】 | **learned of** the affair（漢71） |
| 憚って::忌み～はならない【毋有所諱】 | **without fear of** saying anything that will offend me（漢71） |
| 弾劾::吉を～する上奏をした | drawing up an **indictment** against Ping Chi（漢74） |
| 弾劾し::みずから【上書自劾】 | heaping **blame on** himself（漢71） |
| 弾劾して奏上した【劾奏】 | submitted a memorial to the throne **accusing** the brothers（漢92） |
| 知っていながら | **knowingly**（漢78） |
| 知らない | I am **at a loss to know**（漢74） |
| 地::天～は和合し【天地和洽】 | Heaven and **earth** will attain peace and harmony（漢65） |
| 地位 | **posts**（漢74） |
| 地位::公卿宰相の～におり【卿相之位】 | won the **position** of highest ministers（漢65） |
| 地位におり::公卿宰相の【卿相之位】 | **won the position of** highest ministers（漢65） |
| 地位につく::丞相の | **took over the duties of** chancellor（漢74） |

## 第4章 職官名関連和英表現集

| | |
|---|---|
| 置く::士人を〜【更置士人】 | the office be **staffed** once more **with** ordinary officials（漢78） |
| 遅し::それ来ることの〜【其来遅】 | **how long** she is **in coming**!（漢97A） |
| 答二五〇 | two hundred and fifty **blows of the stick**（漢78） |
| 秩序 | were carried out in **proper fashion**（漢74） |
| 嫡嗣として::漢室の | is the **rightful heir** to the throne of the Han（漢63） |
| 着::繡衣を〜【衣繡衣】 | **donned** embroidered robes（漢71） |
| 中尉::相や〜以下を従え | led the prime minister, the **military commander**, and the other officials of the state（漢63） |
| 中尉と左右内史に詔して | ordered the **commanders** and prefects in charge of the eastern and western areas of the capital（漢65） |
| 中謁者趙堯 | The **middle master of guests** Chao Yao（漢74） |
| 中黄門となり | became **an attendant of the Yellow Gate in the inner palace**（漢97A） |
| 中黄門の宦官たち | eunuchs from the **Yellow Gate of the inner palace**（漢68） |
| 中黄門王舜・・・::故の | the former **eunuch attendants of the Yellow Gate** Wang Shun, Wu Kung, and Chin Yen（漢97B） |
| 中黄門田客 | the **eunuch attendant of the Yellow Gate** T'ien K'o（漢97B） |
| 中宮から来た | had just come back from the **empress's palace**（漢97B） |
| 中宮に属して【属中宮】 | was formerly attached to the **empress's palace**（漢97B） |
| 中宮史::故の〜曹宮 | the former **female scribe of the empress's palace** Ts'ao Kung（漢97B） |
| 中興 | **revival**（漢74） |
| 中御府令高昌【使中御府令高昌奉】 | the **keeper of the imperial treasury** Kao-ch'ang（漢68） |
| 中行の人 | a **man who is absolutely equitable in his behavior**（漢67） |
| 中書令に下して直接受け取らせ【下中書令出取之】 | having the **chief of palace writers** come out of the inner palace so they could put the letter directly into his hands（漢68） |
| 中書令石顕 | the **chief of palace writers** Shih Hsien（漢92） |
| 中書令石顕が政事を執り【中書令石顯用事】 | the eunuch Shih Hsien, who was **chief of palace writers**, exercised great influence in the government |

| | (漢 67) |
|---|---|
| 中丞::御史〜に下される | the matter be referred to the **middle aide** to the imperial secretary(漢 67) |
| 中丞::御史〜に遷任され | advanced to the post of **middle aide to** the imperial secretary(漢 71) |
| 中丞::御史〜王忠 | the **middle aide** to the imperial secretary Wang Chung (漢 78) |
| 中丞::御史〜従事となり | to serve under the **middle aide** to the imperial secretary(漢 71) |
| 中丞::御史〜陳咸 | Ch'en Hsien, the **middle aide** to the imperial secretary (漢 67) |
| 中丞::大司農〜 | Keng Shou-ch'ang, the **middle aide** to the minister of agriculture(漢 78) |
| 中丞〈御史〜〉の印で封印して【封御史中丞印】 | sealed with the seal of the **middle aide to the imperial secretary**(漢 97B) |
| 中人::太子〜となり | became a **lady in waiting to** the heir apparent(漢 54) |
| 中人以上 | Those whose talents are above **mediocrity**(漢 65) |
| 中正の道をとって | dwells in **between these two**(漢 74) |
| 中大夫を京師につかわし | sent his **palace counselor** to the capital(漢 63) |
| 中朝で仰ぎ見られ【本朝所仰】 | looked up to by the **entire court**(漢 78) |
| 中庭は彤朱く彩られ【其中庭彤朱】 | Its **courtyards** were painted vermilion(漢 97B) |
| 中都官 | the **various ministries in the capital**(漢 74) |
| 中都官に守備兵として来る【戍中都官者】 | fulfilling a term of service as guards at the **various administrative offices in the capital**(漢 74) |
| 中二千石 | officials of the **middle two thousand picul class**(漢 68) |
| 中二千石::詔して公卿, 将軍, 〜らに識別させ【詔使公卿將軍中二千石雜識視】 | sent down an order for the high ministers, generals, and **officials of the two thousand picul class** to go in a group(漢 71) |
| 中二千石::丞相・御史大夫・〜たちは誰一人発言しようとしなかった【丞相御史中二千石至者並莫敢發言】 | The chancellor, the imperial secretary, and the **two thousand picul officials** all arrived on the spot but none dared to speak up.(漢 71) |
| 中二千石::秩禄〜とし | a post drawing the salary of a **full two thousand picul official**(漢 54) |
| 中二千石が・・・幕府を塚のほとりに設け【治莫府塚上】 | while **officials of the middle two thousand picul class** prepared the tents to be erected on the grave |

148

## 第4章 職官名関連和英表現集

| | |
|---|---|
| | mound（漢 68） |
| 中二千石の役人 | the officials of the **two thousand picul class**（漢 63） |
| 中府に命じ | gave instructions to the **manager of her household**（漢 65） |
| 中塁校尉となった：：末子高は | his youngest son Ping Kao became **commander of the gate for the northern garrison**（漢 74） |
| 中郎：：推薦して〜諫大夫とした | recommending him as a **palace attendant** and admonisher（漢 67） |
| 中郎：：拝して〜となす | were all appointed **palace gentlemen**（漢 54） |
| 中郎となり | was restored to the post of **palace attendant**（漢 65） |
| 中郎になり | became a **palace attendant**（漢 92） |
| 中郎将 | a **general of palace attendants**（漢 54） |
| 中郎将：：侍中・〜・長水校尉となった | was made attendant in the inner palace, **general of palace attendants**, and commander of the Ch'ang-shui garrison（漢 71） |
| 中郎将：：諸吏〜羽林監任勝 | who held the titles of official in charge, **general of palace attendants**, and superintendent of the Feather and Forest Guard（漢 68） |
| 中郎将：：副〜 | his subordinate **general of palace attendants**（漢 54） |
| 中郎将となり | served as **generals of palace attendants**（漢 68） |
| 中郎将雲を封じて・・・侯とする | let the **general of palace attendants** Ho Yün … be enfeoffed as marquis of Kuan-yang（漢 68） |
| 中郎将王漢を・・・郡の太守とし | made the **general of palace attendants** Wang Han, the husband of one of Ho Kuang's granddaughters, the governor of Wu-wei（漢 68） |
| 中郎将関内侯昌 | the **general of palace attendants** and marquis within the Pass Ping Ch'ang（漢 74） |
| 中郎将舜 | **general of palace attendants** Hsü Shun（漢 71） |
| 中郎将蘇武を匈奴につかわし | dispatched Su Wu, a **general of palace attendants**, as his envoy to the Hsiung-nu（漢 63） |
| 中郎将利漢 | the **general of palace attendants** Li-han（漢 63） |
| 仲がいい【相善】 | **was on close terms with** Ping Chi（漢 74） |
| 忠義を成しとげた【以成其忠】 | thereby **manifesting the utmost loyalty**（漢 68） |
| 忠孝の節【忠孝節】 | **loyalty and devotion**（漢 68） |
| 誅して：：武を立てて衆に威を示し，悪を〜もって邪を禁ず【立武以威衆，誅悪以禁邪】 | make a display of military force in order to inspire awe, and one should **punish** evildoers in order to prevent malefaction（漢 67） |
| 誅す | **have** these two men **done away with**.（漢 68） |

| | |
|---|---|
| 誅する::暴を【誅暴】 | **punish** violence（漢 74） |
| 誅に伏す | they **were** all **put to death**（漢 74） |
| 誅殺した | had her **put to death**（漢 97B） |
| 廚::長安〜の三太牢を出し | had the Ch'ang-an **Kitchen** supply the animals for three t'ai-lao sacrifices（漢 68） |
| 兆民 | the **members of the populace**（漢 74） |
| 寵愛 | **favor**（漢 63） |
| 寵愛され::大いに | **enjoying great favor with** the emperor（漢 97A） |
| 寵幸されて::天子に〜いた幸倡の郭舎人 | an actor named Courtier Kuo who **enjoyed great favor with** the emperor（漢 65） |
| 寵幸され身って［みごもって］【御幸有身】 | have **received the imperial favor** and I am pregnant（漢 97B） |
| 寵幸をこうむり【御幸】 | **enjoyed the attentions of** Emperor Ch'eng the Filial（漢 97B） |
| 寵幸を受けた::史皇孫の | **gained favor with** the imperial grandson Shih（漢 97A） |
| 寵姫の鉤弋趙倢伃 | **reserved all his favor for** Lady Chao, the Beautiful Companion of the Hook and Dart Palace（漢 68） |
| 徴して【徴】 | **summoned** the governor of Hsi-ho Tu Yen-nien **to the capital**（漢 74） |
| 懲らし::悪を〜義を崇ぶ【懲悪崇誼示四方也】 | in **censuring** evil and displaying respect for right（漢 97B） |
| 朝賀::珍宝を奉じて〜して来た【奉珍朝賀】 | **offers** his rarest treasures **in tribute to the court**（漢 78） |
| 朝見した::群臣が | the various ministers were **attending audience in the palace**（漢 67） |
| 朝見する | **appear in court**（漢 78） |
| 朝廷で師傅を辱めた | insulting the imperial tutor **in the presence of the court**（漢 67） |
| 朝廷に::名声は〜高まり【名声重於朝廷】 | won considerable fame and reputation **at court**（漢 71） |
| 調べて罪を認定する【案致其罪】 | **conducting an investigation**（漢 74） |
| 長安令 | the **magistrate of Ch'ang-an**（漢 74） |
| 長安廚の三太牢を出し | had the **Ch'ang-an Kitchen** supply the animals for three t'ai-lao sacrifices（漢 68） |
| 長楽宮 | the **Palace of Lasting Joy**（漢 74） |
| 長公主を侵害侮辱し【侵辱長主】 | insulting and mistreating an **imperial princess, the eldest daughter of** Emperor Wu（漢 67） |

## 第4章　職官名関連和英表現集

| | |
|---|---|
| 長使であった | held the rank of **Superior Attendant**（漢 97B） |
| 長史 | **chief clerk** Ping Chi（漢 78） |
| 長史∷もと禹の～であった任宣【禹故長史任宣】 | his former **chief clerk** Jen Hsüan（漢 68） |
| 長史∷大将軍～敞 | Yang Ch'ang, **head secretary to** the general in chief Ho Kuang（漢 68） |
| 長史∷大将軍の | his **clerks**（漢 54） |
| 長史∷大将軍の～ | the **chief secretary** of the general in chief（漢 54） |
| 長史∷大将軍の～楊敞 | Yang Ch'ang, who was acting as **head secretary** to the general in chief Ho Kuang（漢 63） |
| 長史に遷り∷大将軍の | was promoted to the post of **chief clerk** to the general in chief Ho Kuang（漢 74） |
| 長者と交わって【交長者】 | in his friendships with **prominent people**（漢 92） |
| 長丞に法のとおり奉守させた【長丞奉守如法】 | with **officials** appointed to guard and maintain it according to the law（漢 97A） |
| 長丞に法の通り奉守させた∷三百戸の邑を置いて【置邑三百家, 長丞奉守如】 | with a village of three hundred households set up and **officials** appointed to guard and maintain the grave in accordance with the law（漢 97A） |
| 長信∷貢禹に代って～少府となる【代貢禹為長信少府】 | replaced Kung Yu, first as privy treasurer of the Palace of **Lasting Trust**（漢 71） |
| 長信少府臣嘉 | the privy treasurer of the **Palace of Lasting Trust** Chia（漢 68） |
| 長水校尉∷侍中・中郎将・～となった | was made attendant in the inner palace, general of palace attendants, and **commander of the Ch'ang-shui garrison**（漢 71） |
| 長門宮 | **the Long Gate Palace**（漢 65） |
| 長吏∷二千石や～を攻め殺し【攻殺二千石長吏】 | killed the officials of the two thousand picul class and **senior officers**（漢 92） |
| 長吏∷辺郡の | the **senior officials** in the border provinces（漢 74） |
| 長吏老病で兵馬の任にたえない | the **senior officials** are in some cases too old or sickly to take up arms and ride a horse（漢 74） |
| 冢宰∷政事は～の手により行われ【政繇冢宰】 | and government proceeded instead from the hands of its **high minister**（漢 74） |
| 直∷主が聖なれば, 臣は～なり【主聖臣直】 | if the ruler is a sage, his ministers will **speak frankly**（漢 71） |
| 直言諫争した【直言諫争】 | did **not hesitate to speak out boldly in reprimand**（漢 71） |
| 直指使者として | Pao Sheng-chih acting as a **directly appointed** envoy |

| | |
|---|---|
| | of the emperor（漢 71） |
| 朕が微賤だったころ【朕微眇時】 | In the past when **I was living in humble and obscure circumstances**（漢 74） |
| 珍宝を奉じて朝賀して来た【奉珍朝賀】 | offers his **rarest treasures** in tribute to the court（漢 78） |
| 追念 | **continued to keep** him **in his thoughts**（漢 78） |
| 追放::聖賢が〜されたり殺戮されたりする【放戮聖賢】 | To **banish** and slaughter worthy ministers（漢 65） |
| 通じあわない::たがいに【不与通】 | **refused to have anything more to do with** him（漢 78） |
| 通じて::［だれそれを］〜 | **acting through** Hsü Kuang-han（漢 74） |
| 通じて::許伯を〜【因平恩侯許伯】 | **enlisting the aid of** Hsü Kuang-han（漢 74） |
| 通じている::政事に【通政事】 | **were versed in** government affairs（漢 78） |
| 通じる | has **acquired a thorough knowledge of**（漢 74） |
| 通じる::国の故事先例に【暁国家故事】 | **understands** the precedents that govern the nation（漢 74） |
| 通義::古の〜【古之通義】 | the **accepted practice** of antiquity（漢 78） |
| 通暁::大義に【通大義】 | **mastered** their principles（漢 74） |
| 通暁し::『春秋』に【明春秋】 | was **an expert on** the *Spring and Autumn Annals*（漢 71） |
| 通明し::経術に【経術通明】 | **thoroughly versed in** the teachings of the Classics（漢 67） |
| 帝女夷安公主を尚［めと］った | married a **daughter of the emperor**, Princess I-an（漢 65） |
| 廷尉 | the **commandant of justice**（漢 54） |
| 廷尉::処理が〜に下る【事下廷尉】 | the matter was turned over to the **commandant of justice** for investigation（漢 68） |
| 廷尉::張釈之が〜となって | Chang Shih-chih **was commandant of justice**（漢 71） |
| 廷尉が取り調べた【廷尉験治】 | the **commandant of justice** had been conducting an investigation（漢 71） |
| 廷尉と大鴻臚をつかわし | dispatched the **commandant of justice** and the director of foreign vassals to go to Kuang-ling（漢 63） |
| 廷尉に至った | later advanced to the office of **commandant of justice**（漢 92） |
| 廷尉の獄に下す【下相廷尉獄】 | had Wei Hsiang sent to prison† **for prosecution**（漢 74）［†prison は court と訳すべきであろう］ |
| 廷尉右監になった | reached the post of superintendent of the right under |

## 第4章 職官名関連和英表現集

| | |
|---|---|
| | the **commandant of justice**(漢 74) |
| 廷尉監として | as **superintendent under the commandant of justice**(漢 74) |
| 廷尉李种・王平 | The **commandants of justice** Li Ch'ung and Wang P'ing(漢 68) |
| 廷尉于定国は法を執行するに詳かで公平であり【執憲詳平】 | The **commandant of justice** Yü Ting-kuo administers the law with fairness and exactitude(漢 74) |
| 詆欺∷天子の従官を〜 | to **hoodwink and humiliate** an attendant of the Son of Heaven(漢 65) |
| 適[せ]められ | have been **given a demerit**(漢 92) |
| 適[せ]める∷某[しかじか]のことで【以某事適】 | **give him a demerit** for such behavior(漢 92) |
| 適任の者∷公卿や位はすべて〜を得て【公卿在位得其人矣】 | Every high post has been filled with exactly the **right man**(漢 65) |
| 偶儻大節を好み | liked to behave in a very **lofty and imperturbable** manner, caring only for the larger concerns of honor(漢 67) |
| 典属国 | **Director of dependent states**(漢 54) |
| 典属国∷右曹の〜とした | was appointed **director of dependent states**, with the additional title of officer of the right(漢 54) |
| 典属国∷拝して〜となす | was appointed **director of dependent states**(漢 54) |
| 典属国∷百里奚を〜とし | Po-li Hsi your **director of dependent states**(漢 65) |
| 典属国となしたにすぎず | was given only the post of **director of dependent states**(漢 68) |
| 典属国にしかなれなかった【乃爲典属国】 | was only given the post of **director of dependent states**(漢 54) |
| 典属国になったにすぎない | was given only the post of **director of dependent states**(漢 63) |
| 典属国公孫昆邪 | The **director of dependent states** Kung-sun K'un-yeh(漢 54) |
| 典属国臣蘇武 | the **director of dependent states** Su Wu(漢 68) |
| 天にあり∷死生命あり, 富貴, 〜【死生有命, 富貴在天】 | life and death are decreed by Fate, and wealth and eminence are **decided by Heaven**(漢 97B) |
| 天の道∷功遂りて[なりて]身退くは〜なり【功遂身退, 天之道】 | When deeds have been accomplished, one should retire -- that is **the Way of Heaven**(漢 71) |
| 天を尊ぶことを謹み | diligent in **paying honor to Heaven**(漢 74) |
| 天下に広める∷太子の徳を【広太子徳於天下】 | to **enhance** the prince's reputation for virtue **in the world**(漢 71) |

153

| | |
|---|---|
| 天下に背いて主上殺しの汚名を負わなくてはならない【令我負天下,有殺主名】 | would be guilty of betraying the **empire** and would be branded as a regicide!（漢 68) |
| 天下に冤罪の民なく【天下無冤民】 | there were in fact no people **in the empire** who suffered injustice（漢 71) |
| 天下を傾け混乱させる【傾乱天下】 | the **empire** will be in danger of chaos and subversion（漢 97B) |
| 天下幸甚 | the **whole empire** enjoy the blessings thereof（漢 74) |
| 天火によって城門が焼かれ | … could not be opened; **fire from the sky** burned up the city gate（漢 63) |
| 天子が国を建て【天子建国】 | the **Son of Heaven** founded the state（漢 92) |
| 天子に寵幸されていた幸倡の郭舎人 | an actor named Courtier Kuo who enjoyed great favor with the **emperor**（漢 65) |
| 天子の衣を賜い【賜御衣】 | present him with **robes from the imperial treasury**（漢 68) |
| 天子の大義【天子之義】 | The actions of **the Son of Heaven**（漢 74) |
| 天子の大臣たるにふさわしい | I am fit to become a great minister to **the Son of Heaven**（漢 65) |
| 天寿をまっとうした【以寿終】 | lived to a **ripe old age**（漢 71) |
| 天性::上,〜を変えず【不変天性】 | on the higher plane he does not pervert **the nature of Heaven**（漢 65) |
| 天性を変え::上,〜ず【不変天性】 | on the higher plane he does not **pervert the nature of Heaven**（漢 65) |
| 天地に則る【法天地】 | abide by the **pattern of heaven and earth**（漢 74) |
| 天地に法を取る【取法天地】 | take **Heaven and earth** as their sole pattern（漢 74) |
| 天地は和合し【天地和洽】 | **Heaven and earth** will attain peace and harmony（漢 65) |
| 天道なり | have their basis in **the Way of Heaven**（漢 74) |
| 天変を察す【察於天変】 | had been careful to observe the **portents sent by Heaven**（漢 78) |
| 天佑をもって::たまたま〜【適有天幸】 | met with **extraordinary luck**（漢 92) |
| 天誅::一族が〜に伏するのは当然【家属當伏天誅】 | her family and associates deserve to suffer the **punishment of Heaven**（漢 97B) |
| 伝 | **lodging house**（漢 74) |
| 伝::外戚〜 | **Accounts** of the Families Related to the Emperors by Marriage（漢 97A) |
| 伝え::国を子孫に【伝国子孫】 | their states **pass down to** their sons and grandsons（漢 |

154

第4章　職官名関連和英表現集

| | |
|---|---|
| | 65) |
| 殿最::評定::彼らの〜を【課其殿最】 | decide **whether they have done a proper job or not**（漢 74） |
| 殿中に入り::暁が | her mother Ts'ao Hsiao came to the **apartments**（漢 97B） |
| 田も家も::以前からの〜ある【顧自有旧田廬】 | have the **fields and cottages** that have been in the family all along（漢 71） |
| 田や家を買うよう説き勧めて【君買田宅】 | urge him to buy some **land and houses**（漢 71） |
| 徒〈任侠の〉::軽薄な【軽侠之徒】 | this **class of worthless knights**（漢 92） |
| 登用 | **appoint** you **to an important post**（漢 74） |
| 登用され…太原の太守になった【稍遷至太原太守】 | **advanced him to the post of** governor of T'ai-yuan（漢 92） |
| 登用されない【不除用】 | was not **taken into service**（漢 78） |
| 都尉::右輔〜に命じて…を巡回警備させ | instructed the **chief commandant** in charge of the western area of the capital to inspect and alert the area（漢 65） |
| 都尉::延年を協律〜とした【延年為協律都尉】 | appointed her brother Li Yen-nien as a **chief commandant** with the title "Harmonizer of the Tones."（漢 97A） |
| 都尉::騎〜 | a **chief commandant** of cavalry（漢 54） |
| 都尉::騎〜の印綬 | the seal and seal cord of **chief commandant** of regular cavalry（漢 68） |
| 都尉::京輔〜臣趙広漢 | the **chief commandant** of the capital area Chao Kuang-han（漢 68） |
| 都尉::協律〜 | the **chief commandant** Li Yen-nien, the Harmonizer of the Tones（漢 54） |
| 都尉::彊弩〜 | the **chief commandant** of strong crossbowmen（漢 54） |
| 都尉::彊弩〜 | the **chief commandant** of strong crossbowmen Lu Po-te（漢 54） |
| 都尉::九江郡および河内郡の〜となり | took office, acting as **chief commandant** of Chiu-chiang and Ho-nei（漢 92） |
| 都尉::塞外〜 | a **chief commandant** beyond the border（漢 54） |
| 都尉::諸官署の大夫・騎〜・給事中になった【為諸曹大夫, 騎都尉, 給事中】 | being clerks, counselors, **colonels** of the cavalry, or stewards of the palace（漢 68） |

155

| | |
|---|---|
| 都尉::水衡～に遷り | was shifted to the post of **director** of waterworks（漢 71） |
| 都尉::捜粟～となり | was appointed **chief commandant** for requisitioning grain（漢 54） |
| 都尉::弟をもって関～とし【以丞相弟為関都尉】 | have appointed the younger brother of the late chancellor as **colonel** of the Han-ku Pass（漢 74） |
| 都尉::拝せられて騎～となる | was appointed a **chief commandant** of cavalry（漢 54） |
| 都尉::奉車～ | a **chief commandant** in charge of carriage（漢 54） |
| 都尉::驍騎～となり | served as a cavalry **commander**（漢 54） |
| 度遼将軍の印綬 | the seal and seal cord that had been given him when he was made **general who crosses the Liao**（漢 68） |
| 度遼将軍臣范明友 | the **general who crosses the Liao**, Fan Ming-yu（漢 68） |
| 度遼将軍未央衛尉平陵侯范明友 | who held the titles of **general who crosses the Liao** and marquis of P'iug-ling and who was a colonel of the guard in the Eternal Palace（漢 68） |
| 奴 | his **slaves**（漢 92） |
| 奴僕のかしら善 | Shan, his **chief slave**,（漢 63） |
| 奴僕や食客など大勢 | a large body of **slaves** and retainers（漢 67） |
| 怒る | you **fly into a rage** over it（漢 97B） |
| 冬を越す【踰冬】 | **passing the winter in jail**（漢 74） |
| 東園の温明秘器 | a "warm bright" supplied by the **Eastern Garden Office**（漢 68） |
| 東織室の令史張赦 | the clerk of the **eastern weaving rooms** Chang She（漢 68） |
| 東曹を召して | ordered the **clerk in charge of such matters to examine**（漢 74） |
| 彤朱く::中庭は～彩られ【其中庭彤朱】 | Its courtyards were painted **vermilion**（漢 97B） |
| 當る::死罪に | I **deserve** to die（漢 65） |
| 当世の | **of the day**（漢 74） |
| 統べる::胡越の軍隊を【領胡越兵】 | **having charge of** the soldiers of the Hu and Yüeh tribes（漢 68） |
| 踏みつけ::大夫家の門を～よう と【欲躢大夫門】 | threatened to **kick open** the gate to the secretary's quarters（漢 68） |
| 堂皇::監御史と護軍の諸部校が～に列座した | the superintendent of the garrison took his seat on the **reviewing platform** along with the various company commanders attached to the garrison（漢 67） |

## 第4章 職官名関連和英表現集

| | |
|---|---|
| 道徳の道に入らず | could not have proceeded in accordance with **the Way and virtue**（漢92） |
| 道理に暗く【闇於大理】 | was blind to **fundamental principles**（漢68） |
| 徳::太子の〜を天下に広める【広太子徳於天下】 | to enhance the prince's **reputation for virtue** in the world（漢71） |
| 徳を施し | spread **virtue** abroad（漢78） |
| 督察し::郡国を【督課郡国】 | **inspecting** the provinces and feudal states（漢71） |
| 督笞 | a **beating**（漢74） |
| 篤実と慎み深さ::彼の〜は【篤慎】 | how **devoted and circumspect** he was（漢68） |
| 屯田::漢の車師に〜する【漢屯田車師者】 | the Han **garrison and farm** in Chü-shih（漢74） |
| 屯兵 | **garrison troops**（漢68） |
| 頓首して | **bowed his head** and said,（漢65） |
| 頓首して | **bowed his head**（漢71） |
| 頓首死罪 | **I bow my head, confessing that my fault deserves death.**（漢65） |
| 貪兵 | a **campaign of greed**（漢74） |
| 内謁者令郭穣 | The **master of guests in the inner palace** Kuo Jang（漢74） |
| 内官に拘束される | held in confinement in the **Inner Office**（漢65） |
| 内史::右〜より下民をつかわして | had the **prefect** in charge of the western area muster a force of commoners（漢65） |
| 内者令欧侯 | Ou-hou, the **supervisor of the inner palace**（漢97A） |
| 内心みずから納得しかね【内不自得】 | was **not at all happy** serving as the governor of a distant province（漢78） |
| 内臣::朝廷の〜として | appoint them **ministers of the court**（漢78） |
| 難詰する::法度をまもる士を〜【難法度士】 | **criticizes** a strait-laced gentleman（漢92） |
| 二千石 | the position of a **two thousand picul official**（漢54） |
| 二千石 | **two thousand picul officials**（漢68） |
| 二千石 | the **two thousand picul officials**（漢74） |
| 二千石 | the **two thousand picul officials**（漢78） |
| 二千石::もとの〜の身分をもって | As a former official of the **two thousand picul class**（漢54） |
| 二千石::宰相〜らに謝し | apologized to the prime minister and other **officials of the two thousand picul class**（漢63） |
| 二千石::子はもともと吏〜の大 | You started out as the heir of an official of the **two** |

| | |
|---|---|
| 官の子孫で【子本吏二千石之世】 | **thousand picul class**（漢 92） |
| 二千石となる | became an **official of the two thousand picul rank**（漢 92） |
| 二千石の選挙が不実である【二千石選挙不実】 | The process of selecting the **two thousand picul officials** has not been carried out judiciously（漢 71） |
| 二千石や長吏を攻め殺し【攻殺二千石長吏】 | killed the **officials of the two thousand picul class** and senior officers（漢 92） |
| 二年::後元〜 | In the **second year** of *hou-yüan* (87 B.C.)（漢 74） |
| 弐師将軍 | the **Sutrishna general** Li Kuang-li（漢 54） |
| 弐師将軍として海西侯に封じ【為貳師將軍, 封海西侯】 | enfeoffed her eldest brother Li Kuang-li, the **Sutrishna general**, as marquis of Haihsi（漢 97A） |
| 入れない::宮門内に〜【無入霍氏禁闥】 | be **barred from entering** the inner palace（漢 68） |
| 任える〈職責に〉【在位多不任職】 | there are many men in office who are not **competent to fulfill their duties**（漢 71） |
| 任侠::軽薄な〜の徒【軽侠之徒】 | this class of worthless **knights**（漢 92） |
| 任侠をもって顕われた::劇孟は【以侠顕】 | Chu Meng won a name by his deeds of **chivalry**（漢 92） |
| 任侠をもって名声をえる【用侠聞】 | won fame as a **knight**（漢 92） |
| 任務::重大な〜に耐え,社稷を任せられる【任大重, 可属社稷】 | could be entrusted with such a grave **responsibility** and counted on to protect the altars of the soil and grain（漢 68） |
| 任用::郎に〜した | **made** him a palace attendant（漢 68） |
| 佞臣一人を斬って【斷佞臣一人】 | strike down one of these **mealymouthed ministers**（漢 67） |
| 年間::甘露〜 | during the *kan-lu* era (53-50 B.C.)（漢 74） |
| 念い::深く【深念】 | To **ponder** deeply（漢 65） |
| 納れ::諫言を〜【納諫】 | is **willing to listen to** admonition（漢 78） |
| 馬監に拝し【拜為馬監】 | appointed him **superintendent of horses**（漢 68） |
| 廃す::天子を【廃天子】 | **depose** the emperor（漢 74） |
| 廃れ::私家の権力は〜【私權廃】 | **an end to the exercise of** private **authority**（漢 78） |
| 廃錮 | being **barred from public service**（漢 67） |
| 廃錮::終身〜 | be **barred from holding office**（漢 92） |
| 拝し::馬監に〜【拜為馬監】 | **appointed** him superintendent of horses（漢 68） |

第 4 章　職官名関連和英表現集

| | |
|---|---|
| 拝し〈朔を夫給事中に〉 | honored Shuo by making him a palace counselor（漢 65） |
| 拝して中郎となす | were all appointed palace gentlemen（漢 54） |
| 拝して典属国となす | was appointed director of dependent states（漢 54） |
| 拝して郎となす | appointed Ch'en Pu-lo as a palace attendant（漢 54） |
| 拝せられて騎都尉となる | was appointed a chief commandant of cavalry（漢 54） |
| 拝謁 | pay his respects（漢 74） |
| 拝謁し | bowed in salute（漢 67） |
| 排斥する【斥逐】 | hound his son out of office（漢 74） |
| 輩::邪諂の〜が並び進んで【邪諂之人並進】 | vicious and sycophantic men crowd forward side by side（漢 65） |
| 配［あたる］ | assist one another（漢 74） |
| 陪臣が命令をつかさどった【陪臣執命】 | the ministers of the feudal lords began to issue commands（漢 92） |
| 博士::諫大夫・〜をつかわし | dispatched the admonishers and erudits（漢 74） |
| 博士となった | was made an erudit（漢 67） |
| 発し::長楽宮の衛兵を〜 | called out the guard from the Palace of Lasting Joy（漢 63） |
| 発し::反乱ともに | rebellion broke out both within the state and abroad（漢 63） |
| 発覚 | came to light（漢 74） |
| 伐［ほこ］らない::謙遜して〜【謙退不伐】 | behaving in a modest and retiring fashion and not boasting of their deeds（漢 92） |
| 抜擢されて天水郡の太守となった【擢為天水太守】 | the emperor was pleased and promoted him to the post of governor of T'ien-shui（漢 92） |
| 反す::江充が | Chiang Ch'ung had revolted（漢 63） |
| 反逆者の獄を治める【治反者獄】 | to investigate persons charged with treason（漢 71） |
| 反乱ともに発し | rebellion broke out both within the state and abroad（漢 63） |
| 叛く | revolted（漢 78） |
| 卑賎徒歩であっても【卑賎徒歩】 | might be men of the humblest station who were obliged to go about on foot（漢 71） |
| 妃妾 | his consort and concubines（漢 63） |
| 罷卒 | soldiers who had seen long service in the army（漢 74） |
| 罷免 | relieved the three marquises of the Ho family, Yü, Yün, and Shan, of their duties（漢 74） |
| 罷免し::守備警衛を掌る右将軍 | relieved him of the garrison troops and officials that |

| | |
|---|---|
| の官職を【罷其右將軍屯兵官屬】 | had been under his command as general of the right（漢 68） |
| 避け∷世を【避世】 | **shunned** the world（漢 65） |
| 避けて濁世を【避濁世】 | **fled from** a muddy age（漢 65） |
| 非る[そしる] | **criticize**（漢 74） |
| 婢∷官～曹曉・道房・張棄【官婢】 | the government **slave women** Ts'ao Hsiao, Tao Fang, and Chang Ch'i（漢 97B） |
| 婢が六人 | with six **slave women** in attendance（漢 97B） |
| 裨益するところがない∷主上の治世に【無益於主上之治】 | are **of no help** to the ruler in his government（漢 65） |
| 備えた∷弟子の礼を【備弟子禮】 | waiting on his teacher in accordance with the ritual **demanded of** a disciple（漢 71） |
| 備えを図る【図其備】 | **Preparations should be made** as soon as possible **to cope with the emergency**（漢 74） |
| 備わる∷官の一員に | **become an official** in the government（漢 74） |
| 微行 | Such **incognito expeditions**（漢 65） |
| 微行して外出し【微行出】 | had left the palace on one of his **incognito** outings（漢 97B） |
| 微行で外出し | going out **on incognito expeditions**（漢 65） |
| 微賤∷その出身のあまりに～なことを嫌い【嫌其所出微甚】 | considering Lady Chao to be of much too **humble** origin for such a position（漢 97B） |
| 微賤∷朕が～だったころ【朕微眇時】 | In the past when I was **living in humble and obscure circumstances**（漢 74） |
| 美わしい∷その徳は【厥德茂焉】 | **Laudable** indeed is his virtue（漢 74） |
| 美人∷許～ | the **Comely Person** Lady Hsü（漢 97B） |
| 美人となり | advanced to that of **Comely One**（漢 97B） |
| 美徳をもっぱら…に帰す【專歸美於組，徵卿】 | gave all the **credit** to Hu Tsu and Kuo Cheng-ch'ing（漢 74） |
| 匹夫【匹夫之細】 | mere **commoners** in rank（漢 92） |
| 必ず | **invariably**（漢 74） |
| 百官に告令して | Issuing an announcement to the **various officials** that（漢 63） |
| 百官以下が | everyone from the **hundred officials** on down（漢 68） |
| 百官有司は法を奉じ令を受け【百官有司奉法承令】 | The **hundred officials** and those in authority obeyed the laws, accepted commands（漢 92） |
| 百金 | **a hundred measures of gold**（漢 92） |
| 百姓に利益をあたえる【便利百姓】 | benefit the **common people**（漢 74） |

## 第4章 職官名関連和英表現集

| | |
|---|---|
| 百姓は皆 | all the **common people**（漢 63） |
| 百適を受けた者【有百適者】 | anyone who got **a hundred demerits**（漢 92） |
| 百僚 | the **hundred officials**（漢 78） |
| 百僚はこれを畏れた【百僚畏之】 | **All the men who held public office** stood in awe of him（漢 67） |
| 票騎は | the **general of swift cavalry** once more proceeded（漢 68） |
| 票騎将軍 | the **general of swift cavalry** Ho Ch'ü-ping（漢 54） |
| 票騎将軍∷兄〜去病 | my elder brother, the **general of swift cavalry** Ho Ch'ü-ping（漢 68） |
| 票騎将軍となり | was appointed **general of swift cavalry**（漢 68） |
| 票騎将軍は銭を貪り嗜む【票騎将軍貪嗜銭】 | the **general of swift cavalry** Wang Ken is only interested in squeezing money out of people（漢 97B） |
| 票騎将軍去病 | the **general of swift cavalry** Ho Ch'u-ping（漢 68） |
| 票騎将軍霍去病 | the **general of swift cavalry** Ho Ch'u-ping（漢 68） |
| 表をもってその状を奏上【表奏状】 | submitted **a report** to the throne describing these various events（漢 97B） |
| 評議∷陛下には〜あそばされ | Your Majesty will **consult with**（漢 74） |
| 評定∷彼らの殿最を【課其殿最】 | **decide** whether they have done a proper job or not（漢 74） |
| 馮翊∷管仲を〜とし【管仲為馮翊】 | Kuan Chung **oversees the eastern reaches of the capital**（漢 65） |
| 賓客 | his own **guests and retainers**（漢 63） |
| 賓客 | his **retainers**（漢 63） |
| 賓客 | **private retainers**（漢 74） |
| 賓客・群臣 | his **guests** and courtiers（漢 63） |
| 賓客∷彼の | Yüan She's **followers**（漢 92） |
| 賓客が盛大∷外戚王氏の〜 | the **guests and retainers** of the Wang families were especially numerous（漢 92） |
| 賓客はいよいよ盛大で【賓客愈盛】 | **Guests** flocked about him in even greater numbers（漢 92） |
| 賓客を招いた | attracted **retainers** to their courts（漢 92） |
| 賓客を避ける【以避客】 | escape from his **followers**（漢 92） |
| 不機嫌で【上不說】 | The emperor **was very put out**（漢 71） |
| 不謹慎 | **careless and lacking in respect**（漢 74） |
| 不敬と劾せられる | had been indicted on charges of **irreverence**（漢 65） |
| 不幸な∷何と〜【非不幸也】 | what a **pity**（漢 92） |
| 不実∷二千石の選挙が〜である | The process of selecting the two thousand picul |

161

| | |
|---|---|
| 【二千石選挙不実】 | officials has **not been carried out judiciously**(漢71) |
| 不臣の愬え[うったえ]を受けつけるわけがない【不受不臣之愬】 | will not listen to the pleas of a **disloyal subject**(漢97B) |
| 不遜::朔の文辞は | Tung-fang Shuo's words were so **lacking in humility**(漢65) |
| 不遜::傲慢〜になり | will become **rebellious**(漢68) |
| 夫人::挙〜は位が進んで婕妤となり【拳夫人進為婕妤】 | The **Lady** of the Fists advanced to the rank of Beautiful Companion(漢97A) |
| 夫人::孝武帝の李〜【孝武李夫人】 | **Madam** Li, a Concubine of Emperor Wu the Filial(漢97A) |
| 夫人::李〜 | **Madam** Li(漢63) |
| 富貴::死生命あり,〜, 天にあり【死生有命, 富貴在天】 | life and death are decreed by Fate, and **wealth and eminence** are decided by Heaven(漢97B) |
| 富貴は少夫のもの【富貴与少夫共之】 | we will share the **wealth and honor** with you, Shao-fu(漢97A) |
| 布衣のやから | **hemp-robed commoners**(漢92) |
| 府::ふたたび・・・郡〜の役人となり【為府吏】 | go back to being a clerk in the **office**(漢92) |
| 府::御史〜に入り | entered the **office** of the imperial secretary Wei Hsiang(漢68) |
| 府::宗正〜に迎え | was taken to the **office** of the director of the imperial clan(漢68) |
| 府庫::掖庭の〜を掌る嗇夫【少内嗇夫】 | the keeper of **stores** for the women's quarters(漢74) |
| 仆し::上官桀を | **overthrew** the Shang-kuan family(漢68) |
| 巫鬼を尊ぶ | is much given to **shamanism and spirit** worship(漢63) |
| 巫蠱 | the so-called **black magic** affair(漢74) |
| 巫蠱::宮中に〜の気がある | there were "airs of **sorcery** in the palace"(漢63) |
| 巫蠱の事件が起こった | the **black magic** affair occurred(漢63) |
| 巫蠱の実情【蠱情】 | the true facts of the **black magic affair**(漢63) |
| 扶風と意見が合わず【與扶風相失】 | having failed to get along with the other **Fu-feng officials**(漢92) |
| 符璽::尚〜郎を召し | summoned the palace attendant who had charge of the **imperial credentials and seals**(漢68) |
| 賦や課税を興す【興賦斂】 | imposing a lot of irresponsible **taxes** and levies(漢78) |
| 賦を課す【加賦】 | imposing any additional **taxes** upon the common |

## 第4章 職官名関連和英表現集

| | |
|---|---|
| | people（漢78） |
| 駙馬::黄門～ | the **keeper of the emperor's auxiliary horse** from the Yellow Gate（漢54） |
| 駙馬を河中につき落として | pushed the **keeper of the horse** into the river（漢54） |
| 駙馬都尉 | was made **commandant of the imperial horses**（漢68） |
| 駙馬都尉::侍中～欽を封じて新成侯とした | enfeoffed her younger brother, the attendant of the inner palace and **commandant of the imperial horses** Chao Ch'in, as marquis of Hsin-ch'eng（漢97B） |
| 駙馬都尉::侍中～光禄大夫に遷した | he advanced to the posts of attendant in the inner palace, **commandant of the imperial horses**, and counselor to the keeper of the palace gate（漢68） |
| 誣妄不道の罪に坐し【坐誣罔不道】 | was accused of **malicious falsehood and unprincipled behavior**（漢71） |
| 侮辱::長公主を侵害～し【侵辱長主】 | **insulting** and mistreating an imperial princess, the eldest daughter of Emperor Wu（漢67） |
| 武を立てて衆に威を示し,悪を誅してもって邪を禁ず【立武以威衆,誅悪以禁邪】 | **make a display of military force** in order to inspire awe, and one should punish evildoers in order to prevent malefaction（漢67） |
| 武騎::侍中常侍～ | was accompanied by the gentlemen in constant attendance and **armed riders**（漢65） |
| 武庫の兵器を出し | issued weapons from the **armory**（漢63） |
| 武庫令 | the **chief of the arsenal**（漢74） |
| 武庫令::子をもって～とした【子為武庫令】 | have appointed the chancellor's son as **chief of the military arsenal**（漢74） |
| 武庫令が官を去った | the **chief of the arsenal** has left his post（漢74） |
| 武庫令が西のかた長安に行くと【武庫令西至長安】 | the **chief of the arsenal** proceeded west until he reached Ch'ang-an（漢74） |
| 武庫令であった::洛陽の | had been appointed **chief of the military arsenal** in Lo-yang（漢74） |
| 武帳の中に坐し | was seated within **military style curtains** of state（漢68） |
| 部における【居部】 | in the post of **provincial director**（漢74） |
| 部校::監御史と護軍の諸～が堂皇に列座した | the superintendent of the garrison took his seat on the reviewing platform along with the various **company commanders** attached to the garrison（漢67） |
| 誣告::自ら～に服す | gave a **false confession**（漢71） |
| 誣告し::先帝が女色に傾惑され | **slandering and defiling** the former emperor with |

163

| | |
|---|---|
| た過ちとして〜【誣汙先帝傾惑之過】 | charges of blind infatuation（漢97B） |
| 封ぜられ::高平侯に | **enfeoffed as** marquis of Kao-p'ing（漢74） |
| 封印::御史中丞の印で〜して【封御史中丞印】 | **sealed with** the seal of the middle aide to the imperial secretary（漢97B） |
| 封書を奏上【奏封事】 | submitted a **sealed memorial** to the throne（漢74） |
| 封邑八百戸を食む | with the revenue from a **town** of eight hundred households（漢74） |
| 封緘させて緑色の厚絹の書嚢にいれて,推しやって屏風の東に置く【使緘封篋及緑綈方底,推置屏風東】 | ordering them to **tie up the hamper and seal it**, push it around to the east side of the screen, and leave it there, along with a message pouch tied with a green cord（漢97B） |
| 風雨 | **unusual spells of wind or rain**（漢74） |
| 風雨::士卒は〜にさらされ【士卒暴露】 | your officers and soldiers are exposed to **the dew of the field**（漢71） |
| 風格がある::伯夷[はくい]・史魚の〜【有伯夷,史魚之風】 | a **match for such ancient paragons of virtue** as Po Yi and Shih Yu（漢67） |
| 風俗 | the **customs and folkways** of the empire（漢74） |
| 風俗をうるわしくする【美風俗】 | beautifying his **ways and customs**（漢65） |
| 風俗を観る【察風俗】 | observing the **customs and folkways**（漢74） |
| 風俗教化が頽廃し【俗化陵夷】 | its **customs** have fallen into sad decline（漢71） |
| 伏し::海浜に【竊伏海濱】 | **live at the faraway border of the sea**（漢71） |
| 伏して思いみますに【伏念】 | **venture to ask if**（漢74） |
| 伏す〈罪に〉 | **admitted their guilt**（漢68） |
| 副と署す【署其一日副】 | marked "**duplicate**"（漢74） |
| 副君 | the **ruler's aide**（漢71） |
| 副将::光の〜となった | ended by **acting as** Ho Kuang's **assistant**（漢68） |
| 副中郎将 | his **subordinate general of palace attendants**（漢54）［中郎将は本プロジェクト訳で senior officer of palace corridor attendants に改めた］ |
| 副封 | **duplicate copy**（漢74） |
| 復讐心に満ち | **vindictive**（漢92） |
| 服す::自ら誣告に【自誣服】 | **gave** a false confession（漢71） |
| 服従す::民は | his people **submissive**（漢74） |
| 服喪を実行する::三年の【行三年喪】 | observed the old three-year **mourning period**（漢92） |
| 墳墓::大将軍の | the general's **grave mound**（漢68） |
| 忿兵 | a **campaign of anger**（漢74） |

164

## 第4章 職官名関連和英表現集

| | |
|---|---|
| 文学::郡の〜となり | was recognized by his province as a **man of learning**（漢71） |
| 文辞::朔の〜は不遜 | Tung-fang Shuo's **words** were so lacking in humility（漢65） |
| 文書をしりぞけ奏上しない【屏不奏其書】 | I used to put such **letters** aside and not allow them to be submitted to the throne（漢68） |
| 文吏の議を用いれば【用文吏議】 | were turned over to the **civil officials** for trial（漢67） |
| 聞き知る::海内に誰ひとり〜聞き知らぬ者はない【海内莫不聞知】 | there is no one within the four seas who does not **know of** his reputation（漢67） |
| 兵を出す【遣兵】 | **sent some of their armed men**（漢74） |
| 兵官となる【在兵官】 | have **troops** under their command（漢74） |
| 平し::冤獄を【平冤獄】 | **redressing** cases of injustice in the courts（漢74） |
| 平尚書事【平尚書事】 | was put **in charge of** the office of palace writers（漢71） |
| 平定 | **pacified**（漢74） |
| 平定 | **restoring peace** to his nation（漢78） |
| 平反［よく調べて罪を軽くする］したか【有所平反】 | Did you **reverse or lighten any sentences**（漢71） |
| 弊を受け::周・秦の【周秦之敝】 | has **inherited the abuses of** the Chou and Ch'in dynasties（漢71） |
| 陛下のご恩をこうむって【蒙恩】 | have received great blessing from **Your Majesty**（漢92） |
| 陛下の側近【左右】 | those who attend **Your Majesty**（漢74） |
| 屏去［しりぞ］ける | **put** both copies **aside**（漢74） |
| 屏風::封緘させて緑色の厚絹の書嚢にいれて，推しやって〜の東に置き【使緘封篋及緑綈方底，推置屏風東】 | ordering them to tie up the hamper and seal it, push it around to the east side of the **screen**, and leave it there, along with a message pouch tied with a green cord（漢97B） |
| 辺郡 | The **border regions**（漢74） |
| 便嬖の宦官【便嬖宦竪】 | the **vile and glib-tongued** eunuchs（漢78） |
| 保宮に繋がれる | held prisoner in the **Detention Room** of the palace（漢54） |
| 保護::太子家を監督〜 | to supervise and **look after** the household of the heir apparent（漢71） |
| 保身をはかる::丞相韋玄成が地位を維持せんとして【丞相韋玄 | the chancellor Wei Hsuan-ch'eng was concerned only in **looking out for himself**（漢67） |

| | |
|---|---|
| 成容身保位】 | |
| 保任によって::父の【父任】 | Because of his father's **career in public service**（漢 71） |
| 捕らえる::役人は雲を〜ことができない | the officials were unable to **find** Chu Yü **and arrest** him（漢 67） |
| 捕縛::従史を叱って〜させる【叱従吏收縛】 | shouted to his attendants to **seize and arrest** the young man（漢 71） |
| 補す::地方の吏に〜【補任補吏】 | **transferring** all their relatives and followers **to posts** outside the capital（漢 74） |
| 補任::郡の役人に【以補郡吏】 | **fill posts** as provincial officials（漢 78） |
| 補任した::郁夷県の令に〜 | was **assigned to the post of** magistrate of Yu-i（漢 92） |
| 補任する::郡国の太守・宰相に | **fill posts** that had come vacant as governors of provinces or prime ministers of the feudal states（漢 78） |
| 輔佐 | **assist**（漢 68） |
| 輔佐::少主を〜する | to **assist** his youthful successor（漢 68） |
| 輔弼の臣::推薦して〜とする | recommended Yün Ch'ang as a **man who was capable of assisting the government**（漢 67） |
| 輔弼の臣は瓦解し【補弼之臣瓦解】 | **ministers who might aid and assist** you fall away like broken tiles（漢 65） |
| 奉じる::法を〜【奉法】 | **uphold** the law（漢 78） |
| 奉車都尉 | a **chief commandant in charge of carriage**（漢 54） |
| 奉車都尉 | was **in charge of the imperial carriage**（漢 54） |
| 奉車都尉, 光禄大夫となり | became **chief commandant in charge of the imperial carriage** and counselor to the keeper of the palace gate（漢 68） |
| 奉車都尉::太僕か〜に当たり | correspond to the master of carriage or the **chief commandant in charge of the imperial carriage**（漢 68） |
| 奉車都尉として | as **chief commandant in charge of the imperial carriage**（漢 68） |
| 奉車都尉に | was appointed **chief commandant in charge of the imperial carriage**（漢 68） |
| 奉車都尉山 | the **chief commandant in charge of the imperial carriage** Ho Shan（漢 68） |
| 奉車都尉侍中となって | was **chief commandant in charge of the imperial carriage** and an attendant in the inner palace（漢 68） |
| 奉車都尉霍光 | the **chief commandant in charge of the imperial** |

166

## 第4章　職官名関連和英表現集

| | |
|---|---|
| | **carriage** Ho Kuang（漢 97A） |
| 奉祀::宗廟に〜【奉宗廟】 | **attending** the ancestral temples（漢 74） |
| 奉祠::吏卒が〜した【吏卒奉祠】 | with officials and soldiers to tend it and **offer sacrifices**（漢 68） |
| 崩ず::帝が〜れば | On the **demise** of the emperor（漢 68） |
| 崩御 | Emperor Wu **passed away**（漢 68） |
| 崩御::皇帝がにわかに〜された【皇帝暴崩】 | His Imperial Majesty has **passed away** with great suddenness（漢 97B） |
| 崩御::昼の漏の十刻に〜した【晝漏上十刻而崩】 | By the time the water clock pointed to the tenth notch [8:30 A.M.], he had **passed away**（漢 97B） |
| 放縦で何ものにも拘束されない【放縦不拘】 | was quite **unrestrained** and did just as he pleased（漢 92） |
| 放态::驕慢〜 | very arrogant and **unruly**（漢 67） |
| 方正の科に挙げられ【舉方正】 | was chosen as a **man of honesty and uprightness**（漢 67） |
| 方正の科に推挙【挙護方正】 | recommended Lou Hu as **a man of honesty and uprightness**（漢 92） |
| 法に触れ【坐法】 | **accused of an offense**（漢 74） |
| 法を取る::天地に〜【取法天地】 | **take** Heaven and earth **as their sole pattern**（漢 74） |
| 法を奉じ::百官有司は〜令を受け【百官有司奉法承令】 | The hundred officials and those in authority **obeyed the laws**, accepted commands（漢 92） |
| 法を奉じる【奉法】 | **uphold the law**（漢 78） |
| 法冠::少史も〜をかり【少史冠法冠】 | has his petty clerks dressed up in their **official caps**（漢 78） |
| 法度をまもる士を難詰する【難法度士】 | criticizes a **strait-laced** gentleman（漢 92） |
| 法令を変改し【変易大將軍時法令】 | changed the **laws and regulations**（漢 68） |
| 胞人::館陶公主の〜臣偃，昧死再拝して謁す【館陶公主胞人臣偃昧死再拜謁】 | Your servant Yen, **cook** to the Kuan-t'ao Princess, braving death, bows twice and presents himself for an interview.（漢 65） |
| 亡国秦の鐘をつき【撞亡秦之鐘】 | strikes the bells of the **fallen** Ch'in dynasty（漢 71） |
| 暴を誅する【誅暴】 | punish **violence**（漢 74） |
| 暴室の獄に置き【置暴室獄】 | confine them all to the **sickroom** jail（漢 97B） |
| 暴室嗇夫となった | was later made an orderly† in charge of the **women's sickroom**（漢 97A）[†当番兵（三コ）] |

| | |
|---|---|
| 暴騰::穀価は【穀暴騰踊】 | grain prices are **climbing wildly**(漢 74) |
| 謀りごと::許后を殺した〜【殺許后之謀】 | **contrived** the murder of Empress Hsü(漢 74) |
| 謀叛::莽何羅が〜した【謀為逆】 | Ma Ho-lo has **revolted**(漢 68) |
| 謀慮の::機微があり〜士【幾微謀慮之士】 | men of subtle understanding who are **skilled at laying plans**(漢 78) |
| 防ぐ::壅ぎ蔽われることを【以防雍蔽】 | **foil any attempts** at concealment(漢 74) |
| 僕射::侍中〜莽何羅 | the **archery captain** of the inner palace attendants Ma Ho-lo(漢 68) |
| 僕射::郎官・〜 | The attendants and **archery captains**(漢 68) |
| 僕射をして命じ | had her **archery captain** submit a letter of complaint(漢 67) |
| 牧::州〜となる | has been made **administrator** of Ching-chou(漢 92) |
| 牧となる::荊州の | **was made provincial administrator** of Ching-chou(漢 92) |
| 牧官::郡国の守相もろものの〜【郡國守相群牧】 | the **provincial governors and administrators** and the prime ministers of the feudal states, making sure that(漢 71) |
| 本意は朝廷にあり【雅意在本朝】 | Wang-chih's **thoughts were centered constantly about** the court(漢 78) |
| 本業の農に背いて【背本趨末】 | turned their backs on the **basic pursuits** of agriculture(漢 74) |
| 凡人とかけ離れている【有絶異之姿】 | we recognize in them qualities that are far removed from **the ordinary**(漢 92) |
| 凡庸な人物でない【非庸人】 | was no **ordinary** man(漢 71) |
| 昧死再拝して::館陶公主の胞人臣偃、〜謁す【館陶公主胞人臣偃昧死再拝謁】 | Your servant Yen, cook to the Kuan-t'ao Princess, **braving death, bows twice** and presents himself for an interview.(漢 65) |
| 昧死上聞いたし | **Braving death**, I make this report(漢 67) |
| 末業の商に赴き【背本趨末】 | hastened after the **secondary concerns of trade**(漢 74) |
| 末年::武帝の | **Toward the end of** Emperor Wu's reign(漢 63) |
| 末年::武帝の | In the **late years** of Emperor Wu's reign(漢 71) |
| 末年::武帝の | **Towards the end of** Emperor Wu's reign(漢 74) |
| 末流をほしいままにし【放縱於末流】 | allowed themselves to drift into a **shabby and inferior way of life**(漢 92) |

## 第4章 職官名関連和英表現集

| | |
|---|---|
| 万死::罪,〜に当たり【罪當萬死】 | Truly my blame is such that I deserve **ten thousand deaths**(漢74) |
| 万死に当たる | **deserve to die ten thousand deaths**(漢65) |
| 万世の基を固め【固万世之基】 | the foundations of the state may be made firm for **ten thousand ages to come**(漢74) |
| 万民の仰ぎみるところ【万姓所瞻仰】 | men whom the **myriad commoners** look up to with awe(漢67) |
| 満百回になってから | When I have been given **a full hundred of them**(漢92) |
| 未央宮 | the **Eternal Palace**(漢68) |
| 未然の[禍い]::公卿は〜を防ぎ【公卿有可以防其未然】 | You, the high officials, are supposed to be able to take steps to prevent **future disasters**(漢71) |
| 民::天下に冤罪の〜なく【天下無冤民】 | there were in fact no **people** in the empire who suffered injustice(漢71) |
| 民〈吏〜〉 | any **officials or private citizens**(漢78) |
| 民〈吏〜〉 | the **officials and common people**(漢78) |
| 民は禁を知り正道にかえる【知禁而反正】 | the **people** come to understand the prohibitions and return to what is correct -- that is, to the correct laws of ancient times(漢92) |
| 民和睦す【民和睦】 | the **people** enjoy peace and harmony(漢74) |
| 名と実を正す【核名実】 | making certain that the **title** they held was in conformity with their actual performance(漢74) |
| 名を後世に顕わし【名顕後世】 | their **names are well known** to later ages(漢65) |
| 名儒 | **eminent Confucian scholars**(漢78) |
| 名声::はなはだ〜があった | was widely **praised for** the way he managed administrative affairs(漢67) |
| 名声は朝廷に高まり【名声重於朝廷】 | won considerable **fame and reputation** at court(漢71) |
| 名目 | what **name to assign to** a campaign such as this(漢74) |
| 名誉::すこぶる〜を得る【甚得名誉】 | attaining great **honor and fame**(漢92) |
| 命あり::死生〜,富貴,天にあり【死生有命,富貴在天】 | life and death are **decreed by Fate**, and wealth and eminence are decided by Heaven(漢97B) |
| 命じ::中府に | **gave instructions to** the manager of her household(漢65) |
| 命じる | **instructing** them to(漢74) |
| 明るい | **was an expert in**(漢74) |

169

| | |
|---|---|
| 明るい::法律制度に〜【明於法度】 | **is versed in** matters pertaining to the laws and regulations（漢 74） |
| 明るく::経術に【明経術】 | **are versed in** the principles of the Classics（漢 78） |
| 明るく::経書に【明経】 | **are versed in** the Classics（漢 74） |
| 明王・聖王でないかぎり | If one is not a truly **enlightened** and sage-like **ruler**（漢 65） |
| 明王・聖主に遭遇させる | had met up with **an enlightened king**, a sage ruler（漢 65） |
| 明王が慎重に選ぶところ【明王所慎択】 | whom [men] the **enlightened sovereign** chooses with care（漢 67） |
| 明主 | an **enlightened sovereign**（漢 74） |
| 明主 | an **enlightened ruler**（漢 74） |
| 明主 | An **enlightened ruler**（漢 78） |
| 明詔 | an **enlightened edict**（漢 78） |
| 明詔によって救済【頼明詔振捄】 | an **enlightened edict** came down from the sovereign providing relief（漢 74） |
| 明知::争うて力を致し将軍の高い〜を輔けたいと願う【争願自効, 以輔高明】 | vying with one another in volunteering their services to assist in this **lofty and enlightened undertaking**（漢 78） |
| 滅ぶ | doomed to **annihilation**（漢 74） |
| 免ぜられ::官を〜 | **retired** from office（漢 92） |
| 免ぜられ::昌邑の郎官や奴を〜た者【昌邑郎官者免奴】 | his palace attendants and **freed** slaves from Ch'ang-i（漢 68） |
| 免ぜられ::職を | **retired from** office（漢 71） |
| 免ぜられる | Wei Hsien, who had been serving as chancellor, **retired**（漢 74） |
| 免ぜられる::職を | was **dismissed**（漢 92） |
| 免冠して::群臣がみな | The courtiers all **removed their hats**（漢 63） |
| 免官する | **relieved** Chao Chin, the marquis of Hsin-ch'eng, and his elder brother's son Chao Hsin, the marquis of Ch'eng-yang, **of their titles**（漢 97B） |
| 茂才 | **men of outstanding talent**（漢 78） |
| 木簡を削る【削牘】 | cut up a number of **writing slips**（漢 92） |
| 問責 | **berated** them for having presented such an unwise proposal（漢 78） |
| 門下 | a **student in his household**（漢 78） |
| 門下掾::県の〜となり | was a **minor official** in the district office（漢 92） |
| 役所の仕事を放り出し【曹事数】 | neglected his **duties as a clerk**（漢 92） |

## 第4章 職官名関連和英表現集

| | |
|---|---|
| 廃】 | |
| 役人：：およそ～たるものは剛に過ぎれば【凡為吏太剛則折】 | if an **official** is too unbending（漢71） |
| 役人：：郡の～に補任【以補郡吏】 | fill posts as provincial **officials**（漢78） |
| 役人：：三公の府の | the **officials** in the three highest ministries（漢74） |
| 役人：：丞相・御史, 事件取調べの～匿して【丞相, 御史案事之吏匿不言邪】 | the **officials** under your jurisdiction hiding the truth（漢71） |
| 役人：：中二千石の | the **officials** of the two thousand picul class（漢63） |
| 役人：：追捕の～を射た【犇射追吏】 | shooting as they went along at the law **officials** who pursued them（漢67） |
| 役人：：不疑は～として | Ch'üan Pu-i in exercising his **official duties**（漢71） |
| 役人となり：：ふたたび・・・郡府の～ | go back to being a **clerk** in the office（漢92） |
| 役人に下して論議させ：：願わくは【願下有司議】 | I beg that this memorial be handed down to the **authorities** for discussion（漢97B） |
| 役人に訴えた | reported to the **officials** that（漢71） |
| 役人はすみやかに追わない【吏不亟追】 | the **officials** make no haste to pursue them（漢71） |
| 役人は雲を捕らえることができない | the **officials** were unable to find Chu Yü and arrest him（漢67） |
| 役人を遣わし【遣吏】 | dispatched one of his **clerks**（漢71） |
| 踰える：：公主や貴人で礼制を【踰礼制】 | the princesses and nobles took to **overstepping** the rites and regulations（漢65） |
| 勇：：もともと～を好み | was originally noted for his love of **daring**（漢67） |
| 憂え：：政事を～【憂政】 | is **deeply concerned about** the problems of government（漢78） |
| 憂患：：その～は些細ではない【其憂不細】 | the **damage** will be far from slight（漢71） |
| 憂国の意：：先帝～に逆らい【逆負先帝憂国之意】 | frustrating all his **plans to save the nation** from distress（漢97B） |
| 憂慮：：陛下の | a **cause of concern** to Your Majesty（漢74） |
| 有司 | the **officials**（漢63） |
| 有司 | the **officials**（漢78） |
| 有司 | The **authorities**（漢78） |
| 有司 | the **authorities** for investigation（漢78） |
| 有司：：事案が～に下げ渡され | the case was handed over to the **authorities** for |

171

| | |
|---|---|
| 【事下有司】 | investigation（漢 74） |
| 有司::百官〜は法を奉じ令を受け【百官有司奉法承令】 | The hundred officials and **those [officials] in authority** obeyed the laws, accepted commands（漢 92） |
| 有司に下して案験し，善悪を明らかにする【下有司案験以明好悪】 | to refer the matter to **the authorities** for investigation so that they may determine the right and wrong of it（漢 67） |
| 有司は・・・の疑いで取り調べた | **the authorities** began investigating Chu Yün on the suspicion of（漢 67） |
| 有識者 | **knowledgeable persons**（漢 74） |
| 遊侠::村里の | among the **knights of the streets and alleys**（漢 92） |
| 遊侠劇孟・郭解 | the **wandering knights** Chü Meng and Kuo Hsieh（漢 92） |
| 遊撃将軍 | **scouting and attacking general**（漢 54） |
| 遊士を招致した | gathered about him a number of **wandering scholars**（漢 63） |
| 邑::三百戸の〜を置いて長丞に法の通り奉守させた【置邑三百家,長丞奉守如】 | with a **village** of three hundred households set up and officials appointed to guard and maintain the grave in accordance with the law（漢 97A） |
| 邑里をかけめぐって【馳鶩於閭閻】 | galloped through the **lanes and byways**（漢 92） |
| 与り聞く::政事を〜【与聞政事】 | **take part in** affairs of government（漢 78） |
| 幼君を擁き【擁幼君】 | guarded the **young ruler**（漢 68） |
| 幼弱::少主が〜であれば【少主幼弱】 | when a ruler is still a **mere child**（漢 97B） |
| 幼主 | the **child successor**（漢 68） |
| 幼主 | the ruler is **still young**（漢 74） |
| 幼主を輔佐 | to assist the **young ruler**（漢 97A） |
| 用いる::公卿・大臣を〜 | **appointing** high ministers and major officials（漢 71） |
| 養う::刺客を〜【養刺客】 | **gave support to** professional killers（漢 92） |
| 養う〈馬を〉::黄門に送られて〜た【輸黄門養馬】 | was assigned as a **keeper of the horses** of the Yellow Gate（漢 68） |
| 夭折 | **premature death**（漢 74） |
| 欲する::義を好み利を〜心があり【好義欲利之心】 | possess hearts moved both by concerns of benevolence and righteousness and by the **longing for** personal profit（漢 78） |
| 欲望に際限がなく【耆欲無極】 | there is no end to her **cravings and desires**（漢 97B） |
| 邏卒::県令の〜が傷つけた | his **patrols** had inflicted injury on some of the slaves |

## 第4章 職官名関連和英表現集

| | |
|---|---|
| | （漢67） |
| 来朝 | **pay his respects at the Han court**（漢78） |
| 乱し::漢の制度を〜【乱漢制度】 | **throwing into confusion** the statutes and regulations of the Han（漢68） |
| 乱し::国家を〜危うくする【危乱国家】 | danger and **disorder** to the state resulted in both cases（漢74） |
| 乱す::四国を | **bring confusion to** the lands of the four quarters（漢65） |
| 乱を起こす::近習が | those close to the ruler **turned against** him（漢63） |
| 乱を救う【救乱】 | rectify **disorder**（漢74） |
| 乱脈::奢侈で〜【奢淫】 | given to extravagant and **disorderly** ways（漢78） |
| 利::義を好み〜を欲する心があり【好義欲利之心】 | possess hearts moved both by concerns of benevolence and righteousness and by the longing for **personal profit**（漢78） |
| 吏::悪〜 | Evil **officials**（漢71） |
| 吏::悪〜が法を無視し | villainous **officials** ignore the law（漢63） |
| 吏::京兆尹の〜になる | became an **official** in the office of the prefect of the capital（漢92） |
| 吏::宰相の〜にする | to make me one of your **officials**（漢67） |
| 吏::諸〜中郎将羽林監任勝 | who held the titles of **official** in charge, general of palace attendants, and superintendent of the Feather and Forest Guard（漢68） |
| 吏卒が奉祠した【吏卒奉祠】 | with **officials and soldiers** to tend it and offer sacrifices（漢68） |
| 吏卒を率い【將吏卒】 | led his **officials and soldiers**（漢67） |
| 吏二千石の大官::子はもともと〜の子孫で【子本吏二千石之世】 | You started out as the heir of an **official of the two thousand picul class**（漢92） |
| 吏民 | any **officials or private citizens**（漢78） |
| 吏民 | the **officials and common people**（漢78） |
| 吏民::京師の | The **officials and people** of the capital（漢71） |
| 吏民::長安の | **officials and citizens** of Ch'ang-an（漢71） |
| 吏民に対処する【行於吏民】 | carry considerable weight among the **officials and common people**（漢71） |
| 李法::黄帝〜 | the Yellow Emperor's **Rules of the Adjudicator**†（漢67）[† adjudication 1 司法的判断；裁判；判決；決定；裁決 2（英）破産宣告—田中英夫編「BASIC 英米法辞典」] |
| 律令を修得し【治律令】 | studied the **laws and ordinances**（漢74） |

173

| | |
|---|---|
| 率先::士大夫に〜しない【亡以帥先士大夫】 | lacks the qualities that would entitle him to be a **leader of** officers and gentlemen（漢 67） |
| 立った::太子が | this son **succeeded to the throne**（漢 63） |
| 立てた::故の太子建を | **enfeoffed** the son of Liu Tan's heir, Liu Chien, who had died（漢 63） |
| 立てて::鉤弋子を〜皇太子とし【立鉤弋子為皇太子】 | **appointed** the son of the Hook and Dart Palace **as** heir apparent to the throne（漢 97A） |
| 立てられ::皇太子が〜【立皇太子】 | the heir apparent of Emperor Hsüan **was officially designated**（漢 74） |
| 立てられ::皇太子に〜 | had **been made** imperial heir（漢 68） |
| 立身::小役人から〜【起獄法小吏】 | **started out** as a petty clerk（漢 74） |
| 流され::伯奇は | Po-ch'i was **banished**（漢 63） |
| 流離::人民 | many of the people had **taken to vagrancy**（漢 71） |
| 慮り〈遠く〜〉【遠慮】 | **plan far ahead**（漢 65） |
| 虜::羌〜 | the Ch'iang **barbarians**（漢 78） |
| 良家子::侍詔の隴西郡・北地郡の〜 | **the sons of good families** from Lung-hsi and Pei-ti who had been assigned to await his command（漢 65） |
| 領尚書 | was in charge of the **office of palace writers**（漢 78） |
| 領尚書【領尚書】 | was still **in charge of** the office of palace writers（漢 68） |
| 領尚書事【領尚書事】 | was **in charge of** the office of palace writers（漢 71） |
| 力田::孝弟・〜の者 | those who had behaved in a filial or brotherly fashion or had **worked hard in the fields**（漢 74） |
| 令::県の守〜として | In your capacity as acting **magistrate**（漢 92） |
| 令::真〜が赴任してくれば【真令至】 | the permanent **magistrate** will come to take over（漢 92） |
| 令::谷口県の〜となる | was appointed **magistrate** of Ku-k'ou（漢 92） |
| 令::茂陵の | become acting **magistrate** of Mou-ling（漢 74） |
| 令::茂陵県の〜 | **magistrate** of Mou-ling（漢 74） |
| 令::茂陵県の守〜尹公 | the acting **magistrate** of Mou-ling Lord Yin（漢 92） |
| 令に補任した::郁夷県の | was assigned to the post of **magistrate** of Yu-i in the region of Fu-feng（漢 92） |
| 令史::新安県の〜李寿 | Li Shou, the **secretary to the magistrate of** Hsin-an（漢 63） |
| 令史::東織室の〜張赦 | the **clerk** of the eastern weaving rooms Chang She（漢 68） |
| 礼::皇后の〜をもって葬った【上 | the emperor had her buried with the **honors** |

第4章 職官名関連和英表現集

| | |
|---|---|
| 以后禮葬焉】 | appropriate to an empress（漢 97A） |
| 礼::進退がかならず～に基づいていた【進退必以禮】 | in all his comings nor goings he invariably abided by the dictates of **ritual**（漢 71） |
| 礼なく::丞相を遇するに【遇丞相亡礼】 | treated the chancellor **with discourtesy**（漢 78） |
| 礼に・・・とあるので | since **ritual** tells us that one who is（漢 68） |
| 礼に率いて越えず【率禮不越】 | Obeying **ritual**, never overstepping（漢 78） |
| 礼の服喪 | the **rituals of mourning**（漢 78） |
| 礼を好み恭謙で【好礼恭謹】 | paid the strictest attention to **ritual** and good manners（漢 71） |
| 礼を行う | observe the **dictates of ritual**（漢 78） |
| 礼を制定した【制禮】 | devised certain **rules and rituals** for their [a man's] parents] burial（漢 67） |
| 礼を責め::使者の【責使者礼】 | **accused** an imperial envoy **of a breach of etiquette**（漢 78） |
| 礼を備えた::弟子の【備弟子禮】 | waiting on his teacher in accordance with **the ritual demanded of** a disciple（漢 71） |
| 礼意をもって接し【接以禮意】 | treated him with utmost **courtesy**（漢 71） |
| 礼儀 | **ritual**（漢 78） |
| 礼儀にかない【如礼】 | in exact accordance with **ritual**（漢 71） |
| 礼儀は諸侯王のごとくにし【礼儀宜如諸侯王】 | be received with the **ritual** appropriate to a king or marquis（漢 78） |
| 礼誼::民に～が乏しく【民寡禮誼】 | The people pay scant heed to **ritual and right**（漢 71） |
| 礼経 | the **ritual texts**（漢 74） |
| 礼譲 | **ritual and courtesy**（漢 74） |
| 礼譲を興す【礼譲可興】 | men will be ready to listen to the dictates of **humility and proper conduct**（漢 74） |
| 礼譲を好んだ【好礼譲】 | liked to do things in a **courteous and self-effacing manner**（漢 74） |
| 礼制::公主や貴人で～を踰える【踰礼制】 | the princesses and nobles took to overstepping the **rites and regulations**（漢 65） |
| 列侯 | **land-holding lords**（漢 74） |
| 列侯::爵～として郡守に備わり【遵爵列侯, 備郡守】 | has been ennobled as a **feudal lord** and appointed governor of a province（漢 92） |
| 列侯として長安に帰った【以列侯帰長安】 | returned to live as **feudal lords** in Ch'ang-an（漢 92） |
| 列座::監御史と護軍の諸部校 | the superintendent of the garrison **took his seat on** the |

175

| | |
|---|---|
| が堂皇に〜した | reviewing platform along with the various company commanders attached to the garrison（漢67） |
| 廉潔倹約 | was **careful to conduct himself with integrity and temperance**（漢92） |
| 連坐::その兄弟は当然〜すべきであった【同産當坐】 | all the members of her family were scheduled to **be tried along with** her（漢97B） |
| 輦閣::天子の車の通る道[〜]を永巷に通じ【輦閣通屬永巷】 | built a **covered road for hand-drawn carriages** connecting it with the women's quarters of the grave keeper's house（漢68） |
| 漏::昼の〜の十刻に崩御した【晝漏上十刻而崩】 | By the time the **water clock** pointed to the tenth notch [8:30 A.M.], he had passed away（漢97B） |
| 老病をもって【以老病免】 | **on grounds of old age and poor health**（漢74） |
| 郎・羽林の閲兵を行う | hold an inspection and drill of the **palace attendants** and the Feather and Forest Guard（漢68） |
| 郎・羽林の属を総検閲した | called out the **palace attendants** and the Feather and Forest Guard for inspection（漢63） |
| 郎::尚符璽〜を召し | summoned the **palace attendant** who had charge of the imperial credentials and seals（漢68） |
| 郎::他の〜の鞍を取って【取它郎鞍】 | took the saddle belonging to another **attendant**（漢97A） |
| 郎となり | had begun their careers as **attendants at the court**（漢54） |
| 郎となり | being made **palace attendants**（漢54） |
| 郎にとどめられ | remained a **palace attendant**（漢65） |
| 郎になった | were **palace attendants**（漢54） |
| 郎に任ぜられ | was made a **palace attendant**（漢68） |
| 郎に任用した | made him a **palace attendant**（漢68） |
| 郎は剣に手をかけ【按剣】 | The **attendant**, his hand on his sword（漢68） |
| 郎謁者五十余人 | fifty or more of the king's **palace attendants** and masters of guests（漢63） |
| 郎官・僕射 | The **attendants** and archery captains（漢68） |
| 郎官::昌邑の〜や奴を免ぜられた者【昌邑郎官免奴】 | his **palace attendants** and freed slaves from Ch'ang-i（漢68） |
| 郎官となり騎常侍を授かる【為郎, 騎常侍】 | was rewarded with the position of cavalry attendant **in the inner palace**（漢54） |
| 郎官に東方から来た者あり【郎有從東方來者】 | **Palace attendants** returning from the east（漢71） |
| 郎中の侍従する者 | The **palace attendants** who accompanied him（漢63） |

## 第4章 職官名関連和英表現集

| | |
|---|---|
| 郎中韓義ら | The **palace attendant** Han Yi and others（漢 63） |
| 郎中成軫 | The **palace attendant** Ch'eng Chen（漢 63） |
| 郎中令 | asked his **chief of palace attendants** Kung Sui about them（漢 63） |
| 郎中令龔遂 | His **chief of palace attendants** Kung Sui（漢 63） |
| 郎中令::李広に代わって～となった | replace his father Li Kuang as **chief of palace attendants**（漢 54） |
| 郎中令とした | summoned Li Kuang to take his place as **chief of palace attendants**（漢 54） |
| 郎中令として | as **chief of palace attendants**（漢 54） |
| 郎中令遂 | his **chief of palace attendants** Kung Sui（漢 63） |
| 陋劣なこと | a **disgrace**（漢 74） |
| 禄[さいわい]が去る【禄去】 | **fortune** deserted（漢 74） |
| 勒す::車騎～ | **called out** his carriage and horsemen（漢 63） |
| 論告::鬼薪の刑を～され【論為鬼薪】 | was **condemned to** become a provider of "firewood for the spirits."（漢 97A） |
| 和やかな::寛やか[ゆるやか]で～気色【寛和之色】 | had been granted ... a benign and **sympathetic** glance |
| 和を得る::人の【得人和】 | **be in harmony with** man（漢 74） |
| 和合し::天地は【天地和洽】 | Heaven and earth will **attain peace and harmony**（漢 65） |
| 和睦::民～す【民和睦】 | the people **enjoy peace and harmony**（漢 74） |
| 話がじょうず::機敏で～【敏而有辞】 | was alert and **well-spoken**（漢 71） |
| 話が徐々に泄れた【語稍泄】 | … had passed away, **word of the affair** gradually began to leak out（漢 68） |

# 付　録

## 付録 1　職官名英訳参照英文集

### 参照文献名略語

| | |
|---|---|
| 無表記または Br | Encyclopædia Britannica 2006 Ultimate Reference Suite DVD. |
| Gr | Grolier Encyclopedia. |
| LDOCE | Longman Dictionary of Contemporary English |
| LgAm | Longman Advanced American Dictionary. |
| NSOED | New Shorter Oxford English Dictionary. |
| OAD | Oxford American Dictionary. |
| RH | Random-House Webster's Unabridged. |
| 三コ | 三省堂コンサイス和英または英和。 |
| 法律用語対訳集 | 法務省刑事局外国法令研究会，商事法務研究会，1995。 |
| その他 | Black's Law Dictionary Digital (Thomson West, 2008). |
| | Oxford Dictionary of Law (Oxford University Press, 2006). |
| | The British Museum Dictionary of Ancient Egypt (The British Museum Press, 1995). |

### 凡例

| | |
|---|---|
| ● | 項目見出し |
| ===== abc ===== | Britannica Encyclopaedia 2006 DVD の記事見出し。 |
| ===== abc, Gr ===== | Grolier Encyclopedia の記事見出し。 |
| ===== abc, Web ===== | Web 掲載記事のタイトル。 |
| 〈　〉 | 辞典名。 |
| [ ] | 備考。 |
| A ⇒ B | A については項目見出し B を参照せよの意。A が自明のときは省略。 |

● armoury (武器，刀剣，甲冑類の総称)
〈NSOED〉　1 Arms or armour collectively (arch.); an array of weapons or (fig.) resources etc.　2 A place where arms and armour are kept or (chiefly US) made; an arsenal; N. Amer. a drill hall.

● artisan
〈NSOED〉　1 A skilled (esp. manual) worker; a mechanic; a craftsman.　2 A person who practises or cultivates an art.

● bannerman

Fig. 34  Bannerman (*hatasashi*) of a feudal warrior. (After a scroll of the Kamakura period)
George Sansom, *A Short Cultural History of Japan*, p. 290

● battalion
⇒ unit

● brigade
⇒ unit

● butler (単にワインと皿の管理人ではない)

===== butler =====

chief male servant of a household who supervises other employees, receives guests, directs the serving of meals, and performs various personal services. The title originally applied to the person who had charge of the wine cellar and dispensed liquors, the name being derived from Middle English boteler (and various other forms), from Old French bouteillier, "bottle bearer." In the European Middle Ages it meant precisely this, but in time it came to mean an official of the crown, who nominally had charge of the wine but who in fact was a person of high rank, having different duties in different countries at different times.

===== public administration =====

Early European administrative structures developed from the royal households of the medieval period. Until the end of the 12th century official duties within the royal

## 付録 1 職官名英訳参照英文集

households were ill-defined, frequently with multiple holders of the same post. Exceptions were the better-defined positions of **butler** (responsible for the provision of wine), **steward** (responsible for feasting arrangements), **chamberlain** (often charged with receiving and paying out money kept in the royal sleeping chamber), and chancellor (usually a priest with responsibilities for writing and applying the seal in the monarch's name). With the 13th century a separation began between the purely domestic functions of the royal household and the functions connected with governing the state. The older household posts tended to disappear, become sinecures, or decline in importance. The office of chancellor, which had always been concerned with matters of state, survived to become the most important link between the old court offices and modern ministries, and the development of the modern treasury or finance ministry can be traced back to the **chamberlain**'s office in the royal household.

===== Europe, history of: =====
The royal household

The seed from which all medieval institutions of central administration were to grow was the immediate personal household of the king; its members were the only permanent staff he had. The essential elements of the early royal household therefore provided the framework of the first departments of state.

The chief elements of the royal household were four—the hall, the chamber, the chapel, and the courtyard, with its horses and stables. The whole household, but in particular the **hall**, which was at once **palace, law court, and dining room**, was directly governed by the **steward** (dapifer, seneschal, or drost), under whose direction the **guests** were **seated** and the **feasting conducted**, while the wine was under the charge of a butler (pincerna, or Oberschenk). Under the later Merovingians in Gaul, the **mayor of the palace** (literally chief of the house) became a figure **so powerful as first to overshadow and then replace his king**; elsewhere, though less powerful, the **steward** was the usual **chief deputy of the king**. Under the Capetians of France, he was charged with the annual scrutiny of the accounts tendered by the king's local bailiffs, the provosts; in Normandy, Jerusalem, and elsewhere he was the natural choice as regent in his lord's absence.

The chamber, the room in which the king slept or took private counsel, was also the natural place to store **his treasure**; hence, the **chamberlains** were often specially charged with **the collection of revenue and handing it out** as the king had need. The papal treasury was known as the Apostolic Chamber, and the papal **chamberlain**s were widely entrusted with financial missions.

The chapel, containing the royal altar and relics (the term chapel derives from the capella, the short cloak of St. Martin preserved among the chief relics of the Carolingian royal treasury), was served by chaplains, to say the daily mass, assisted by a body of clerical assistants. As the chief and sometimes only literate members of the household, these men were responsible for drawing up such documents as the earlier kings required; among their number and often at the head stood the **chancellor**, whose special task was the authentication of royal acts, usually with the seal, which he kept.

This royal household was constantly on the move, carried on carts or packhorses—hence the great importance of the last two major household offices, those of the **constable** and **marshal**. The duty of the count of the stable (**constable**) was closely associated with the organization of the army, and hence the term came to be used of commanders of garrisons as well as the central household officer. The office of the **marshal** was originally more humble but shared the military fortunes of that of **constable**. In the 14th and 15th centuries, the **constable** and **marshal** came to a new importance as military commanders and correspondingly acquired judicial competence as presidents of the courts of chivalry, which dealt especially with military discipline, the division of ransoms, and the right to bear a coat of arms.

The growth of a permanent bureaucracy
These early household offices, with characteristically unspecialized duties, changed greatly under the impact of two forces. First, they had a tendency to become hereditary, much as the local offices of count or duke had done. Since the domestic service of the king, at least on public occasions, was itself a very great dignity, the most powerful families claimed the right to perform it, so that the office came to be the prerogative of great magnates who were too preoccupied elsewhere to perform their duties in person. Even the **chancellor**ship sometimes became attached to certain archbishoprics—Reims or Mainz, for instance. Since the king's domestic needs continued, a distinction evolved between the hereditary dignitaries such as high **steward** or arch**chancellor** and the men of much humbler rank who actually performed the routine duties of the household. Second, the increasing volume of business done in the king's name—judicial, administrative, or financial—demanded ever more elaborate records and a more extensive staff; therefore, the offices of government were less mobile, and a physical distinction became common between the constantly itinerant household about the king's person and the more cumbrous (though rarely wholly static) departments of permanent officials. Furthermore, the processes of government, especially in the chancery or (particularly well documented) the English exchequer, became arts or mysteries that demanded a staff of financial or legal experts with a specialized training. Thus were born the chief departments of state; well beyond the end of the medieval period, however, their principal officers were still considered the king's servants in a literal sense. This household character of public office made the

distinction between loyalty to the king's person and loyalty to the office extremely hard to draw and frustrated many early efforts at "constitutionalism."

===== United Kingdom, history of: Government and justice =====
William hoped to be able to rule England in much the same way as his Anglo-Saxon predecessors had done, though in many respects the old institutions and practices had to be changed in response to the problems of ruling a conquered land. The Anglo-Saxon witan, or council, became the king's curia regis, a meeting of the royal tenants in chief, both lay and ecclesiastical. William was said by chroniclers to have held full courts three times a year, at Christmas, Easter, and Whitsuntide, to which all the great men of the realm were summoned and at which he wore his crown. These were similar to the great courts he held in Normandy. Inevitably there were many disputes over land, and the curia regis was where justice was done to the great tenants in chief. William himself is said to have sat one Sunday "from morn till eve" to hear a plea between William de Braose and the abbot of Fecamp.

William at first did little to change Anglo-Saxon administrative organization. The royal household was at the centre of royal government, and the system, such as it was, under Edward the Confessor had probably been quite similar to that which existed in Normandy at the same period, although the actual titles of the officers were not the same. Initially under William there also was little change in personnel. But, by the end of his reign, all important administrative officials were Norman, and their titles corresponded to those in use in Normandy. There were a **steward**, a **butler**, a **chamberlain**, a **constable**, a **marshal**, and a head of the royal scriptorium, or **chancellor**. This scriptorium was the source from which all writs (i.e., written royal commands) were issued. At the start of William's reign the writs were in English, and by the end of it, in Latin.

In local government the Anglo-Saxon shire and hundred courts continued to function as units of administration and justice, but with important changes. Bishops and earls ceased to preside over the shire courts. Bishops now had their own ecclesiastical courts, while earls had their feudal courts. But although earls no longer presided over shire courts, they were entitled to take a third of the proceeds coming from them. The old Anglo-Saxon office of sheriff was transformed into a position resembling that of the Norman vicomte, as native sheriffs were replaced by Norman nobles. They controlled the shire and hundred courts, were responsible for collecting royal revenue, and controlled the royal castles that had been built both to subdue and protect the country.

William made the most of the financial system he had inherited. In addition to customary dues, such as revenues from justice and income from royal lands, his predecessors had been able to levy a geld, or tax, assessed on the value of land and originally intended to provide funds to buy off Danish invaders. The Confessor had abandoned this tax, but the Conqueror collected it at least four times. Profits from the ample royal estates must have been significant, along with those from royal mints and towns.

● captain
⇒ 軍組織

● carriage

===== Becket, Saint Thomas =====
Whether Becket was fully satisfied with his life as chancellor is another matter. Throughout his life Thomas gave with prodigality and acted with panache. The description of the procession of men, beasts, and **carriages** laden with objects of luxury that accompanied him as envoy to Paris in 1158 is one of the highlights of William FitzStephen's Life of Thomas Becket.

● chamberlain
⇒ butler
〈RH〉 chamberlain, 1. an official charged with the management of the living quarters of a sovereign or member of the nobility.　2. an official who receives rents and revenues, as of a municipal corporation; treasurer.　3. the high steward or factor of a member of the nobility.　4. a high official of a royal court.

● chancellor
概説
　1. 西ヨーロッパで重要度がさまざまに異なる各種職責保有者の称号。主に秘書的, 法的, 行政的性質, 最終的には政治的性質を帯びる。
　2. ドイツでは 1871 年から, オーストリアでは 1918 年から, Kanzler（英語では chancellor）という称号（title）は, 首相 prime minister が保持している。
　3. イギリスでは神聖ローマ帝国とは異なり, head of the government にならなかった。これは lord **chancellor** が司法義務が多かったことによる。
起源
　1. ローマ帝国 cacellarii＝下級法律官僚
　2. tribune と民衆とを隔てる, cancellus と呼ぶ横木のそばに立つ官であった。
　3. のちに帝国の crinia（書記局 writing departments）で雇用される。
　4. 帝国滅亡後は, これを継承した蛮族の統治者がローマ式行政慣行をまねたため, 中世領主（世俗, 聖職両方）の書記局が **chancellor** に司られるようになる。
　5. ほぼ 13 世紀までは, 司祭, 牧師, 修道院僧以外で読み書きできる人間は少数であったため, **chancellor** といえば教会関係者であった。

付録1　職官名英訳参照英文集

6. 王室文書を認証する great seal の保管者として，大半の中世王国では，最も権勢の強い官僚であった。

chancellor と prime minister
Watson 史記英訳注 (I 巻 p. 127) ＝ 陳丞相世家の陳丞相は Prime Minister Chen。この時代，prime minister の old position は chancellor と呼んでいたが，chancellor と prime minister は interchangeably に使われていた。

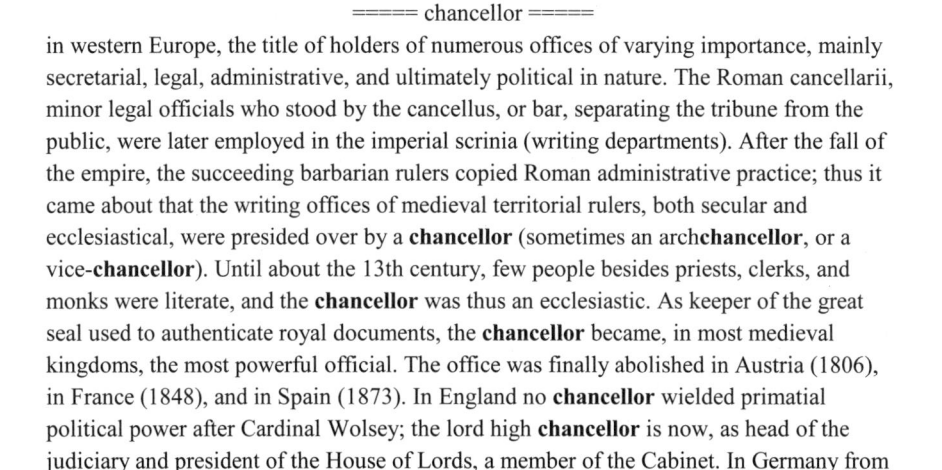

===== chancellor =====
in western Europe, the title of holders of numerous offices of varying importance, mainly secretarial, legal, administrative, and ultimately political in nature. The Roman cancellarii, minor legal officials who stood by the cancellus, or bar, separating the tribune from the public, were later employed in the imperial scrinia (writing departments). After the fall of the empire, the succeeding barbarian rulers copied Roman administrative practice; thus it came about that the writing offices of medieval territorial rulers, both secular and ecclesiastical, were presided over by a **chancellor** (sometimes an arch**chancellor**, or a vice-**chancellor**). Until about the 13th century, few people besides priests, clerks, and monks were literate, and the **chancellor** was thus an ecclesiastic. As keeper of the great seal used to authenticate royal documents, the **chancellor** became, in most medieval kingdoms, the most powerful official. The office was finally abolished in Austria (1806), in France (1848), and in Spain (1873). In England no **chancellor** wielded primatial political power after Cardinal Wolsey; the lord high **chancellor** is now, as head of the judiciary and president of the House of Lords, a member of the Cabinet. In Germany from 1871 and in Austria from 1918, the title Kanzler ("**chancellor**") has been held by the prime minister.

The title **chancellor** is also the name in many countries of the heads of small archive offices, of the heads of universities, and of some orders of chivalry.

In England the member of the Cabinet in charge of finance is called the **chancellor** of the Exchequer; another Cabinet member, the **chancellor** of the duchy of Lancaster, is a minister without departmental responsibility whose title derives from that of the official originally employed by the crown to manage the palatine duchy of Lancaster.

===== Bismarck, Otto von =====
Imperial **chancellor**
It is important to note that the Germany Bismarck created was not the result of strong popular currents of nationalist sentiment but of cabinet diplomacy and war. Not all German-speaking areas of Europe were included but only as many as Prussia could unite

while retaining hegemony. The new constitution was a revision of the Prussian constitution from 1867; it included the position of **chancellor**, designed with Bismarck specifically in mind. Bismarck also remained prime minister of Prussia until 1890, apart from a brief period in 1872-73.

===== diplomatics =====

Under the Ottonian dynasty, which came to power in the eastern division of the original Carolingian empire early in the 10th century, the German royal chancery developed the organization that was to characterize it throughout the remainder of the Middle Ages. The heads of the chancery were the arch**chancellor**s, but the office was entirely honorary and soon came to be automatically held, as far as Germany was concerned, by whoever was archbishop of Mainz. When the German kings or emperors established administrations in Italy, Italian bishops were at first made arch**chancellor**s for Italy, but in 1031 the office was attached to the archbishopric of Cologne. From the 11th century, Burgundian bishops were arch**chancellor**s for Burgundy, but, in the second half of the 13th century, the archbishop of Trier took over the office.

The actual heads of the chancery were the **chancellor**s. At first there was a **chancellor**, as well as an arch**chancellor**, for each separate part of the empire--Germany, Italy, and Burgundy--but from 1118 there was only one **chancellor** for all three kingdoms. But even the **chancellor**s, all of whom were clerics, were rarely involved in the actual composition and engrossing of documents, being usually engaged, as important advisers to the king or emperor, in much weightier matters. They do seem to have been especially concerned, however, with decisions about the granting of charters, and they supervised the work of the scribes or notaries. From among the ranks of these notaries, a group of protonotaries gradually developed after the mid-12th century, as a result of influence from the chancery of the Norman rulers of Sicily. Often called upon to deputize for the **chancellor**, the protonotaries, from the late 13th century onward, frequently titled themselves vice **chancellor**s.

From the 12th century onward, the documents issued by the German royal chancery were divided into various classifications. The diploma, by then usually called a privilege, existed in two categories, the solemn and the simple privilege. A solemn privilege included the invocatio, the signum and recognition line, and a detailed dating or at least one of these three elements, which were entirely lacking in simple privileges. Gradually, simple privileges merged into documents called mandates; it is not always easy to distinguish between them, but, in general, privileges were concerned with rights in perpetuity, while the mandates dealt mainly with matters of only temporary importance. From the early 14th century, mandates were superseded by the use of letters patent and letters close (open or

付録 1　職官名英訳参照英文集

closed letters). Privileges continued to be sealed with a hanging seal; the seal on letters patent was impressed on the document and was used to seal up letters close.

As the power of the German kings declined during the later Middle Ages, so that of the arch**chancellor**s increased, and in the 14th century they attempted to win control of the chancery. But, despite fluctuations in the power struggle, the king retained control of the **chancellor**, who, by the end of the 15th century, held the title of imperial vice **chancellor**.

Under the Carolingians and the first Capetians in France, various bishops and archbishops, especially the archbishops of Reims, held the office of royal **chancellor**. But at that time the office was merely titular, and, by the end of the 11th century, it disappeared entirely. From the 12th century onward, the title of **chancellor** became reserved to the head of the chancery. These new **chancellor**s became so powerful that in 1185 King Philip II Augustus left the office vacant, and, during almost the whole of the 13th century, the chancery was administered by subordinate officials. **Chancellor**s, often laymen, were appointed again in the 14th century, however, and the office remained important until 1789. As in other parts of Europe, the French **chancellor** merely directed the work of the notaries, and it was they who were responsible for drawing up the documents. From 1350 onward, the notaries were called secretaries, and both their numbers and their importance steadily increased. From the 15th century, the tremendous expansion of business occupying the Grande **Chancellerie** led to the establishment of several subsidiary petites chancelleries, all issuing royal documents sealed with the king's signet. Until the reign of Henry I (1031-60), the old Frankish type of diploma was issued almost exclusively.

===== North German Confedration =====
German NORDDEUTSCHER BUND, union of the German states north of the Main River formed in 1867 under Prussian hegemony after Prussia's victory over Austria in the Seven Weeks' War (1866). Berlin was its capital, the king of Prussia was its president, and the Prussian **chancellor** was also its **chancellor**. Its constitution served as a model for that of the German Empire, with which it merged in 1871.

⇒ butler

● chief
chief = 本部長，参謀長など高位
director-general = 局長
director = 部長（局長の下）

===== 行政機構（日本）=====

189

| 日本語 | 英語 |
|---|---|
| 内閣官房 | |
| 内閣官房長官(国務大臣) | **Chief** Cabinet Secretary(Minister of State) |
| 総務主幹, 内閣法制局 | **Chief** of the Administration Office |
| | |
| 人事院 | |
| 首席試験専門官, 任用局 | **Chief** Examiner |
| | |
| 自衛隊 | |
| 幕僚長 | **Chief** of Staff(陸上, 海上, 航空) |
| | |
| 外務省 | |
| 儀典長, 外務事務次官 | **Chief** of Protocol |
| | |
| 大蔵省 | |
| 主計監査官, 主計局 | **Chief** Budget Inspector |
| | |
| 国税庁 | |
| 首席国税庁監察官, 長官官房 | **Chief** Personnel Inspector |
| | |
| 特許庁 | |
| 審査長, 審査第一部・第二部 | **Chief** Examiner |
| | |
| 運輸省 | |
| 首席船舶検査官, 海上技術安全局 | **Chief** Ship Inspector |
| 首席海技試験官, 船員部 | **Chief** Marine Technic Examiner |
| 首席安全監察官, 航空局 | **Chief** Safety Inspection Officer |
| | |
| 海難審判庁 | |
| 海難審判書記官 | **Chief** Clerk of the Marine Accidents Inquiry |
| | |
| 最高裁判所 | |
| 最高裁判所長官 | **Chief** Justice of the Supreme Court |
| 高等裁判所長官 | **Chief** Judge of the High Court |
| 大法廷 | **Grand** Bench of the Supreme Court |
| | |
| 警視庁 | |

付録 1　職官名英訳参照英文集

| 警視総監 | **Superintendent**-General (**Chief** of Police) (警視庁公式サイト組織図) |

===== イギリス国防省（UK Government 公式サイト）=====

| | **UK Government 公式サイト** | ジャパンタイムズ「主要国行政機構ハンドブック」 |
|---|---|---|
| 国務大臣 | Secretary of State | Secretary of State for Defence |
| 担当大臣 | Ministers of State<br>- Minister of State (also in the Department for Business, Innovations and Skills)<br>- Minister of State (Armed Forces) | Minister of State for Defence |
| 国防政務次官 | - Parliamentary Under-Secretary (International Defence and Security) (also in Foreign and Commonwealth Office)<br>- Parliamentary Under-Secretary (Defence Equipment & Support)<br>- Parliamentary Under-Secretary (Veterans) | Parliamentary Under-Secretary of State (海軍，陸軍，空軍) |

===== イギリス国防省和英対訳 =====
（ジャパンタイムズ「主要国行政機構ハンドブック」）

| 日本語 | 英語 |
|---|---|
| 国防省 | Ministry of Defence |
| 参謀本部長 | **Chief** of the Defence Staff |
| 首席科学顧問 | **Chief** Scientific Adviser |
| 人事・兵站長 | **Chief** of Personnel and Logistics |
| 参謀本部 | Defence Staff |
| … | |
| 海軍参謀長兼海軍本部第一委員 | **Chief** of Naval Staff and First Sea Lord |
| … | |
| 総務参謀長 | **Chief** of the General Staff |
| 作戦部長 | **Director** of Military Operations |

| | |
|---|---|
| 陸軍軍務部長 | **Director** of Army Staff Duties |
| 戦闘展開部長 | **Director** of Combat Development |
| 装備部長 | Arms **Director**s |
| 空軍参謀長 | **Chief** of the Air Staff |
| … | |
| 科学スタッフ | Scientific Staff |
| … | |
| 首席科学官(海軍) | **Chief** Scientist (Royal Navy) |
| 首席科学官(陸軍) | **Chief** Scientist (Army) |
| 首席科学官(空軍) | **Chief** Scientist (RAF) |
| 補給調整局長 | **Director**-General of Supply Co-ordination |
| 海軍人事局兼海軍委員会第二委員 | **Chief** of Naval Personnel and Second Sea Lord |
| 海軍事務局長 | Naval Secretary |
| 医務局長(海軍) | Medical **Director**-General (Naval) |
| 海軍教育部長 | **Director** of Womens Royal Naval Service |
| … | |
| 艦船支援局長 | **Chief** of Fleet Support |
| 海軍工廠長 | **Chief** Executive, Royal Dockyards |
| 工廠要員生産性部長 | **Director** of Dockyard Manpower and Productivity |

===== アメリカ陸軍省和英対訳 =====
(ジャパンタイムズ「主要国行政機構ハンドブック」)

| 日本語 | 英語 |
|---|---|
| 陸軍省 | Department of the Army |
| 装備・兵站・財務管理担当陸軍次官補 | Assistant Secretary (Installations, Logistics and Financial Management) |
| 管理システム担当副次官補 | Deputy for Management Systems |
| 陸軍長官行政補佐官 | Administrative Assistant to the Secretary of the Army |
| 管理課(長) | Management Office (**Chief**) |
| 文官職員保安プログラム(主任) | Civilian Employees Security Program (**Director**) |
| 参謀長 | **Chief** of Staff |
| 作戦・計画担当副参謀長 | Deputy **Chief** of Staff Operations and Plans |
| 人事担当副参謀長 | Deputy **Chief** of Staff Personnel |
| 兵站担当副参謀長 | Deputy **Chief** of Staff Logistics |

付録 1　職官名英訳参照英文集

| 情報担当参謀長補 | Assistant **Chief** of Staff Intelligence |
| … | |
| 軍務局長 | The Adjutant General |
| 技師長 | **Chief** of Engineers |
| 州兵局長 | **Chief**, National Guard Bureau |
| 陸軍予備役部長 | **Chief**, Army Reserve |

⇒ 宮内庁

● colonel
⇒ 軍組織

● command

===== army military organization =====

The current administrative structure of the U.S. Army was established by the National Security Act of 1947 and amendments to it in 1949. The Department of the Army is organized as a military section of the Department of Defense. It is headed by the Office of the Secretary of the Army. The Army Staff gives advice and assistance to the secretary and administers civil functions, including the civil works program of the Corps of Engineers.

The major army field **command**s are: Forces **Command**, which is responsible for all army forces in the continental United States, the Army Reserve, and the Army National Guard; Training and Doctrine **Command**; Materiel **Command**, which is responsible for supply logistics and research, development, and evaluation of new materiel; Intelligence and Security **Command**; Medical **Command**; Criminal Investigation **Command**; Corps of Engineers, which oversees a variety of military and civil development projects; Special Operations **Command**; Military Traffic Management **Command**; Military District of Washington, which is charged with defense of the national capital; the Space and Missile Defense **Command**; U.S. Army Europe; U.S. Army Pacific; Eighth Army (stationed in South Korea); and U.S. Army South. The army also administers the U.S. Military Academy at West Point, New York.

===== army United Kingdom =====

British army
in the United Kingdom, the military force charged with national defense and the fulfillment of international mutual defense commitments. The army of England before the Norman Conquest consisted of the king's household troops (housecarls) and all freemen able to bear arms, who served under the fyrd system for two months a year. After 1066 the Normans introduced feudalism and mounted troops (knights) and their auxiliaries, infantry,

and military artisans. Mercenaries were employed during the Hundred Years' War (1337–1453) and the Wars of the Roses (1455–85) in combination with the militia. With the Battle of Crécy in 1346, archers became important, the longbow being a major innovation of warfare.

The first English standing army was formed by Oliver Cromwell in 1645 during the Civil War. His New Model Army was highly disciplined and well-trained. Associated with the excesses of Cromwell's Commonwealth, however, it was disbanded by Charles II in 1660 except for a household **brigade** (now the Coldstream Guards). After the Glorious Revolution (1688–89), the English Bill of Rights (1689) gave Parliament the control of the army that it maintains today.

During the 18th and 19th centuries, as Britain consolidated its colonial empire, the army grew in size and developed as an effective fighting force. The army established standing forces in the colonies and distinguished itself during the Napoleonic Wars (1800–15). Reforms were carried out to improve its organization and efficiency in the late 1800s. Between 1905 and 1912 the Territorial Force (after 1921, Territorial Army) and Special Reserve were established. The army was greatly increased in size by conscription during World War I but was reduced to a minimum with an end to conscription after 1919. In July 1939, however, conscription was again enforced.

Major changes in the British army occurred after 1945. Troops stationed overseas were returned home as the British colonies gained independence, and the military forces were placed in Europe or absorbed into the Home Guard. In 1960 conscription was ended and an all-volunteer army again created. With the introduction of nuclear weapons, the Territorial Army was greatly reduced.

In 1964 the Ministry of Defense was established to administer all the armed forces, and in 1972 all army forces were placed under Headquarters United Kingdom Land Forces. The secretary of state for defense is responsible to the prime minister and the cabinet. He is advised by the chief of defense staff, who is aided by the three service chiefs.

===== tokugawa =====

**censor**
in traditional East Asia, governmental official charged primarily with the responsibility for scrutinizing and criticizing the conduct of officials and rulers.［cenor＝ 目付］

The office originated in China, where, under the Ch'in (221–206 BC) and Han (206 BC–AD 220) dynasties, the **censor**'s function was to criticize the emperor's acts; but, as

付録 1　職官名英訳参照英文集

the imperial office gained prestige, the **censorate** became mainly an instrument for imperial control of the bureaucracy, investigating acts of official corruption and misgovernment for the emperor. By the T'ang dynasty (618–907), the **censorate**, or Yü-shih-t'ai, as it was then known, had thus become a major organ of the government. It expanded even further during the Sung dynasty (960–1279) and reached the apogee of its power during the Ming (1368–1644) and Ch'ing (1644–1911) dynasties, when the imperial institution became extremely autocratic. Retitled the Tu-ch'a-yüan in 1380, it was then a huge governmental bureau controlled by two chief **censor**s and composed of four subdivisions.

The **censor**s checked important documents, supervised construction projects, reviewed judicial proceedings, kept watch over state property, and maintained a general lookout for cases of subversion and corruption. Usually recruited from the civil bureaucracy, the **censor**s were generally younger men of relatively low rank who were tenured for a maximum of nine years, after which they resumed their former posts. Their chief power derived from their direct access to the emperor. Some **censor**s, however, were punished for their overzealous criticisms of favoured imperial policies, and this induced others to mute their criticisms and ignore many cases of misgovernment. The major effect of the office was to spread fear throughout the bureaucracy, preventing officials from instituting any kind of radically new or innovative policies.

Although the functions of the **censorate** were maintained in the Chinese Nationalist and, to a lesser extent, the Chinese Communist governments, the institution effectively ended in China with the overthrow of the Ch'ing dynasty in 1911.

A **censorate** apparatus was adopted by all the East and Central Asian states that copied the Chinese bureaucratic system. In Korea, because of the relatively weak position of the Korean king and the strength of the aristocracy, the **censorate** became a highly important organ that not only scrutinized corruption but directly criticized the policies of the mon*arch*. In Korea the original boards of **censor**s (Sahŏnbu and Saganwŏn) were supplemented by the Hongmun'gwan (Office of Special Counselors) and Kyŏngyŏn (Office of Royal Lectures), which eventually became a forum for evaluating state policy and the conduct of the king and officials.

The Tokugawa government (1603–1867) of Japan instituted a **censorial** system (metsuke) in the 17th century for the surveillance of affairs in every one of the feudal fiefs (han) into which the country was divided. Many daimyos (lords of fiefs) were transferred to smaller han or lost their domains altogether as a result of the unfavourable judgments of the **censorate**.

● commandant

===== commandant =====

commander of a single place or body of men, such as a military school or training unit, or of a larger organization such as a naval district in the United States. The rank of a **commandant** depends upon the size and importance of his command: in the British Army a colonel **commandant** is the **senior officer** of a regiment; in the French Army a **commandant** is the commanding officer of a battalion, a rank equivalent to major; and the **commandant** of the United States Marine Corps is a four-star general. Headquarters **commandant** denotes a staff officer in charge of the internal administration of a military headquarters, with emphasis on maintenance and security of buildings and grounds.

===== Lake Erie, Battle of =====

- On Sept. 10, 1813, Master **Commandant** Oliver Hazard Perry's fleet of nine ships engaged six British warships under Capt. Robert Heriot Barclay in Lake Erie.

===== Egypt, history of =====

- Military controls were established, with garrisons under Libyan **commandant** serving to quell local insurrections, so that the structure of the state became more feudalistic.

===== China: Han Dynasty =====

The armed forces

The command of the armed forces was also arranged so as to avoid giving excessive powers to a single individual. General officers were usually appointed in pairs, and, in times of emergency or when a campaign was being planned with a defined objective, officers were appointed for a specific task; when their mission was fulfilled, their commands were brought to a close. At a lower level there existed a complement of colonels whose duties were defined so as to cover smaller scale activities. In addition, the governors and **commandant**s of the commanderies were sometimes ordered to lead forces. The **commandant**s were also responsible for training conscript soldiers and setting them to maintain internal discipline and to man the static lines of defense in the north and northwest.

Provincial government

At the outset of the Han dynasty very large areas were entrusted as kingdoms to the emperor's kinsmen while the central government administered the interior provinces as commanderies. But by c. 100 BC the Imperial government had deprived the kingdoms of their strength, and most of their lands had been incorporated as commanderies under the central government. Although the kingdoms survived in a much reduced form until the end

付録 1　職官名英訳参照英文集

of the period, their administration came to differ less and less from that of the commanderies, which formed the regular provincial units. Each commandery was controlled by two senior officials, the governor and the **commandant**, who were appointed by the central government. Commanderies could be established at will: by dividing larger into smaller units, by taking over the lands of the kings, or by establishing organs of government in regions only recently penetrated by Chinese officials. Provincial government was not necessarily pervasive throughout the lands where commandery offices existed, but there was a steady advance in provincial government during the Han period. During Kao-tsu's reign 16 commanderies existed, but by the end of the Hsi Han there were 83 commanderies and 20 kingdoms. ((Jack L. Dull))

- The executive committee set up a central headquarters in Canton. It also decided to strengthen the party throughout the country by deputizing most of its leaders to manage regional and provincial headquarters and by recruiting new members. A military academy was planned for training a corps of young officers, loyal to the party, who would become lower level commanders in a new national revolutionary army that was to be created. Borodin provided funds for party operations, and the Soviet Union promised to underwrite most of the expenses of, and to provide training officers for, the military academy. Chiang Kai-shek was chosen to be the first **commandant** of the academy and Liao Chung-k'ai to be the party representative, or chief political officer. (Reorganization of the KMT*, China, C. Martin Wilbur, George Sansom Professor of Chinese History, Columbia University)

* KMT = The Nationalist Party (Kuomintang; KMT)

〈NSOED〉commandant, 1 A commanding officer, esp. of a particular force, a military academy, etc. L17.　2 In S. Afr. *Hist.*, the leader of a Boer commando. Now, an officer in the South African armed forces ranking between a major and a colonel. L18.　2 commandant-general a commander-in-chief.

〈LgAm〉commandant, the chief officer in charge of a military organization:・*the commandant of a prison camp*

〈RH〉 commandant, 1. the commanding officer of a place, group, etc.: the commandant of a naval base.　2. the title of the **senior officer** and head of the U.S. Marine Corps.　3. U.S. Army. a title generally given to the heads of military schools.　4. a commander. [1680・0; < F, n. use of prp. of commander to COMMAND; see -ANT]

〈NSOED〉 -ant, Forming adjs. denoting existence of action, as pendant, repentant, or state, as arrogant, expectant, and ns. denoting an agent, as assistant, celebrant, deodorant, usu. f.

vbs. Conflicting Eng., Fr., & L analogies have produced much inconsistency of use of -ant and -ent.

〈RH〉-ant, a suffix forming adjectives and nouns from verbs, occurring originally in French and Latin loanwords (pleasant; constant; servant) and productive in English on this model; -ant has the general sense 田haracterized by or serving in the capacity of ・that named by the stem (ascendant; pretendant), esp. in the formation of nouns denoting human agents in legal actions or other formal procedures (tenant; defendant; applicant; contestant). In technical and commercial coinages, -ant is a suffix of nouns denoting impersonal physical agents (propellant; lubricant; deodorant). In general, -ant can be added only to bases of Latin origin, with a very few exceptions, as coolant. See also -ent.
[< L -ant-, prp. s. of verbs in -!re; in many words < F -ant < L -ant- or -ent- (see -ENT); akin to ME, OE -and-, -end-, prp. suffix]

===== 主要国行政機構(ジャパンタイムズ) =====
国防総省
統合参謀本部 Joint Chiefs of Staff[chief of staff=高位ではない。国防通信庁スタッフ主任も chief of staff]
　陸軍参謀長 Chief of Staff, Army
　空軍参謀長 Chief of Staff, Air Force
　海軍軍令部長 Chief of Naval Operations
　海兵隊司令長官 **Commandant**, Marine Corps

空軍
主要司令部 Major Commands
　防空司令部 Aerospace Defence Command
　太平洋空軍司令部 Pacific Air Forces

陸軍省
合衆国陸軍司令部司令長官 Commanding General, U.S. Army Force Command

海軍省
海軍太平洋艦隊司令長官 **Commander** in Chief, U.S. Pacific Fleet
軍事輸送司令部司令官 **Commander**, Military Sealift Command
合衆国海兵隊司令長官 **Commandant**, U.S. Marine Corps

国防総省所管機関・共通教育機関 Department of Defense Agencies and Joint Service Schools
　国防通信庁 Defense Communications Agency

付録 1　職官名英訳参照英文集

スタッフ主任 Chief of Staff

● commander
⇒ commandant

● company
⇒ unit

● compulsory labour
⇒ labour 労役

● constable
〈NSOED〉 constable, 1 *Hist.* The principal officer of the household, administration, or army of a monarch or nobleman; *spec.* one of the chief officers of the French, English, or Scottish royal household. ME.　2 The governor or warden of a royal fortress or castle. ME. 3 A military officer. Long rare. ME.　4 An officer of the peace. ME.b A police officer of the lowest rank. Also more fully police constable. M19.

● control/management
management = 経営的管理
control = 備品・産物・産品などの具象物(モノ)の保管、移動記録、購入、貸し出し、支給といった実務作業的管理。例, control of iron goods

● credential
〈NSOED〉 credentials, A adj. Recommending or entitling to credit or confidence. *rare.* B n. A letter of recommendation or introduction, esp. of an ambassador; an indication of trustworthiness or achievement. *Usu. in pl.*

● curio
===== Jerusalem =====
Industry and trade
The establishment of heavy industries has not been encouraged, in the interest of preserving the traditional character of the city. Combined with transport and marketing difficulties, this has limited the city to a number of small industries. They include diamond cutting and polishing and the manufacture of home appliances, furniture, shoes, pencils, plastics, textiles, clothing, and pharmaceuticals and chemicals. There are also printing and publishing houses, as well as workshops producing jewelry, giftware, religious articles, **curios**, and printed fabrics

● director
⇒ chief
⇒ director of music

===== Handel, George Frideric =====
In 1718 Handel became **director of music** to the duke of Chandos, for whom he composed the 12 *Chandos Anthems* and the English masque *Acis and Galatea*, among other works.

===== Schumann, Robert =====
Schumann's attempts to obtain posts in Leipzig and Vienna had also been abortive, and in the end he accepted the post of municipal **director of music** at Düsseldorf. ... and in 1853 he lost his post as **music director** at Düsseldorf.
[director of music と music director は完全同義]

===== Brahms, Johannes =====
Brahms remained in Vienna for the rest of his life. He resigned as **director of the Society of Friends of Music** in 1875, and from then on devoted his life almost solely to composition.

===== Vivaldi, Antonio =====
Vivaldi had dealings with the Pietà for most of his career: as violin master (1703–09; 1711–15), **director of instrumental music** (1716–17; 1735–38), and paid external supplier of compositions (1723–29; 1739–40).

===== Bach, Johann Sebastian =====
As **director of church music** for the city of Leipzig, Bach had to supply performers for four churches.

===== Karajan, Herbert von =====
He helped found the London Philharmonia in 1948, and in 1955 he became **music director** of the Berlin Philharmonic.
[後ろに of ~ orchestra / ~ harmonic のようなオーケストラの名前が来るとき music director となる率高]

===== Ozawa, Seiji =====
Subsequently, he was music director of the Ravinia Festival in Chicago (1964–68). He became **music director** of the Toronto Symphony Orchestra in 1965 and of the San Francisco Symphony Orchestra in 1970. In 1973 he was appointed conductor and **music director** of the Boston Symphony Orchestra, for years the exclusive preserve of European conductors.

付録 1　職官名英訳参照英文集

===== New York Philharmonic =====
Its **music directors**, music advisers, and principal conductors have been Ureli Corelli Hill (1842–47), ..., Leonard Bernstein (1958–69; laureate conductor 1969–90), George Szell (1969–70), Pierre Boulez (1971–77), Zubin Mehta (1978–91), and Kurt Masur (from 1991).

● divination
⇒ diviner
⇒ invoke

● diviner

===== China =====
Late Shang **divination** and religion
Although certain complex symbols painted on Late Neolithic pots from Shantung suggest that primitive writing was emerging in the east in the 3rd millennium, the Shang **divination** inscriptions that appear at Hsiao-t'un form the earliest body of Chinese writing yet known. In Late Shang **divination** as practiced during the reign of Wu-ting (c. 1200-1180 BC), cattle scapulae or turtle plastrons, in a refinement of Neolithic practice, were first planed and bored with hollow depressions to which an intense heat source was then applied. The resulting T-shaped stress cracks were interpreted as lucky or unlucky. After the prognostication had been made, the day, the name of the presiding **diviner** (some 120 are known), the subject of the charge, the prognostication, and the result might be carved into the surface of the bone. Among the topics divined were sacrifices, campaigns, hunts, the good fortune of the 10-day week or of the night or day, weather, harvests, sickness, childbearing, dreams, settlement building, the issuing of orders, tribute, divine assistance, and prayers to various spirits. Some evolution in divinatory practice and theology evidently occurred. By the reigns of the last two Shang kings, Ti-i and Ti-hsin (c. 1100 to 1045 BC), the scope and form of Shang **divination** had become considerably simplified: prognostications were uniformly optimistic, and **divination** topics were limited mainly to the sacrificial schedule, the coming 10 days, the coming night, and hunting.

⟨NSOED⟩　divine, 1 Make out or interpret by supernatural or magical insight; disclose, make known.　2 Make out by sagacity, intuition, or fortunate conjecture; conjecture successfully; guess.　3 Have supernatural or magic insight into (things to come); have a presentiment of; predict or prophesy by some special intuition.　4 Conceive of, devise, or contrive by special inspiration or extraordinary sagacity.　5 Of a thing: foreshadow, prognosticate, portend; point out.　6 Make divine; canonize; divinize.

⟨RH⟩ divine, 13. to discover or declare (something obscure or in the future) by divination; prophesy.    14. to discover (water, metal, etc.) by means of a divining rod.    15. to perceive by intuition or insight; conjecture.

⟨RH⟩ divination, 1. the practice of attempting to foretell future events or discover hidden knowledge by occult or supernatural means.    2. augury; prophecy: The divination of the high priest was fulfilled.    3. perception by intuition; instinctive foresight.

● division
⇒ unit

● forced labour
⇒ labour 劳役

● foster
⟨LDOCE⟩ 1 [ transitive ] to help a skill, feeling, idea etc develop over a period of time SYN encourage , promote : *The bishop helped foster the sense of a community embracing all classes.*    2 [ intransitive and transitive ] to take someone else's child into your family for a period of time but without becoming their legal parent → adopt : *The couple wanted to adopt a black child they had been fostering.*

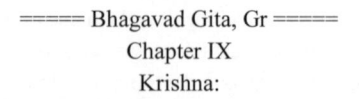

===== Bhagavad Gita, Gr =====
Chapter IX
Krishna:

...
· I am the Sacrifice! I am the Prayer!
· I am the Funeral-Cake set for the dead!
· I am the healing herb! I am the ghee,
· The Mantra, and the flame, and that which burns!
· I am--of all this boundless Universe--
· The Father, Mother, Ancestor, and Guard!
· The end of Learning! That which purifies
· In lustral water! I am Om! I am
· Rig-Veda, Sama-Veda, Yajur-Ved;
· The Way, the **Fosterer**, the Lord, the Judge,
· The Witness; the Abode, the Refuge-House,
· The Friend, the Fountain and the Sea of Life
· Which sends, and swallows up; Treasure of Worlds
· And Treasure-Chamber! Seed and Seed-Sower,

付録1 職官名英訳参照英文集

- Whence endless harvests spring! Sun's heat is mine;
- Heaven's rain is mine to grant or to withhold;
- Death am I, and Immortal Life I am,
- Arjuna! Sat and Asat, Visible Life,
- And Life Invisible!

● garment

===== dress ====

Byzantine dress strongly influenced that of eastern Europe, especially the Balkans and Russia. Some of the bejeweled silk formal **garments** were gradually adopted by the church to become **vestments** in the Middle Ages.[この記事中 garment は 125 回出現し，vestment はここ1回のみ]

===== vestment =====

Ceremonial and ritualistic objects as indicators or bearers of the sacred or holy Liturgical and ceremonial objects can also indicate or lead to the sacred or holy. Not only holy pictures and symbols (e.g., the cross in Christianity or the mirror in Japanese Shintō) but also lights, candles, lamps, vessels for holy materials, liturgical books, holy writings, **vestment**s, and sacred ornaments are indicators of the sacred or holy. Liturgical **vestment**s and masks are intended to transform the wearer, to remove him from the realm of the this-worldly, and to adapt him to the sphere of the sacred or holy; they help him to come into contact with the divine—for example, by obscuring his sexual characteristics. The **vestment**s may be covered with symbols, such as those worn by Arctic shamans (medicine men with psychic transformation abilities). They are signs of the function of the wearer and his relationships to the sacred or holy and to the profane world. Such **vestment**s are frequently derived from those of rulers or from ceremonial court dress; e.g., Japanese Shintō and Roman Catholic and Eastern Orthodox Christianity. They are supposed to create a fitting atmosphere of solemnity and dignity. In Western Christianity, the liturgical **vestment**s have a very specific symbolism: the alb (a tunic) symbolizes purity of heart; the stole, the raiment of immortality; and the chasuble (an outer eucharistic, or holy communion, **vestment**), the yoke of Christ. The liturgical **vestment**s of the Eastern Christian churches have a similar symbolism. The ritual headdress and the crown express the sacred dignity of the wearer. The **vestment**s of the various religious orders (Oriental and Occidental) express the holiness of the members of the community, their nearness to the sacred or holy, and the significance of religious life for them. In the reception ritual of Jainism and Buddhism, the monastic **vestment**s are put on as a sign of an entrance in a new state of life. This ritual in Jainism resembles that of a wedding ceremony. The taking over of the monastic garb is an essential part of becoming a sādhu. The monks of the Jainistic Śvetāmbara sect wear five objects (e.g., shells) as symbols of the five monastic virtues. In early Christianity the white baptismal **vestment** was a symbol of rebirth, new life, and innocence.

===== fur (pelt), Gr =====
Garment Making

In the production of a fur **garment** the dressed furs are matched for uniformity. The waste parts -- the head, tail, and paws -- are cut away. In mink and other costly furs an additional process called letting-out is employed, whereby the skin of the pelt is cut down the center, and each half is sliced into narrow diagonal strips ranging in width from 1.5 to 13 mm ( 1/16 to 1/2 in). These strips are resewn to produce a longer, narrower pelt that will give the finished **garment** a more graceful line.

- Maldives, Republic of

Tourism has become the leading source of foreign exchange, followed by the export of fresh, frozen, and canned fish, especially tuna. In 1997 about 350,000 tourists visited the Maldives. **Garment** making, boatbuilding, and handicrafts are other important industries.

- clothing industry

Often the **garment** workers owned their machines and carried them from the workshop to their homes.

● grain tax

● grand
［重厚, 壮麗, 威厳ある great］
===== Ssu-ma Ch'ien =====

The standard study of Ssu-ma Ch'ien is the extremely perceptive work of Burton Watson, Ssu-ma Ch'ien, **Grand** Historian of China (1958), which gives a full critical analysis of Ssu-ma Ch'ien's works and also translates all the relevant biographical material from early sources.

===== **Grand** Army of the Republic =====

patriotic organization of American Civil War veterans who served in the Union forces, one of its purposes being the "defense of the late soldiery of the United States, morally, socially, and politically."

===== **Grand** Union Flag =====

also called <u>Great</u> Union Flag, or Cambridge Flag, American colonial banner first displayed by George Washington on Jan. 1, 1776. It showed the British Union Flag of 1606 in the

付録 1　職官名英訳参照英文集

canton. Its field consisted of seven red and six white alternated stripes representing the 13 colonies. The Stars and Stripes officially replaced it on June 14, 1777.

===== grand duke =====

feminine **grand** duchess, also called (in Russia) **grand** prince and **grand** princess title of sovereign princes ranking between kings and dukes and of certain members of the Russian imperial family.

The first **grand** duchy of western Europe was that of Tuscany, the title of **grand** duke being accorded by Pope Pius V to Cosimo de' Medici in 1569 and recognized, for Cosimo's son Francesco, by the Holy Roman Emperor Maximilian II in 1575. The title passed with Tuscany to the house of Habsburg-Lorraine in the 18th century. The reorganization of Germany and eastern Europe in the period of the Napoleonic Wars gave rise to new **grand** duchies; the Congress of Vienna respected some of the Napoleonic creations (notably Hesse-Darmstadt and Baden) and created others (including Saxe-Weimar, the two Mecklenburgs [east and west], Luxembourg, and Oldenburg).

〈NSOED〉　grand, 2b Designating a (now only foreign) monarch or an official who is senior to others of the same general rank. Now chiefly *Hist.* L16.　3 Great, large; main or principal by virtue of greatest size. Now only, (of a specified part of a large building) main or principal by virtue of size and magnificence.　4 Law. (Of a tribunal etc.) of great importance, chief, principal; (of a crime) serious, on a large scale. Cf. PETTY a. Now chiefly *Hist.* E16.　5 Of most or great importance, value, or scope; great, vital. L16.　6 (Esp. of architecture, a natural object, etc.) imposing, impressive, magnificent; (of an idea, style, design, etc.) lofty and dignified in conception or expression.　7 (Of a person) stately, dignified; now esp. imposing, superior, haughty; (of appearance) rich, splendid. M18.　8 Of a ceremony, occasion, etc.: conducted with great solemnity and splendour esp. on a large scale. M18.　9 Splendid, excellent; (of a person) in good health, well. colloq. E19.

⇒ 宮内庁

● imperial tomb

===== arts, East Asian =====
Ming dynasty
Architecture

In 1402, a son of the founding Ming emperor enfeoffed at the old Yüan capital usurped the throne from his nephew, the second Ming ruler, and installed himself as the Yung-lo Emperor. He rebuilt the destroyed Mongol palaces and moved the Ming capital there in 1421, renaming the city Peking (Pei-ching, "Northern Capital"). His central palace cluster,

205

the Forbidden City, is the foremost surviving Chinese palace compound, maintained and successively rebuilt over the centuries. ...

Central to this entire arrangement are three great halls of state, situated on a high, triple-level marble platform (the number three, here and elsewhere, symbolic of heaven and of the Imperial role as chief communicant between heaven and earth). ... The grandeur of this palatial scheme was matched by the layout of a vast **Imperial burial ground** on the southern slopes of the mountain range to the north of Peking, ...

Sculpture

Colossal figures lining the approaches to early Ming **Imperial tombs** at Nanking reflect a deliberate revival of T'ang style.

===== Anthropology and Archaeology, Year in Review 2004 =====
Archaeology
Eastern Hemisphere.

What was thought to be an **imperial tomb group** of the Western Zhou dynasty (1046–771 BC) was unearthed at the Zhougong Temple site in northwestern Shaanxi province. According to Lei Xingshan of Beijing University, 12 multichambered tombs had been excavated along with seven chariot pits.

● interrogator 獄吏

===== Europe, history of =====

魔女狩りについて，魔女の実態を解明することはむつかしい。彼女らが行っていた魔術（witchcraft）の中身さえよくわからない。その理由について考えられることは・・・として，下の英文が続く。要旨は以下の通り。

魔女裁判の証人たちは［事件に巻き込まれることか裁判そのものへの］恐怖を感じて，interrogator が喜びそうな固定観念を中心に証言し，魔女が本当に信じていたこと，あるいは実践いたことを明らかにしなかった［実はこっちのほうが魔術とは呼べないまともなことであった可能性がある］。だから残っている記録は欠陥のないものとは言えないが，それでも文化史を脈打つ豊かな情報源であることに変りはない。皮肉なことに court officials（今の場合裁判書記官）たちは，［これら証言のなかで］自分たちの感覚として消滅すればよいと願った考え方や価値観［魔女を魔女と判決できなくする不都合な証言か］を記録に残したのだが，これが歴史のためになった。

Terrorized witnesses tended to respond in ways they thought would please their **interrogators**; thus they reinforced stereotypes rather than revealing what they truly believed or did. Court records of this kind are not flawless sources, but they remain a rich vein of cultural history. Ironically, the **court officials** saved for history the

付録 1　職官名英訳参照英文集

thoughts and values they had hoped to extirpate. (Br Europe, history of / Aspects of early modern society)

- court officials は法律用語対訳集では「裁判所職員」であり，獄吏より事務職的意味合いが強そうである。

⇒ judicial officer（法律用語対訳集では「司法官憲」。獄吏より地位が高いか）

● invocation

===== invocation =====

a convention of classical literature and of epics in particular, in which an appeal for aid (especially for inspiration) is made to a muse or deity, usually at or near the beginning of the work. Homer's Odyssey, for instance, begins

Tell me, Muse, of the man of many ways, who was driven
far journeys, after he had sacked Troy's sacred citadel.
Many were they whose cities he saw, whose minds he learned of,
many the pains he suffered in his spirit on the wide sea,
struggling for his own life and the homecoming of his companions.

The word is from the Latin invocatio, meaning "to summon" or " to call upon." (Br invocation)

===== Jesus prayer =====

Eastern Christianity, a mental **invocation** of the name of Jesus Christ, considered most efficacious when repeated continuously. The most widely accepted form of the prayer is "Lord Jesus Christ, Son of God, have mercy on me." It reflects the biblical idea that the name of God is sacred and that its **invocation** implies a direct meeting with the divine.

===== Obaku =====

Chinese Huang-po, one of the three Zen sects in Japan, founded in 1654 by the Chinese priest Yin-yüan (Japanese Ingen); it continues to preserve elements of the Chinese tradition in its architecture, religious ceremonies, and teachings. Although the methods of achieving sudden insight as developed by the Rinzai sect are practiced by Ōbaku monks, **invocation** of the name of the Buddha Amida (nembutsu) is also used. The head temple of the sect is the Mampuku-ji in Kyōto.［invocation ＝ 称名？］

===== Buddhism =====

The basic doctrines of the Pure Land sects differ considerably from the doctrines of the early Buddhists. The Pure Land's leaders have generally taught that a person reaches salvation from this Earth not by individual effort or the accumulation of merit but through faith in the grace of the Buddha Amitābha. The main practice of those who follow the Pure Land teachings is not the learning of the texts nor meditation on the Buddha but rather the constant **invocation** of the name Amitābha. This practice, based on the 18th vow of Dharmākara, the future Amitābha, is called *nien-fo* in Chinese and ***nembutsu*** in Japanese. Furthermore, in Pure Land Buddhism, the attainment of nirvana is not the primary goal; it is rather to become reborn in the Pure Land of Amitābha.

These doctrines and the practice of **invoking** the name Amitābha gained great popularity in China and Japan, where it was believed that the world had reached a degenerate period in which the Buddhist doctrines were no longer clear and humans no longer possessed the purity of heart or determination to attain salvation by self-endeavour. Therefore, all people of every section of society could only hope to be saved by the grace of Amitābha. As the Pure Land sect spread from India to China and then to Japan, this doctrine of grace became more and more radical until individual actions were said to play no part in the attainment of salvation.

…

One of Hōnen's disciples, Shinran, who was exiled at the same time, was the founder of a more radical sect named the True Pure Land sect (Jōdo Shinshū, or Shin). Shinran married, with Hōnen's consent, proving that one need not be a monk to attain the Pure Land; and he popularized his doctrines by preaching in Japanese villages. In his teachings he rejected all sutras except the *Pure Land Sutra* and rejected the vows of Dharmākara in the *Pure Land Sutra* that stress individual merit. Basing his doctrines on the 18th vow, Shinran discouraged any attempt to accumulate merit, for he felt that this stood in the way of absolute faith and dependence on Amida. Furthermore, he rejected Hōnen's practice of continual **invocation** of Amida, believing that the faithful need only say the *nembutsu* once in order to attain salvation. Any repetition after this *nembutsu* must be seen as praise of Amida and not as bringing merit or affecting one's salvation. Thus, with Shinran, the doctrine of grace gained total ascendancy. A third Pure Land sect grew up around the itinerant teacher Ippen. He traveled throughout Japan, advocating the chanting of Amida's name at set intervals throughout the day; hence, his school was called the Ji ("Times") sect, or Jishū.

All Souls festival
During the Japanese festival of Bon, two altars are constructed, one to make offerings to the spirits of dead ancestors and the other to the souls of those dead who have no peace. Odorinembutsu (the chanting of **invocation**s accompanied by dancing and singing) and **invocation**s to Amida are features of the Bon celebrations.

付録 1　職官名英訳参照英文集

===== Anatolian religion =====

Gods and men
The gods were imagined to have their own lives, though also needing the service of their worshipers, who in turn were dependent on the gods for their well-being. They lived in their temples, where they had to be fed, clothed, washed, and entertained. Part of their time, however, might be spent in heaven or in roaming the sea or the mountains. They might withdraw in anger and so cause life on Earth to wither and cease. <u>One of the most characteristic rituals of the Hittites was the **invocation** by which a god who had absented himself was induced to return and attend to his duties by a combination of prayer and magic.</u> ヒッタイト人の最も特徴的なリチュアルに invocation がある。invocation とは，それによって，自分たちから離れ留守をしていた神が自分たちのところへ戻ってくるよう促し，祈祷と魔術の組み合わせることで神に神本来の仕事に就かせようとすることである。

The relation between man and god resembled that between servant and master. "If a servant has committed an offence and confesses his guilt before his master, his master may do with him whatever he pleases; but because he has confessed his guilt . . . his master's spirit is appeased and he will not call that servant to account." Confession and expiation form the main theme of the extant royal prayers.

**Divination**
**Divination**, through which the cause of divine displeasure was ascertained, was mainly of three kinds: augury (**divination** by flight of birds), haruspicy (**divination** by examining the entrails of sacrificial animals), and an enigmatic procedure using tokens with symbolic names, arts said to be practiced respectively by the "bird-watcher," the seer, and the "old woman." The omens, as interpreted by these experts, were either favourable or unfavourable and would give a yes or no answer according to the sense of the question put to them. In this way, by a lengthy process of elimination, it was possible to determine the precise offence that required expiation. Haruspicy was a science inherited by the Hittites from the Babylonian seers. The other two methods of **divination** seem to have been indigenous to Asia Minor.

===== witchcraft =====

the exercise or **invocation** of alleged supernatural powers to control people or events, practices typically involving sorcery or magic. Although defined differently in disparate historical and cultural contexts, witchcraft has often been seen, especially in the West, as the work of crones who meet secretly at night, indulge in cannibalism and orgiastic rites with the Devil, and perform black magic.

===== Soka-gakkai =====

In common with other Nichiren movements (*see* Nichiren Buddhism), Sōka-gakkai places great emphasis on the benefits effected by the chanting of the phrase *namu Myōhō renge kyō* ("Salutation to the *Lotus Sūtra*"), which is an **invocation** of its chief scripture, the *Lotus Sūtra*.

===== myth =====

Throughout the world music is played at religious ceremonies to increase the efficacy and appeal of prayers, hymns, and **invocation**s to divinities. The power of music to charm the gods is movingly expressed in the Greek story of Orpheus. This mythical figure goes to the underworld to try to have his dead wife, Eurydice, restored to life. By means of his lyre playing and singing he is able to win over even the god of death, so that Eurydice is allowed to leave the underworld. The continuing potency of the myth (including its tragic conclusion—Orpheus is forbidden to look back at his wife but does so and thus loses her again) is shown by the fact that it has been retold in Europe by numerous composers of opera since the early 17th century.

===== arts, East Asian =====

Amidism

An expression of faith in the Amida Buddha through the **invocation** of his name in the *nembutsu* prayer was the single requirement for salvation. Iconography served mainly as a reminder of the coming consolations rather than as the tool for a meditative journey to enlightenment.

===== Hinduism =====

Bhakti movements
...
Much has been said about the synthesis of Hinduism and Islām in the period of Muslim dominance, ...

What synthesis did take place came from the Muslims, most of whom were Indian by blood. In Hindi, Bengali, Gujarati, Punjabi, and Marathi there is much poetic literature, written by Muslims and commencing with the Islāmic **invocation** of Allāh, which nevertheless betrays strong Hindu influence.

⟨NSOED⟩ betray, 1 Show incidentally; constitute evidence or a symptom of.
⟨LgAm⟩ 1. to show the true condition, origin etc. of something, especially when this is not easily noticed:   2. The documents betray a deep anti-Semitism in the country.

⇒ invoke

付録1　職官名英訳参照英文集

● invoke

===== Pure Land Buddhism =====

Chinese (Wade–Giles romanization) Ch'ing-t'u, Pinyin Qingtu, Japanese Jōdo, devotional cult of the Buddha Amitābha ("the Buddha of Infinite Light"). Known in China as O-mi-t'o-fo and in Japan as Amida, it is one of the most popular forms of Mahāyāna Buddhism in eastern Asia today. Pure Land schools believe that rebirth in Amitābha's Western Paradise, Sukhāvatī (known as the Pure Land, or Pure Realm), is ensured all those who **invoke** Amitābha's name with sincere devotion (nembutsu, referring to the Japanese formula of **invocation**, namu Amida Butsu).

In the larger Pure Land sutra, Buddha tells the story of Amitābha: many eons ago, as a monk, he learned from the 81st Buddha about the glories of innumerable Buddha Lands, whereupon he vowed to create his own Buddha Land (which he is now doing), making it 81 times more excellent than all the others and drawing into it all creatures who **invoked** his name. According to this sutra, in addition to calling upon Amitābha, one needs to accumulate merit and concentrate on Enlightenment. In the later, smaller Pure Land sutra, however, the Blessed Land is not a reward for good works but is accessible to anyone who **invokes** Amitābha at the hour of death.

⇒ invocation

● judicial officer
⇒ magistrate

● labour 労役

===== crime and punishment =====

Other penalties

The concept of reparation has gained in popularity in a number of jurisdictions. Under this method, the offender makes good the damage he has done through his crime, not by paying money but by providing services to the victim directly or indirectly through the community. In England this takes the form of the community service order, under which the court is empowered to order anyone who is convicted of an offense that could be punished with imprisonment to perform up to 240 hours of unpaid work for the community, usually over a period of not more than 12 months. The consent of the offender is necessary before the court can make such an order, to avoid allegations that it amounts to **forced labour**. ... in some cases it may involve **heavy physical labour**, but in others it may require such work as the provision of help to handicapped people.

211

China
The state is keenly interested in changes in the offender's thinking during imprisonment. Thus, reform through **labour** and political study generally accompanies imprisonment for criminal offenses.

===== Chinese civil service =====
Under the Ming dynasty (1368–1644), the civil-service system reached its final form, and the succeeding Qing dynasty (1644–1911/12) copied the Ming system virtually intact. During this period no man was allowed to serve in his home district, and officials were rotated in their jobs every three years. The recruitment exam was divided into three stages: the *xiucai* ("cultivated talent"), or bachelor's degree, held on the local-prefecture level; the *juren* ("recommended man"), given at the prefectural capital; and the *jinshi*, held at Beijing. Although only the passage of the *jinshi* made one eligible for high office, passage of the other degrees gave one certain privileges, such as exemption from **labour service** and corporal **punishment**, government stipends, and admission to upper-gentry status (*juren*). 徭役？

> labour service = 労働奉仕？
> corporal punishment = 体刑（法律用語対訳集）
> stipend, 1 A soldier's pay. Now *rare* or *obs*. LME.   2 A salary or fixed regular sum paid for the services of a teacher, public official, or (esp.) a minister of religion. LME. (NSOED)

===== statute labour =====
unpaid work on public projects that is required by law. Under the Roman Empire, certain classes of the population owed personal services to the state or to private proprietors—for example, **labour** in lieu of taxes for the upkeep of roads, bridges, and dikes; unpaid **labour** by coloni (tenant farmers) and freedmen on the estates of landed proprietors; and **labour** requisitioned for the maintenance of the postal systems of various regions. The feudal system of corvée—regular work that vassals owed their lord—developed from this Roman tradition. (The term corvée, meaning contribution, is now often used synonymously with statute **labour**.)［statute labour = 徭役？］

Similar **labour** obligations have existed in other parts of the world. In Japan the yō system of imposing **compulsory labour** on the farmers was incorporated in the tax system in the 7th century. The Egyptians used the corvée for centuries to obtain **labour** to remove the mud left at the bottom of the canals by the rising of the Nile River. In various times and places the corvée has been used when money payment did not provide sufficient **labour**

付録1　職官名英訳参照英文集

for public projects. In wartime the corvée was sometimes used to augment regular troops in auxiliary capacities.

The corvée differs from **forced labour** in being a general and periodic short-term obligation; **forced labour** is usually prescribed for a long or indefinite period as a method of punishment or of discrimination.

===== Mesopotamia, history of =====

The penal laws of the time were generally more severe in Assyria than in other countries of the East. The death penalty was not uncommon. In less serious cases the penalty was forced **labour** after flogging.

===== Tasmania =====

International whalers made use of Hobart's superb harbour; it became a major port for whaling ships. **Convict labour** assisted in all this and in constructing public works and handsome buildings, both urban and rural.

〈法律用語対訳集〉convicted prisoner 受刑者; convict; prisoner; inmate 既決囚。
〈Black's Law Dic.〉forced labour, Int'l law. Work exacted from a person under threat of penalty; work for which a person has not offered himself or herself voluntarily. • Under the U.N. Convention on Civil and Political Rights (article 8), exemptions from this definition include (1) penalties imposed by a court, (2) compulsory military service, (3) action taken in an emergency, (4) normal civil obligations, and (5) minor communal services. -- Also termed compulsory labour.

● land tax 年貢

===== Japan =====
The Hideyoshi regime

At the core of Hideyoshi's unification policy was its firm establishment in the principle of the separation between warriors and peasants. ... Moreover, this kokudaka now came within the landlord's grasp in every village, and land taxes were levied on the village as a unit. In addition to this definition of the rights held by the farming population, the kokudaka system also applied to the landholdings of the daimyo for distribution among their retainers. In place of previous **land taxes (nengu)** assessed in money as so many hundred or ten thousand kan of silver, an assessment of kokudaka was made as so many hundred or ten thousand koku of rice. A koku represented the amount of rice consumed by one person in one year (about five bushels); the amount also was used as a standard on which military services were levied in proportion.

● lead motorcycle
===== lead motorcycle marathon race, Web =====
- NEW YORK CITY MARATHON; Masterful Is Word For Campbell's Run
By GERALD ESKENAZI
Published: Monday, November 5, 1990
But a few moments later, the police officer on the lead motorcycle fell while the entourage was in the Brooklyn-Battery Tunnel. The first bus stopped short to avoid the police officer, causing a chain-reaction collision among several other buses.
http://www.nytimes.com/1990/11/05/sports/new-york-city-marathon-masterful-is-word-for-campbell-s-run.html
- Then the lead motor cycle turned onto to North Quincy and the runners had about one-sixth of a mile of firmly downhill to the finish.
http://www.runwashington.com/news/2206/314/Acumen-Solutions-Race-for-a-Cause-8K.htm

● magistrate
⟨NSOED⟩ 1 The office or dignity of a **magistrate**. 2 gen. A civil officer administering the law, a member of the executive government. 3 spec. A person conducting a court of summary jurisdiction (see **magistrate**s・court below); a justice of the peace; (freq. w. specifying wd) a salaried official carrying out such duties. In pl. also, the provost and councillors of a Scottish burgh, as forming a court for police jurisdiction and the granting of licences. L17.
⟨Black's Law Dic.⟩ accusation, 1. A formal charge of criminal wrongdoing. • The accusation is usu. presented to a court or **magistrate** having jurisdiction to inquire into the alleged crime.

奉行 ⇒ Tokugawa bakufu

===== triumph =====
The **magistrate**s and members of the Senate came first in the processions followed by musicians, the sacrificial animals, the spoils of war, and the captured prisoners in chains.

===== Spotlights The Romans, OUP =====
The consuls were the most senior **magistrate**s. (Spotlights The Romans, OUP, p. 11)

===== Oxford Dic. of Law =====
A justice of the peace sitting in a **magistrate** court. Most **magistrate**s are lay persons and have no formal legal qualification: they receive no payment for their services but give their time vountarily. There are also, however, district judges (**magistrate**s' court) (formerly

214

付録1 職官名英訳参照英文集

called stipendiary **magistrate**s) in London and other major cities.

[justice of the peace = A person holding a commission from the Crown to Exercise certain judicial functions for a particular commission area. JPs are appointed on behalf of and in the name of the Queen by the Lord Chancellor and may by removed from office in the same way. ...(Oxford Dic. of Law)]

===== Black's Law Dic. ------
A local judicial officer having jurisdiction over minor criminal offenses and minor civil disputes, and authority to perform routine civil functions (such as administering oaths and performing marriage ceremonies). Abbr. J.P.
]

===== Black's Law Dic. =====
1. The highest-ranking official in a government, such as the king in a monarchy, the president in a republic, or the governor in a state. -- Also termed *chief **magistrate***; *first **magistrate***. 2. A local official who possesses whatever power is specified in the appointment or sateutory grant of authority. 3. A judicial officer with strictly limited jurisdiction and authority, often on the local level and often restricted to criminal cases. Cf. JUSTICE OF THE PEACE.[治安判事= **magistrate**; justice of the peace (法律用語対訳集)]

committing **magistrate**. A judicial officer who conducts preliminary criminal hearings and may order that a defendant be released for lack of evidence, sent to jail to await trial, or released on bail. See examining court under COURT.

district-court **magistrate**. In some states, a quasi-judicial officer given the power to set bail, accept bond, accept guilty pleas, impose sentences for traffic violations and similar offenses, and conduct informal hearings on civil infractions. [Cases: Justices of the Peace 31. C.J.S. Justices of the Peace §§ 26, 47.]

United States **Magistrate** Judge. A federal judicial officer who hears civil and criminal pretrial matters and who may conduct civil trials or criminal misdemeanor trials. 28 USCA §§ 631-639. -- Also termed federal **magistrate**; (before 1990) United States **Magistrate**. -- Sometimes also termed parajudge. [Cases: United States **Magistrate**s 11-12. C.J.S. United States Commissioners §§ 2-7, 13-15.]

investigating **magistrate**. A quasi-judicial officer responsible for examining and sometimes ruling on certain aspects of a criminal proceeding before it comes before a judge.

metropolitan stipendiary **magistrate** (stI-pen-dee-er-ee). English law. A stipendiary **magistrate** with jurisdiction in inner London areas. • Under the Access to Justice Act 1999, these **magistrate**s have been renamed district judges (**magistrate**s' courts). See stipendiary **magistrate**.

stipendiary **magistrate** (stI-pen-dee-er-ee). English law. A salaried **magistrate** that performs either in the place of or along with Justices of the Peace, and is appointed from barristers and solicitors of seven years' standing.

● marshal

===== **marshal** =====

also called Field **Marshal**, in some past and present armies, including those of Britain, France, Germany, Russia or the Soviet Union, and China, the highest ranking officer. The rank evolved from the title of *marescalci* (**masters of the horse**) of the early Frankish kings. The importance of cavalry in medieval warfare led to the **marshal**ship being associated with a command position; this rank came to include the duties of keeping order at court and in camp and of deciding questions of chivalry. As a military leader the **marshal** was originally subordinate to the constable in the various states of western Europe. By the 13th century, however, the **marshal** was rapidly coming to prominence as a commander of the royal forces and a great officer of state.

⟨NSOED⟩ marshal

1 A person who tends horses; a smith; esp. a person who treats diseases of horses, a farrier. ME 胞 18.
2 One of the chief functionaries of a royal household or court (in the middle ages usually entrusted with the military affairs of the monarch); a high officer of State. Formerly *spec.* (now *Hist.*) = Earl Marshal s.v. EARL. ME.
3 a Orig., any senior army officer; a commander, a general. Later (esp. in **marshal** of the field, **marshal** of the camp), a (senior) officer of a definite rank, which varied according to period and country. Now obs. exc. in Field Marshal s.v. FIELD n. & a. ME. b An officer of the highest rank in any of various armies. ME.
4 An officer of a court of law responsible for the custody of prisoners and for the keeping of order, and frequently entrusted with the keeping of a prison. Also Marshal of the Exchequer, Marshal of the King's Bench, Marshal of the Queen's Bench. obs. exc. *Hist.* ME.b An official (now usually a barrister) who accompanies a judge on circuit to act as secretary and personal assistant. Also judge's **marshal**. M19.
5 A person responsible for arranging ceremonies or controlling people at a race, banquet, etc. ME.b In full City **marshal**. An officer of the corporation of the City of London. M17.

付録1 職官名英訳参照英文集

6 a Orig., an official with certain police duties, or in charge of the infliction of punishment. Now (US), a police officer or sheriff with responsibility for a designated area; the administrative head of a police or fire department. L16. b A legal officer in each judicial district responsible for executing court precepts. US. L18.
7 The chief of the proctors・attendants at Oxford University; either of two officials appointed by the Vice-Chancellor of Cambridge University to act as his messengers, to summon meetings, etc. E19.

⇒ butler (Europe, history of: The royal household); (United Kingdom, history of: Government and justice)
⇒ master of horse
⇒ steward
⇒ 軍組織

● master
===== Scientific American Triumph of Discovery, p. 187 =====
The Theory of Gravity
When he [Isaac Newton] produced his seminal treatise, the *Mathematical Principles of Natural Philosophy*, he was rewarded by being appointed **Master** of the Royal Mint, but he had already transformed gravity from a mythological fancy into a reality of nature.

===== lord steward =====
**lord steward**, also called Lord Steward Of the Household, in England, an official of the royal household, whose duties were originally domestic and who was known as the "chief steward" of the household. The office was of considerable **political importance** under the Tudors and Stuarts, and it carried cabinet rank during the 18th century. In 1924 it ceased to be a political appointment and since then it has been filled at the discretion of the sovereign. In theory the lord steward is responsible for **the day-to-day management and financial affairs** of the royal household; in practice these functions are carried out by the master of the household. Thus, the duties of the lord steward are now **purely ceremonial**, though he is still the **first dignitary** of the court and is always a peer and a privy councillor.
In theory the lord steward is responsible for the day-to-day management and financial affairs of the royal household; in practice these functions are carried out by the **master of the household**.

===== Douglass, Frederick, Narrative (excerpt), Gr =====
By far the larger part of the slaves know as little of their ages as horses know of theirs, and it is the wish of most **master**s within my knowledge to keep their slaves thus ignorant.

===== ballet =====
glossary

ballet **master**/mistress Before the word choreographer was used in its contemporary sense, the ballet **master** was responsible for arranging ballets. Today the term more usually denotes the person who rehearses ballets created by someone else and also performs certain administrative duties such as drawing up rehearsal schedules; casting of minor roles is often the province of the ballet **master**.

===== Japanese art and architecture =====

The works of the 16th-century **master** Sesson, as exemplified in his boldly painted Hawk on a Pine Tree (Tokyo National Museum), presage trends toward more martial styles favored by the warring daimyos (great lords) of the succeeding Momoyama period.

===== Zen Buddhism =====

Zen's roots may be traced to India, but it was in East Asia that the movement became distinct and flourished. Like other Chinese Buddhist sects, Chan first established itself as a lineage of **master**s emphasizing the teachings of a particular text, in this case the Lankavatara Sutra. Bodhidharma, the first Chan patriarch in China, who is said to have arrived there from India · c.470, was a **master** of this text. He also emphasized the practice of contemplative sitting, and legend has it that he himself spent nine years in meditation facing a wall.

With the importance of lineages, Chan stressed the **master**-disciple relationship, and Bodhidharma was followed by a series of patriarchs, each of whom received the dharma (religious truth) directly from his predecessor and teacher.

===== Islam =====

Sufism is organized in the form of numerous orders or brotherhoods, all of which trace their origins to the same source but which differ on various points of doctrine and on their method of reaching the Divine Reality. The most important orders are the Chishtiyya (South Asia), the Nakshbandiyya (Central Asia, Turkey, Syria, Iran), the Nimataliyya (Iran), the Qadiriyya (West Africa, Middle East, South Asia), and the Shadhiliyya (North Africa). A Sufi order governs the practice of Sufism and is often centered in a hospice (khanaqa). It organizes Sufi members into a hierarchy, at the head of which is the Sufi **master** (shaikh, pir, or murshid). The hierarchy is symbolic of the Sufi's spiritual journey from novice to **master**. The community's organization promotes concentration, learning, and character. To join the Sufi order, a novice must undergo initiation, declare his commitment to the spiritual path, and submit his soul to the guidance of the Sufi **master**, who leads the novice to the realization of Absolute Truth, which is God.

付録 1　職官名英訳参照英文集

===== Tokugawa Ieyasu =====
This triumph left Ieyasu the undisputed **master of Japan**, ...［国家の頭］

===== United Kingdom, history of =====
He [Charles II] was now fully **master of his state**--financially independent of Parliament ...［国家の頭］

⇒ marshal
⇒ 宮内庁

● master of horse［イギリス，ローマは master of the horse, フランスは master of horse の傾向］

===== ancient Rome: The dictatorship =====
He [dictator] was also termed the **master** of the army (*magister populi*), and he appointed a **subordinate** cavalry commander, the **master** of **horse** (*magister equitum*).

===== Somerset, Charles Seymour [ 6th duke of, born August 12, 1662] =====
Having befriended Princess Anne in 1692, he became a great favourite with her after her accession to the throne, receiving the post of **master of the horse** in 1702.

===== Antony, Mark =====
Caesar left him in charge of Italy, a post he again occupied in 48–47 as **Master of the Horse** (the dictator's assistant) after the decisive battle at ...

===== Elizabeth: The woman ruler in a patriarchal world =====
Elizabeth was courted by English suitors as well, most assiduously by her principal favourite, Robert Dudley, Earl of Leicester. As **master of the horse** and a member of the Privy Council, Leicester was constantly in attendance on the queen, ...

===== Caulaincourt, Armand(-Augustin-Louis) =====
marquis de [born Dec. 9, 1773, Caulaincourt, Fr.] French general, diplomat, and ultimately foreign minister under Napoleon. As the Emperor's loyal **master of horse** from 1804, Caulaincourt was at Napoleon's side in his great battles, and his Mémoires provide an important source for the period 1812 to 1814.

⇒ marshal

● mausoleum

===== mausoleum =====

large and impressive sepulchral monument. The word is derived from Mausolus, ruler of Caria, in whose memory his widow Artemisia raised a splendid tomb at Halicarnassus c. 353–c. 350 BC. Some remains of this monument are now in the British Museum. Probably the most ambitious **mausoleum** is the famous white marble Tāj Mahal at Āgra, in India, built by the Mughal emperor Shāh Jahān for his favourite wife, who died in 1631. He originally intended to build another in black marble, opposite the Tāj Mahal, but died before work could begin. Other notable examples include the **mausoleum** called Hadrian's Tomb, now the Castel Sant'Angelo, Rome; that of Frederick William III and Queen Louisa of Mecklenburg-Strelitz at Charlottenburg, near Berlin; of Napoleon III at Farnborough, Hampshire, Eng.; and of Vladimir Lenin at Moscow.

===== architecture =====

Funerary art
... Monumental tombs have been produced in ancient Egypt (pyramids), Hellenistic Greece (tomb of Mausolus at Halicarnassus, which is the source of the word **mausoleum**), ancient Rome (tomb of Hadrian), Renaissance Europe (Michelangelo's Medici Chapel, Florence), and Asia (Tāj Mahal, Āgra, Uttar Pradesh, India). Modern tomb design has lost vitality, though it remains as elabourate (Monument to Victor Emmanuel II, Rome) or as meaningful in terms of power (Lenin **Mausoleum**, Moscow) as before.

===== Nikko =====

Since the 17th century, however, the city has been dominated by the great Tōshō Shrine, which contains the **mausoleum** of Tokugawa Ieyasu, the first Tokugawa shogun. Also important is the Daiyuin **mausoleum**, dedicated to Tokugawa Iemitsu, the third Tokugawa shogun, who died in 1651.

⟨NSOED⟩ mausoleum
1 The magnificent tomb of Mausolus, King of Caria, erected in the 4th cent. BC at Halicarnassus by his queen Artemisia.   2 *gen.* A large and stately place of burial.

⟨RH⟩ mausoleum, 1. a stately and magnificent tomb.   2. a burial place for the bodies or remains of many individuals, often of a single family, usually in the form of a small building.   3. a large, gloomy, depressing building, room, or the like.   4. (cap.) the tomb erected at Halicarnassus in Asia Minor in 350?B.C.Cf. Seven Wonders of the World. [1375·425; late ME < L < Gk Mausoleîn the tomb of Mausolus, king of Caria]

● military unit
===== army military organization =====

付録 1 職官名英訳参照英文集

military **unit**
also called **Unit**, a group having a prescribed size and a specific combat or support role within a larger military organization. The chief military **unit**s in the ancient classical world were the phalanx (q.v.) of the Greeks and the legion (q.v.) of the Romans. The **unit**s used in modern armies have their origins in the 16th–18th centuries, when professional armies reemerged in Europe after the end of the Middle Ages. The basic **unit**s of the **company**, **battalion**, **brigade**, and **division** have been retained since then.

Armies, navies, and air forces are organized hierarchically into progressively smaller units commanded by officers of progressively lower rank. The prototypical units are those of the army. The smallest unit in an army is the squad, which contains 7 to 14 soldiers and is led by a sergeant. (A slightly larger unit is a **section**, which consists of 10 to 40 soldiers but is usually used only within headquarters or support organizations.) Three or four squads make up a platoon (q.v.), which has 20 to 50 soldiers and is commanded by a lieutenant. Two or more platoons make up a **company** (q.v.), which has 100 to 250 soldiers and is commanded by a captain or a major. The function of administration is introduced at this level, in the form of a headquarters platoon administered by a sergeant and containing supply, maintenance, or other sections.

Two or more companies make up a **battalion** (q.v.), which has 400 to 1,200 troops and is commanded by a lieutenant colonel. The **battalion** is the smallest unit to have a staff of officers (in charge of personnel, operations, intelligence, and logistics) to assist the commander. Several **battalion**s form a **brigade**, which has 2,000 to 8,000 troops and is commanded by a brigadier general or a colonel. (The term regiment [q.v.] can signify either a **battalion** or a **brigade** in different countries' armies.) A **brigade** is the smallest unit to integrate different types of combat and support units into a functional organization. A combat **brigade**, for example, usually has infantry, armour, artillery, and reconnaissance units.

Two or more **brigade**s, along with various specialized **battalion**s, make up a **division** (q.v.), which has 7,000 to 22,000 troops and is commanded by a major general. A **division** contains all the arms and services needed for the independent conduct of military operations. Two to seven **division**s and various support units make up an army corps, or a corps, which has 50,000 to 300,000 troops and is commanded by a lieutenant general. The army corps is the largest regular army formation, though in wartime two or more corps may be combined to form a field army (commanded by a general), and field armies in turn may be combined to form an army group.

Naval units follow somewhat more flexible organizational guidelines. Administratively, several ships of the same type (e.g., destroyers) are organized into a squadron. Several squadrons in turn form a flotilla, several of which in turn form a fleet. For operations, however, many navies organize their vessels into task units (3–5 ships), task or battle groups (4–10 ships), task forces (2–5 task groups), and fleets (several task forces).

The basic fighting unit in an air force is the squadron, which consists of several aircraft of the same type—e.g., fighters, and often of the same model—e.g., F-16s. Three to six flying squadrons and their support squadrons make up a wing. (An intermediate unit between the squadron and the wing is the air group or group, which consists of two to four squadrons.) Several wings are sometimes combined to form an air **division** or an air force.

● mortuary
〈NSOED〉 mortuary, 2 A funeral.   3 A burial place, a sepulchre.   4 A place where dead bodies are kept for a time, either for purposes of examination or pending burial or cremation.

===== mortuary temple =====
in ancient Egypt, place of worship of a deceased king and the depository for food and objects offered to the dead mon*arch*. In the Old and Middle Kingdoms (c. 2575–c. 2130 BC; and 1938–c. 1600? BC) the **mortuary temple** usually adjoined the pyramid and had an open, pillared court, storerooms, five elongated shrines, and a chapel containing a false door and an offering table. In the chapel, priests performed the daily funerary rites and presented the offerings to the dead king's ka (protective spirit). In the New Kingdom (1539–1075 BC) the kings were buried in **rock-cut tombs**, but separate **mortuary temples** continued to be built nearby. All were provided with a staff of priests and assured of supplies through endowments of estates and lands to ensure religious services and offerings in perpetuity.［墓窟。葬祭殿。ともに平凡社国民百科エジプト 411］

● music
1. 楽, 魯に帰ると魯の〜は正され returned to Lu from Wei, the **music** was reformed（史 121）
2. 礼楽を習って絃歌の声が絶えない practising rites and **music**, and never allowing the sound of strings and voices to die out（史 121）
3. 礼楽を好む国柄 the state of Lu loves rites and **music** so（史 121）
4. 楽, 民を導くに礼をもってし, これを化するに〜をもってす the people are to be guided by rites and led to the practice of virtue through **music**（史 121）
5. 楽, 礼もすたれ〜も崩れ, 現今は at the present time rites have fallen into disuse and **music** has declined（史 121）
6. Historical development / ... the tong gu (t'ung ku) ("metal drum"), a **ritual** instrument

of southeast Asia that was introduced to China during the Han dynasty's military
expeditions (Confucianism, Gr)

● musician［語感が軽薄か］

===== arts, East Asian =====

Painting and related arts
Surviving Han painting includes chiefly tomb paintings and painted objects in clay and
lacquer, ... and at Liao-yang in Liaoning, where the themes include a feasting scene,
**musicians**, jugglers, chariots, and horsemen.

Painting
Among the first named painting masters, Ts'ao Pu-hsing and Tai K'uei painted chiefly
Buddhist and Taoist subjects. Tai K'uei was noted as a poet, painter, and **musician** and
was one of the first to establish the tradition of scholarly amateur painting (wen-jen hua).

Ceramics
Tomb figurines were produced in such enormous quantities that ... Among the human
figures are servants and actors, female dancers, and **musicians** of exquisite grace. ... There
are also many figurines of Central Asian grooms and Semitic merchants, whose deep-set
eyes and jutting noses are caricatured. Of the camels and horses, the most remarkable are
glazed camels bearing on their backs a group of four or five singers and **musicians**.

Han dynasty: musical events and foreign influences
Modern information on all these elements of music has suffered because of the destruction
of many books and musical instruments under the order of Shih Huang-ti, emperor of the
Ch'in dynasty. Yet there are several survivals from the Han dynasty that do give some
insight into how the musical events took place. In the court and the Confucian temples
there were two basic musical divisions: banquet music (yen-yüeh) and **ritual music**
(ya-yüeh). Dances in the Confucian rituals were divided into military (wu-wu) and civil
(wen-wu) forms. The ensembles of **musicians** and dancers could be quite large, and
ancient listings of their content were often printed in formation patterns in a manner
analogous in principle to those of football marching bands in America today.

T'ang dynasty
Thriving of foreign styles
In addition to all the commercial musical enterprises of the T'ang dynasty period, there was
another equally extensive system under government supervision. The T'ang emperor
Hsüan-tsung seemed particularly keen on music and took full advantage of the various
musical "tributes" or "captives" sent to him by all the nations of Asia. This plethora of

sounds was further enriched by the special area in Ch'ang-an called the Pear Garden (Li-yüan), in which hundreds of additional **musicians** and dancers were trained and in which the emperor himself was most active.

===== Taoism =====

Influence
Taoism and Chinese culture
Taoist contributions to Chinese science
The Taoist secret of efficacy is to follow the nature of things; this does not imply scientific experimentation but rather a sensitivity and skill obtained by "minute concentration on the Tao running through natural objects of all kinds." This knowledge and skill cannot be handed down but is that which the men of old took with them when they died (Chuang-tzu). The image for it is the skill of the artisan admired by the Taoists in their numerous parables on wheelwrights, meatcutters, sword makers, carvers, animal tamers, and **musicians**.

Early eclectic contributions
The idea of Yin and Yang
First conceived by **musicians**, astronomers, or diviners and then propagated by a school that came to be named after them, Yin and Yang became the common stock of all Chinese philosophy.

===== Handel, George Frideric =====
In England, Handel was accorded the status of a classic composer even in his own lifetime, and he is perhaps unique among **musicians** in never having suffered any diminution of his reputation there since.

===== Mendelssohn, Felix =====
In 1821 Mendelssohn was taken to Weimar to meet J.W. von Goethe, for whom he played works of J.S. Bach and Mozart and to whom he dedicated his Piano Quartet No. 3. in B Minor (1825). A remarkable friendship developed between the aging poet and the 12-year-old **musician**.

- offer = priesthood; Day of Atonement; Polynesian culture; master of ceremonies (jp hand 皇室)
attend = British Museum Dic. of Ancient Egypt 228 priest

- of the

付録 1　職官名英訳参照英文集

| the ありの例 | the なしの例 |
|---|---|
| secretaries of the chancellor | 謁者令＝master of guests（漢 74） |
| secretary of the censorate | 典客＝director of guests（史 9.9.10.11.118） |
| director of rectitude in the office of the chancellor | 典属国＝director of dependent states（漢 54.63.65.68） |
| officials of the middle two thousand picul class | 大行令＝chief of grand messengers（史 11） |
| aide of the imperial secretary | |
| nine lower offices of the government | |
| officials of the middle two thousand picul class | |
| chief commandant of the imperial carriage | |
| ほか多数 | |

● palace garden

===== Buckingham Palace =====

By order of George IV, John Nash initiated the conversion of the house into a **palace** in the 1820s. Nash also reshaped the Buckingham **Palace Garden**s and designed the Marble Arch entryway, which was later removed (1851) to the northeast corner of Hyde **Park**.
...
Leading northeast from the **palace** and the Queen Victoria Memorial, the straight avenue of the Mall divides St. James's **Park** from Green **Park**, skirts the grounds of St. James's **Palace**, and eventually reaches the Admiralty Arch, gateway to Charing Cross.

===== Hui Tsung =====

Politically, Hui Tsung's reign was fatal to the Northern Sung dynasty. He promoted Taoism at the court and sought comfort and amusement in the arts, in amorous affairs, and in the construction of an extravagant new **palace garden**. He busied himself with requisitioning colourful stones, rare plants, and exotic pets for this **garden** while leaving the administration of the state to others.

===== Versailles =====

The first scenes of the French Revolution were also enacted at the **palace**, whose **garden**s, the masterpiece of André Le Nôtre, have become part of the national heritage of France and one of the most visited historic sites in Europe.

===== Fontainebleau =====

Famed craftsmen, including the Italian painter Francesco Primaticcio and the Italian sculptor Benvenuto Cellini, were called to the court to further embellish the **palace**; these artists, collectively referred to as the School of Fontainebleau, blended Italian and French styles. Henry II (reigned 1547–59), Catherine de Médicis (1519–89), and Henry IV (reigned 1589–1610) enlarged the **palace**. The spacious **garden**s were redesigned by André Le Nôtre, the 17th-century French landscape architect, during the reign of Louis XIV.

===== Paris =====

Catherine de Médicis began to build the Tuileries **Palace**, the **garden**s of which became a meeting place for elegant society.

===== Williamsburg =====

The exhibition buildings—which include the Capitol, Governor's **Palace** and **Garden**s, Public Gaol, and Raleigh Tavern—are furnished as they were in the 18th century, and the entire area is landscaped as it was in colonial times.

===== Bonn =====

The former Electoral **Palace** (now the Rhenish Friedrich Wilhelm University of Bonn [founded 1786]) and the Poppelsdorf **Palace**, with its botanical **garden**s, along with the city's beautiful avenues and **park**s are reminders of the electoral and archiepiscopal capital.

===== Liechtenstein =====

Year in Review 2004

Liechtenstein princely family, which fully financed the ユーロ 23 million (about $27.8 million) renovations of the museum's Baroque **Garden Palace**.

===== Prague =====

Outstanding architects created magnificent **palace**s and **garden**s, and churches in the Prague version of the Baroque style sprang up throughout the city.

===== Copenhagen =====

The old quarter of Christianshavn is on the harbour to the south. It contains the 17th-century Church of Our Saviour. The western quarter contains the Frederiksberg **Park**, with its **palace** and a zoological **garden**.

===== Leonardo da Vinci =====

Finally, there was his big project for the **palace** and **garden** of Romorantin in France (1517–19).

付録 1　職官名英訳参照英文集

===== Athens =====
Below the well-sited but very plain **palace**, a large **garden** square, Síntagma (Constitution) Square, was laid out.

===== Minamoto Yoritomo =====
Defying the emperor, Yoritomo established shugo (constables) and jitō (district **steward**s) throughout the Japanese provinces, thus undermining the central government's local administrative power, and in 1192 he acquired the title of supreme commander (shogun) over the shugo and jitō.

● picked troop
===== Christianity =====
In the Johannine apocalypse the 144,000 "... who have not defiled themselves with women" (Revelation 14:4) constituted the **picked troops** of the Kingdom of God.

● prefect[政府内高官ではなく, prefectus urbi はローマ市警司法官, prefectus praetorio は皇帝 SP, 知事監督官, 地方司法財政官, 軍小単位指揮官機能を有し, 帝国最高位の役人]
===== prefect =====
Latin Praefectus, plural Praefecti, in ancient Rome, any of various high officials or magistrates having different functions.

In the early republic, a prefect of the city (praefectus urbi) was appointed by the consuls to act in the consuls' absence from Rome. The position lost much of its importance temporarily after the mid-4th century BC, when the consuls began to appoint praetors to act in the consuls' absence. The office of prefect was given new life by the emperor Augustus and continued in existence until late in the empire. Augustus appointed a prefect of the city, two praetorian prefects (praefectus praetorio), a prefect of the fire brigade, and a prefect of the grain supply. The prefect of the city was responsible for maintaining law and order within Rome and acquired full criminal jurisdiction in the region within 100 miles (160 km) of the city. Under the later empire he was in charge of Rome's entire city government. Two praetorian prefects were appointed by Augustus in 2 BC to command the praetorian guard; the post was thereafter usually confined to a single person. The praetorian prefect, being responsible for the emperor's safety, rapidly acquired great power. Many became virtual prime ministers to the emperor, Sejanus being the prime example of this. Two others, Macrinus and Philip the Arabian, seized the throne for themselves.

By AD 300 the praetorian prefects virtually directed the civil administration of the empire. They executed judicial powers as delegates of the emperor, organized tax levies, and supervised provincial governors. They also commanded troops and served as quartermasters general to the emperor's court. Under the emperor Constantine I the Great (reigned 312–337), the praetorian prefects were stripped of their military commands, but they retained their judicial and financial functions and remained the highest officers of the empire.

● priest

===== British Museum Dictionary of Ancient Egypt =====
priests

The Egyptian title we usually translate as **priest** means 'god's **servant**'. ... The Egyptian **priest**, literally described as a '**servant** of god' (*hem netjer*). ... the chief **priest**, who was supported by lesser **priest**s who would have **attended to offerings** and minor parts of the temple ritual. (p. 228)

===== shinshoku =====

**priest** in the Shintō religion of Japan. The main function of the shinshoku is to officiate at all shrine ceremonies on behalf of and at the request of worshippers. He is not expected to lecture, preach, or act as spiritual leader to his parishioners; rather, his main role is to ensure the continuance of a satisfactory relationship between the kami (god or **sacred power**) and the worshipper through **offerings**, evocation of the kami, and mediation of the deity's blessing to the parishioners.

The highest rank of shinshoku is the gūji (chief **priest**). In large shrines he generally has serving under him the gon-gūji (associate chief **priest**), negi (**priest**, or senior **priest**), and gon-negi ( junior **priest**).

In the Grand Shrine of Ise, the supreme **priest**ess, the saishu ("**chief of the religious ceremonies**"), ranks even above the supreme **priest**, the dai-gūji. Formerly the post of supreme **priest**ess was always filled by an unmarried princess of the Imperial family. She devoted herself entirely to the religious ceremonies (matsuri, q.v.) of the Ise Shrine.

To qualify as a shinshoku, a novice must attend a school approved by the Jinja Honchō (Association of Shintō Shrines), usually the Kokugakuin University in Tokyo, or pass a qualifying examination. At one time the office of high **priest** was inherited. The **priest**hood of some **temples** is said to have remained within the same families for as many as 100 generations. Although the hereditary status of the office has been abolished, the practice continues in many shrines by local preference.

**Priest**s may marry and have families. Women may also be admitted to the **priest**hood, and widows often succeed their husbands. The **priest**s are supported by offerings of the parishioners and worshippers.

In modern Japan an alternative name for the Shintō **priest** is kannushi, which traditionally referred only to a head **priest** who, through the observance of purificatory practices, had become qualified to serve as a medium for a deity.

===== priesthood =====

harai-gushi: Shinto **priest** blessing children
[お祓い写真 oharai.jpg]
A Shintō **priest** blessing children during the Shichi-go-san (Seven-Five-Three) festival at the Meiji Shrine, Tokyo, Japan. The **priest** waves a haraigushi, a wooden wand with folded-paper pendants, symbolically purifying the children and assuring them of good health and prosperity.

● privy (王室の私的な, 私用に供する)

===== China =====

The administration of the Han Empire
The structure of government
The civil service

There was a total of 12 grades in the Han civil service, ranging from that of clerk to the most senior minister of state. No division in principle existed between men serving in the central offices or the provincial units. Promotion could be achieved from one grade of the service to the next, and, in theory, a man could rise from the humblest to the highest post. In theory and partly in practice, the structure of Han government was marked by an adherence to regular hierarchies of authority, by the division of specialist responsibilities, and by a duplication of certain functions. By these means it was hoped that excessive monopoly of power by individual officials would be avoided. The uppermost stratum of officials or statesmen comprised the chancellor, the Imperial counselor, and, sometimes, the commander in chief. These men acted as the emperor's highest advisers and retained final control over the activities of government. Responsibility was shared with nine ministers of state who cared for matters such as religious cults, security of the palace, adjudication in criminal cases, diplomatic dealings with foreign leaders, and the collection and distribution of revenue. Each minister of state was supported by a department staffed by directors and subordinates. There were a few other major agencies; these ranked slightly below the nine ministries and were responsible for specialist tasks. Functions were duplicated so as to check the growth of power. Occasionally, for example, two chancellors were appointed concurrently. Similarly, financial matters were controlled by two permanent ministries: the **Department of Agriculture and Revenue** and the **Privy**

Treasury.

⟨NSOED⟩ 3. = PRIVATE a. 4. Sharing in the knowledge of something secret or private. Foll. by *to, of*. LME. II 5. Secret, concealed; clandestine, surreptitious. *arch*. ME. 6. Not visible; hidden. Special collocations: **privy chamber** *Hist.* (a) a room reserved for the private use of a particular person or persons; (b) *spec*. a private apartment in a royal residence. **privy council** (a) (with cap. initials) a body of advisers appointed by the British monarch, usu. as a personal honour but automatically in the case of Cabinet Ministers, and including those who hold or have held high political, legal, or ecclesiastical office in Britain or the Commonwealth (Judicial Committee of the Privy Council: see JUDICIAL a.); (b) any similar select body of advisers, *spec*. (chiefly *Hist.*) that of a (foreign) monarch, governor-general, etc. **privy councillor** = privy counsellor below. **privy counsellor** (a) (with cap. initials) a member of the **Privy Council**; (b) *gen*. a private or confidential adviser. **privy member**(s): see MEMBER n. **privy parts** *arch*. the genitals. **privy purse** (a) the allowance from the public revenue for the private expenses of the monarch; (b) (with cap. initials) an officer of the royal household in charge of this. **privy seal** (a) a seal affixed to documents that are afterwards to pass the Great Seal or that do not require it; in Scotland, a seal authenticating a royal grant of personal or assignable rights; (b) (with cap. initials) the keeper of this (now called **Lord Privy Seal** and having chiefly nominal official duties) (see also **Keeper of the Privy Seal** *s.v.* KEEPER n.); (c) *Hist*. a document to which the privy seal was affixed.    B n. 2 Law. A person who has a part or interest in any action, matter, or thing. Opp. stranger.    b A person privy to a secret matter.    c A native or inhabitant of a place, as opp. to a stranger.    II 3 A lavatory, esp. an outside one or one without plumbing.    4 Secrecy. Only in in privy.

● proffer

===== Williams, William Carlos =====

Characteristic poems that ¥proffer Williams' fresh, direct impression of the sensuous world are the frequently anthologized "Lighthearted William,""By the Road to the Contagious Hospital," and "Red Wheelbarrow."

===== Charles II =====

but poverty ¥doomed this nucleus of a royalist army to impotence. European princes took little ¥interest in Charles and his ¥cause, and his ¥proffers of marriage were declined. Even Cromwell's death did little to improve his prospects.

<NSOED> 1 v.t. Bring or put before a person for acceptance; offer, present. Now literary. ME.<unknown>b v.t. Attempt to engage in or inflict (battle, injury, etc.). J. WAINWRIGHT *Barker..took one of the proffered cigarettes*.いかがですかと差し出す

## 付録 1　職官名英訳参照英文集

● regent
〈OAD〉regent, a person appointed to rule a country while the monarch is too young or unable to rule, or is absent.

● rite/ritual

| Dictionary | ritual | rite |
| --- | --- | --- |
| NSOED | 1 Of, pertaining to, or used in a solemn rite or solemn rites. L16. | 2 Of the nature of or constituting a solemn rite or solemn rites; carried out as a solemn rite. | A formal procedure or act in a religious or other solemn observance. |
| Longman Activator | a special action or a set of related actions that are performed in a fixed pattern, especially in order to mark important religious or social occasions [n C/U]. All cultures have their own rituals for the burying of the dead. | the ritual of I have always been fascinated by the ritual of the Roman Catholic church.　[adj] the ritual slaughter of a goat | a special action that is done as part of an important religious or social ceremony, especially one that only particular people, for example priests, are allowed to perform [n C] Prayers and chants are an integral part of the religious rites of most societies. | The Batak chieftains perform the traditional initiation rite. |
| Longman American | 1 a ceremony that is always performed in the same way, in order to mark an important religious or social occasion: traditional dances and rituals | The Chinese surround silk with myth and ritual. 2 something that you do regularly and in the same way each time: Set up a regular time for homework; make it a ritual. | a ceremony that is always performed in the same way, usually for religious purposes: Buddhist rites | A cleansing rite was performed before building started. |

===== fertility rites =====

**Fertility rites** are ceremonies of a magic-religious nature performed to ensure the continuity of life. From earliest time humans have performed these **rites** in an attempt to control the environment. Expressed as invocations, incantations, prayers, hymns, processions, dances, and sacred dramas, these **ritual** activities were believed to be closely connected with the processes of nature. If the enactment of **fertility rites** could induce

231

fertility in the animal and human worlds, the vegetable world would also be stimulated to reproduction, resulting in an abundant harvest. The basis for such **rites** was usually a belief in sympathetic magic, based on the assumption that the principle of life and fertility was one and indivisible.

A persistent theme of primitive **fertility rituals** was the freeing of the waters and the subsequent regeneration of the earth. Many hymns of the Rig-Veda are supplications to Indra, in his role as god of weather and war, to slay the giant who had imprisoned the great rivers of India (see Vedas). Such personification of natural phenomena was common. Another prevalent myth of pastoral societies, often enacted as sacred drama, was the search of the earth goddess for her lost lover, brother, or child who either has been killed or has disappeared from Earth. Symbolizing death and the return of vegetation and life, this myth was recorded as early as 3000 BC in the Babylonian cult of Ishtar (Inanna) and Tammuz, and it is traceable through the Sabeans at Harran (in present-day Yemen). Another example is the death and resurrection of the Phoenician-Greek deity Adonis, beloved of Aphrodite. The Greek myth of Demeter and Persephone (Kore) represents the same theme, as does the Egyptian myth of Osiris and Isis.

Sacred marriages frequently have formed part of the **fertility ritual**; the effectiveness of this symbolic union at times depended on the chastity of the participants. **Ritual** prostitution, human and animal sacrifice, and displays of phallic symbols were also sometimes believed to stimulate fertility. In a number of preliterate societies the role of the god was combined with that of the king, and the fertility of the land and people was linked with the king's state of perfection and purification.

===== ritual =====
Introduction
ritual

the performance of ceremonial acts prescribed by tradition or by sacerdotal decree. Ritual is a specific, observable mode of behaviour exhibited by all known societies. It is thus possible to view **ritual** as a way of defining or describing humans.
Nature and significance

Human beings are sometimes described or defined as a basically rational, economic, political, or playing species. They may, however, also be viewed as **ritual** beings, who exhibit a striking parallel between their **ritual** and verbal behaviour. Just as language is a system of symbols that is based upon arbitrary rules, **ritual** may be viewed as a system of symbolic acts that is based upon arbitrary rules.

付録1 職官名英訳参照英文集

The intricate, yet complex, relation between **ritual** and language can be seen in the history of various attempts to explain **ritual** behaviour. In most explanations, language becomes a necessary factor in the theory concerning the nature of **ritual**, and the specific form of language that is tied to explanations of **ritual** is the language of myth. Both myth and **ritual** remain fundamental to any analysis of religions.

Three general approaches to a theory about the nature and origin of **ritual** prevail.
The origin approach

The earliest approach was an attempt to explain **ritual**, as well as religion, by means of a theory concerned with historical origin. In most cases, this theory also assumed an evolutionary hypothesis that would explain the development of **ritual** behaviour through history. The basic premise, or law, for this approach is that ontogeny (development of an individual organism) recapitulates phylogeny (evolution of a related group of organisms), just as the human embryo recapitulates the stages of human evolutionary history in the womb—e.g., the gill stage. The solution to explaining the apparently universal scope of **ritual** depended upon the success in locating the oldest cultures and cults. Scholars believed that if they could discover this origin, they would be able to explain the contemporary **rituals** of man.

There are almost as many solutions as authors in this approach. In the search for an origin of **ritual**, research turned from the well-known literate cultures to those that appeared to be less complex and preliterate. The use of the terms primitive religion and primitive cultures comes from this approach in seeking an answer to the meaning of **ritual**, myth, and religion. Various cultures and **rituals** were singled out, sacrifice of either men or animals becoming one of the main topics for speculation, though the exact motivation or cause of sacrificial **ritual** was disputed among the leading authors of the theory. For W. Robertson Smith, a British biblical scholar who first published his theory in the ninth edition of Encyclopædia Britannica (1875–89), sacrifice was motivated by the desire for communion between members of a primitive group and their god. The origin of **ritual**, therefore, was believed to be found in totemic (animal symbolic clan) cults; and totemism, for many authors, was thus believed to be the earliest stage of religion and **ritual**. The various stages of **ritual** development and evolution, however, were never agreed upon. Given this origin hypothesis, **rituals** of purification, gift giving, piacular (expiatory) **rites**, and worship were viewed as developments, or secondary stages, of the original sacrificial **ritual**. The Christian Eucharist (Holy Communion), along with contemporary banquets and table etiquette, were explained as late developments or traits that had their origin and meaning in the totemic sacrifice.

The influence of Robertson Smith's theory on the origin of **ritual** can be seen in the works of the British anthropologist Sir James Frazer, the French sociologist Émile Durkheim, and Sigmund Freud, the father of psychoanalysis. Although they were not in complete agreement with Smith, sacrifice and totemism remained primary concerns in their search for the origin of religion. For Frazer, the search led to magic, a stage preceding religion. Both Smith and Frazer led Durkheim to seek the origin of **ritual** and religion in totemism as exemplified in Australia. Durkheim believed that in totemism scholars would find the original form of **ritual** and the division of experience into the sacred and the profane. **Ritual** behaviour, they held, entails an attitude that is concerned with the sacred; and sacred acts and things, therefore, are nothing more than symbolic representations of society. In his last major work, Moses and Monotheism, Freud also remained convinced that the origin of religion and **ritual** is to be found in sacrifice.

The functional approach

The second approach to explaining **ritual** behaviour is certainly indebted to the work of such men as Smith, Freud, and Durkheim. Yet very few, if any, of the leading contemporary scholars working on the problems of religion, **ritual**, and myth begin with a quest for origins. The origin-evolutionary hypothesis of **ritual** behaviour has been rejected as quite inadequate for explaining human behaviour because no one can verify any of these bold ideas; they remain creative speculations that cannot be confirmed or denied.

Turning from origin hypotheses, scholars next emphasized empirical data gathered by actual observation. Contemporary literature is rich in descriptions of **rituals** observed throughout the world. If the term origin can be used as central to the first approach, the term function can be used as indicative of the primary focus of the second approach. The nature of **ritual**, in other words, is to be defined in terms of its function in a society.

The aim of functionalism is to explain **ritual** behaviour in terms of individual needs and social equilibrium. **Ritual** is thus viewed as an adaptive and adjustive response to the social and physical environment. Many leading authorities on religion and **ritual** have taken this approach as the most adequate way to explain **rituals**. Bronisław Malinowski, A.R. Radcliffe-Brown, E.E. Evans-Pritchard, Clyde Kluckhohn, Talcott Parsons, and Edmund Leach, all English or American anthropologists, adopted a functional approach to explain **ritual**, religion, and myth.

Most functional explanations of **ritual** attempt to explain this behaviour in relation to the needs and maintenance of a society. The strengths of this approach are dependent upon a claim that it is both logical and empirical. It is a claim, however, that is open to serious criticism. If the aim of functionalism is to explain why **rituals** are present in a society, it will be necessary to clarify such terms as need, maintenance, and a society functioning adequately, and this becomes crucial if they are to be taken as empirical terms. From a logical point of view, functionalism remains a heuristic device, or indicator, for describing the role of **ritual** in society. If it is asserted that a society functions adequately only if necessary needs are satisfied; and if it is further asserted that **ritual** does satisfy that need, scholars cannot conclude that, therefore, **ritual** is present in that society without committing the logical fallacy of affirming the consequent. To assert that the need is satisfied "if and only if" **ritual** is present is a tautology and a reversal of the claim to be empirical.

The history of religions approach

A third approach to the study of **ritual** is centred on the studies of historians of religion. The distinction between this approach and the first two is that though many historians of religions agree with functionalists that the origin-evolutionary theories are useless as hypotheses, they also reject functionalism as an adequate explanation of **ritual**. Most historians of religions, such as Gerardus van der Leeuw in The Netherlands, Rudolf Otto in Germany, Joachim Wach and Mircea Eliade in the United States, and E.O. James in England, have held the view that **ritual** behaviour signifies or expresses the sacred (the realm of transcendent or ultimate reality). This approach, however, has never been represented as an explanation of **ritual**. The basic problem with it remains that it cannot be confirmed unless scholars agree beforehand that such a transcendent reality exists (see also religion, study of: History and phenomenology of religion).

Functions of **ritual**

**Ritual** behaviour, established or fixed by traditional rules, has been observed the world over and throughout history. In the study of this behaviour, the terms sacred (the transcendent realm) and profane (the realm of time, space, and cause and effect) have remained useful in distinguishing **ritual** behaviour from other types of action.

Although there is no consensus on a definition of the sacred and the profane, there is common agreement on the characteristics of these two realms by those who use the terms to describe religions, myth, and **ritual**. For Durkheim and others who use these terms, **ritual** is a determined mode of action. According to Durkheim, the reference, or object, of **ritual** is the belief system of a society, which is constituted by a classification of everything into the two realms of the sacred and the profane. This classification is taken as a universal feature of religion. Belief systems, myths, and the like, are viewed as expressions of the nature of the sacred realm in which **ritual** becomes the determined conduct of the individual in a society expressing a relation to the sacred and the profane. The sacred is that aspect of a community's beliefs, myths, and sacred objects that is set apart and forbidden. The function of **ritual** in the community is that of providing the proper rules for action in the realm of the sacred as well as supplying a bridge for passing into the realm of the profane.

Although the distinction between the sacred and profane is taken as absolute and universal, there is an almost infinite variation on how this dichotomy is represented—not only between cultures but also within a culture. What is profane for one culture may be sacred to another. This may also be true, however, within a culture. The relative nature of things sacred and the proper **ritual** conducted in relation to the sacred as well as the profane varies according to the status of the participants. What is set apart, or holy, for a sacred king, priest, or shaman (a religious personage having healing and psychic transformation powers), for example, will differ from the proper **ritual** of others in the community who are related to them, even though they share the same belief systems. The crucial feature that both sustains these relations and sets their limits is the **ritual** of initiation.

Three further characteristics are generally used to specify **ritual** action beyond that of the dichotomy of sacred and profane thought and action. The first characteristic is a feeling or emotion of respect, awe, fascination, or dread in relation to the sacred. The second characteristic of **ritual** involves its dependence upon a belief system that is usually expressed in the language of myth. The third characteristic of **ritual** action is that it is symbolic in relation to its reference. Agreement on these characteristics can be found in most descriptions of the functions of **ritual**.

The scholarly disputes that have arisen over the functions of **ritual** centre around the exact relation between **ritual** and belief or the reference of **ritual** action. There is little agreement, for example, on the priority of **ritual** or myth. In some cases, the distinction between **ritual**, myth, and belief systems is so blurred that **ritual** is taken to include myth or belief (see also myth: Myth and religion).

The function of **ritual** depends upon its reference. Once again, although there is common agreement about the symbolic nature of **ritual**, there is little agreement with respect to the reference of **ritual** as symbolic. **Ritual** is often described as a symbolic expression of actual social relations, status, or the role of individuals in a society. **Ritual** is also described as referring to a transcendent, numinous (spi**ritual**) reality and to the ultimate values of a community.

Whatever the referent, **ritual** as symbolic behaviour presupposes that the action is nonrational. That is to say, the means–end relation of **ritual** to its referent is not intrinsic or necessary. Such terms as latent, unintended, or symbolic are often used to specify the nonrational function of **ritual**. The fundamental problem in all of this is that **ritual** is described from an observer's point of view. Whether **ritual** man is basically nonrational or rational, as far as his behaviour and his belief system are concerned, is largely dependent upon whether he also understands both his behaviour and belief to be symbolic of social, psychological, or numinous realities. It is difficult to imagine a Buddhist, a Christian, or an Australian aborigine agreeing that his **ritual** action and beliefs are nothing but symbols for social, psychological, or ultimate realities. The notion of the sacred as a transcendent reality may, however, come closest to the participant's own experience. The universal nature of the sacred–profane dichotomy, however, remains a disputed issue.

What is needed is a new theory that will overcome the basic weaknesses of functional descriptions of **ritual** and belief. Until such a time, **ritual** will remain a mystery. The progress made in the study of language may be of help in devising a more adequate explanation of nonverbal behaviour in general and of **ritual** in particular.
Types of **ritual**

Because of the complexities inherent in any discussion of **ritual**, it is often useful to make distinctions by means of typology. Although typologies do not explain anything, they do help to identify **rituals** that resemble each other within and across cultures.
Imitative

All **rituals** are dependent upon some belief system for their complete meaning. A great many **rituals** are patterned after myths. Such **rituals** can be typed as imitative **rituals** in that the **ritual** repeats the myth or an aspect of the myth. Some of the best examples of this type of **ritual** include **rituals** of the New Year, which very often repeat the story of creation. In a passage from an Indian Brāhma□a (a Hindu scripture) the answer to the question of why the **ritual** is performed is that the gods did it this way "in the beginning." **Rituals** of this imitative type can be seen as a repetition of the creative act of the gods, a return to the beginning.

This type of myth has led to a theory that all **rituals** repeat myths or basic motifs in myths. A version of this line of thought, often called "the myth-**ritual**" school, is that myth is the thing said over **ritual**. In other words, myths are the librettos for **ritual**. The works of such scholars as Jane Harrison and S.H. Hooke are examples of this theory. Although it cannot be denied that some **rituals** explicitly imitate or repeat a myth (e.g., a myth of creation), it cannot be maintained that all **rituals** do so. The **ritual** pattern of the ancient Near East, which Hooke considers basic to the festival celebrating the creation, is itself a typological construction. In any case, although there is a combat and killing narrated in the festival myth, no known evidence exists of **ritual** killing or of king-sacrifice in the ancient Near

East. Nevertheless, some **rituals** do repeat the story of a myth and represent an important type of **ritual** behaviour, even though the type cannot be universalized as a description of all **ritual** action.

Positive and negative

**Rituals** may also be classified as positive or negative. Most positive **rituals** are concerned with consecrating or renewing an object or an individual, and negative **rituals** are always in relation to positive **ritual** behaviour. Avoidance is a term that better describes the negative **ritual**; the Polynesian word tabu (English, taboo) also has become popular as a descriptive term for this kind of **ritual**. The word taboo has been applied to those **rituals** that concern something to be avoided or forbidden. Thus, negative **rituals** focus on rules of prohibition, which cover an almost infinite variety of **rites** and behaviour. The one characteristic they all share, however, is that breaking the **ritual** rule results in a dramatic change in **ritual** man, usually bringing him some misfortune.

Variation in this type of **ritual** can be seen from within a culture as well as cross-culturally. What is prohibited for a subject, for example, may not be prohibited for a king, chief, or shaman. **Rituals** of avoidance also depend upon the belief system of a community and the **ritual** status of the individuals in their relation to each other. Contact with the forbidden or transgression of the **ritual** rules is often offset by **rituals** of purification.

Negative **ritual**, as noted above, is always in polarity with positive **ritual**. The birth of a child, the consecration of a king, a marriage, or a death are **ritualized** both positively and negatively. The **ritual** of birth or death involves the child or corpse in a **ritual** that, in turn, places the child or the corpse in a prohibitive status and thus to be avoided by others. The **ritual** itself, therefore, determines the positive or negative characteristic of **ritual** behaviour.

Sacrificial

Another type of **ritual** is classified as sacrificial. Its importance can be seen in the assessment of sacrificial **ritual** as the earliest or elementary form of religion. See sacrifice.

The significance of sacrifice in the history of religions is well documented. One of the best descriptions of the nature and structure of sacrifice is to be found in Essai sur la nature et le fonction du sacrifice, by the French sociologists Henri Hubert and Marcel Mauss, who differentiated between sacrifice and **rituals** of **oblation**, offering, and consecration. This does not mean that sacrificial **rituals** do not at times have elements of consecration, offering, or **oblation** but these are not the distinctive characteristics of sacrificial **ritual**. Its distinctive feature is to be found in the destruction, either partly or totally, of the victim.

The victim need not be human or animal; vegetables, cakes, milk, and the like are also "victims" in this type of **ritual**. The total or partial destruction of the victim may take place through burning, dismembering or cutting into pieces, eating, or burying.

Hubert and Mauss have provided a very useful structure for dividing this type of **ritual** into subtypes. Though sacrificial **rituals** are very complex and diverse throughout the world, nevertheless, they can be divided into two classes: those in which the participant or participants receive the benefit of the sacrificial act and those in which an object is the direct recipient of the action. This division highlights the fact that it is not just individuals who are affected by sacrificial **ritual** but in many instances objects such as a house, a particular place, a thing, an action (such as a hunt or war), a family or community, or spirits or gods that become the intended recipients of the sacrifice. The variety of such **rituals** is very extensive, but the unity in this type of **ritual** is maintained in the "victim" that is sacrificed.

Life crisis

Any typology of **rituals** would not be complete without including a number of very important **rites** that can be found in practically all religious traditions and mark the passage from one domain, stage of life, or vocation into another. Such **rituals** have often been classified as **rites** of passage, and the French anthropologist Arnold van Gennep's study of these **rituals** remains the classic book on the subject. See **rite** of passage; death **rite**.

The basic characteristic of the life-crisis **ritual** is the transition from one mode of life to another. **Rites** of passage have often been described as **rituals** that mark a crisis in individual or communal life. These **rituals** often define the life of an individual. They include **rituals** of birth, puberty (entrance into the full social life of a community), marriage, conception, and death. Many of these **rituals** mark a separation from an old situation or mode of life, a transition **rite** celebrating the new situation, and a **ritual** of incorporation. **Rituals** of passage do not always manifest these three divisions; many such **rites** stress only one or two of these characteristics.

**Rituals** of initiation into a secret society or a religious vocation (viz., priesthood, ascetic life, medicine man) are often included among **rites** of passage as characteristic **rituals** of transition. The great New Year's **rituals** known throughout the world also represent the characteristic passage from old to new on a larger scale, that includes the whole society or community.

One of the dominant motifs of the life-crisis **ritual** is the emphasis on separation, as either a death or a return to infancy or the womb. In India, a striking example is the Hindu **rite** of being "twice born." The young boy who receives the sacred thread in the upanayana **ritual**, a ceremony of initiation, goes through an elabourate **ritual** that is viewed as a second birth. **Rituals** such as Baptism in early Christianity, Yoga in India, and the complex puberty **rituals** among North American Indian cultures exemplify this motif of death and rebirth in **rites** of passage.

**Rituals** of crisis and passage are often classified as types of initiation. An excellent description of such **rites** is found in Birth and Rebirth by Mircea Eliade. From Eliade's point of view, **rituals**, especially initiation **rituals**, are to be interpreted both historically and existentially. They are related to the history and structure of a particular society and to an experience of the sacred that is both transhistorical and transcendent of a particular social or cultural context. Culture, from this perspective, can be viewed as a series of cults, or **rituals**, that transform natural experiences into cultural modes of life. This transformation involves both the transmission of social structures and the disclosure of the sacred and spiritual life of man.

Initiation **rituals** can be classified in many ways. The patterns emphasized by Eliade all include a separation or symbolic death, followed by a rebirth. They include **rites** all the way from separation from the mother to the more complex and dramatic **rituals** of circumcision, ordeals of suffering, or a descent into hell, all of which are symbolic of a death followed by a rebirth. **Rites** of withdrawal and quest, as well as **rituals** characteristic of shamans and religious specialists, are typically initiatory in theme and structure. Some of the most dramatic **rituals** of this type express a death and return to a new period of gestation and birth and often in terms that are specifically embryological or gynecological. Finally, there are the actual **rituals** of physical death itself, a **rite** of passage and transition into a spi**ritual** or immortal existence.

The various typologies of **ritual** that can be found in texts on religion and culture often overlap or reveal a common agreement in the way in which **ritual** behaviour can be classified. There is a striking contrast in the use of these typologies to interpret the meaning of **ritual**. In general, this contrast can be described in terms of two positions: the first emphasizes the sociopsychological function of **ritual**; the second, although not denying the first, asserts the religious value of **ritual** as a specific expression of a transcendental reality.

Conclusion

**Ritual** behaviour is obviously a means of nonverbal communication and meaning. This aspect of **ritual** is often overlooked in the stress on the relation of **ritual** to myth. Thus, the

付録 1　職官名英訳参照英文集

meaning of **ritual** is often looked for in the verbal, spoken, or belief system that is taken as its semantic correlate. The spoken elements in a **ritual** setting do often reveal the meaning of a **ritual** by reference to a belief system or mythology, but not always. Such a connection has led to an overemphasis on the importance of the belief system or myth over **ritual**. To assert that myths disclose more than **ritual** ever can is an oversimplification of the complex correlation of these two important aspects of religion. A partial explanation of this emphasis is undoubtedly the fact that a vast amount of data, both primary and secondary, is literary in form. Theories about **ritual** are either deduced from the primary literature of a religious tradition or are translated into written language as a result of observation.

**Ritual** can be studied as nonverbal communication disclosing its own structure and semantics. Scholars have only recently turned to a systematic analysis of this important aspect of human behaviour; and progress in kinesics, the study of nonverbal communication, may provide new approaches to the analysis of **ritual**. This development may well parallel the progress in linguistics and the analysis of myth as an aspect of language.

A complete analysis of **ritual** would also include its relation to art, architecture, and the specific objects used in **ritual** such as specific forms of **ritual** dress. All of these components are found in **ritual** contexts, and all of them are nonverbal in structure and meaning.

Most **rituals** mark off a particular time of the day, month, year, stage in life, or commencement of a new event or vocation. This temporal characteristic of **ritual** is often called "sacred time." What must not be forgotten in the study of **ritual** is a special aspect of **ritual** that is often described as "sacred space." Time and place are essential features of **ritual** action, and both mark a specific orientation or setting for **ritual**. Time and space, whether a plot of ground or a magnificent temple, are **ritual**ly created and become, in turn, the context for other **rituals**. Examples of **ritual** time and **ritual** space orientation can be found in the **rituals** for building the sacrifice in Brahmanic Indian **ritual** texts; for the building of a Hindu temple or a Christian cathedral; and for consecrating those structures that symbolize a definite space–time orientation in which **rituals** are enacted. The shape, spatial orientation, and location of the **ritual** setting are essential features of the semantics of **ritual** action.

When particular **ritual** objects, dances, gestures, music, and dress are included in the study of **ritual**, the total structure and meaning of **ritual** behaviour far exceed any one description or explanation of **ritual** man. Most descriptions are selective and are dependent upon the theory and intent with which **rituals** are to be studied.

In recent years there has been little consensus among scholars on an adequate theory, or framework, for explaining or describing **ritual**. Though the term has often been used to describe the determined, or fixed, behaviour of both animals and men, the future study of **ritual** may disclose that this behaviour, found throughout history and cultures, is as unique to man as his capacity for speaking a language and that change in **ritual** behaviour is parallel to, or correlated with, change in language. Although great progress has been made in the analysis of man as the species who speaks, the syntax and semantics of **ritual** man are yet to be discovered.

===== Confucianism, Gr =====

Confucianism, the philosophical system founded on the teaching of Confucius (551-479 BC), dominated the sociopolitical life of China for most of that country's history and largely influenced the cultures of Korea (see North Korea; South Korea), Japan, and Indochina. The Confucian school functioned as a recruiting ground for government positions, which were filled by those scoring highest on examinations in the Confucian classics. It also blended with popular and imported religions and became the vehicle for articulating Chinese mores to the peasants. The school's doctrines supported political authority using the theory of the mandate of heaven. It sought to help the rulers maintain domestic order, preserve tradition, and maintain a constant standard of living for the taxpaying peasants. It trained its adherents in benevolence, traditional **rituals**, filial piety, loyalty, respect for superiors and for the aged, and principled flexibility in advising rulers.

Confucius

Westerners use Confucius as the spelling for Kong Fuzi (K'ung Fu-tzu; Master Kong), China's first and most famous philosopher. Confucius had a traditional personal name (Qiu, or Ch'iu) and a formal name (Zhongni, or Chung-ni). Confucius's father died shortly after Confucius's birth. His family fell into relative poverty, and Confucius joined a growing class of impoverished descendants of aristocrats who made their careers by acquiring knowledge of feudal **ritual** and taking positions of influence serving the rulers of the fragmented states of ancient China. Confucius devoted himself to learning. At age 30, however, when his short-lived official career floundered, he turned to teaching others. Confucius himself never wrote down his own philosophy, although tradition credits him with editing some of the historical classics that were used as texts in his school. He apparently made an enormous impact on the lives and attitudes of his disciples, however. The book known as the Analects, which records all the "Confucius said, /" aphorisms, was compiled by his students after his death. Because the Analects was not written as a systematic philosophy, it contains frequent contradictions and many of the philosophical doctrines are ambiguous. The Analects became the basis of the Chinese social lifestyle and the fundamental religious and philosophical point of view of most traditionalist Chinese intellectuals throughout history. The collection reveals Confucius as a person dedicated to the preservation of traditional **ritual** practices with an almost spi**ritual** delight in performing **ritual** for its own sake.

● ritual music
⇒ musician

● royal

===== China =====
The first historical dynasty: the Shang
The advent of bronze casting

hinese legends of the 1st millennium BC describe the labours of Yü, the Chinese "Noah" who drained away the floods to render China habitable and established the first Chinese dynasty, called Hsia. Seventeen Hsia kings are listed in the Shih-chi, a comprehensive history written during the 1st century BC, and much ingenuity has been devoted to identifying certain Late Neolithic fortified sites -- such as Wang-ch'eng-kang ("the mound of the **royal** city") in north central Honan and Teng-hsia-feng in Hsia hsien (thus the site of Hsia-hsü, "the ruins of Hsia"?) in southern Shansi -- as early Hsia capitals.

The Late Shang period is best represented by a cluster of sites focused on the village of Hsiao-t'un, west of An-yang in northern Honan. Known to history as Yin-hsü, "the Ruins of Yin" (Yin was the name used by the succeeding Chou dynasty for the Shang), it was a seat of **royal** power for the last nine Shang kings, from Wu-ting to Ti-hsin.

The Chou and Ch'in dynasties
The history of the Chou (1111-255 BC)

The origin of the Chou **royal** house is lost in the mists of time. Although the traditional historical system of the Chinese contains a Chou genealogy, no dates can be assigned to the ancestors. The first ancestor was Hou Chi, literally translated as "Lord of Millet." He appears to have been a cultural hero and agricultural deity rather than a tribal chief.

The T'ang dynasty
Administration of the state

The structure of the new central administration resembled that of Wen-ti's time, with its ministries, boards, courts, and directorates. There was no radical change in the dominant group at court. Most of the highest ranks in the bureaucracy were filled by former Sui officials, many of whom had been the new emperor's colleagues when he was governor in

T'ai-yüan, or by descendants of officials of the Pei Chou, Pei Ch'i, or Sui, or of the **royal** houses of the northern and southern dynasties. The T'ang were related by marriage to the Sui **royal** house, and a majority of the chief ministers were related by marriage to either the T'ang or Sui Imperial family.

- sacred fire

===== Xiuhtecuhtli =====

Aztec god of fire, thought to be the creator of all life. ... One of the important duties of an Aztec priest centred on **the maintenance of the sacred fire**, making sure that it should burn perpetually. A new fire was ritually kindled during the dedication of new buildings.

===== Natchez =====
[North American Indian tribe]

The fire was remade at dawn of the festival day, and all the village fires were then made anew from the **sacred fire**.

===== Zoroastriaism =====

The chief ceremony, the Yasna, essentially a sacrifice of haoma (the sacred liquor), is celebrated before the **sacred fire** with recitation of large parts of the Avesta. There also are offerings of bread and milk and, formerly, of meat or animal fat. / The **sacred fire** must be kept burning continually and has to be fed at least five times a day. Prayers also are recited five times a day. The founding of a new fire involves a very elaborate ceremony. There are also rites for purification and for regeneration of a fire.

===== Iztapalapa =====
[northeastern Federal District, central Mexico]Overlooking the area is Mount Estrella, where Aztecs kindled a **sacred fire** to initiate each cycle of their calendar round of 52 years.

- sacrifice

===== sacrifice =====

In general, it may be said that the one who makes sacrifices is man, either an individual or a collective group—a family, a clan, a tribe, a nation, a secret society. Frequently, special acts must be performed by the **sacrificer** before and sometimes also after the sacrifice. In the Vedic cult, the **sacrificer** and his wife were required to undergo an initiation (dīk☐ā) involving ritual bathing, seclusion, fasting, and prayer, the purpose of which was to remove them from the profane world and to purify them for contact with the sacred world. At the termination of the sacrifice came a rite of "desacralization" (avabh☐ta) in which they bathed in order to remove any sacred potencies that might have attached themselves during the sacrifice.[**sacrificer** = 献納者，献供主。供物の所有者で，お祓いを受ける側であって，神主のようにお祓いを授ける役割を演じる側ではない]

There are sacrifices in which there are no participants other than the individual or collective **sacrificer**. Usually, however, one does not venture to approach sacred things directly and alone; they are too lofty and serious a matter. An intermediary—certain persons or groups who fulfill particular requirements or qualifications—is necessary. In many cases, sacrificing by unauthorized persons is expressly forbidden and may be severely punished; e.g., in the book of Leviticus, Korah and his followers, who revolted against Moses and his brother Aaron and arrogated the priestly office of offering incense, were consumed by fire. The qualified person—whether the head of a household, the old man of a tribe, the king, or the priest—acts as the appointed representative on behalf of a community.

The head of the household as **sacrificer** is a familiar figure in the Old Testament, particularly in the stories of the patriarchs; e.g., Abraham and Jacob. Generally, in cattle-keeping tribes with patriarchal organization, the paterfamilias long remained the person who carried out sacrifices, and it was only at a late date that a separate caste of priests developed among these peoples. In ancient China, too, sacrifices were not presided over by a professional priesthood but by the head of the family or, in the case of state sacrifices, by the ruler.

## Material of the oblation

Any form under which life manifests itself in the world or in which life can be symbolized may be a sacrificial **oblation**. In fact, there are few things that have not, at some time or in some place, served as an **offering**. Any attempt to categorize the material of sacrifice will group together heterogeneous phenomena; thus, the category human sacrifice includes several fundamentally different sacrificial rites. Nevertheless, for convenience sake, the variety of sacrificial **offering**s will be treated as (1) blood **offering**s (animal and human), (2) bloodless **offering**s (libations and vegetation), and (3) a special category, divine **offering**s.

## Blood **offering**s

Basic to both animal and human sacrifice is the recognition of blood as the sacred life-force in man and beast. Through the sacrifice—through the return of the sacred life revealed in the victim—the god lives, and, therefore, man and nature live. The great potency of blood has been utilized through sacrifice for a number of purposes; e.g., earth fertility, purification, and expiation. The letting of blood, however, was neither the only end nor the only mode of human and animal sacrifice.

A wide variety of animals have served as sacrificial **offering**s. In ancient Greece and India, for example, **oblation**s included a number of important domestic animals, such as the goat, ram, bull, ox, and horse. Moreover, in Greek religion all edible birds, wild animals of the hunt, and fish were used. In ancient Judaism the kind and number of animals for the various sacrifices was carefully stipulated so that the **offering** might be acceptable and thus fully effective. This sort of regulation is generally found in sacrificial cults; the **offering** must be appropriate either to the deity to whom or to the intention for which it is to be presented. Very often the sacrificial species (animal or vegetable) was closely associated with the deity to whom it was offered as the deity's symbolic representation or even its incarnation. Thus, in the Vedic ritual the goddesses of night and morning received the milk of a black cow having a white calf; the "bull of heaven," Indra, was offered a bull, and Sūrya, the sun god, a white, male goat. Similarly, the ancient Greeks sacrificed black animals to the deities of the dark underworld; swift horses to the sun god Helios; pregnant sows to the earth mother Demeter; and the dog, guardian of the dead, to Hecate, goddess of darkness. The Syrians sacrificed fish, regarded as the lord of the sea and guardian of the realm of the dead, to the goddess Atargatis and ate the consecrated **offering** in a communion meal with the deity, sharing in the divine power. An especially prominent sacrificial animal was the bull (or its counterparts, the boar and the ram), which, as the representation and embodiment of the cosmic powers of fertility, was sacrificed to numerous fertility gods (e.g., the Norse god Freyr; the Greek "bull of the Earth," Zeus Chthonios; and the Indian "bull of heaven," Indra).

The occurrence of human sacrifice appears to have been widespread and its intentions various, ranging from communion with a god and participation in his divine life to expiation and the promotion of the earth's fertility. It seems to have been adopted by agricultural rather than by hunting or pastoral peoples. Of all the worldly manifestations of the life-force, the human undoubtedly impressed men as the most valuable and thus the most potent and efficacious as an **oblation**. Thus, in Mexico the belief that the sun needed human nourishment led to sacrifices in which as many as 20,000 victims perished annually in the Aztec and Nahua calendrical maize ritual in the 14th century AD. Bloodless human sacrifices also developed and assumed greatly different forms: e.g., a Celtic ritual involved the sacrifice of a woman by immersion, and among the Maya in Mexico young maidens were drowned in sacred wells; in Peru women were strangled; in ancient China the king's retinue was commonly buried with him, and such internments continued intermittently until the 17th century.

In many societies human victims gave place to animal substitutes or to effigies made of dough, wood, or other materials. Thus, in India, with the advent of British rule, human

## 付録1　職官名英訳参照英文集

sacrifices to the Dravidian village goddesses (grāma-devīs) were replaced by animal sacrifices. In Tibet, under the influence of Buddhism, which prohibits all blood sacrifice, human sacrifice to the pre-Buddhist Bon deities was replaced by the **offering** of dough images or reduced to pantomime. Moreover, in some cults both human and animal **oblation**s could be "ransomed"—i.e., replaced by **offering**s or money or other inanimate valuables.

### Bloodless offerings

Among the many life-giving substances that have been used as libations are milk, honey, vegetable and animal oils, beer, wine, and water. Of these, the last two have been especially prominent. Wine is the "blood of the grape" and thus the "blood of the earth," a spiritual beverage that invigorates gods and men. Water is always the sacred "water of life," the primordial source of existence and the bearer of the life of plants, animals, human beings, and even the gods. Because of its great potency, water, like blood, has been widely used in purificatory and expiatory rites to wash away defilements and restore spiritual life. It has also, along with wine, been an important **offering** to the dead as a revivifying force.

**Vegetable offerings** have included not only the edible herbaceous plants but also grains, fruits, and flowers. In both Hinduism and Jainism, flowers, fruits, and grains (cooked and uncooked) are included in the daily temple **offering**s. In some agricultural societies (e.g., those of West Africa) yams and other tuber plants have been important in planting and harvest sacrifices and in other rites concerned with the fertility and fecundity of the soil. These plants have been regarded as especially embodying the life-force of the deified earth and are frequently buried or plowed into the soil to replenish and reactivate its energies.

● salt tax

===== China =====

### Taxation

The Ming laissez-faire policy in agrarian matters had its counterpart in fiscal administration. The Ming state took the collection of land taxes -- its main revenues by far -- out of the hands of civil service officials and entrusted this responsibility directly to well-to-do family heads in the countryside. Each designated tax captain was, on the average, responsible for tax collections in an area for which the land-tax quota was 10,000 piculs (one picul = 107 litres) of grain. In collabouration with the li-chia community chiefs of his fiscal jurisdiction, he saw to it that **tax grains** were collected and then delivered, in accordance with complicated instructions: ...

Many revenues other than land taxes contributed to support of the government. Some, such as mine taxes and levies on marketplace shops and vending stalls, were based on proprietorship; others, such as **salt taxes**, **wine taxes**, and taxes on mercantile goods in transit, were based on consumption. Of all state revenues, more than half always seem to have remained in local and provincial **granaries** and treasuries; and of those forwarded to the capital, about half seem normally to have disappeared into the emperor's personal vaults. ….

● section
⇒ unit

● security force

===== China =====

Armed forces

The role of the Public **Security force**s of China began to change in the late 1970s. The definition and designation of what poses a threat to security, for example, were narrowed, and there was a decline in the scope of activities of the **security force**s. The practice of political suppression, the victims of which once numbered in the tens of millions, was reduced, and in the late 1970s a large (but unknown) number of people were released from labour or other camps run by the Public **Security force**s. Also, during the 1980s the "open-door" policy toward the outside world led to the adoption of a more relaxed attitude by the Public **Security force**s regarding their efforts to control and restrict the activities of foreigners in China. By 1990, however, the trend was again toward a stricter policy and tighter controls.

===== France =====

Police services

The police are responsible primarily for maintaining public law and order. They are responsible to the prefects in the départements and to the prefects of police in Paris, the suburban communes, and Lyon and Marseille. The police force is divided into public **security force**s and specialized police forces, such as the vice squad. The security police include the State Security Police (Compagnies Républicaines de Sécurité; CRS), responsible for public order; the judicial police, who carry out criminal investigations and hunt down suspects; and the complex internal intelligence and antiespionage units. The municipal forces are responsible to the mayor. There is also the national gendarmerie, a kind of state police, which is responsible to the minister of defense and which is of particular importance in the rural areas.

● senior officer

===== actuary =====

one who calculates insurance risks and premiums. Actuaries compute the probability of the

付録 1　職官名英訳参照英文集

occurrence of various contingencies of human life, such as birth, marriage, sickness, unemployment, accidents, retirement, and death. They also evaluate the hazards of property damage or loss and the legal liability for the safety and well-being of others.

Most actuaries are employed by insurance companies. They make statistical studies to establish basic mortality and morbidity tables, develop corresponding premium rates, establish underwriting practices and procedures, determine the amounts of money required to assure payment of benefits, analyze company earnings, and counsel with the company accounting staff in organizing records and statements. In many insurance companies the actuary is a **senior officer**.

　　　　actuary, 保険計理人（保険用語辞典，日経文庫）。上の場合 senior officer = 上級役員か。

⇒　commandant

● servant
⇒　priest

● shrine
⇒　temple/shrine

● steward
〈RH〉 steward, 1. a person who manages another's property or financial affairs; one who administers anything as the agent of another or others.　2. a person who has charge of the household of another, buying or obtaining food, directing the servants, etc.　3. an employee who has charge of the table, wine, servants, etc., in a club, restaurant, or the like. 4. a person who attends to the domestic concerns of persons on board a vessel, as in overseeing maids and waiters.　5. an employee on a ship, train, or bus who waits on and is responsible for the comfort of passengers, takes orders for or distributes food, etc.　6. a flight attendant.　7. a person appointed by an organization or group to supervise the affairs of that group at certain functions.　8. U.S. Navy. a petty officer in charge of officer's quarters and mess.

===== jito =====

in feudal Japan, land **steward** appointed by the central military government, or shogunate, whose duties involved levying taxes and maintaining peace within the manor.

===== domestic service =====

Domestic service, as an occupation, reached its height in Victorian England. The great households of the royalty and gentry employed large numbers of servants of both sexes. The elabourate hierarchy of positions afforded ample opportunity for advancement. A man could work his way up from **groom** 馬丁 to valet 従者・側用人 and then on to butler or even **steward**. Similarly, a woman could rise from scullery maid to cook or from chambermaid to housekeeper. In general, **steward**s and housekeepers had their own private servants. Households of lesser, though well-to-do, families often had in their employ a staff of six or more servants, including a lady's maid, nanny, and butler.

===== Penn, William =====

Penn's final years were unhappy. His eldest son, William, Jr., turned out a scapegrace. Penn's own poor judgment in choosing his subordinates (except for the faithful Logan) recoiled upon him: his deputy governors proved incompetent or untrustworthy, and his **steward**, Philip Ford, cheated him on such a staggering scale that Penn was forced to spend nine months in a debtors' prison.

===== La Fayette, Gilbert Motier de =====

born c. 1380, , Auvergne, Fr.
died Feb. 23, 1462, Auvergne
**marshal** of France during the Hundred Years' War and noted adviser to King Charles VII.

After serving in Italy under **Marshal** Jean le Meingre Boucicaut in 1409, he became **steward** of the Bourbonnais. In the wars with England, Jean I, duc de Bourbon, made him lieutenant general in Languedoc and Guyenne.

===== Craggs, James =====

baptized June 10, 1657, Wolsingham, Durham, Eng.
died March 16, 1721
Following service as **steward** to the 7th Duke of Norfolk, Craggs entered the household of the 1st Duke of Marlborough, whose wife arranged for his election to the House of Commons in 1702.

===== Swift, Jonathan =====

Swift's father, Jonathan Swift the elder, was an Englishman who had settled in Ireland after the Stuart Restoration (1660) and become **steward** of the King's Inns, Dublin.

===== Hojo Family =====

The bakufu's own domain of the Kantō rose in revolt under Nitta Yoshisada (the opposition to %the{ Hojo was, in part, a revolt of the family's own constables and

付録 1　職官名英訳参照英文集

**steward**s, who had become locally powerful).

⇒ butler

● subordinate commander

===== aide-de-camp =====
(French: "camp assistant"), an officer on the personal staff of a general, admiral, or other high-ranking commander who acts as his confidential secretary in routine matters. On Napoleon's staff such officers were frequently of high military qualifications and acted both as his "eyes" and as interpreters of his mind to **subordinate commander**s, even on occasion exercising delegated authority. In modern times aides-de-camp are usually of junior rank and their duties largely social. Military, naval, and air force officers, frequently of high rank, who act as aides to chiefs of state, such as kings or presidents, are also called aides-de-camp. In many countries, the word adjutant is used for aide-de-camp and adjutant general for a royal aide-de-camp.

===== strategy =====
The Prussian-German strategists
…
Recognizing that the field of operations had become too vast to be surveyed by the eye of the **commander**, he introduced a new system of delegating power to **subordinate commander**s.

===== World War II =====
The invasion of northwest Africa, November–December 1942
Thus, the French **commander** in chief in Algeria, General Alphonse Juin, and his counterpart in Morocco, General Charles-Auguste Noguès, were **subordinate** to the supreme **commander** of all Vichy's forces, namely Admiral Jean-François Darlan.

● superintendent
⇒ 宮内庁
⇒ 警察組織

● supervisor
⇒ 宮内庁

● temple/shrine

===== arts, East Asian =====
Sculpture

In the first centuries of Buddhist history in China, **rock-cut cave temples** and monastic cells rivaled timber-built courtyard temples in importance. ... It is the splendour and richness of these rock-cut **shrines** and the almost total absence of sculpture from southern China of this period that have given the wrong impression that this new second phase in Buddhist sculpture was the creation of northern sculptors.［temple＝神殿。岩窟神殿、平凡社国民百科エジプト。岩窟○○］

Shintō music

The indigenous religion of Japan, Shintō, was closely connected with the legendary legitimacy of the emperor. Thus, special Shintō music was devised for use in **Imperial shrines**, a tradition already familiar from the discussion of China and Korea. In Japan such Shintō music is called kagura. The kind of music and ritual used exclusively in the Imperial palace grounds is called mi-kagura, that in large Shintō shrines, o-kagura, and Shintō music for local shrines, sato-kagura.［神宮＝imperial shrine ともできるか］

===== Nagoya =====

Nagoya abounds in cultural assets. Educational institutions include Nagoya University (1939), .... The Tokugawa Art Museum preserves the collection of the Tokugawa family. The **Atsuta Shrine** and the nearby **Grand Shrine of Ise** are the oldest and most highly esteemed Shinto shrines in Japan.
［熱田神宮 Atsuta Shrine, 伊勢神宮 Grand Shrine of Ise。「神宮」訳不正確］

===== Shinto =====

Types of shrine

In the beginning Shintō had no shrine buildings. At each festival people placed a tree symbol at a sacred site, or they built a temporary shrine to invite kami. Later they began to construct permanent shrines where kami were said to stay permanently. The honden of the Inner Shrine at Ise and of Izumo-taisha (**Grand Shrine of Izumo**, in Shimane prefecture) illustrate two representative archetypes of shrine construction.［出雲大社］

===== art and architecture, Egyptian =====

Temple architecture

Two principal kinds of temple can be distinguished—**cult temples** and **funerary or mortuary temples**. The former accommodated the images of deities, the recipients of the daily cult; the latter were the shrines for the funerary cults of dead kings.

付録1 職官名英訳参照英文集

The cult temple achieved its most highly developed form in the great sanctuaries erected over many centuries at Thebes. Architecturally the most satisfying, and certainly the most beautiful, is the **Luxor Temple**, started by Amenhotep III of the 18th dynasty. The original design consists of an imposing open court with colonnades of graceful lotus columns, a smaller offering hall, a **shrine** for the ceremonial boat of the god, an inner sanctuary for the cult image, and a room in which the divine birth of the king was celebrated. ［ルクソル神殿, 平凡社国民百科エジプト 405。shrine＝祠か］

The great precinct of the **Temple of Karnak** (the longest side, 1,837 feet [560 metres]) contains whole buildings, or parts of buildings, dating from the early 18th dynasty down to the Roman Period. ［カルナクのアモン神殿, 平凡社国民百科エジプト 404］

Mention should also be made of the immense temple dedicated to the god Amon-Re at Tanis in the delta by the kings of the 21st and 22nd dynasties. Much of the stone for the so-called northern Karnak, along with colossal statues and a dozen obelisks, was appropriated from other sanctuaries in Egypt, making this a remarkable assemblage of earlier work. It was not only a cult temple but the **funerary temple** for the kings who were buried within the precinct.

Funerary temples
Most of the New Kingdom **funerary temples** were built along the desert edge in western Thebes. An exception, and by far the most original and beautiful, was **Queen Hatshepsut's temple**, designed and built by her **steward** Senenmut near the tomb of **Mentuhotep II** at Dayr al-Ba□rī. ［ハトシェプスト女王葬祭殿, 平凡社国民百科エジプト 405。メントゥヘテプ2世, 同］］

The largest conventionally planned **funerary temple** was probably that of **Amenhotep III**, now to be judged principally from the two huge quartzite statues, the Colossi of Memnon. These and other royal sculptures found in the ruins of the temple's courts and halls testify to the magnificence now lost. Its design, as well as much of its stone, was used by Ramses II for his own **funerary temple**, the Ramesseum.［ルクソルではアメンホテプ（アメノフィス）3世の宮殿, 神殿などが残り］

Ramses III's **funerary temple** at Madīnat Habu contains the best preserved of Theban mortuary chapels and shrines, as well as the main temple components.

As with most New Kingdom temples, the **mural** decorations on the outer walls of **funerary temples**, including that at Madīnat Habu, dealt mainly with the military campaigns of the king, while the inner scenes were mostly of ritual significance.［壁面装

253

飾？]

===== Greek religion =====

The Parthenon and other Athenian **temples** of the late 5th century proclaim the taste and power of the Athenians rather than their awe of the gods. ... Fundamental was the precinct (temenos) allotted to the deity, containing the altar, temple (if any), and other sacral or natural features, such as the sacred olive in the temenos of Pandrosos on the Athenian Acropolis. Naoi (temples -- literally "dwellings" -- that housed the god's image) were already known in Homeric times and, like models discovered at Perachora, were of wood and simple design.

In the earliest times deities were worshiped in awesome places such as groves, caves, or mountain tops. ... The image, crude and wooden at first, was placed in the central chamber (cella), which was open at the eastern end. No ritual was associated with the image itself, though it was sometimes paraded. **Hero shrines** were far less elaborate and had pits for offerings. Miniature shrines also were known. **Miniature shrines** also were known.

Most **oracular shrines** included a subterranean chamber, but no trace of such has been found at Delphi, though the Pythia was always said to "descend." At the oracle of Trophonius, discovered in 1967 at Levadhia, incubation was practiced in a hole. The most famous centre of incubation was that of Asclepius at Epidaurus. His **temple** was furnished with a hall where the sick were advised by the demigod in dreams.
...
Priesthood
Even in the state cults, priesthoods were frequently ancestral prerogatives. ... The mysteries at Eleusis were administered by the Eumolpids and Kerykes. The latter assembled the initiates (mystae), while the former provided the Hierophant, who revealed the mysteries in the torchlit Anaktoron (king's **shrine**) within the great Telesterion, or entrance hall.
...
The precise details of many festivals are obscure. Among the more elaborate was the Panathenaea, which was celebrated at high summer, and every fourth year (the Great Panathenaea) on a more splendid scale. Its purpose, besides offering sacrifice, was to provide the ancient wooden image of Athena, housed in the "Old **Temple**," with a new robe woven by the wives of Athenian citizens.
...
The skill of the Greek sculptor reached an almost unparalleled height in the new **temples** on the **Acropolis** of Athens;

付録 1　職官名英訳参照英文集

● Tokugawa bakufu

===== Cambridge History of Japan =====

| 将軍 Shogun | | | |
|---|---|---|---|
| | | | The Great Corridor<br>The Antechamber<br>Regent (*hosa*; *koken*; etc.) |
| | 大老 *tairo* 1<br>Great Councilor<br>老中 *roju* 4-5<br>Senior Councilors | | |
| | | 右筆 *yuhitsu* about 60<br>Secretaries | |
| | | 側衆 *sobashu* 6-7<br>Chamberlains | |
| | | 高家 *koke* 16-26<br>Masters of Court Ceremony | |
| | | 御三家家老 Tayasu-*karo*, Hitotsubashi-*karo*, Shimizu-*karo*<br>Councilors for the Three Lords | |
| | | 留守居 *rusui* 5<br>Keepers of Edo Castle | |
| | | 大番頭 *oban gashira* 12<br>Captains of the Great Guards | |
| | | 大目付 *ometsuke* 4-5<br>Inspectors General | |
| | | 江戸町奉行 *Edo machi bugyo* 2<br>Edo City Magistrates | |
| | | 勘定奉行 *kanjo bugyo* 4<br>Superintendents of Finance | |
| | | | 郡代・代官 3 *gundai*; 40-50 *daikan*<br>Deputies |

255

|  |  |  |
|--|--|--|
|  |  | 金奉行 *kane bugyo* 4<br>Superintendents of the Treasury |
|  |  | 蔵奉行 *kura bugyo* 2<br>Superintendents of Cereal Stores |
|  |  | 金座 *kinza*<br>Gold Monopoly |
|  |  | 銀座 *ginza*<br>Silver Monopoly |
|  |  | 銅座 *doza*<br>Copper Monopoly |
|  |  | 朱座 *shuza*<br>Cinnabar* Monopoly |
|  | 勘定吟味役 *kanjo gimmiyaku* 4<br>Comptrollers of Finance |  |
|  | 関東郡代 *Kanto gundai* i<br>Kanto Deputy |  |
|  | 作事奉行 *sakuji bugyo* 2<br>Superintendents of Works |  |
|  | 普請奉行 *fushin bugyo* 2<br>Superintendents of Public Works |  |
|  | 京都町奉行 *Kyoto machi bugyo* 2<br>Kyoto City Magistrates |  |
|  | 大坂町奉行 *Osaka machi bugyo* 2<br>Osaka City Magistrates |  |
|  | 長崎奉行・浦賀奉行など<br>*Nagasaki bugyo, Uraga bugyo* 2-4)(1-2<br>Magistrates of Nagasaki |  |
| 側用人<br>*sobayonin* 1<br>Grand Chamberlain |  |  |
| 若年寄 |  |  |

付録 1　職官名英訳参照英文集

| | |
|---|---|
| *wakadoshiyori* 4-5 Junior Councilors | |
| | 書院番頭 *shoimban gashira* 6 Captains of the Body Guard |
| | 小姓組番頭 *koshogumiban gashira* 6 Captains of the Inner Guards |
| | 新番頭 *shimban gashira* 6 Captains of the New Guards |
| | 小普請奉行 *kobushin bugyo* Superintendents of Construction and Repair |
| | 小姓頭取 *kosho-todori* 6 Chiefs of the Pages |
| | 小納戸頭取 *konando-todori* 3 Chiefs of the Attendants |
| | 目付 *metsuke* Inspectors |
| | 納戸頭 *nando gashira* 2 Chiefs of the Castle Accountants |
| | 医師 *ishi* Attendant Physicans |
| | 儒者 *jusha* Attendant Confucianists |
| | 膳奉行 *zen bugyo* 3-5 Superintendents of the Kitchen |
| 宗者番 *sojaban* 20 or more Masters of Shogunal Ceremony | |
| 寺社奉行 *jisha* | |

| |
|---|
| *bugyo* 4 Superintendents of Temples and Shrines |
| 京都所司代 *Kyoto-shoshidai* 1 Kyoto Deputy |
| 大坂城代 *Osaka-jodai* 1 Keeper of Osaka Castle |

| |
|---|
| 評定所 *hyojosho* Supreme Court of Justice |

常勤職 Regular duty:
    寺社奉行 Superintendents of Temples and Shrines
    江戸町奉行 Edo City Magistrates
    勘定奉行 Superintendents of Finance
非常勤職 Irregular duty:
    老中 A Senior Councilor
    側用人 The Grand Chamberlain
    江戸詰め時その他奉行 Other Magistrates and Superintendents when residing in Edo
これらの補佐 Assisted by:
    勘定吟味役 Comptrollers of Finance
    大目付ほか Inspectors General and others

\* Cinnabar = シン砂（水銀の硫化鉱物、鮮赤〜暗赤色で金剛光沢をもつ）（エッセンシャル化学辞典）

Figure 4.2 Main offices of the Tokugawa bakufu. [Source: John W. Hall, *Tanuma Okitsugu: Forerunner of Modem Japan* (Cambridge, Mass.: Harvard University Press, 1955), pp. 28-9.]

● tomb

付録1 職官名英訳参照英文集

⇒ imperial tomb

● water patrol
〈Web〉Missouri State **Water Patrol** is an Internationally Accredited Law Enforcement Agency
Our Mission: ...to protect and serve the public through law enforcement and education so that citizens and visitors can safely enjoy the waters of the state.

● water police
〈Web〉Victoria Police: 20 Jun 2007 ... The **Water Police** has the primary role of coordinating all marine incidents involving recreational vessels, yachts and fishing vessels and commercial vessels in port. These incidents often involve overdue vessels, flare sightings, broken down boats, missing divers, injured crewmembers and distress calls. (www.police.vic.gov.au/content.asp?)

〈Web〉The Western Australia **Water Police** was established in 1851 and is located on the Swan River in North Fremantle. Thirty one sworn police officers and civilian staff operate and maintain five patrol vessels and are responsible for Western Australia's 13,000 kilometres of coastline, and more than 85,000 registered pleasure craft.
(www.police.wa.gov.au/Specialistunits/WaterPolice/.../Default.aspx)

〈Web〉The original **Water Police** was developed in 1789 when Governor Phillip established the "Row Boat Guard" with 12 well behaved convicts. (NSW Police Force, New South Wales Government)
(www.police.nsw.gov.au/recruitment/police_career/role_and_careers/careers/water_police)

● waterway watch
〈Web〉America's Waterway Watch (AWW)
America's **Waterway Watch** (AWW), a combined effort of the Coast Guard and its Reserve and Auxiliary components, continues to grow, enlisting the active participation of those who live, work or play around America's waterfront areas. Coast Guard Reserve personnel concentrate on connecting with businesses and government agencies, while Auxiliarists focus on building AWW awareness among the recreational boating public. (www.americaswaterwaywatch.org/)

● 外構・緑地
外構工事 = external work and landscaping (和英建築用語辞典)
exterior work は外壁や建物の壁面装飾など。
緑地 greens = Although all modern football sports evolved from medieval folk football,

they derive more directly from games played in schoolyards rather than village **greens** or open fields. (Br football)

緑地 green field = The city [Phoenix] occupies a semiarid, saucer-shaped valley that is surrounded by mountains and **green irrigated fields**. (Br Phoenix)

緑野 green fields = It has towering snow-clad mountains divided by deep valleys with thick woods, **green fields**, lakes, and cascading streams.

野 fields = It has enough rain in all seasons to keep **fields** green. (Br climate / European Plain)

畑 fields = The "age of trisection" was the bleakest in all Hungarian history. Fighting and slave raiding, which went on even in times of nominal peace, reduced the whole south of the country to a wasteland occupied by only a few seminomadic Vlach herdsmen; villages disappeared and **fields** reverted to swamp and forest. (Br Hungary)

● 雅楽

===== gagaku =====

court music, ancient court music

===== arts, East Asian =====

The general term for **court orchestra music**, gagaku, is merely a Japanese pronunciation for the same characters used in China for ya-yüeh and in Korea for a-ak., Br

● 軍組織

| 和英翻訳ハンドブック | | | **Army Rank (Grolier)** | 三省堂コンサイス |
|---|---|---|---|---|
| 旧陸軍 | 自衛隊 | | British Army Officers | |
| 元帥 | - | Field **Marshal**(英) General of the Army(米) | Field **Marshal** | 元帥 |
| 大将 | 陸・空将(甲) | General | General | 大将 |
| 中将 | 陸・空将(乙) | Lieutenant General | Lieutenant General | 中将 |
| 少将 | 陸・空将補 | Major General | Major General | 少将 |
| - | - | - | Brigadier | 准将, 代将 |
| 大佐 | 一等陸・空佐 | **Colonel** | **Colonel** | 大佐 |
| 中佐 | 二等陸・空佐 | Lieutenant **Colonel** | Lieutenant **Colonel** | 中佐 |
| 少佐 | 三等陸・空佐 | Major | Major | 少佐 |

付録1 職官名英訳参照英文集

| 和英翻訳ハンドブック | | | Army Rank (Grolier) | 三省堂コンサイス |
|---|---|---|---|---|
| 大尉 | 一等陸・空尉 | Captain | Captain | 大尉 |
| 中尉 | 二等陸・空尉 | First Lieutenant | Lieutenant | 中尉 |
| 少尉 | 三等陸・空尉 | Second Lieutenant | Second Lieutenant | |
| 准尉 | 准陸・空尉 | Warrant Officer | Warrant Officer I | |
| - | - | - | Warrant Office II | |
| 曹長 | 一等陸・空曹 | **Master Sergeant** | Staff Sergeant | |
| 軍曹 | 二等陸・空曹 | Sergeant First Class | Sergent | 軍曹 |
| 伍長 | 三等陸・空曹 | Sergeant Second Class | Corporal | 伍長 |
| 兵長 | 陸・空士長 | Lance Corporal | Lance-Corporal | |
| 上等兵 | 一等陸・空士 | Private First Class | Private | 兵卒 |
| 一等兵 | 二等陸・空士 | Private Second Class | | Private First Class |
| 二等兵 | 三等陸・空士 | Recruit | | |

米陸軍組織（ジャパンタイムズ「和英翻訳ハンドブック」）

| 英語 | 日本語 |
|---|---|
| Field army | 軍 |
| Corps | 軍団 |
| Division | 師団 |
| Brigade | 旅団 |
| Regiment** | 連隊** |
| Battalion | 大隊 |
| Company | 中隊 |
| Platoon | 小隊 |
| Squad (Section) | 分隊 Squad Section) |

** 1963年廃止

===== military rank, Gr =====

| MILITARY RANK IN GREAT BRITAIN AND FRANCE |||||||
|---|---|---|---|---|---|
| British Army | French Army | British Army | French Army | British Navy | French Navy |

| British Army Officers | French Army Enlisted Personnel | British Army Officers | French Army | British Navy | French Navy |
|---|---|---|---|---|---|
| Field Marshal | Maréchal de France* | Warrant Officer I | Adjutant-chef | Admiral of the Fleet | |
| General | Général d'Armée | Warrant Officer II | Adjutant | Admiral | Amiral |
| Lieutenant General | Général de Corps d'Armée | Staff Sergeant | Sergent-major | Vice-Admiral | Vice-amiral |
| Major General | Général de Division | Sergeant | Sergent | Rear-Admiral | Contre-amiral |
| Brigadier | Général de Brigade | Corporal | Caporal-chef | Commodore | Chef d'escadre |
| Colonel | Colonel | Lance-Corporal | Caporal | Captain | Capitaine de vaisseau |
| Lieutenant Colonel | Lieutenant Colonel | | Soldat, 1ere Classe | Commander | Capitaine de frégate |
| Major | Commandant † | Private | Soldat, 2eme Classe | Lieutenant Commander | Capitaine de corvette |
| Captain | Capitaine | | | Lieutenant | Lieutenant de vaisseau |
| Lieutenant | Lieutenant | | | Sublieutenant | Enseigne de vaisseau |
| Second Lieutenant | Sous Lieutenant | | | Midshipman | Aspirant |

\* The title is technically not a rank but a "state dignity."

† It should be noted that the Commandant is called chef de bataillon in the infantry, chef d'escadrons in cavalry/armor, and chef d'escadron in the artillery.

Military rank is the system of titles that forms the hierarchy of the armed services.

Army Rank

Modern army rank traces its origins to the mercenary companies of Renaissance Italy (see condottieri), at the time when professional soldiers began to replace part-time feudal warriors. At the head of the company stood the headman (Latin, caput, "head"), from which is derived the title captain or, later, in Germany, Hauptmann. The captain was assisted by a deputy, or lieutenant (Latin, locum tenens, "place holder"). Both depended on

付録 1　職官名英訳参照英文集

a number of trustworthy soldiers who carried the title of sergeant, which was derived from that of the feudal warrior's personal attendants (Latin, servientem, "serving"). All modern ranks, with minor exceptions, are derived from these three. As armies grew larger, companies were organized into columns. The modern rank of colonel is derived from the head of each column (Old Italian, colonnello). When armies grew larger still in the 17th century, superior officers were generally appointed to command the whole army; for them general was added to the original company titles. In this way evolved the ranks of lieutenant general, captain general, and colonel general. At the same time the title major was attached to some of the lower ranks to indicate special responsibility. The ranks of captain major (now major) and sergeant major developed in this way. The latter could also be a general rank (sergeant major general), but that title was found to be cumbersome and was abbreviated to major general. This abbreviation explains why a (sergeant) major general in modern armies is subordinate to a lieutenant general.

The rank of **marshal** is derived from two Old High German words, Marah, "horse," and Scalc, "caretaker" or "servant." In the Teutonic tribes that overran the Roman Empire, the tribal chief's principal servant was his horse **master** (Marah Scalc). When the chiefs became kings of their conquered territories, the **master** of horse became a high court officer and, in wartime, the head of the cavalry. Later, in some countries, the courtly and military offices were divided; in Britain, for example, the earl **marshal** became, effectively, a civilian, and field **marshal**s were appointed to command armies in the field.

When armies became permanent state organizations during the 17th century, the grant of rank became a royal prerogative, usually conferred by a commission from the king to a trusted subject. These commissioned officers in turn appointed suitable soldiers in their regiments to hold the minor ranks, which thus became known as noncommissioned. In Britain the commissioned ranks were salable until 1870, a practice that survived from mercenary days. General rank was, however, by official appointment, as was all rank in most other armies. During the 19th century armies everywhere began to apply tests of efficiency for promotion or to require officers to complete a course of training for the next rank. Officers of outstanding ability for whom a superior rank could not be immediately found were sometimes awarded a brevet to the next rank, which guaranteed them promotion when a vacancy occurred. It also became common practice to issue a warrant to the most senior of the noncommissioned officers, henceforth called warrant officers, which ensured that they could not arbitrarily be demoted. In most countries warrant officers now constitute an intermediate rank between commissioned and noncommissioned officers.

By 1900 the system of officer ranks was standard throughout the major armies, although some national variations existed. In the French army, for example, the major is known as commandant. General's titles in the French army and in those of most other Latin countries followed the Napoleonic pattern of conforming to that of the appropriate formation commanded ʌ general of brigade, for example. Few changes have been made in the system since 1900. The U.S. Army created for World War I hero Gen. John J. Pershing the field-**marshal** equivalent of general of the armies (subsequently army), whereas the former USSR, which originally scorned rank titles, had a more elabourate hierarchy than did any other country. Air force titles in most countries are similar to army ranks.

Navy Rank

Naval rank was slower to formalize than army rank because permanent navies came into being some time after permanent armies. The first title to acquire general currency was that of admiral, which was derived from the Arabic amir-al-bahr, "prince of the sea," by which the leader of the Muslim fleet in the Mediterranean was known as early as the 12th century. The term was brought back to Europe by the Crusaders, who spelled it by analogy with the Latin admirabilis, "admirable." As late as the 16th century, however, the word was applied as often to the commander's ship as to the man, who was more often called general, captain, or captain general. For this reason establishing a distinctive title for the ship's commander was delayed. In the British Royal Navy of the 17th century a man held title only while in post and on a ship of the line. He therefore came to be called a post captain, and naval vessels smaller than a sixth-rate ship were commanded by a **master** and commander, the common merchant title (abbreviated in 1794 to commander). Not until 1860 did Britain officially accord titles of rank to naval officers who were not actually in post. Custom, however, had long done so ʌ to include also the captain's deputy, the lieutenant, and the apprentice officers, the midshipmen. During the 19th century the extra rank of lieutenant commander was invented to distinguish senior lieutenants in larger ships. In 1861 the rank sublieutenant was added. These additions recognized that the steam navy required on the same ship a considerable hierarchy of officers to perform a variety of functions unknown in simple sailing-ship days. In the French and German navies the names of types of ships were attached to officers' ranks. Capitaine de frŽgate, for example, outranked capitaine de corvette.

In the higher naval ranks, the old divisions of the line of battle ʌ rear and van, the latter always commanded by the admiral's deputy, or vice admiral ʌ had become attached to flag (admiral's) rank to give the titles in use today. In the Royal Navy the most senior officer had also long been known as admiral of the fleet, a title that became a rank in 1863. Its equivalent was Grossadmiral in the German Navy, which also used the unusual next rank of Generaladmiral. The U.S. Navy, which had generally followed British usage in these forms, adopted the title of fleet admiral in World War II.

付録 1　職官名英訳参照英文集

● 警察組織
警視庁
警視総監 Superintendent-General of the Metropolitan Police Department (Chief of Police)
副総監 Deputy Superintendent-General
警視監？Police Superintendent Supervisor

大阪府警
警視監 Superintendent Supervisor
警視長 Chief Superintendent
警視正 Senior Superintendent
警視 Superintendent

〈Web〉警察組織
http://www.police.pref.osaka.jp/01sogo/koho/digital/images/p01-p02.pdf
http://www.keishicho.metro.tokyo.jp/foreign/gaiyo2/image1/MPD1.pdf

| 大阪府警察本部 Osaka Prefectural Police Headquarters | 警視庁 Metropolitan Police Department |
|---|---|
| 警視監 Superintendent Supervisor | 警視総監 Superintendent-General of the Metropolitan Police Department (Chief of Police) 副総監 Deputy Superintendent-General 警視監？Police Superintendent Supervisor |
| 警視長 Chief Superintendent | Chief Police Superintendent |
| 警視正 Senior Superintendent | Senior Police Superintendent |
| 警視 Superintendent | Police Superintendnent |
| 警部 Police Inspector | Police Inspector |
| 警部補 Assistant Police Inspector | Assistant Police Inspector |
| 巡査部長 Police Sergeant | Police Sergent |
| 巡査長 Senior Police Officer | Senior Policeman |
| 巡査 Police Officer | Policeman |
| 警察署 Police Station | General Affairs Section / Finance Section / Community Safety Section / Community Affairs Section (Police Box: KOBAN / Residential Police Box) / Criminal Investigation Section / Traffic Section / Security Section |

● 宮内庁

| 日本語 | 英語 |
| --- | --- |
| 宮内庁 | Imperial Household Agency |
| 宮内庁長官 | **Grand** Steward of the imperial Household |
| 侍従長, 侍従職 | **Grand** Chamberlain to H.M. The Emperor (cf. 東宮職東宮侍従長＝**Chief** Chamberlain to H.I.H The Crown Prince) |
| 皇太后宮大夫, 皇太后宮職 | **Grand** Master or the Empress Dowager's Household |
| 東宮大夫, 東宮職 | **Grand** Master of the Crown Prince's Household |
| 式部官長, 式部職 | **Grand** Master of the Ceremonies |
| 皇太后宮大夫, 皇太后宮職 | Grand **Master** of the Empress Dowager's Household |
| 東宮大夫, 東宮職 | Grand **Master** of the Crown Prince's Household |
| 式部官長, 式部職 | Grand **Master** of the Ceremonies |
| 式部官 | **Master** of the Ceremonies |
| 宮務主管, 宮内庁長官官房 | **Supervisor** of the Imperial Princes' Household Affairs |
| 皇室医務主管, 宮内庁長官官房 | Medical **Supervisor** of the Imperial Household |
| 女官長, 侍従職 | **Chief** Lady-in-Waiting to H.M. The Empress |
| 侍医長, 侍従職 | **Chief** Court Physician |
| 皇太后宮女官長, 皇太后宮職 | **Chief** Lady-in-Waiting to the Empress Dowager |
| 皇太后宮侍医長, 皇太后宮職 | **Chief** Physician of the Empress Dowager's Household |
| 東宮侍従長, 東宮職 | **Chief** Chamberlain to H.I.H The Crown Prince (cf. 侍従職侍従長＝Grand Chamberlain to H.M. The Emperor) |
| 東宮女官長, 東宮職 | **Chief** Lady-in-Waiting to H.I.H. The Crown Princess |
| 東宮侍医長, 東宮職 | **Chief** Physician of the Crown Prince's Household |
| 宮殿管理官, 管理部 | **Superintendent** of the Imperial Palace |

● 水利

===== agricultural science, the =====

Soil and **water control** engineering deals with soil drainage, irrigation, conservation, hydrology, and flood **control**.

===== water control =====

In 1811 Lin passed the highest of the examinations, the chin-shih, and joined the Hanlin Academy, which advised the emperor and helped him to draft documents. In 1820 Lin

付録1　職官名英訳参照英文集

took up his first regular administrative post and rose through a number of the most responsible offices in the bureaucracy. After starting in the salt monopoly, he supervised **water-control systems** in several localities, administered the collection of taxes, and served a term as a local judge, during which he earned the respectful nickname "Lin the Clear Sky." Lin's quick rise showed him to be an effective organizer and ambitious bureaucrat. (Rise as administrator, Lin Tse-hs'u', Pinyin Lin Zexu leading Chinese scholar and official of the Ch'ing (Manchu) dynasty, known for his role in the events leading up to the Anglo-Chinese Opium War (1839–42). He was a proponent of the revitalization of traditional Chinese thought and institutions, a movement that became known as the Self-Strengthening Movement.)

===== river control =====
The spring melt leads to extensive flooding, which makes the control of water difficult. (Water development, Water resources, North America)

===== Tigris-Euphrates river system: Agriculture and irrigation =====
The economic life of the Tigris-Euphrates basin remains dependent on the waters of the rivers, even though oil revenues now play a dominant role in Iraq. Modern **water-control** technology has reduced the devastating effects of the flood-and-drought cycle, but at a cost of desiccated marshlands and decreased natural replenishment of soil nutrients. ...

The sheer volume of floodwater endangers the bunds (embankments) within which the rivers are confined in their lower courses. The primary requirement of **river control**, therefore, is to maintain an effective system of diversion and storage, both as a precaution against the kind of inundation that threatened Baghdad as recently as 1954 and as a means of retaining the floodwaters for distribution in the hot season. Damming and water diversion in Iraq, Syria, and Turkey will undoubtedly lead to future conflicts unless water-sharing schemes can be worked out.

===== agricultural technology =====
Drainage, irrigation, and other special techniques of **water management** are important in tropical agriculture. An example is the cultivation of rice and sugarcane in the fertile coastal areas of Guyana. Originally through private enterprise and later by government efforts, large coastal areas were "empoldered" (diked) to keep back the sea in front and floods from the rivers in the rear. With a mean annual rainfall of 90 inches (2,300 millimetres), drainage is a critical factor; in fact, the system cannot discharge all possible floodwater, and so the crops must tolerate occasional drowning. With gravity drainage effective only at low tide, the drainage gates are opened on the ebbing tide and closed on the rising tide. Great difficulty is encountered in keeping the outlets unclogged by the

heavy sediment discharge. Since rain does not always fall when it is needed, many fields are irrigated. Most of the rice soil is specially tilled after plowing in order to create a better seedbed under the water, using tractors operating in water four to six inches (10 to 15 centimetres) deep. After this special tillage, the seeds are broadcast in one to two inches (2.5 to five centimetres) of water. Though maintenance and operation of such an intricate **water-control** system are not simple, Guyana rice production has been doubled through its use.［Water management＝水利用の運営面に力点ありか］

● 太祝太宰ほか
◇ ceremony
- Master of the Ceremonies 式部官長
- Grand Master of the Ceremonies 式部職（雅楽部が所属）
- master of ceremonies 式部官
⇒ 宮内庁
◇ attend ⇒ priest
◇ server
奉車 carrier server（史 028）
◇ priest
- 祝宰 priest（史 028）
⇒ priest
◇ feast 饗宴，祝宴
◇ offering ⇒ sacrifice
◇ procurer＝軍・企業の物資調達人。またポン引き（pander; pimp）の意あり。ただし公職にも使用。
- financial officials under a **procurer**- general. (Br Belgium, history of)
- their own government is the major **procurer** of military systems (Br aerospace indusry)
- his role as Stalin's **procurer**（⇒ Br Union of the Soviet Socialist Republics）

［祠官はだいたいにおいて sacrificial official。 祝官はだいたいにおいて religious official か］
===== 史記卷二十八 封禪書 第六 =====
　　［即帝位三年，東巡郡県，祠騶嶧山，頌秦功業。・・・］其禮頗采**太祝**之祀雍上帝所用，［而封藏皆祕之，世不得而記也。］
… In both of these ceremonies he followed on the whole the procedure used by the **master of invocations** in sacrificing to the Lord on High at Yong, … (p. 12)

　　［於是始皇遂東遊海上，・・・琅邪在齊東方，］蓋歳之所始。皆各用一牢具祠，而巫祝所損益，珪幣雜異焉。

付録 1　職官名英訳参照英文集

It is said that at the beginning of each year **sacrifices were offered** at all of these places consisting of one set of **sacrificial animals**, though the jade and silk offerings presented by the shamans and **invocators** who directed the ceremonies were of various kinds and number. (p. 13-14)

［昔三代之皆在河洛之間,···］及秦並天下, 令祠官所常奉天地名山大川鬼神可得而序也。
When the First Emperor united the world, he instructed the **officials in charge of sacrifices** to put into order the worship of Heaven and Earth, the famous mountains, the great rivers, and the other spirits that had customarily been honoured in the past. (p. 16)

［於是自殽以東, 名山五, 大川祠二。曰太室。太室, 嵩高也。恆山, 泰山, 會稽, 湘山。水曰濟, 曰淮。春以脯酒為歲祠, 因泮凍, 秋涸凍, ］冬塞禱祠。其牲用牛犢各一, 牢具珪幣各異。
..., and in the winter prayers and **sacrifices were offered** to recompense the gods for their favour during the year. A cow and a calf were invariably used as sacrifices, but the **sacrificial implements** and the offerings of jade and silk differed with the time and place. (p. 16)［この下何段落か下にも同一表現 1 箇所あり（其牲用牛犢各一, 牢具珪幣各異］

［唯雍四時上帝為尊···黃犢羔各四, 珪幣各有數, ］皆生瘞埋, 無俎豆之具。
... All the sacrifices were buried alive in the ground and no sacrificial **implements** such as stands or platters were used. (p. 18)

諸此祠皆太祝常主, 以歲時奉祠之。···郡県遠方神祠者, 民各自奉祠, 不領於天子之祝官。祝官有祕祝, 即有菑祥, 輒祝祠移過於下。
All of these **places of worship** were customarily under the jurisdiction of the **master of invocations**, who saw to it that **offerings and sacrifices** were made at the appropriate seasons of the year. ... The spirits and holy places of the various provinces and other distant regions were **worshipped** by the people of their respective localities and were not under the control for the emperor's religious officials. Among the **religious officials** of the court was one called the private **invocator**. If any disaster or evil omen appeared, it was his duty to **offer sacrifices** with all speed and **pray** that the blame for the mishap might be transferred from the ruler to the officials or the people. (p. 18)

［二年, 東擊項籍而還入關, 問:「故秦時上帝祠何帝也？」對曰:「四帝, 有白, 青, 黃, 赤帝之祠。」高祖曰:「吾聞天有五帝, 而有四, 何也？」」莫知其說。於是高祖曰:「吾知之矣, 乃待我而具五也。」乃立黑帝祠, 命曰北畤。有司進祠, 上不親往。悉召故秦祝官, 複置太祝, 太宰, 如其故儀禮。因令県為公社。下詔曰:「吾甚重祠而敬祭。今上帝之祭及山川諸神当祠者, 各以其時禮祠之如故。」

269

... When no one was able to offer an explanation, Gaozu replied: "I know the reason: They were waiting for me to come and **complete** the five!" He accordingly set up a place for the Black Emperor, called the Alter of the North, with officials appointed to **carry out its sacrifices**; Gaozu did not go in person to perform sacrifices. He then summoned all of the former **religious officials** of the Qin dynasty and restored the posts of **master of invocations** and **grand supervisor**, ordering these officials to carry out the rites and ceremonies as they had in the past. He also gave instructions for altar of the dynasty to be erected in all the provinces and issued an edict saying: "I hold the **places of worship** in highest regard and deeply respect the **sacrifices**. Whenever the time comes for **sacrifices** to the Lord on High or for the **worship** of the mountains, rivers, or other spirits, let the **ceremonies** be performed in due season as they were in the past!" (p. 19)

其後二歲，或曰周興而邑邰，立後稷之祠，至今血食天下。於是高祖制詔禦史：「其令郡国県立靈星祠，常以歳時祠以牛。」

Two years later ... Gaozu accordingly issued an edict to the imperial secretary ordering placed of worship set up in all the provinces, districts, and feudal kingdoms, called **Shrines** of the Sacred Start, and dedicated to Hou Ji, where oxen should be **sacrificed** at the appropriate seasons each year. (p. 20)

始名山大川在諸侯，諸侯祝各自奉祠，[天子官不領。及齊，淮南国廢，]令太祝盡以歳時致禮如故。

Originally it had been left to the **religious officials** of the feudal lords to perform **sacrifices and offerings** to an of the famous mountains or great rivers that happened to be within their domains; ... Emperor Wen ordered his **master of invocations** to see to it that all the proper ceremonies were carried out in these regions at the proper times. (p. 20)

[文帝出長門，若見五人於道北，[遂因其直北立五帝壇，祠以五牢具。

Because of this he had an altar to the Five Emperors set up on the spot, where he **offered** five sets of **sacrificial animals**. (p. 23)

...

[亳人謬忌奏祠太一方，曰：「天神貴者太一，太一佐曰五帝。古者天子以春秋祭太一東南郊，用太牢，七日，為壇開八通之鬼道。」]於是天子令太祝立其祠長安東南郊，[常奉祠如忌方。其後人有上書，言「古者天子三年壹用太牢祠神三一：天一，地一，太一」。]天子許之，令太祝領祠之於忌太一壇上，如其方。

The emperor accordingly ordered the **master of invocations** to set up such a **place of worship** southeast of Chang'an ... The emperor gave his consent to the ritual and ordered the **master of invocations** to see to it that such sacrifices were carried out at Miu Ji's altar of the Great Unit in the manner recommended (p. 26)

270

付録1 職官名英訳参照英文集

其後, 天子苑有白鹿, 以其皮為幣, 以發瑞應, 造白金焉。
…
［上遂郊雍, 至隴西, 西登崆峒, 幸甘泉。］令祠官寬舒等具太一祠壇…祭日以牛, 祭月以羊彘特。太一祝宰則衣紫及繡。
There he gave orders to Kuan Shu and the other **officials in charge of sacrifices** to **fit out** an altar to the Great Unity. … An ox was offered to the sun and a ram or a pig to the moon. The **priest** who presented the offerings to the Great Unity wore robes of purple with brocade; (p. 38)

太史公曰：［余從巡祭天地諸神名山川而封禪焉。入壽宮侍祠神語,］究觀方士祠官之意, 於是退而論次自古以來用事於鬼神者, 具見其表裏。
The Grand Historian remarks: … and I thus had an opportunity to study and examine the ways of the magicians and the **sacrificial officials**. Later I retired and write down in order all that I knew about the worship of the spirits from ancient times on, **setting forth** both the outside and the inside stories of these affairs. (p. 51-52)

271

## 付録 2　Dubs ほかの研究者による職官名英訳比較表

（各研究者に対する参照文献については「作業の要約」に列挙した）

| 職官名 | 英語対訳 | [1]Dubs [2]Bielenstein [3]Dull | [1]Loewe [2]Giele | 備考（Hucker） |
|---|---|---|---|---|
| 三公 | three highest ministers* | [1] Gentleman to the Three Dukes（三公曹郎） | [1] – [2] Executive Council | |
| 丞相〔大司徒〕 | chancellor* 〔master of government〕 | [1] The Lieutenant Chancellor〔The Grand Minister over the Masses〕 [2] Chancellor 〔Grand Minister over the Masses〕 [3] imperial chancellor | [1] Chancellor〔同〕 [2] Chief Minister〔同〕 | (1) CH'IN-N-S DIV: Counselor-in-chief ; (2) T'ANG: Vice Director of the Department of State Affairs; (3) SUNG-MING: Grand Councilor 483〔Grand Minister of Education 6052〕 |
| 長史 | chief secretary* | [1] Chief Clerk [to the Commander-in-Chief] [2] Chief Clerk | | Lit., senior scribe. (1) CH'IN-SUNG: Aide; (2) N-S DIV—CH'ING: Administer; (3) T'ANG, CH'ING: Administrator; (4) T'ANG: Administrator; (5) YÜAN: Administrator 185 |

付録2 Dubsほかの研究者による職官名英訳比較表

| 職官名 | 英語対訳 | [1]Dubs [2]Bielenstein [3]Dull | [1]Loewe [2]Giele | 備考（Hucker） |
|---|---|---|---|---|
| 司直 | director of rectitude* | [1] Director of Uprightness [2] Director of Uprightness | | Rectifier 5585 |
| 太尉〔大司馬〕 | **grand commandant*** 〔**grand marshal***〕 | [1] The Grand Commandant〔Commander-in-Chief〕 [2] Grand Commandant〔Commander-in-Chief〕 [3] grand commandant〔grand minister of war〕 | [1] Supreme Commander〔-〕 [2] Chief of Staff〔1 (office nominally held by) Regent. 2 Chief of Staff〕 | 〔(1) CHOU: Minister of War; (2) HAN-N-S DIV: Commander-in-Chief; (3) N-S DIV (Chou) : Minister of War; (4) CH'ING: Minister of War 6039〕 |
| 長史 | chief secretary* | [1] Chief Clerk [to the Commander-in-Chief] [2] Chief Clerk | | Lit., senior scribe. (1) CH'IN-SUNG: Aide; (2) N-S DIV—CH'ING: Administer; (3) T'ANG, CH'ING: Administrator; (4) T'ANG: Administrator; (5) YÜAN: Administrator 185 |
| 御史大夫〔大司空〕 | **imperial secretary*** 〔**secretary of government**〕 | [1] The Imperial Clerk Grandee 〔The Grand Minister of Works〕 [2] randee | [1] Imperial Counsellor〔同〕 [2] Chief Prosecutor〔同〕 | Censor-in-chief 8181〔Grand Minister of Works 6037〕 |

273

| 職官名 | 英語対訳 | ¹Dubs ²Bielenstein ³Dull | ¹Loewe ²Giele | 備考（Hucker） |
|---|---|---|---|---|
| | | Secretary〔Grand Minister of Works〕³ grandee secretary〔grand minister of works〕 | | |
| 丞 | aide | | | |
| 中丞—侍御史 | middle aide*—secretary of the censorate* | ¹ __—Attendant Imperial Clerks ² __—Attending Secretary | | ——Attending Secretary |
| 繡衣直指 | imperial inquisitor in brocade robe | ¹ Specially Commissioned Messengers Wearing Embroidered Garments ² Special Commissioner Clad in Embroidered Garments | | Bandit-suppressing Censor; Bandit-suppressing Commissioner (繡衣直指 hsiu-i chih-chih) 2621 |
| 九卿 | **nine highest ministers*** | | | |
| 中二千石 | **officials of the middle two thousand picul class*** | ¹ Fully Two Thousand Piculs [Officials with nominal salary of] | ¹ ---Ministers ("Fully ² 2,000 bushels," zhong erqianshi 中二千石) | |
| 太常〔奉常〕 | **master of ritual*** 〔**imperial master of ritual**〕 | ¹ The Grand Master of Ceremonies〔The Upholder of Ceremonies〕² The Grand | ¹ Superintendent of Ceremonial〔同〕² Minister of Ceremonial〔同〕 | Chamberlain for Ceremonials 6137〔-〕 |

274

付録2  Dubsほかの研究者による職官名英訳比較表

| 職官名 | 英語対訳 | ¹Dubs<br>²Bielenstein<br>³Dull | ¹Loewe<br>²Giele | 備考（Hucker） |
|---|---|---|---|---|
|  |  | Master of Ceremonies<br>³ grand minister of ceremonies |  |  |
| 太楽令 | grand musician | ¹ Prefect Grand Musician<br>² Prefect Grand Musician |  | (1) CH'IN-N-S DIV: Grand Director of Music; (2) N-S DIV (N. Ch'i)-Yüan: Directorof the Imperial Music Office (太樂令) 6268 |
| 太祝令 | grand invocator* | ¹ Prefect Grand Supplicator<br>² Prefect Grand Supplicator |  | HAN-N-S DIV: Great Supplicator 6154 |
| 太宰令 | grand servant（史28） | ¹ Prefect Grand Butcher<br>² Prefect Grand Butcher |  | Great Sacrificial Butcher 6226 |
| 太史令 | grand historian*（漢54） | ¹ Prefect Grand Clerk<br>² Prefect Grand Astrologer |  | (1) CH'IN-N-S DIV: Grand Astrologer; (2) SUI-Yüan: Director; (3) CH'ING: Chancellor of the Hanlin Academy and a Director of the Directorate of Astronomy 6218 |
| 太卜令 | grand diviner*（史127） | ¹ Prefect Grand Augur |  | Imperial Diviner 6199 |

275

| 職官名 | 英語対訳 | ¹Dubs ²Bielenstein ³Dull | ¹Loewe ²Giele | 備考（Hucker） |
|---|---|---|---|---|
| | | ² Prefect Grand Augur | | |
| 太医令 | grand physician*（史110） | ¹ Prefect Grand Physician [under the Upholder of Ceremonies/Grand Master of Ceremonies]<br>² Prefect Grand Physician | | Imperial Physician (太医令 t'ai-i ling) 6180 |
| 均官長 | head of the office of imperial burial places | ¹ Chief of Price Adjustment [under the Grand Master of Ceremonies]<br>² Chief of the Office of Adjustment | | Fair Tax Office, headed by a Director (chang 長)(均官) 1766 |
| 都水長 | head of water control at the imperial parks | ¹ Chief Director of Waters [under the Upholder of Cerennonies/Grand Master of Ceremonies]<br>² Chief Director of the Waters | | Director of Waterways 7277 |
| 諸廟寝官令 | chief of the inner chamber of the funerary temple | | | |
| 諸廟園官令 | chief of the park of the funerary temple | | | |
| 諸廟食官令 | chief of food offerings at the funerary temple | | | |
| 博士 | erudit* | ¹ Erudit | ¹ --- | Erudite 4746 |

276

付録2　Dubsほかの研究者による職官名英訳比較表

| 職官名 | 英語対訳 | ¹Dubs<br>²Bielenstein<br>³Dull | ¹Loewe<br>²Giele | 備考<br>（Hucker） |
|---|---|---|---|---|
|  |  | ² Erudit | ² Academician |  |
| 光禄勲〔郎中令〕 | **keeper of the palace gate*** (漢68.71.78.97)〔**chief of palace corridor attendants**（漢54.63)〕 | ¹ The Superintendent of the Imperial Household〔Prefect of the Gentlemen of the Palace〕<br>² Superintendent of the Imperial Household〔Prefect of the Gentleman-of-the Palace〕<br>³〔prefect of the gentlemen of the palace〕 | Superintendent of the Palace〔同〕<br><br>Minister of Palace〔同〕 | (1) HAN-N-S DIV: Chamberlain for Attendants (2) N-S DIV-CH'ING: Chief Minister (ch'ing) of the Court of Imperial Entertainments (光禄勲) 3347〔Chamberlain for Attendants 3570〕 |
| 太中大夫 | grand palace counselor | ¹ Grand Palace Grandee<br>² Grand Palace Grandee<br>³ grand palace grandee |  | Superior Grand Master of the Palace 6155 |
| 中大夫〔光禄大夫〕 | palace counselor* (漢63)〔counselor to the keeper of the palace gate* (漢63.68.71.74)〕 | ¹ Palace Grandee〔Imperial Household Grandee〕<br>²〔Imperial Household Grandee〕 | Palace Advisor〔同〕 | 〔Grand Master for Splendid Happiness, ただし光禄大夫3349〕 |
| 諫大夫 | admonisher* | ¹ Grandee-remonstrant<br>² Grandee Remonstrant | ¹ ---<br>² Advisor | Grand Master of Remonstrance 865 |
| 五官中郎 | senior officer of | ¹ General of the | ¹ --- | Leader of Court |

277

| 職官名 | 英語対訳 | [1]Dubs [2]Bielenstein [3]Dull | [1]Loewe [2]Giele | 備考（Hucker） |
|---|---|---|---|---|
| 将 | palace corridor attendants at the "Five Bureaus" | Gentlemen of the Household for All Purposes [2] General of the Gentlemen-of-the- Household for All Purposes | [2]［中郎将］ Leader of the Courtiers-in-waiting | Gentleman for Miscellaneous Users 7787 |
| 左中郎将 | senior officer of palace corridor attendants of the left | [1] General of the Gentlemen of the Household on the Left [2] General of the Gentlemen-of-the-Hou-sehold of the Left | [1] --- [2]［中郎将］ Leader of the Courtiers-in-waiting | (1) HAN-N-S DIV: Leader of Court Gentlemen, differentiated by the prefixes tso (of the Left), yu (of the Right); (2) T'ANG-SUNG: Commandant（中郎將）1581 |
| 右中郎将 | senior officer of palace corridor attendants of the right | [1] General of the Gentlemen of the Household on the Right [2] General of the Gentlemen-of-the-Household of the Right | [1] --- [2]［中郎将］ Leader of the Courtiers-in-waiting | (1) HAN-N-S DIV: Leader of Court Gentlemen, differentiated by the prefixes tso (of the Left), yu (of the Right); (2) T'ANG-SUNG: Commandant（中郎將）1581 |
| 中郎 | palace gentleman*（漢 54） | [1] Gentleman of the Household | [1] --- [2] Courtier-in-waiting (high-ranking) | |
| 侍郎 | attendant in the | [1] Gentleman in | [1] --- | (1) |

278

付録2 Dubsほかの研究者による職官名英訳比較表

| 職官名 | 英語対訳 | ¹Dubs<br>²Bielenstein<br>³Dull | ¹Loewe<br>²Giele | 備考<br>（Hucker） |
|---|---|---|---|---|
|  | inner palace*（漢65） | Attendance<br>² Gentleman-in-Atten-dance | ² Courtier-in-waiting (middle-ranking) | HAN-T'ANG: Attendant Gentleman (2) N-S DIV-SUNG: Vice Director (3) N-S DIV-CH'ING: Vice Minister 5278 |
| 郎中 | palace corridor attendant | ¹ Gentleman of the Palace<br>² Gentleman-of-the-Palace | ¹ ---<br>² Courtier-in-waiting (low-ranking) | (1) HAN-N-S DIV: Gentleman of the Interior; (2) N-S DIV-CH'ING: Director of a Section (ts'ao) or Bureau (pu, ssu, ch'ing-li ssu) in a Ministry (pu) or in some agency of comparable status, e.g. 3565 |
| 車将 | senior officer of carriage |  |  |  |
| 戸将 | senior officer of watch gates |  |  |  |
| 騎将 | senior officer of cavalry（史7） |  |  |  |
| 郎中 | palace corridor attendant（漢63） | ¹ Gentleman of the Palace<br>² Gentleman-of-the-Palace | ¹ ---<br>² Courtier-in-waiting (low-ranking) | (1) HAN-N-S DIV: Gentleman of the Interior; (2) N-S DIV-CH'ING: Director of a |

279

| 職官名 | 英語対訳 | [1]Dubs [2]Bielenstein [3]Dull | [1]Loewe [2]Giele | 備考（Hucker） |
|---|---|---|---|---|
|  |  |  |  | Section (ts'ao) or Bureau (pu,ssu,ch'ing-li ssu) in a Ministry (pu) or in some agency of comparable status, e.g. 3565 |
| 謁者僕射 | chief master of guests（史 101.102） | [1] Supervisor of the Internuncios [2] Supervisor of the Internuncios | [1] [2] Vice Director of the Imperial Receptionists | Receptionist（謁者）; they were commonly organized under one or more Supervisors (pu' yeh) chosen from among their ranks 7908 |
| 謁者 | master of guests（漢 63.65.74.74.78） | [1] nternuncio [2] Internuncio |  | Receptionist 7908 |
| 期門僕射〔虎賁中郎将〕 | archery captain at the Rendezvous Gate（漢 67.68）〔senior officer of palace corridor attendants for the picked troops（漢 54.63.68.71.74.史 103.123）〕 | [1]〔General of the Gentlemen of the Household As Rapid As a Tiger〕 [2]〔General of the Gentlemen-of-the-Household Rapid as Tigers〕 | [1] --- [2]〔中郎将〕 Leader of the Courtiers-in-waiting |  |
| 期門〔虎賁郎〕 | keeper of the Rendezvous Gate*（漢 65）〔junior officer of the picked troops〕 | [1] Attendants of the Gates〔-〕 [2] Attendant at the Gates〔-〕 |  | Gate Guardsman, as many as 1000 Court Gentlemen (lang) led by a Supervisor |

付録2　Dubsほかの研究者による職官名英訳比較表

| 職官名 | 英語対訳 | [1]Dubs [2]Bielenstein [3]Dull | [1]Loewe [2]Giele | 備考（Hucker） |
|---|---|---|---|---|
| | | | | (p'u-yeh) 629 〔Gentleman Braves as Tigers 2788 or 2787〕 |
| 羽林中郎将 | senior officer of palace corridor attendants for the Feather and Forest Guard | [1] General of the Gentlemen of the Household of the Feathered Forest [2] General of the Gentlemen-of-the-Household of the Feathered Forest | [2]〔中郎将〕 Leader of the Courtiers-in-waiting | 上に参照 |
| 羽林騎都尉 | chief commandant of cavalry for Feather and Forest Guard | [1] Chief Commandant of the Cavalry of the Feathered Forest [2]〔羽林騎〕 Cavalry of the Feathered Forest | | Palace Guard Cavalry (羽林騎 yü-lin ch'i); they were originally commanded by a Director (ling 令), then by a Leader of Court Gentlemen (chung-lang chiang 中郎将) with rank=2000 bushels also refer to a Supervisor (tu-wei 都尉) of the same rank 8150 |
| 羽林郎 | horseman of the Feather and Forest Guard* （漢68） | | | |
| 衛尉 | colonel of the | [1] The Command- | [1] Superintendent | Chamberlain for |

281

| 職官名 | 英語対訳 | ¹Dubs<br>²Bielenstein<br>³Dull | ¹Loewe<br>²Giele | 備考<br>(Hucker) |
|---|---|---|---|---|
| | guard*(漢 54.63.65.68.74.78) | ant of the Palace Guard<br>² Commandant of the Guards | of the Guards<br>² Minister of the Guards | the Palace Garrison7681 |
| 公車司馬令 | chief marshal of the palace gates | ¹ Prefect of the Major in Charge of Official Chariots[-]<br>² [公車司馬] Prefect of the Majors in Charge of Official Carriages[-] | | 公車司馬門 Gate Traffic Control Office。Directors 2 名 (公車司馬令 k'ung-ch'e ssu-ma ling および公車令 kung-ch'e ling)により統率 3394 |
| 衛士令 | chief of the palace guard | ¹ Prefect of the Guards<br>² Prefect of the Guards | | |
| 旅賁令 | chief of envoys | ¹ Prefect of the Emergency Cohort<br>² Prefect of the Emergency Cohort | | Imperial Escort (旅賁), led by a Director (ling 令) in HAN 3889 |
| 屯司馬 | marshal of the stationed unit | | | |
| 衛司馬 | marshal of the palace guard | | | |
| 候司馬 | marshal of scouts | | | |
| 太僕 | master of carriage*(漢 65.68.74) | ¹ The Grand Coachman<br>² Grand Coachman<br>³ grand keeper of equipages | ¹ Superintendent of Transport<br>² Minister of the Stables | (1) CHOU: Royal Groom; (2) CH'IN-N-S DIV: Chamberlain for the Imperial Stud |

付録2 Dubsほかの研究者による職官名英訳比較表

| 職官名 | 英語対訳 | ¹Dubs<br>²Bielenstein<br>³Dull | ¹Loewe<br>²Giele | 備考<br>(Hucker) |
|---|---|---|---|---|
| | | | | 6201 |
| 大廏令 | chief of the imperial stables | | | |
| 未央令 | chief of carriage and horses for the Eternal Palace | ¹ Prefect of the Wei-yang Palace Stables<br>² Prefect of the Stables of the Eternal Palace (Former Han); Prefect of the Eternal Stables (Later Han) | | Director of the Inner Compound Stable (未央令) |
| 家馬令〔挏馬令〕 | chief of the imperial household's horses〔chief of the emperor's horses〕 | ¹ Prefect of the Stables for the Imperial Household Mares〔Prefect of the Mare Milkers〕<br>² Prefect of the Stables for the Imperial Household Mares〔Prefect of the Mare Milkers〕 | | 〔Director of the Imperial Mares 7495〕 |
| 車府令 | chief of the office of carriage | ¹ Prefect of the Coachhouses for Imperial Equipages<br>² Prefect of the Coachhouses for Imperial Equipages (chü-fu ling) | | Director of the Livery Office 357 |

283

| 職官名 | 英語対訳 | ¹Dubs ²Bielenstein ³Dull | ¹Loewe ²Giele | 備考（Hucker） |
|---|---|---|---|---|
| 路軨令 | chief of light hunting chariots | ¹ Prefect of the Coach houses for Imperial Chariots ² Prefect of the Coach Houses for Imperial Chariots | | 路れい令 or 輅れい令 Director of the Imperial Hunting Chariots 3852 |
| 騎馬令 | chief of cavalry horses | ¹ Prefect of the Stable for Riding Horses ² Prefect of the Stable for Riding Horses | | Director of Cavalry Mounts 570 |
| 駿馬令 | chief of famous steed | ¹ Prefect of the Stables for Fine Horses ² Prefect of the Stables for Fine Horses | | Director of the Finest Steeds 1772 |
| 廷尉〔大理〕 | **commandant of justice*〔grand examiner*（史11）〕** | ¹ The Commandant of Justice〔The Grand Judge〕 ² Commandant of Justice | ¹ Superintendent of Trials〔同〕 ² Minister of Trials〔同〕 | Chamberlain for Law Enforcement 6767 |
| 正監 | superintendent of the center（史30） | | | |
| 左監〔左平〕 | superintendent of the left〔judge of the left〕 | ¹ Inspector on the Left〔Referee on the Left〕 ² Inspector of the Left〔Referee on the Left〕 | | (1) Directorate; (2) Supervisor or Director; (3) T' ANG: Horse Pasturage; (4) SUNG: Industrial |

284

付録2 Dubsほかの研究者による職官名英訳比較表

| 職官名 | 英語対訳 | ¹Dubs<br>²Bielenstein<br>³Dull | ¹Loewe<br>²Giele | 備考<br>(Hucker) |
|---|---|---|---|---|
| 右監〔右平〕 | superintendent of the right（漢74）〔judge of the right〕 | ¹ Inspector on the Right〔Referee on the Right〕<br>² Inspector of the Right〔Referee of the Right〕 | | Prefecture (監) 786〔平 Arbiter 4698〕<br>(1) Directorate; (2) Supervisor or Director; (3) T'ANG: Horse Pasturage; (4) SUNG: Industrial Prefecture (監) 786 |
| 典客〔大鴻臚〕 | **director of foreign guests**（史9.9.10.11.118）〔**director of foreign vassals***（漢63.68.78）〕 | ¹ The Director of Guests〔The Grand Herald〕<br>² Director of Guests〔Grand Herald〕 | ¹ Superintendent of State Visits〔同〕<br>² Minister of Feudal Relations〔同〕 | (1) CH'IN-HAN: Chamberlain for Dependencies; (2) T'ANG-SUNG: Custodian of Foreign Visitors; (3) CH'ING: Minister of the Court of Colonial Affairs 6600〔Chamberlain for Dependencies 5947〕 |
| 行人令〔大行令〕 | chief of messengers〔grand messenger*（漢78.史11.49.108.111.114.116.118.120. | ¹ Prefect Usher〔The Prefect Grand Usher〕<br>² Prefect Usher〔Prefect Grand Usher〕 | 〔典客と同じ〕<br>〔典客と同じ〕 | Messenger (行人), (1) HAN: designation of couriers subordinate to the Chamberlain for |

285

| 職官名 | 英語対訳 | ¹Dubs<br>²Bielenstein<br>³Dull | ¹Loewe<br>²Giele | 備考<br>（Hucker） |
|---|---|---|---|---|
| | 123)〕 | 〔以下同様に1段目から3段目にかけて Dubs, Bielenstein, Dull の順〕 | | Dependencies, headed by a Director (ling 令); (2) MING: Messenger Office, a central government agency attached to the Ministry of Rites, headed by a director (cheng 丞) (hsing-jen) 2574 〔大行 Messenger Office, headed by a Director (*ling*) 5955〕 |
| 訳官令 | chief of interpreters | Prefect of the Office for Interpreting<br><br>Prefect of the Office of Interpreters | | Director of interpreters (譯官令 i-kuan ling) 2966 |
| 別火令 | chief of the maintenance of the sacred fire | Prefect of the Fresh Fire<br><br>Prefect of the Fresh Fire | | Director of Fire Renewal 4626 |
| 郡邸長 | head of the provincial offices in the capital | Chief of the Lodges for the Commanderies<br><br>Chief of the Commandery | | Liaison Hostel for the Commandery, each headed by a Director (ling 令) and an Aide (ch' |

286

付録2  Dubsほかの研究者による職官名英訳比較表

| 職官名 | 英語対訳 | ¹Dubs<br>²Bielenstein<br>³Dull | ¹Loewe<br>²Giele | 備考<br>(Hucker) |
|---|---|---|---|---|
|  |  | Quarters |  | eng) (郡邸) 1974 |
| 宗正〔宗伯〕 | **director of the imperial clan*** （漢54.63.68.74）〔master of the imperial clan〕 | The Superintendent of the Imperial House〔Elder of the Imperial House〕<br><br>Director of the Imperial Clan〔Elder of the Imeperial Clan〕 | Superintendent of the Imperial Clan〔一〕<br><br>Minister of Ancestral Worship〔同〕 | 〔(1) CHOU: Minister of Rites (2) HAN: Chamberlain for the Imperial Clan (3) N-S DIV-CH'ING Chief Minister or Director of the Court of the Imperial Clan (4) CH'ING: Chief Minister of the Court of Imperial Sacrifices 7147〕 |
| 都司空令 | chief of criminal affairs in the imperial family | Prefect of the Central Capital District Director of Works<br><br>Prefect Director of Works in the Central District of the Capital | ²〔御史大夫/司空〕Chief Prosecutor | Prison for Imperial Kinsman (都司空獄), headed by a Director (ling) 7286 |
| 内官長 | head of the office of weights and measures | Chief of the Inner Palace Office<br><br>Chief of the Inner Palace Office |  | (1) From antiquity, one of many terms for eunuch; (2) From antiquity, a variant of nü-kuan (Palace Woman); (3) Throughout history may be |

287

| 職官名 | 英語対訳 | ¹Dubs ²Bielenstein ³Dull | ¹Loewe ²Giele | 備考（Hucker) |
|---|---|---|---|---|
| | | | | encountered in reference to personnel in palace service as opposed to central government personnel; (4) HAN: Palace Manager; (5) HAN: Inner Official; (6) SUI: Inner Officials (内官) 4203 |
| 諸公主家令 | steward in the household of the princess | | | |
| 諸公主門尉 | commander of gatekeepers in the household of the princess | | | |
| 大司農〔治粟内史〕 | **minister of revenue〔secretary in charge of grain\***(史11.56)〕 | The Grand Minister of Agriculture〔The Clerk of the Capital for Supplies〕<br><br>Grand Minister of Agriculture〔Clerk of the Capital for Supplies〕<br><br>grand minister of agriculture | 治粟内史/大司農 Superintendent of Agriculture〔同〕<br><br>治粟内史/大司農 Minister of Agriculture〔同〕 | (1) HAN-N-S DIV: Chamberlain for the National Treasury; (2) T'ANG-CH'ING: Minister of Revenue 6042〔Chamberlain for the National Treasury 1069〕 |

288

付録 2  Dubs ほかの研究者による職官名英訳比較表

| 職官名 | 英語対訳 | [1]Dubs [2]Bielenstein [3]Dull | [1]Loewe [2]Giele | 備考（Hucker） |
|---|---|---|---|---|
| 太倉令 | chief of the central granary | Prefect of the Grand Granary<br><br>Prefect of the Grand Granary<br><br>太倉長 chief ot the grand granary | | Director of the Imperial Granaries 6230 |
| 均輸令 | chief of the transport office for equalizing prices | Prefect of Price Adjustment and Transportation [under the Grand Minister of Agriculture]<br><br>Prefect of Price Adjustment and Transportation | | Office of Tax Substitutes (Each headed by a Director (ling 令) and an Aide (ch'eng) (均輸) 1787 |
| 平準令 | chief of the office for the balanced standard | Prefect of the Bureau of Equalization and Standards<br><br>Prefect of the Bureau of Equalization and Standards | | Bureau of Standards (平準), headed by a Director (ling 令) 4705 |
| 都内令 | chief of granaries in the capital | The Prefect over the Imperial Treasury<br><br>Prefect of the Imperial Treasury | | Imperial Treasury (都内), headed by a Director (ling) 7260 |
| 籍田令 | chief of the | Prefect Over the | | Sacred fields |

289

| 職官名 | 英語対訳 | ¹Dubs<br>²Bielenstein<br>³Dull | ¹Loewe<br>²Giele | 備考<br>（Hucker） |
|---|---|---|---|---|
| | sacred field in the palace | Sacred Field<br><br>Prefect of the Sacred Field | | (籍田); In Han there was a Director of the Sacred Fields (chi-t'ien ling) 602 |
| 斡官長 | head of the office of salt, iron, and liquor taxes | Chief Controlling the Office<br><br>Chief of the Controlling Office | | chief Administrative Clerk(斡官長) 3134 |
| 鉄市長 | head of the control of iron monopoly | Chief of the Market for Iron<br><br>Chief of the Market of Iron | | Iron Market (鉄市), headed by a Director (chang 長) 6510 |
| 捜粟都尉 | chief commandant for requisitioning grain*（漢 54.63.68） | Chief Commandant Who Searches for Grain<br><br>Chief Commandant Who Searches for Grain | | Commandant-in-chief for Foraging (捜粟都尉) 5532 |
| 少府 | **privy treasurer*** | The Privy Treasurer<br><br>Privy Treasurer | Minister of Resources | (1) CH'IN-N-S DIV: Chamberlain for the Palace Revenues (2) T'ANG-Yüan: District Defender (3) CH'ING: Grand |

290

付録2　Dubsほかの研究者による職官名英訳比較表

| 職官名 | 英語対訳 | [1]Dubs [2]Bielenstein [3]Dull | [1]Loewe [2]Giele | 備考（Hucker） |
|---|---|---|---|---|
| | | | | Minister of the Imperial Household Department (4) CH'ING: District Jailor 5097 |
| 尚書令 | master of palace writers | Prefect of the Masters of Writing | Director (尚書台 Imperial Secretariat --尚書令) | |
| 符節令 | chief of the imperial credentials | Prefect of Insignia and Credentials<br><br>Prefect of Insignia and Credentials | | Manager of Credentials 2042 |
| 太医令 | grand physician for the imperial household | Prefect Grand Physician [under the Upholder of Ceremonies/Grand Master of Ceremonies]<br><br>Prefect Grand Physician | | Imperial Physician (太医令 t'ai-i ling) 6180 |
| 太官令 | grand butler of the imperial household | Prefect Grand Provisioner<br><br>Prefect Grand Provisioner | | (1) CH'IN-N-S DIV: Provisioner (2) CH'ING: Chief Minister of the Court of Imperial Entertainments |

| 職官名 | 英語対訳 | ¹Dubs ²Bielenstein ³Dull | ¹Loewe ²Giele | 備考（Hucker） |
|---|---|---|---|---|
| | | | | 6185 |
| 湯官令 | chief of the emperor's patisserie | Prefect of the Office for Liquors<br><br>Prefect of the Office of Liquors<br><br>湯官 provisioner of wines and fruits | | Office of Drinks and Delicacies (湯官), headed by a Director (ling 令) assisted by 2 Aide (ch'eng) 6298 |
| 導官令 | chief of the grain selectors | Prefect of the Office for Selecting Grain<br><br>道官令 Prefect of the Office for Selection of Grain | | 道 (下に禾がある) 官署 Office of Grain Supplies, headed by a Director (ling 令) 6318 |
| 楽府令 | chief of the Music Bureau | Prefect of the Bureau of Music<br><br>Prefect of the Bureau of Music | | Music Bureau (樂府), headed by a Director (ling 令) 8262 |
| 若盧令 | chief of the *Ruolu* court | Prefect of the Hunting Dog Office<br><br>［若盧獄令］Prefect of the Hunting Dog Prison | | Central Prison (若盧獄), with a eunuch Director (ling) 3061 |
| 考工室令 | chief of the government artisans | | | |

292

付録2 Dubsほかの研究者による職官名英訳比較表

| 職官名 | 英語対訳 | ¹Dubs ²Bielenstein ³Dull | ¹Loewe ²Giele | 備考（Hucker） |
|---|---|---|---|---|
| 左弋令〔佽飛令〕 | chief of the emperor's hunting assistants〔chief of hunting archery for the emperor〕 | Prefect of the Bird Shooting Aides〔Prefect of the Sharpshooters〕<br><br>Prefect of the Bird Shooting Aides〔Prefect of the Sharpshooters〕 |  | 左弋 Duck Hunter, headed by a Director (ling 令) (tso-i) 6972〔Duck Hunter, headed by a Director (ling 令). (し飛) 7555〕 |
| 居室令〔保宮令〕 | chief of the detention room in the palace〔supervisor of the detention room〕 | Prefect of the Convict Barracks〔Prefect of the Protective Enclosure〕<br><br>Prefect of the Convict Barracks〔Prefect of the Protective Enclosure〕 |  | Palace Prison, headed by a Director (ling 令) (居室) 1685 〔Palace Prison (保宮), headed by a Director (ling 令) (pao-kung) 4487〕 |
| 昆台令〔甘泉居室令〕 | chief of the *Kuntai* detention room〔chief of the detention room in the Palace of Sweet Springs〕 | Prefect of the K'un Terrace〔Prefect of the Convict Barracks of the Kan-ch'üan Palace〕<br><br>Prefect of the K'un Terrace〔Prefect of the Convict Barracks of the Palace of Sweet |  | Pavilion of Kinsmen (昆臺), headed by a Director (ling 令) 3386〔-〕 |

293

| 職官名 | 英語対訳 | [1]Dubs [2]Bielenstein [3]Dull | [1]Loewe [2]Giele | 備考（Hucker） |
|---|---|---|---|---|
| | | Springs] | | |
| 左司空令 | chief of compulsory labour of the left | | | |
| 右司空令 | chief of compulsory labour of the right | Prefect of the Office of Director of Works in the Western District of the Capital<br><br>Prefect Director of Works in the Western District of the Capital | [2]［御史大夫/司空］Chief Prosecutor | Director of Convict Labor (司空令), the latter 2 prefixed Left and Right, in reference to the eastern and western sectors 5689 |
| 東織令 | chief of the eastern weaving room | Prefect of the Eastern Weaving Chamber<br><br>Prefect of the Eastern Weaving House | | East Weaving Shop (東織), headed by a Director (ling 令) 7424 |
| 西織令 | chief of the western weaving room | | | |
| 東園匠令 | chief of the craftsmen of the imperial tombs | Prefect of the Artisans of the Eastern Enclosure<br><br>Prefect of the Artisans of the Eastern Garden | | Capenter of the Eastern Park (東園匠), headed by a Director (ling) with an Aide (ch'eng) 7462 |
| 胞人長 | head of cooks | | | |
| 都水長 | head of water control at the | Chief Director of Waters [under | | Director of Waterways 7277 |

294

付録 2　Dubs ほかの研究者による職官名英訳比較表

| 職官名 | 英語対訳 | ¹Dubs ²Bielenstein ³Dull | ¹Loewe ²Giele | 備考（Hucker） |
|---|---|---|---|---|
|  | imperial parks | the Upholder of Cerennonies/Grand Master of Ceremonies] <br><br> Chief Director of the Waters |  |  |
| 均官長 | head of the office of imperial burial places | Chief of Price Adjustment [under the Grand Master of Ceremonies] <br><br> Chief of the Office of Adjustment |  | Fair Tax Office, headed by a Director (chang 長) (均官) 1766 |
| 上林十池監 | supervisor of the maintenance of ponds at the Imperial Forest Park |  |  |  |
| 中書謁者令〔中書令〕 | master of documents and guests〔chief of palace writers*（漢 67.68.78.92）〕 | Prefect of the Palace Writer Internuncios 〔—〕 <br><br> Prefect of the Palace Writers and Internuncios 〔—〕 | Director of the Palace Secretaries and Receptionists 〔—〕 |  |
| 黄門令 | chief the Yellow Gate | Prefect of the Yellow Gates <br><br> Prefect of the Yellow Gates |  | Director of Eunuch Attendants 2844 |
| 鉤盾令 | chief of the | Prefect Intendant |  | Office of |

295

| 職官名 | 英語対訳 | ¹Dubs<br>²Bielenstein<br>³Dull | ¹Loewe<br>²Giele | 備考<br>（Hucker） |
|---|---|---|---|---|
| | control of the imperial parks | of the Imperial Palace Parks<br><br>鉤盾監 Inspector of the Intendant of the Imperial Palace Gardens | | Imperial Parks Products, headed by one or more Directors (chien, rank 600 bushes, in Han; ling, rank 8a, in T'ang) (鉤盾署 kou-tun shu) 3218 |
| 尚方令 | chief of the royal craftsmen | Prefect of the Master of the Recipes<br><br>Prefect of the Masters of Techniques | | Directorate for Imperial Manufactories (尚方), headed by a Director (ling 令) 4992 |
| 御府令 | chief of royal garments | Prefect of the Imperial Wardrobe<br><br>Prefect of the Imperial Wardrobe | | 御府 Palace Wardrobe, headed by a eunuch Director (ling 令) 8129 |
| 永巷令〔掖庭令〕 | chief of the Long Halls Palace〔chief of the women's quarters〕 | Prefect of the Long Lanes〔一〕<br><br>Prefect of the Long Lanes〔一〕 | | Palace Discipline Service (永巷), a eunuch agency with a Director (ling 令) 8097〔一〕 |
| 内者令 | chief of the palace interior（漢 97） | Prefect of the Valets<br><br>Prefect of the Valets | | Palace Servant (内者), headed by a Director (ling 令) 4143 |

付録2 Dubsほかの研究者による職官名英訳比較表

| 職官名 | 英語対訳 | ¹Dubs ²Bielenstein ³Dull | ¹Loewe ²Giele | 備考（Hucker） |
|---|---|---|---|---|
| 宦者令 | chief of eunuchs（史9） | Prefect of the Eunuchs<br><br>Prefect of the Eunuchs | | Director of Eunuchs 2823 |
| 中尉〔執金吾〕 | **military commander of the capital***（史122）〔**chief of the capital police***（漢63.68.78.97）〕 | The Commandant of the Capital〔The Bearer of the Golden Mace〕<br><br>Commandant of the Capital〔Bearer of the Gilded Mace〕 | Superintendent of the Capital〔同〕<br><br>Minister of Capital Security〔同〕 | (1) HAN: Chamberlain for the Imperial Insignia; (2) HAN: Commandant-in-ordinary of the Nobles; (3) HAN-N-S DIV, Yüan: Commaandant-in-ordinary 1638〔Chamberlain for the Imperial Insignia 964〕 |
| 候 | scout*（史109.123） | | | |
| 司馬 | marshal*（史7.8.48.101.102.111） | Major [under the Commandant of the Capital/Bearer of the Golden Mace]<br><br>Major | | Lit., to be in charge of horses, i.e., of cavalry; a title deriving from high antiquity and used through most of imperial history; (1) CHOU: Minister of War; (2) CHOU: Commander; (3) (1) HAN-N-S |

297

| 職官名 | 英語対訳 | ¹Dubs ²Bielenstein ³Dull | ¹Loewe ²Giele | 備考（Hucker） |
|---|---|---|---|---|
| | | | | DIV: Defender-in-chief; (4) : (1) HAN-N-S DIV: Commander; (5) N-S DIV-SUNG: Vice or Assistant; (6) SUI-T'ANG: Adjutant; (7) CHIN-YÜAN: Adjutant; (8) MINg-CH'ING: Vice Prefect; (9) MING-CH'ING: Minister of War 5713 |
| 千人 | head of a battalion of 1,000 men*（史107） | Millarian [under the Commandant of the Capital/Bearer of the Golden Mace]<br><br>Millarian | | Battalion Commander 903 |
| 中壘令 | commander of the security force | Prefect of the Capital Encampment<br><br>Prefect of the Capital Rampart | | Director of the Capital Garrison, assisted by a Vice Director (ch'eng) and associated with Commandants (wei, Hsiao-wei 校尉) (chung-lei ling) 1582 |

298

付録2　Dubsほかの研究者による職官名英訳比較表

| 職官名 | 英語対訳 | ¹Dubs<br>²Bielenstein<br>³Dull | ¹Loewe<br>²Giele | 備考（Hucker） |
|---|---|---|---|---|
| 寺互令 | chief of interoffice liaison | Prefect of the Ssu-hu<br><br>Prefect of the Ssu-hu | | Director of the Ssu-hu 5645 |
| 武庫令 | chief of the arsenal*（漢74） | Prefect of the Arsenal<br><br>Prefect of the Arsenal | | (1) HAN-N-S DIV: Director of the Armory; (2) CH'ING: Chief Minister of the Court of Imperial Armaments 7781 |
| 都船令 | chief of the water police | Prefect of the Director of Boats<br><br>Prefect of the Director of Boats | | Director of the Capital Boats 7215 |
| 式道候 | captain of the lead bannermen | Captains of the Standard Bearers<br><br>式道中候<br>Captain of the Centre of the Standard Bearers<br>式道左候<br>Captain of the Left of the Standard Bearers<br>式道右候<br>Captain of the Right of the Standard Bearers | | Commandant of the Imperial Escort (式道侯 shih-tao hou) 5318 |
| 左中候 | captain of the left bannermen | | | |
| 右中候 | captain of the | | | |

299

| 職官名 | 英語対訳 | ¹Dubs ²Bielenstein ³Dull | ¹Loewe ²Giele | 備考（Hucker） |
|---|---|---|---|---|
|  | right bannermen |  |  |  |
| 左京輔都尉 | chief commandant of the left of the capital |  |  |  |
| 右京輔都尉 | chief commandant of the right of the capital |  |  |  |
| 二千石 | official of the two thousand picul rank* | [Officials with nominal salary of] Two Thousand Piculs | Other top-ranking officials (about "2,00 bushels," erqianshi 二千石) |  |
| 太子太傅 | grand tutor to the heir apparent* (漢書 74.78) | Grand Tutor to the Heir-apparent<br><br>Grand Tutor to the Heir-apparent | Senior Tutor to the Heir Apparent | Grand Mentor of the Heir Apparent 6256 |
| 太子少傅 | lesser tutor to the heir apparent* (漢書 67) | Junior Tutor to the Heir-apparent<br><br>Junior Tutor of the Heir-apparent | Junior Tutor to the Hair Apparent | Junior Mentor of the Heir Apparent 6251 |
| 太子門大夫 | lord of the gate to the heir apparent | Grandee at the Gate of the Heir-apparent<br><br>Grandee at the Gate of the Heir-apparent |  | Grand Master of the Gates (門大夫), commonly serving in the household of the Heir Apparent 3951 |

付録2 Dubsほかの研究者による職官名英訳比較表

| 職官名 | 英語対訳 | [1]Dubs [2]Bielenstein [3]Dull | [1]Loewe [2]Giele | 備考（Hucker） |
|---|---|---|---|---|
| 太子庶子 | secretary to the heir apparent | | | |
| 太子先馬 | mounted guard to the heir apparent*（史120） | Forerunner of the Heir-apparent<br><br>Forerunner of the Heir-apparent | | |
| 太子舍人 | retainer in the household of the heir apparent*（史120） | Member of the Heir-apparent's Suite<br><br>Member of the Suite of the Heir-apparent | | |
| 将作大匠 | **master of construction works** | The Court Architect<br><br>Court Architect | 将作少府/将作大匠 Court Architect<br><br>将作少府/将作大匠 Superintendent of Construction | Chamberlain for the Palace Buildings (將作大匠) 712 |
| 石庫令 | chief of stone materials | Prefect of the Stoneyard<br><br>Prefect of the Stoneyard | | Stoneyard (石庫), headed by a Director (ling 令) 5268 |
| 東園主章令〔木工令〕 | chief of wooden materials at the Eastern Garden〔chief of woodworkers〕 | Prefect of the Eastern Park for Large Timbers〔一〕<br><br>Prefect of Large Timbers for the | | Woodsman of the Eastern Park (東園主章), headed by a Director (ling 令) with an Aide (ch'eng) 7463 |

301

| 職官名 | 英語対訳 | ¹Dubs ²Bielenstein ³Dull | ¹Loewe ²Giele | 備考（Hucker） |
|---|---|---|---|---|
|  |  | Eastern Garden 〔一〕 |  | 〔一〕 |
| 左校令 | commander of the left over compulsory labour | Prefect Controller of the Left<br><br>Prefect of the Enclosure of the Left |  | Director of a Construction (校令 hsiao-ling) 2422 |
| 右校令 | commander of the right over compulsory labour | Prefect Controller of the Right<br><br>Prefect of the Enclosure of the Right |  | Director of a Construction (校令 hsiao-ling) 2422 |
| 前校令 | commander of the front over compulsory labour |  |  |  |
| 後校令 | commander of the rear over compulsory labour |  |  |  |
| 中校令 | commander of the middle over compulsory labour |  |  |  |
| 詹事 | **chamberlain to the empress and the heir apparent**(史107.120) | The Supplier<br><br>Supervisor of the Household | Supervisor of the Household |  |
| 太子率更令 | chief of the night guard in the household of the |  |  |  |

付録2 Dubs ほかの研究者による職官名英訳比較表

| 職官名 | 英語対訳 | ¹Dubs ²Bielenstein ³Dull | ¹Loewe ²Giele | 備考（Hucker） |
|---|---|---|---|---|
| | heir apparent | | | |
| 太子家令 | steward in the household of the heir apparent* （史101） | Prefect of the Household of the Heir-apparent<br><br>Prefect of the Household of the Heir-apparent | | Household Provisioner (家令), normally in the household of an Heir Apparent 669 |
| 太子僕 | chief of the heir apparent's horses | Chief Driver of the Heir-apparent<br><br>Coachman of the Heir-apparent | | Coachman of the Heir Apparent 6245 |
| 太子中盾 | chief of patrol in the household of the heir apparent | Chief of the Palace Patrol of the Heir-apparent<br><br>Palace Patroller of the Heir-apparent | | Palace Patrolman (中盾), normally prefixed with t'ai-tzu 1636 |
| 太子衛率 | chief of the gatekeepers in the household of the heir apparent | Chief Generalssimo of the Guard of the The Heir-apparent<br><br>Leader of the Guard of the Heir-apparent | | |
| 太子厨廄 | chief of the kitchen and stables in the household of the heir apparent | | | |

303

| 職官名 | 英語対訳 | ¹Dubs ²Bielenstein ³Dull | ¹Loewe ²Giele | 備考（Hucker） |
|---|---|---|---|---|
| 中長秋 | steward in the household of the empress | The Empress's Long Autumn Palace<br><br>Prefect of the Empress's Palace of Prolonged Autumn | | Domestic Service of the Empress 1531 |
| 私府令 | chief of ritual implements | Prefect of the Private Treasury [of the Empress]<br><br>Prefect of the Private Storehouse | | Private Storehouse, supervised by a Director (ling 令 in Former Han, chang in Later Han) (私府) 5624 |
| 永巷令 | chief of the Long Halls Palace | | | |
| 倉廄令 | chief of the warehouses | | | |
| 祠祀令 | chief of performing sacrifices | | | |
| 食官令 | chief of food（漢 68） | | | |
| 大長秋 | **supervisor of the harem***（漢 65） | The Grand Prolonger of Autumn<br><br>Grand Prolonger of Autumn | 将作/大長秋 Empress' Chamberlain | (1) HAN-N-S DIV: Director of the Palace Domestic Service; (2) CH'ING: palace eunuch 5886 |
| 典属国 | **director of dependent states***（漢 54.63.65.68.史 | The Director of Dependent States | Director of the Dependent States | Supervisor of Dependent Countries (典屬國) 6646 |

付録2 Dubsほかの研究者による職官名英訳比較表

| 職官名 | 英語対訳 | ¹Dubs ²Bielenstein ³Dull | ¹Loewe ²Giele | 備考（Hucker） |
|---|---|---|---|---|
|  | 109) | Director of Dependent States | Superintendent of Colonies |  |
| 九訳令 | chief of foreign languages | Prefect of the Nine Successive Interpreters<br><br>Prefect of the Nine Successive Interpreters |  | Director of Translations from Afar (九譯令) 1302 |
| 候 | scout*（史123） |  |  |  |
| 千人 | head of a battalion of 1,000 men*（史107） | Millarian [under the Commandant of the Capital/Bearer of the Golden Mace]<br><br>Millarian |  | Battalion Commander 903 |
| 水衡都尉 | chief commandant of the palace gardens | The Chief Commandant of Waters and Parks<br><br>Chief Commandant of Waters and Parks | Superintendent of Waterways and Parks<br><br>Superintendent of the Imperial Hunting Park | (1) HAN-N-S DIV: Commandant of the Imperial Gardens; (2) N-S DIV: Commandant of Waterways; (3) T'ANG: Commissioner of the Directorate of Waterways 5497 |
| 上林令 | chief of the Imperial Forest Park |  |  |  |
| 均輸令 | chief of the | Prefect of Price |  | Office of Tax |

305

| 職官名 | 英語対訳 | [1]Dubs [2]Bielenstein [3]Dull | [1]Loewe [2]Giele | 備考（Hucker） |
|---|---|---|---|---|
|  | transport office for equalizing prices | Adjustment and Transportation [under the Grand Minister of Agriculture]<br><br>Prefect of Price Adjustment and Transportation |  | Substitutes (Each headed by a Director (ling 令) and an Aide (ch'eng) (均輸) 1787 |
| 御羞令 | chief of the imperial farm of curio offerings |  |  |  |
| 禁圃令 | chief of the fields of the imperial household |  |  |  |
| 輯濯令 | chief of the control of boatmen |  |  |  |
| 鍾官令 | chief of metal casting |  |  |  |
| 技巧令 | chief of craftwork |  |  |  |
| 六廏令 | chief of the six kinds of domestic animals |  |  |  |
| 辯銅令 | chief of copper assessment |  |  |  |
| 左馮翊〔左內史〕 | **left prefect of the capital\***（漢68.97）〔**prefect in charge of the eastern area of the capital\***（漢65）〕 | The Eastern Supporter〔Clerk of the Eastern Part of the Capital〕<br><br>Eastern | Metropolitan Superintendent of the Left (Eastern Supporter)〔Metropolitan Superintendent | Guardian of the Left (左馮翊 tso p'ing-i) 6985 |

306

付録 2　Dubs ほかの研究者による職官名英訳比較表

| 職官名 | 英語対訳 | ¹Dubs ²Bielenstein ³Dull | ¹Loewe ²Giele | 備考 (Hucker) |
|---|---|---|---|---|
| | | Supporter〔Clerk of the Eastern Part of the Capital〕 | of the Left〕 Governor of the Capital East 〔Governor of the Estern Capital Area〕 | |
| 廩犧令 | chief of grain offerings and animal sacrifices | Prefect of the Office of Sacrificial Oblations and Victims [under the Eastern Supporter] Prefect of the Office of Sacrificial Oblations and Victims | | Section (Office) of Sacrificial Grains and Animals (廩犧), headed by a Director (ling 令) 3724 |
| 左都水長 | head of water control of the left at the imperial parks | | | |
| 鉄官長 | head of the office of iron goods | Chief of the Office for Iron [under the Governor of the Capital] Chief of the Office of Iron | | Iron Monopoly Office (鉄官), headed by a Director (ling 令) 6508 |
| 長安四市長 | head of the Chang'an four marketplaces | Chiefs of the Four Markets in Ch'ang-an [under the Eastern | | |

307

| 職官名 | 英語対訳 | ¹Dubs<br>²Bielenstein<br>³Dull | ¹Loewe<br>²Giele | 備考<br>(Hucker) |
|---|---|---|---|---|
| | | Supporter]<br><br>Chiefs of the Four Markets in Ch'ang-an | | |
| 京兆尹〔右内史〕 | **prefect of the capital\***(漢54.67.71.74.78.92)〔**prefect in charge of the western area of the capital\***(漢65)〕 | The Governor of the Capital 〔Clerk of the Western Part of the Capital〕<br><br>Governor of the Capital〔Clerk of the Western part of the Capital〕 | Governor of the Capital 〔Metropolitan Superintendent of the Right〕<br><br>Governor of the Capital Center 〔Governor of the Western Capital Area〕 | Metropolitan Governor (京兆尹) 1192 |
| 長安東市令 | chief of the Chang'an East Marketplace | | | |
| 長安西市令 | chief of the Chang'an West Marketplace | | | |
| 長安廚令 | chief of the Chang'an Kitchen | | | |
| 都水長 | head of water control at the imperial parks | Chief Director of Waters [under the Upholder of Cerennonies/Grand Master of Ceremonies]<br><br>Chief Director of the Waters | | Director of Waterways 7277 |
| 鉄官長 | head of the office of iron | Chief of the Office for Iron | | Iron Monopoly Office (鉄官), |

308

付録2　Dubsほかの研究者による職官名英訳比較表

| 職官名 | 英語対訳 | ¹Dubs<br>²Bielenstein<br>³Dull | ¹Loewe<br>²Giele | 備考<br>（Hucker） |
|---|---|---|---|---|
| | goods | [under the Governor of the Capital]<br><br>Chief of the Office of Iron | | headed by a Director (ling 令) 6508 |
| 右扶風〔主爵中尉・主爵都尉〕 | **right prefect of the capital\***（漢54.68）〔**master of titles military commander**（史11）/ **master of titles chief commandant\***（史11.107.111.113.120.122）〕 | The Western Sustainer〔The Palace Commandant Over Noble Ranks / The Chief Commandant Over the Nobility〕<br><br>Western Sustainer〔Palace Commandant Over the Nobility / Chief Commandant over the Nobility〕 | Metropolitan Superintendent of the Right (Western Sustainer)《Metropolitan Superintendent of the Right は右内史に同じ。また左内史は Metropolitan Superintendent of the Left》〔Director, Orders of Honour (Palace Commandant over the Nobility) / Commandant, Orders of Honour (Chief Commandant over the Nobility)〕<br><br>Governor of the Capital West〔-〕 | 〔Commandant of the Nobles (主爵), a prefix found before tu-wei Commandant-in-chief) and chung-wei (Commandant-in-ordinary) 1379〕 |
| 掌畜令 | chief of animal husbandry | Prefect in Charge of | | Keeper of Sacrificial |

309

| 職官名 | 英語対訳 | ¹Dubs ²Bielenstein ³Dull | ¹Loewe ²Giele | 備考（Hucker） |
|---|---|---|---|---|
| | | Sacrificial Domestic Animals [under the Western Sustainer]<br><br>Prefect in Charge of Sacrificial Domestic Animals | | Animals (掌畜), headed by a Director (ling 令) 124 |
| 都水長 | head of water control at the imperial parks | Chief Director of Waters [under the Upholder of Cerennonies/Grand Master of Ceremonies]<br><br>Chief Director of the Waters | | Director of Waterways 7277 |
| 鉄官長 | head of the office of iron goods | Chief of the Office for Iron [under the Governor of the Capital]<br><br>Chief of the Office of Iron | | Iron Monopoly Office (鉄官), headed by a Director (ling 令) 6508 |
| 廄長 | head of stables | | | |
| 廱廚長 | head of cooking | | | |
| 司隷校尉 | **superintendent-general of the capital \| *subordinate* commander in charge of** | The Colonel Director of the Retainers<br><br>Colonel Director of the Retainers | Commissioner of the Capital Region | Metropolitan Commandant 5697 |

310

付録 2  Dubs ほかの研究者による職官名英訳比較表

| 職官名 | 英語対訳 | ¹Dubs<br>²Bielenstein<br>³Dull | ¹Loewe<br>²Giele | 備考<br>（Hucker） |
|---|---|---|---|---|
|  | convicts（漢 68.74） | colonel-director of retainers |  |  |
| 城門校尉 | company commander of the city gate | The Colonel of the City Gates<br><br>Colonel of the City Gates | Colonel of the City Gates | Commandant of the Capital Gates 504 |
| 司馬 | marshal*（史 48.7.8.101.102.111） | Major [under the Commandant of the Capital/Bearer of the Golden Mace]<br><br>Major |  | Lit., to be in charge of horses, i.e., of cavalry; a title deriving from high antiquity and used through most of imperial history; (1) CHOU: Minister of War; (2) CHOU: Commander; (3) (1) HAN-N-S DIV: Defender-in-chief; (4) : (1) HAN-N-S DIV: Commander; (5) N-S DIV-SUNG: Vice or Assistant; (6) SUI-T'ANG: Adjutant; (7) CHIN-YÜAN: Adjutant; (8) MINg-CH'ING: |

311

| 職官名 | 英語対訳 | ¹Dubs<br>²Bielenstein<br>³Dull | ¹Loewe<br>²Giele | 備考<br>（Hucker） |
|---|---|---|---|---|
| | | | | Vice Prefect; (9) MING-CH'ING: Minister of War 5713 |
| 城門候 | city gate scout | | | |
| 中壘校尉 | company commander of the gate for the northern garrison | The Colonel of the Capital Encampment<br><br>Colonel of the Capital Rampart | Colonel of the Capital Garrison | |
| 屯騎校尉 | company commander of the stationed cavalry | The Colonel of the Garrison Cavalry<br><br>Colonel of the Garrison Cavalry | Colonel of the Garrison Cavalry | Commandant of Garrison Cavalry; assisted by one or more Aides (ch'eng), Commanders (ssu-ma 司馬) 7405 |
| 步兵校尉 | company commander of the guard of the Imperial Forest Park | The Colonel of Footsoldiers<br><br>Colonel of Foot Soldiers | Colonel of the Garrison Infantry | Infantry Commandant 4794 |
| 越騎校尉 | company commander of cavalrymen of the Yueh tribe | The Colonel of the Elite Cavalry<br><br>Colonel of the Picked Cavalry | Colonel of the Elite Cavalry | |
| 長水校尉 | company ommander of the Ch'ang-shui garrison | The Colonel of the Ch'ang River Encampments<br><br>Colonel of the | Colonel of the Ch/a/ng River Garrison | |

付録 2  Dubs ほかの研究者による職官名英訳比較表

| 職官名 | 英語対訳 | [1]Dubs [2]Bielenstein [3]Dull | [1]Loewe [2]Giele | 備考（Hucker） |
|---|---|---|---|---|
|  |  | Ch'ang River Encampments |  |  |
| 胡騎校尉 | company commander of nomadic horsemen | The Colonel of the Northern Barbarian Cavalry<br><br>Colonel of Hu Cavalry | Colonel of the Auxiliary Cavalry |  |
| 射声校尉 | company commander of archers | The Colonel of the Archers Who Shoot at a Sound<br><br>Colonel of the Archers Who Shoot by Sound | Colonel of the Archers | Bowmen Shooter by Sound (射聲) 5142 |
| 虎賁校尉 | company commander of the picked troops | The Colonel of the Troops As Rapid As a Tiger<br><br>Colonel of the Rapid as Tigers | Colonel of the Charioteers | Brave as Tigers (虎賁): throughout history occurs as a prefix to military titles associated with guarding the ruler, especially such Han-T'ang titles as chung-lang chiang (Leader of Court Gentleman 中郎將) and Hsiao-wei (commandant 校尉) 2787 |
| 比二千石 | official of the |  |  |  |

| 職官名 | 英語対訳 | [1]Dubs [2]Bielenstein [3]Dull | [1]Loewe [2]Giele | 備考（Hucker） |
|---|---|---|---|---|
| | **two thousand picul or over rank** | | | |
| 奉車都尉 | chief commandant of the imperial carriage | | | |
| 駙馬都尉 | chief commandant of the imperial horses | | | |

## 付録3　職官名対訳確定作業の要約

官名の英訳では Burton Watson による漢書訳および史記訳を参照英訳に採用した。理由は三つに大別できる。1) Watson の漢語理解は深い。2) その深い原意理解に基づき、忠実かつ柔軟な英訳を心がけている。3) 官名に一定の体系が見られる。

Dubs, Bielenstein, Loewe と続く Dubs 系、および Bielenstein を参考文献にあげながらも、漢代研究者とは相当に語彙を異にする Hucker は、第一義的参照の外に置いた。Dubs の官名訳は、「令」に一律 prefect をあてるなど機械的であり、その prefect という語の選択も原意に合わない。Bielenstein は Dubs の忠実な継承者である。

Loewe は Bielenstein をもとに独自の英訳を試みてはいるが、九卿を superintendent で統一するなど、原官制を現代風に体系づけようとしている風がある。

この方式は名称単独でも序列がわかりやすいという利点はあるが、本プロジェクトでは原言語の語感を保存しながら原意をできるかぎり正確に反映した中国古代官制の英訳を試みることとした。

参照英訳の採用・不採用を判断した予備調査において、Watson 訳から下記のような各職位に特徴的な要素語を集約することができた。当プロジェクトではこれを原則として官名英訳を進めた。ただし職掌に合わない場合には応変に語を選択した。

| | |
|---|---|
| 九卿 | master, director, minister |
| 太〜 | grand〜（九卿配下の令） |
| 令 | chief |
| 長 | head |
| 監 | superintendent, supervisor |
| 都尉 | chief commandant |
| 校尉 | company commander |

**A. 参照英訳候補**

1. Dubs, Homer H., *History of the Former Han Dynasty, A critical translation with annotations*: 3 vols.: I, 1938; II, 1944; III, 1955. Waverly Press, Baltimore. (Official Titles of the Former Han Dynasty by Rafe De Crespigny, Australian National University Press, 1967)
2. Bielenstein, Hans, *The Bureaucracy of Han Times*, Cambridge University Press, 1980.
3. Loewe, Michael, *The Men Who Governed Han China.*, Handbook of Oriental Studies Section Four China, vol. 17, ed. S. F. Teiser & M. Kern, Koninklijke Brill NV, Leiden, The Netherlands, 2004.［特に第11章 The Kingdoms of

Western Han 中の The powers of the kings and the government of the kingdoms (p. 371-394)および巻末 Principal Officials of the Central Government, p. 650-652]
4. Twitchett, Denis and Michael Loewe, *Cambridge Ancient History of China*, Cambridge University Press, 2006. [p. xxv-xxxvii Official Titles and Institutional Terms]
5. Giele, Enno, *Imperial Decision-Making and Communication in Early China.*, Otto Harrassowitz GmbH & Co. KG, Wiesbaden, 2006.
6. Hucker, Charles O., *A Dictionary of Official Titles in Imperial China*, SMC Publishing Inc., Taipei, by arrangement with Stanford University Press, 1985.
7. Dull, Jack L., *Han Social Structure: Han Dynasty China, Volume 1*, University of Washington Press, 1972.
8. Watson, Burton, tr.(漢書部分英訳), Courtier and Commoner in Ancient China, Columbia University Press, 1974.
9. Watson, Burton, tr.(史記英訳), Records of the Grand Historian, Han Dynasty I & II, revised edition, Columbia University Press, 1961 (Pinyin 表記に改訂 1993).

これら研究者間の文献参照関係を図示すると，次ページのようになる。

付録3 職官名対訳確定作業の要約

## 職官名研究者間の文献参照関係

点線＝参考文献に名があることから，参照していると推測される
二重実線＝参照の域を越えて，ほとんどそのまま踏襲している

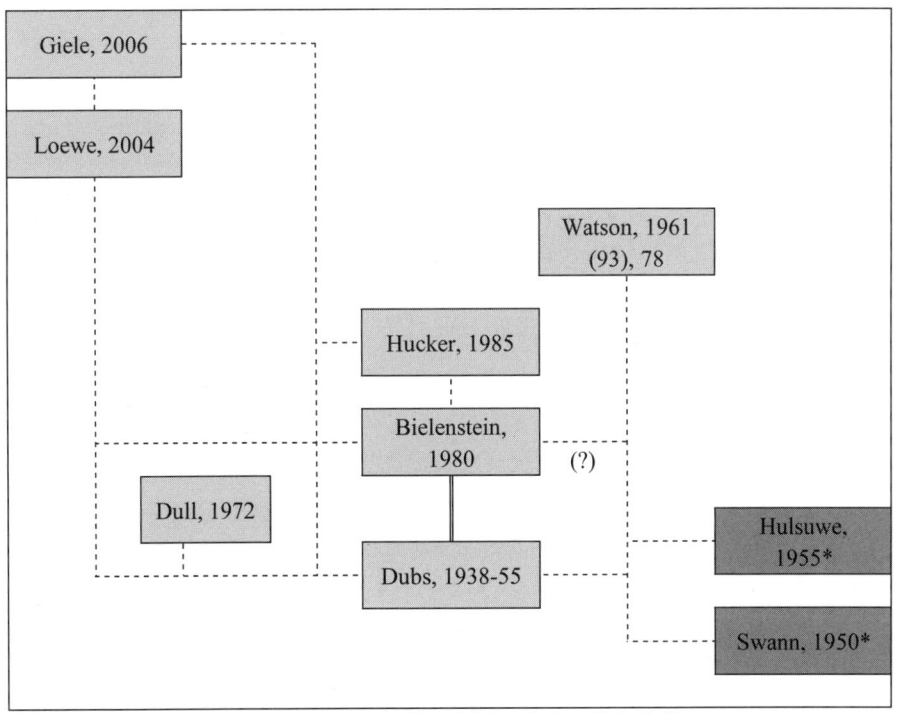

```
Giele, 2006

Loewe, 2004

                              Watson, 1961
                               (93), 78

              Hucker, 1985

              Bielenstein,
                1980           (?)
                                            Hulsuwe,
  Dull, 1972                                 1955*

              Dubs, 1938-55
                                            Swann, 1950*
```

＊ Watson の Hulsuwe および Swann 参照は，漢書，史記の英訳全般について。
‡ Giele の上にさらに 2006 年刊第7版 Cambridge Ancient History of China (Loewe)があるが，Loewe による別書と内容重複につき省略した。

B. 予備調査の結果—Watson 以外を第一義的参照英訳から除外した理由

1) Dubs
予備調査の結果 Dubs を第一義的参照英訳から外すこととした。理由は大きく二つある。
(1)職務内容を正確に反映していない，(2)逐語訳（Word for word 訳）が目立つ。

(1) 職務内容を正確に反映していない
1 例を挙げれば，太宰令を Prefect Grand Butcher としている。太宰令は肉屋の大将ではない。屠殺人は，供物としての動物の屠殺をさすのであれば遠くはないが，butcher は肉屋という印象に強く引かれる。供物としての食物の準備が職務であり，屠殺ばかりではない。また屠殺が主でもない。

(2) 逐語訳（Word for word 訳）が目立つ
大夫 grandee と令 prefect について見る。

(a) 大夫 grandee

| 御史大夫 | The Imperial Clerk Grandee |
| 太中大夫 | Grand Palace Grandee |
| 中大夫 | Palace Grandee |
| 光禄大夫 | Imperial Household Grandee |
| 諫大夫 | Grandee-remonstrant |
| 太子門大夫 | Grandee at the Gate of the Heir-apparent |

大夫を grandee に置き換えることで，一見容易に体系化できるかのような印象を与えるが，御史大夫は国務長官，太中大夫は現代日本の官僚機構でいう局長である。このように大夫＝grandee として行政組織を体系化するには，大夫がすべて同ランクに位置づけられていなければならない。課長のなかに大臣を名乗る職位があり，大臣のなかに大臣を名乗らない職位があるのは体系とは言えない。国務長官も大夫，局長も大夫では体系にならない。逐語訳（Word for word 訳）は最も安易は翻訳法であり，たいていの場合成功しない。

そもそも grandee は中世後期にスペインで発生した貴族の尊号のようなものであり，広大な影響力と，王の前でも帽子着用を許されたほどの特権を誇った特殊な地位を示す語であった。いわば貴族間のステータスを強く意識させられる語であり，その意味で職官名にはいびつな感がある。何か古めかしさ，いかめしさを出そうとしているのであろうか。
(Britannica 2006 *grandee*: Spanish　Grande,　a title of honour borne by the highest class of the Spanish nobility. The title appears first to have been assumed during the late Middle Ages by certain of the ricos hombres, or powerful magnates of the realm, who had by then acquired vast influence and considerable privileges, including one—that of wearing a hat in the king's presence—which later became characteristic of the dignity of grandee.)。

(b) 令 prefect
「令」を一律 prefect とする訳し方も同じである。Britannica は prefect を次のように説明して

付録 3　職官名対訳確定作業の要約

いる。「政府内高官ではなく, prefectus urbi はローマ市警司法官, prefectus praetorio は皇帝 SP, 知事監督官, 地方司法財政官, 軍小単位指揮官機能を有し, 帝国最高位の士官」(付録 1　職官名英訳参照英文集の prefect の項) であり, 令を一律機械的に prefect と訳すことで成り立っている Dubs-Bielenstein 体系は拒否せざるを得ない。この点, 左馮翊〔左内史〕, 京兆尹〔右内史〕および右扶風にのみ prefect を適用した Watson の判断は, すぐれて学術的である。

2) Bielenstein, Dull
Bielenstein はごくごく一部の修正を除いて, ほぼ 100 パーセント Dubs をそのまま踏襲している。Dull の対訳は部分的でしかなく, 訳されている官名はほとんど Dubs そのままである。両者も第一義的参照英訳から除外した。

3) Hucker
Hucker は独自の英訳も試みているが, 氏は漢から清に至るあまりに広大な時代スパンを包括する辞典を目指しており, 漢代については Bielenstein しか参考文献に挙げていない。その訳語は字義の語学辞書的解釈を主体にして, 各職務内容に踏み込んだ解釈を欠いている感があり, また専門を明代に置いて, 丞相を Counselor-in-chief, 太尉を Minister of War, 御史大夫を Censor-in-chief とするなど, 他の研究者らとは語彙が相当に異質である。これらの理由から, 本作業では Hucker もまた第一義的参照の外に置いた。

4) Loewe, Giele
Giele を参照するには官名の数が限られているため, われわれが目指す官制を体系的にとらえることがむつかしい。Loewe の弊については, その形式論的側面を冒頭に記したが, 職掌理解にも同意できない点が多い。詳細は付録 2「比較表」に示した。そのごく一例を挙げれば水衡都尉の職掌を Waterways and Parks とする点は, Dubs, Bielenstein から抜け出せていないであろう。

C.　Watson 訳がすぐれている理由

　それは「原文解釈が深い」の一点に尽きる。このことは「史記」というタイトルが historical records と, 字面のみを訳されることの多いなか, Watson はこれを Records of the Grand Historian とする点にすでに象徴的であるが, ほかに一例だけあげよう。

　　広漢刑人 (漢書巻 97 上)
　　Hsü Kuang-han had in the past been condemned to corporal punishment.

「広漢」と「刑」との 2 語を聞いて, その刑に corporal punishment (身体刑, 肉刑) を思う訳者がどれほどいるだろうか。刑必ずしも肉刑でないにせよ, あとに「不宜君国」と続くとき, corporal は広漢が蚕室に下った者であることを意識させて文脈をより一層闡明にする。

Watsonの古代中国文化・歴史に対する知識は該博なのである。乞われるなら，私（藤田）はこの種の例をいくつでも紹介して差し上げることができる。
　Watsonが西欧言語から遠く異質な漢語，中国語そして日本語をも学び習得してくれたおかげで，われわれはいくつもの貴重な対訳を持つことができた。「司直」に対するrectitudeなど，日本人が容易に思いつける語ではない。和英辞典に「志士」は見出せても，「志士仁人」がない。仮にあったとして，日本人編者から出る出典のない訳と，漢籍に裏打ちされた日本語を了解し，日本語で漢文を講義できる英語ネイティブの訳と，われわれは果たしてどちらを選ぶであろう。Watsonがいなければ世界は，漢語・日本語と英語をつなぐ膨大な数の架け橋を永遠に失ったのである。
　場違いを承知のうえで，私はここに一日本人として，コロンビア大学Burton Watson Adjunct教授がこれらの難言語を習得しおきくれたことに対し，心からの敬意と感謝の意を表したい。

# 職官名和英索引

( ) 内は組織図

斡官長 head of the office of salt, iron, and liquor taxes 26 (3)
右監 superintendent of the right 23 (2)
右京輔都尉 chief commandant of the right of the capital 36 (3)
右校令 commander of the right over compulsory labour 38 (7)
右司空令 chief of compulsory labour of the right 30 (4)
右中候 captain of the right bannermen 36 (3)
右中郎将 senior officer of palace corridor attendants of the right 16 (3)
右内史 **prefect in charge of the western area of the capital\*** 44 (6)
右扶風 **right prefect of the capital\*** 45 (6)
右平 judge of the right 23 (2)
羽林騎都尉 chief commandant of cavalry for Feather and Forest Guard 18 (4)
羽林中郎将 senior officer of palace corridor attendants for the Feather and Forest Guard 18 (4)
羽林郎 horseman of the Feather and Forest Guard\* 18 (4)
永巷令 chief of the Long Halls Palace 33 (6)
永巷令 chief of the Long Halls Palace 40 (7)
衛尉 **colonel of the guard\*** 18 (2)
衛司馬 marshal of the palace guard 19 (2)
衛士令 chief of the palace guard 19 (2)
掖庭令 chief of the women's quarters 33 (6)

謁者 master of guests 17 (3)
謁者僕射 chief master of guests 17 (3)
越騎校尉 **company commander of cavalrymen of the Yueh tribe** 47 (8)
黄門令 chief the Yellow Gate 31 (5)
家馬令 chief of the imperial household's horses 20 (2)
楽府令 chief of the Music Bureau 28 (3)
甘泉居室令 chief of the detention room in the Palace of Sweet Springs 30 (4)
宦者令 chief of eunuchs 33 (6)
諫大夫 admonisher\* 16 (2)
期門 junior officer of the picked troops 18 (4)
期門僕射 archery captain at the Rendezvous Gate 17 (4)
騎将 senior officer of cavalry 17 (3)
騎馬令 chief of cavalry horses 22 (3)
廱厨長 head of cooking 45 (7)
廄長 head of stables 45 (7)
技巧令 chief of craftwork 43 (7)
居室令 chief of the detention room in the palace 30 (4)
京兆尹 **prefect of the capital\*** 44 (6)
均官長 head of the office of imperial burial places 13 (3)
均官長 head of the office of imperial burial places 30 (5)
均輸令 chief of the transport office for equalizing prices 26 (2)
均輸令 chief of the transport office for equalizing prices 41 (7)
禁圃令 chief of the fields of the imperial household 42 (7)

321

九卿 nine highest ministers* 11 (1)
九訳令 chief of foreign languages 40 (6)
郡邸長 head of the provincial offices in the capital 23 (2)
戸将 senior officer of watch gates 17 (3)
胡騎校尉 company commander of nomadic horsemen 47 (8)
虎賁校尉 company commander of the picked troops 47 (8)
虎賁中郎将 senior officer of palace corridor attendants for the picked troops 17 (4)
虎賁郎 junior officer of the picked troops 18 (4)
五官中郎将 senior officer of palace corridor attendants at the "Five Bureaus" 16 (2)
後校令 commander of the rear over compulsory labour 38 (7)
御史大夫 imperial secretary* 10 (1)
御府令 chief of royal garments 32 (6)
御羞令 chief of the imperial farm of curio offerings 41 (7)
候 scout* 34 (2)
候 scout* 40 (6)
候司馬 marshal of scouts 19 (2)
光禄勲 keeper of the palace gate* 16 (2)
光禄大夫 counselor to the keeper of the palace gate* 16 (2)
公車司馬令 chief marshal of the palace gates 19 (2)
考工室令 chief of the government artisans 29 (4)
行人令 chief of messengers 23 (2)
鉤盾令 chief of the control of the imperial parks 31 (6)
昆台令 chief of the *Kuntai* detention room 30 (4)
左監 superintendent of the left 22 (2)
左京輔都尉 chief commandant of the left of the capital 36 (3)
左校令 commander of the left over compulsory labour 37 (7)
左司空令 chief of compulsory labour of the left 30 (4)
左中候 captain of the left bannermen 36 (3)
左中郎将 senior officer of palace corridor attendants of the left 16 (3)
左都水長 head of water control of the left at the imperial parks 44 (7)
左内史 prefect in charge of the eastern area of the capital* 43 (6)
左平 judge of the left 22 (2)
左弋令 chief of the emperor's hunting assistants 29 (4)
左馮翊 left prefect of the capital* 43 (6)
三公 three highest ministers* 10 (1)
司直 director of rectitude* 10 (1)
司馬 marshal* 34 (2)
司馬 marshal* 46 (8)
司隷校尉 superintendent-general of the capital 45 (8)
私府令 chief of ritual implements 40 (7)
佽飛令 chief of hunting archery for the emperor 29 (4)
祠祀令 chief of performing sacrifices 40 (8)
侍御史 secretary of the censorate* 11 (1)
侍郎 attendant in the inner palace* 16 (3)
寺互令 chief of interoffice liaison 35 (2)
治粟内史 secretary in charge of grain* 26 (2)
式道候 captain of the lead bannermen 35 (3)
執金吾 chief of the capital police* 34 (2)
射声校尉 company commander of archers 47 (8)
車将 senior officer of carriage 17 (3)

322

## 職官名和英索引

車府令 chief of the office of carriage 20 (2)
若盧令 chief of the *Ruolu* court 28 (4)
主爵中尉 master of titles military commander 45 (6)
主爵都尉 master of titles chief commandant*〕45 (6)
宗正 director of the imperial clan* 24 (2)
宗伯 master of the imperial clan 24 (2)
繡衣直指 imperial inquisitor in brocade robe 11 (1)
輯濯令 chief of the control of boatmen 42 (7)
駿馬令 chief of famous steed 22 (3)
諸公主家令 steward in the household of the princess 25 (2)
諸公主門尉 commander of gatekeepers in the household of the princess 25 (2)
諸廟園官令 chief of the park of the funerary temple 15 (4)
諸廟食官令 chief of food offerings at the funerary temple 15 (4)
諸廟寢官令 chief of the inner chamber of the funerary temple 15 (4)
将作大匠 master of construction works 37 (6)
少府 privy treasurer* 27 (2)
尚書令 master of palace writers 27 (2)
尚方令 chief of the royal craftsmen 31 (6)
掌畜令 chief of animal husbandry 45 (6)
鍾官令 chief of metal casting 43 (7)
上林十池監 supervisor of the maintenance of ponds at the Imperial Forest Park 31 (5)
上林令 chief of the Imperial Forest Park 41 (6)
丞 aide 10 (1)
丞 assistant* 40 (6)

丞相 chancellor* 10 (1)
城門候 city gate scout 46 (8)
城門校尉 company commander of the city gate 46 (8)
食官令 chief of food 40 (8)
水衡都尉 chief commandant of the palace gardens 40 (6)
正監 superintendent of the center 22 (2)
西織令 chief of the western weaving room 30 (5)
石庫令 chief of stone materials 37 (6)
籍田令 chief of the sacred field in the palace 26 (3)
千人 head of a battalion of 1,000 men* 34 (2)
千人 head of a battalion of 1,000 men* 40 (6)
詹事 chamberlain to the empress and the heir apparent 38 (6)
前校令 commander of the front over compulsory labour 38 (7)
倉廄令 chief of the warehouses 40 (7)
搜粟都尉 chief commandant for requisitioning grain* 27 (4)
太尉 grand commandant* 10 (1)
太医令 grand physician* 13 (3)
太医令 grand physician for the imperial household 27 (2)
太樂令 grand musician 12 (2)
太官令 grand butler of the imperial household 27 (2)
太宰令 grand servant 13 (2)
太史令 grand historian* 13 (2)
太子衛率 chief of the gatekeepers in the household of the heir apparent 39 (7)
太子家令 steward in the household of the heir apparent* 39 (7)
太子舍人 retainer in the household of the heir apparent* 37 (7)

太子庶子 secretary to the heir apparent 37 (7)
太子少傅 **lesser tutor to the heir apparent*** 37 (6)
太子先馬 mounted guard to the heir apparent* 37 (7)
太子太傅 **grand tutor to the heir apparent*** 36 (6)
太子中盾 chief of patrol in the household of the heir apparent 39 (7)
太子僕 chief of the heir apparent's horses 39 (7)
太子門大夫 lord of the gate to the heir apparent 37 (6)
太子率更令 chief of the night guard in the household of the heir apparent 39 (6)
太子廚廄 chief of the kitchen and stables in the household of the heir apparent 39 (7)
太祝令 grand invocator* 12 (2)
太常 **master of ritual*** 12 (2)
太倉令 chief of the central granary 26 (2)
太僕 **master of carriage*** 19 (2)
太卜令 grand diviner* 13 (3)
大行令 grand messenger* 23 (2)
大鴻臚 **director of foreign vassals*** 23 (2)
大司空 **secretary of government** 10 (1)
大司徒 **master of government*** 10 (1)
大司農 **minister of revenue** 26 (2)
大司馬 **grand marshal*** 10 (1)
大長秋 **supervisor of the harem*** 40 (6)
大理 **grand examiner*** 22 (2)
大廄令 chief of the imperial stables 19 (2)
中尉 **military commander of the capital*** 34 (2)
中校令 commander of the middle over compulsory labour 38 (7)

中書謁者令 master of documents and guests 31 (5)
中書令 chief of palace writers* 31 (5)
中丞 middle aide* 11 (1)
中大夫 palace counselor* 16 (2)
中長秋 steward in the household of the empress 39 (7)
中二千石 **officials of the middle two thousand picul class*** 12 (1)
中壘校尉 **company commander of the gate for the northern garrison** 46 (8)
中壘令 commander of the security force 34 (2)
中郎 palace gentleman* 16 (3)
長安四市長 head of the Chang'an four marketplaces 44 (7)
長安西市令 chief of the Chang'an West Marketplace 45 (7)
長安東市令 chief of the Chang'an East Marketplace 45 (6)
長安廚令 chief of the Chang'an Kitchen 45 (7)
長史 chief secretary* 10 (1)
長史 chief secretary* 10 (1)
長水校尉 **company commander of the Ch'ang-shui garrison** 47 (8)
廷尉 **commandant of justice*** 22 (2)
鐵官長 head of the office of iron goods 44 (7); 45 (7)
鐵市長 head of the control of iron monopoly 27 (3)
典客 **director of foreign guests** 23 (2)
典屬國 **director of dependent states*** 40 (6)
都司空令 chief of criminal affairs in the imperial family 24 (2)
都水長 head of water control at the imperial parks 14 (4); 30 (5); 45 (7)
都船令 chief of the water police 35 (2)

324

## 職官名和英索引

都內令 chief of granaries in the capital 26 (2)
東園主章令 chief of wooden materials at the Eastern Garden 37 (7)
東園匠令 chief of the craftsmen of the imperial tombs 30 (5)
東織令 chief of the eastern weaving room 30 (5)
湯官令 chief of the emperor's patisserie 28 (3)
挏馬令 chief of the emperor's horses 20 (2)
導官令 chief of the grain selectors 28 (3)
屯騎校尉 **company commander of the stationed cavalry** 46 (8)
屯司馬 marshal of the stationed unit 19 (2)
內官長 head of the office of weights and measures 24 (2)
內者令 chief of the palace interior 33 (6)
二千石 **official of the two thousand picul rank*** 36 (3)
博士 erudit* 16 (4)
比二千石 **official of the two thousand picul or over rank** 47 (8)
符節令 chief of the imperial credentials 27 (2)
武庫令 chief of the arsenal* 35 (2)
駙馬都尉 chief commandant of the imperial horses 47 (8)

平準令 chief of the office for the balanced standard 26 (2)
別火令 chief of the maintenance of the sacred fire 23 (2)
辯銅令 chief of copper assessment 43 (7)
保宮令 supervisor of the detention room 30 (4)
步兵校尉 **company commander of the guard of the Imperial Forest Park** 47 (8)
奉車都尉 chief commandant of the imperial carriage 47 (8)
奉常 **imperial master of ritual** 12 (2)
胞人長 head of cooks 30 (5)
未央令 chief of carriage and horses for the Eternal Palace 20 (2)
木工令 chief of woodworkers 37 (7)
譯官令 chief of interpreters 23 (2)
旅賁令 chief of envoys 19 (2)
廩犧令 chief of grain offerings and animal sacrifices 44 (6)
路軨令 chief of light hunting chariots 21 (3)
郎中 palace corridor attendant 17 (3)
郎中令 **chief of palace corridor attendants** 16 (2)
六廄令 chief of the six kinds of domestic animals 43 (7)

# 職官名英和索引

( ) 内は組織図

admonisher*諫大夫 16 (2)
aide 丞 10 (1)
archery captain at the Rendezvous Gate 期門僕射 17 (4)
assistant*丞 40 (6)
attendant in the inner palace*侍郎 16 (3)
captain of the lead bannermen 式道候 35 (3)
captain of the left bannermen 左中候 36 (3)
captain of the right bannermen 右中候 36 (3)
**chamberlain to the empress and the heir apparent** 詹事 38 (6)
**chancellor**\*丞相 10 (1)
chief commandant for requisitioning grain*搜粟都尉 27 (4)
chief commandant of cavalry for Feather and Forest Guard 羽林騎都尉 18 (4)
chief commandant of the imperial carriage 奉車都尉 47 (8)
chief commandant of the imperial horses 駙馬都尉 47 (8)
chief commandant of the left of the capital 左京輔都尉 36 (3)
**chief commandant of the palace gardens** 水衡都尉 40 (6)
chief commandant of the right of the capital 右京輔都尉 36 (3)
chief marshal of the palace gates 公車司馬令 19 (2)
chief master of guests 謁者僕射 17 (3)
chief of animal husbandry 掌畜令 45 (6)
chief of carriage and horses for the Eternal Palace 未央令 20 (2)
chief of cavalry horses 騎馬令 22 (3)
chief of compulsory labour of the left 左司空令 30 (4)
chief of compulsory labour of the right 右司空令 30 (4)
chief of copper assessment 辯銅令 43 (7)
chief of craftwork 技巧令 43 (7)
chief of criminal affairs in the imperial family 都司空令 24 (2)
chief of envoys 旅賁令 19 (2)
chief of eunuchs 宦者令 33 (6)
chief of famous steed 駿馬令 22 (3)
chief of food offerings at the funerary temple 諸廟食官令 15 (4)
chief of food 食官令 40 (8)
chief of foreign languages 九訳令 40 (6)
chief of grain offerings and animal sacrifices 廩犧令 44 (6)
chief of granaries in the capital 都內令 26 (2)
chief of hunting archery for the emperor 佽飛令 29 (4)
chief of interoffice liaison 寺互令 35 (2)
chief of interpreters 訳官令 23 (2)
chief of light hunting chariots 路軨令 21 (3)
chief of messengers 行人令 23 (2)
chief of metal casting 鍾官令 43 (7)
**chief of palace corridor attendants** 郎中令 16 (2)
chief of palace writers*中書令 31 (5)
chief of patrol in the household of the heir apparent 太子中盾 39 (7)

chief of performing sacrifices 祠祀令 40 (8)
chief of ritual implements 私府令 40 (7)
chief of royal garments 御府令 32 (6)
chief of stone materials 石庫令 37 (6)
chief of the Chang'an East Marketplace 長安東市令 45 (6)
chief of the Chang'an Kitchen 長安廚令 45 (7)
chief of the Chang'an West Marketplace 長安西市令 45 (7)
chief of the Imperial Forest Park 上林令 41 (6)
chief of the *Kuntai* detention room 昆台令 30 (4)
chief of the Long Halls Palace 永巷令 33 (6)
chief of the Long Halls Palace 永巷令 40 (7)
chief of the Music Bureau 樂府令 28 (3)
chief of the *Ruolu* court 若盧令 28 (4)
chief of the arsenal*武庫令 35 (2)
**chief of the capital police*執金吾 34 (2)**
chief of the central granary 太倉令 26 (2)
chief of the control of boatmen 輯濯令 42 (7)
chief of the control of the imperial parks 鉤盾令 31 (6)
chief of the craftsmen of the imperial tombs 東園匠令 30 (5)
chief of the detention room in the Palace of Sweet Springs 甘泉居室令 30 (4)
chief of the detention room in the palace 居室令 30 (4)
chief of the eastern weaving room 東織令 30 (5)
chief of the emperor's horses 駧馬令 20 (2)
chief of the emperor's hunting assistants

左弋令 29 (4)
chief of the emperor's patisserie 湯官令 28 (3)
chief of the fields of the imperial household 禁圃令 42 (7)
chief of the gatekeepers in the household of the heir apparent 太子衛率 39 (7)
chief of the government artisans 考工室令 29 (4)
chief of the grain selectors 導官令 28 (3)
chief of the heir apparent's horses 太子僕 39 (7)
chief of the imperial credentials 符節令 27 (2)
chief of the imperial farm of curio offerings 御羞令 41 (7)
chief of the imperial household's horses 家馬令 20 (2)
chief of the imperial stables 大廄令 19 (2)
chief of the inner chamber of the funerary temple 諸廟寢官令 15 (4)
chief of the kitchen and stables in the household of the heir apparent 太子廚廄 39 (7)
chief of the maintenance of the sacred fire 別火令 23 (2)
chief of the night guard in the household of the heir apparent 太子率更 39 (6)
chief of the office for the balanced standard 平準令 26 (2)
chief of the office of carriage 車府令 20 (2)
chief of the palace guard 衛士令 19 (2)
chief of the palace interior 內者令 33 (6)
chief of the park of the funerary temple 諸廟園官令 15 (4)
chief of the royal craftsmen 尚方令 31 (6)
chief of the sacred field in the palace 籍田令 26 (3)

chief of the six kinds of domestic animals 六廐令 43 (7)
chief of the transport office for equalizing prices 均輸令 26 (2)
chief of the transport office for equalizing prices 均輸令 41 (7)
chief of the warehouses 倉廐令 40 (7)
chief of the water police 都船令 35 (2)
chief of the western weaving room 西織令 30 (5)
chief of the women's quarters 掖庭令 33 (6)
chief of wooden materials at the Eastern Garden 東園主章令 37 (7)
chief of woodworkers 木工令 37 (7)
chief secretary*長史 10 (1)
chief secretary*長史 10 (1)
chief the Yellow Gate 黄門令 31 (5)
city gate scout 城門候 46 (8)
**colonel of the guard***衛尉 18 (2)
**commandant of justice***廷尉 22 (2)
commander of gatekeepers in the household of the princess 諸公主門尉 25 (2)
commander of the front over compulsory labour 前校令 38 (7)
commander of the left over compulsory labour 左校令 37 (7)
commander of the middle over compulsory labour 中校令 38 (7)
commander of the rear over compulsory labour 後校令 38 (7)
commander of the right over compulsory labour 右校令 38 (7)
commander of the security force 中壘令 34 (2)
**company commander of archers** 射声校尉 47 (8)
**company commander of cavalrymen of the Yueh tribe** 越騎校尉 47 (8)
**company commander of nomadic horsemen** 胡騎校尉 47 (8)
**company commander of the Ch'ang-shui garrison** 長水校尉 47 (8)
**company commander of the city gate** 城門校尉 46 (8)
**company commander of the gate for the northern garrison** 中壘校尉 46 (8)
**company commander of the guard of the Imperial Forest Park** 步兵校尉 47 (8)
**company commander of the picked troops** 虎賁校尉 47 (8)
**company commander of the stationed cavalry** 屯騎校尉 46 (8)
counselor to the keeper of the palace gate* 光禄大夫 16 (2)
**director of dependent states***典属国 40 (6)
**director of foreign guests** 典客 23 (2)
**director of foreign vassals***大鴻臚 23 (2)
director of rectitude*司直 10 (1)
**director of the imperial clan***宗正 24 (2)
erudit*博士 16 (4)
grand butler of the imperial household 太官令 27 (2)
**grand commandant***太尉 10 (1)
grand diviner*太卜令 13 (3)
**grand examiner***大理 22 (2)
grand historian*太史令 13 (2)
grand invocator*太祝令 12 (2)
**grand marshal***大司馬 10 (1)
grand messenger*大行令 23 (2)
grand musician 太楽令 12 (2)
grand physician for the imperial household 太医令 27 (2)
grand physician*太医令 13 (3)
grand servant 太宰令 13 (2)

328

grand tutor to the heir apparent*太子太傅 36 (6)
head of a battalion of 1,000 men*千人 34 (2)
head of a battalion of 1,000 men*千人 40 (6)
head of cooking 靡廚長 45 (7)
head of cooks 胞人長 30 (5)
head of stables 廄長 45 (7)
head of the Chang'an four marketplaces 長安四市長 44 (7)
head of the control of iron monopoly 鉄市長 27 (3)
head of the office of imperial burial places 均官長 13 (3)
head of the office of imperial burial places 均官長 30 (5)
head of the office of iron goods 鉄官長 44 (7); 45 (7)
head of the office of salt, iron, and liquor taxes 斡官長 26 (3)
head of the office of weights and measures 内官長 24 (2)
head of the provincial offices in the capital 郡邸長 23 (2)
head of water control at the imperial parks 都水長 14 (4); 30 (5); 45 (7)
head of water control of the left at the imperial parks 左都水長 44 (7)
horseman of the Feather and Forest Guard*羽林郎 18 (4)
imperial inquisitor in brocade robe 繡衣直指 11 (1)
**imperial master of ritual** 奉常 12 (2)
**imperial secretary***御史大夫 10 (1)
judge of the left 左平 22 (2)
judge of the right 右平 23 (2)
junior officer of the picked troops 期門 18 (4)
junior officer of the picked troops 虎賁郎 18 (4)
**keeper of the palace gate***光禄勲 16 (2)
**left prefect of the capital***左馮翊 43 (6)
**lesser tutor to the heir apparent***太子少傅 37 (6)
lord of the gate to the heir apparent 太子門大夫 37 (6)
marshal of scouts 候司馬 19 (2)
marshal of the palace guard 衛司馬 19 (2)
marshal of the stationed unit 屯司馬 19 (2)
marshal*司馬 34 (2)
marshal*司馬 46 (8)
**master of carriage***太僕 19 (2)
**master of construction works** 将作大匠 37 (6)
master of documents and guests 中書謁者令 31 (5)
master of guests 謁者 17 (3)
master of palace writers 尚書令 27 (2)
**master of ritual***太常 12 (2)
**master of the imperial clan** 宗伯 24 (2)
**master of titles chief commandant***主爵都尉 45 (6)
**master of titles military commander** 主爵中尉 45 (6)
middle aide*中丞 11 (1)
**military commander of the capital***中尉 34 (2)
**master of government***大司徒 10 (1)
**minister of revenue** 大司農 26 (2)
mounted guard to the heir apparent*太子先馬 37 (7)
**nine highest ministers***九卿 11 (1)
**official of the two thousand picul or over rank** 比二千石 47 (8)
**official of the two thousand picul rank*** 二千石 36 (3)
**officials of the middle two thousand**

picul class*中二千石 12 (1)
palace corridor attendant 郎中17 (3)
palace counselor*中大夫 16 (2)
palace gentleman*中郎 16 (3)
**prefect in charge of the eastern area of the capital**\*左內史 43 (6)
**prefect in charge of the western area of the capital**\*右內史 44 (6)
**prefect of the capital**\*京兆尹 44 (6)
**privy treasurer**\*少府 27 (2)
retainer in the household of the heir apparent*太子舍人37 (7)
**right prefect of the capital**\*右扶風 45 (6)
scout*候34 (2)
scout*候40 (6)
**secretary in charge of grain**\*治粟內史 26 (2)
**secretary of goverment** 大司空 10 (1)
secretary of the censorate*侍御史 11 (1)
secretary to the heir apparent 太子庶子37 (7)
senior officer of carriage 車將 17 (3)
senior officer of cavalry 騎將 17 (3)
senior officer of palace corridor attendants at the "Five Bureaus" 五官中郎將 16 (2)
senior officer of palace corridor attendants for the Feather and Forest Guard 羽林中郎將 18 (4)
senior officer of palace corridor attendants for the picked troops 虎賁中郎將 17 (4)
senior officer of palace corridor attendants of the left 左中郎將16 (3)
senior officer of palace corridor attendants of the right 右中郎將16 (3)
senior officer of watch gates 戶將 17 (3)
steward in the household of the empress 中長秋39 (7)
steward in the household of the heir apparent*太子家令39 (7)
steward in the household of the princess 諸公主家令 25 (2)
superintendent of the center 正監22 (2)
superintendent of the left 左監 22 (2)
superintendent of the right 右監23 (2)
**superintendent-general of the capital** 司隸校尉45 (8)
supervisor of the detention room 保宮令 30 (4)
**supervisor of the harem**\*大長秋 40 (6)
supervisor of the maintenance of ponds at the Imperial Forest Park 上林十池監 31 (5)
**three highest ministers**\*三公 10 (1)

# 職官名キーワード索引

凡例
1. ( )内は組織図のページ。
2. chief, grand, master など語頭に来る語については，上記職官名英和索引参照。

■ admonisher
admonisher*諫大夫 16 (2)
■ affair
chief of criminal affairs in the imperial family 都司空令 24 (2)
■ aide
aide 丞 10 (1) | middle aide*中丞 11 (1)
■ animal
chief of animal husbandry 掌畜令 45 (6) | chief of grain offerings and animal sacrifices 廪犠令 44 (6) | chief of the six kinds of domestic animals 六廄令 43 (7)
■ archer
company commander of archers 射声校尉 47 (8)
■ archery
archery captain at the Rendezvous Gate 期門僕射 17 (4) | chief of hunting archery for the emperor 佽飛令 29 (4)
■ archery
archery captain at the Rendezvous Gate 期門僕射 17 (4) | chief of hunting archery for the emperor 佽飛令 29 (4)
■ arsenal
chief of the arsenal*武庫令 35 (2)
■ artisan
chief of the government artisans 考工室令 29 (4)
■ assessment
chief of copper assessment 辯銅令 43 (7)
■ balanced

chief of the office for the balanced standard 平準令 26 (2)
■ bannermen
captain of the lead bannermen 式道候 35 (3) | captain of the left bannermen 左中候 36 (3) | captain of the right bannermen 右中候 36 (3)
■ battalion
head of a battalion of 1,000 men*千人 34 (2), 40 (6)
■ boatman
chief of the control of boatmen 輯濯令 42 (7)
■ brocade
imperial inquisitor in brocade robe 繡衣直指 11 (1)
■ bureau
the "Five Burearus"
■ burial
head of the office of imperial burial places 均官長 13 (3) | head of the office of imperial burial places 均官長 30 (5)
■ butler
grand butler of the imperial household 太官令 27 (2)
■ capital
chief commandant of the left of the capital 左京輔都尉 36 (3) | chief commandant of the right of the capital 右京輔都尉 36 (3) | chief of granaries in the capital 都内令 26 (2) | chief of the capital police*執金吾

34 (2) | head of the provincial offices in the capital 郡邸長 23 (2) | left prefect of the capital*左馮翊 43 (6) | military commander of the capital*中尉 34 (2) | prefect in charge of the eastern area of the capital*左內史 43 (6) | prefect in charge of the western area of the capital*右內史 44 (6) | prefect of the capital*京兆尹 44 (6) | right prefect of the capital*右扶風 45 (6) | superintendent-general of the capital 司隸校尉 45 (8)

■ **captain**
archery captain at the Rendezvous Gate 期門僕射 17 (4) | captain of the lead bannermen 式道候 35 (3) | captain of the left bannermen 左中候 36 (3) | captain of the right bannermen 右中候 36 (3)

■ **carriage**
chief commandant of the imperial carriage 奉車都尉 47 (8) | chief of carriage and horses for the Eternal Palace 未央令 20 (2) | chief of the office of carriage 車府令 20 (2) | master of carriage*太僕 19 (2) | senior officer of carriage 車將 17 (3)

■ **casting**
chief of metal casting 鍾官令 43 (7)

■ **cavalry**
chief commandant of cavalry for Feather and Forest Guard 羽林騎都尉 18 (4) | chief of cavalry horses 騎馬令 22 (3) | company commander of cavalrymen of the Yueh tribe 越騎校尉 47 (8) | company commander of the stationed cavalry 屯騎校尉 46 (8) | senior officer of cavalry 騎將 17 (3)

■ **cavalrymen**
company commander of cavalrymen of the Yueh tribe 越騎校尉 47 (8)

■ **censorate**

secretary of the censorate*侍御史 11 (1)

■ **center**
superintendent of the center 正監 22 (2)

■ **central**
chief of the central granary 太倉令 26 (2)

■ **chamber**
chief of the inner chamber of the funerary temple 諸廟寢官令 15 (4)

■ **chamberlain**
chamberlain to the empress and the heir apparent 詹事 38 (6)

■ **chancellor**
chancellor*丞相 10 (1)

■ **chariot**
chief of light hunting chariots 路軨令 21 (3)

■ **city**
city gate scout 城門候 46 (8) | company commander of the city gate 城門校尉 46 (8)

■ **clan**
director of the imperial clan*宗正 24 (2) | master of the imperial clan 宗伯 24 (2)

■ **class**
officials of the middle two thousand picul class*中二千石 12 (1)

■ **colonel**
colonel of the guard*衛尉 18 (2)

■ **commandant**
chief commandant for requisitioning grain*搜粟都尉 27 (4) | chief commandant of cavalry for Feather and Forest Guard 羽林騎都尉 18 (4) | chief commandant of the imperial carriage 奉車都尉 47 (8) | chief commandant of the imperial horses 駙馬都尉 47 (8) | chief commandant of the left of the capital 左京輔都尉 36 (3) | chief commandant of the palace gardens 水衡都尉 40 (6) | chief

commandant of the right of the capital 右京輔都尉 36 (3)｜commandant of justice*廷尉 22 (2)｜grand commandant* 太尉 10 (1)｜master of titles chief commandant*]主爵都尉 45 (6)

■ **commander**

commander of gatekeepers in the household of the princess 諸公主門尉 25 (2)｜commander of the front over compulsory labour 前校令 38 (7)｜commander of the left over compulsory labour 左校令 37 (7)｜commander of the middle over compulsory labour 中校令 38 (7)｜commander of the rear over compulsory labour 後校令 38 (7)｜commander of the right over compulsory labour 右校令 38 (7)｜commander of the security force 中壘令 34 (2)｜company commander of archers 射声校尉 47 (8)｜company commander of cavalrymen of the Yueh tribe 越騎校尉 47 (8)｜company commander of nomadic horsemen 胡騎校尉 47 (8)｜company commander of the Ch'ang-shui garrison 長水校尉 47 (8)｜company commander of the city gate 城門校尉 46 (8)｜company commander of the gate for the northern garrison 中壘校尉 46 (8)｜company commander of the guard of the Imperial Forest Park 步兵校尉 47 (8)｜company commander of the picked troops 虎賁校尉 47 (8)｜company commander of the stationed cavalry 屯騎校尉 46 (8)｜master of titles military commander 主爵中尉 45 (6)｜military commander of the capital*中尉 34 (2)

■ **company**

company commander of archers 射声校尉 47 (8)｜company commander of cavalrymen of the Yueh tribe 越騎校尉 47 (8)｜company commander of nomadic horsemen 胡騎校尉 47 (8)｜company commander of the Ch'ang-shui garrison 長水校尉 47 (8)｜company commander of the city gate 城門校尉 46 (8)｜company commander of the gate for the northern garrison 中壘校尉 46 (8)｜company commander of the guard of the Imperial Forest Park 步兵校尉 47 (8)｜company commander of the picked troops 虎賁校尉 47 (8)｜company commander of the stationed cavalry 屯騎校尉 46 (8)

■ **compulsory**

chief of compulsory labour of the left 左司空令 30 (4)｜chief of compulsory labour of the right 右司空令 30 (4)｜commander of the front over compulsory labour 前校令 38 (7)｜commander of the left over compulsory labour 左校令 37 (7)｜commander of the middle over compulsory labour 中校令 38 (7)｜commander of the rear over compulsory labour 後校令 38 (7)｜commander of the right over compulsory labour 右校令 38 (7)

■ **construction**

master of construction works 将作大匠 37 (6)

■ **control**

chief of the control of boatmen 輯濯令 42 (7)｜chief of the control of the imperial parks 鉤盾令 31 (6)｜head of water control at the imperial parks 都水長 14 (4); 30 (5); 45 (7)｜head of the control of iron monopoly 鉄市長 27 (3)｜head of water control of the left at the imperial parks 左都水長 44 (7)

■ **cook**

head of cooking 廱厨長 45 (7)｜head of

cooks 胞人長 30 (5)
■ cooking
head of cooking 麛廚長 45 (7)
■ copper
chief of copper assessment 辯銅令 43 (7)
■ counselor
counselor to the keeper of the palace gate* 光禄大夫 16 (2) | palace counselor*中大夫 16 (2)
■ court
chief of the Ruolu court 若盧令 28 (4)
■ craftsmen
chief of the craftsmen of the imperial tombs 東園匠令 30 (5) | chief of the royal craftsmen 尚方令 31 (6)
■ craftwork
chief of craftwork 技巧令 43 (7)
■ credential
chief of the imperial credentials 符節令 27 (2)
■ criminal
chief of criminal affairs in the imperial family 都司空令 24 (2)
■ curio
chief of the imperial farm of curio offerings 御羞令 41 (7)
■ detention
chief of the Kuntai detention room 昆台令 30 (4) | chief of the detention room in the Palace of Sweet Springs 甘泉居室令 30 (4) | chief of the detention room in the palace 居室令 30 (4) | supervisor of the detention room 保宮令 30 (4)
■ director
director of dependent states*典属国 40 (6) | director of foreign guests 典客 23 (2) | director of foreign vassals*大鴻臚 23 (2) | director of rectitude*司直 10 (1) | director of the imperial clan*宗正 24 (2)

■ diviner
grand diviner*太卜令 13 (3)
■ document
master of documents and guests 中書謁者令 31 (5)
■ domestic
chief of the six kinds of domestic animals 六廄令 43 (7)
■ eastern
chief of the eastern weaving room 東織令 30 (5) | prefect in charge of the eastern area of the capital*左内史 43 (6)
■ emperor
chief of hunting archery for the emperor 佽飛令 29 (4) | chief of the emperor's horses 挏馬令 20 (2) | chief of the emperor's hunting assistants 左弋令 29 (4) | chief of the emperor's patisserie 湯官令 28 (3)
■ empress
chamberlain to the empress and the heir apparent 詹事 38 (6) | steward in the household of the empress 中長秋 39 (7)
■ envoy
chief of envoys 旅賁令 19 (2)
■ equalizing
chief of the transport office for equalizing prices 均輸令 26 (2), 41 (7)
■ erudit
erudit*博士 16 (4)
■ eternal
■ eunuch
chief of eunuchs 宦者令 33 (6)
■ examiner
grand examiner*大理 22 (2)
■ family
chief of criminal affairs in the imperial family 都司空令 24 (2)
■ famous

334

chief of famous steed 駿馬令 22 (3)
■ **farm**
chief of the imperial farm of curio offerings 御羞令 41 (7)
■ **feather**
■ **field**
chief of the fields of the imperial household 禁圃令 42 (7) | chief of the sacred field in the palace 籍田令 26 (3)
■ **fire**
chief of the maintenance of the sacred fire 別火令 23 (2)
■ **food**
chief of food offerings at the funerary temple 諸廟食官令 15 (4) | chief of food 食官令 40 (8)
■ **force**
commander of the security force 中壘令 34 (2)
■ **foreign**
chief of foreign languages 九譯令 40 (6) | director of foreign guests 典客 23 (2) | director of foreign vassals*大鴻臚 23 (2)
■ **forest**
chief commandant of cavalry for Feather and Forest Guard 羽林騎都尉 18 (4) | chief of the Imperial Forest Park 上林令 41 (6) | company commander of the guard of the Imperial Forest Park 步兵校尉 47 (8) | horseman of the Feather and Forest Guard*羽林郎 18 (4) | senior officer of palace corridor attendants for the Feather and Forest Guard 羽林中郎將 18 (4) | supervisor of the maintenance of ponds at the Imperial Forest Park 上林十池監 31 (5)
■ **front**
commander of the front over compulsory labour 前校令 38 (7)

■ **funerary**
chief of food offerings at the funerary temple 諸廟食官令 15 (4) | chief of the inner chamber of the funerary temple 諸廟寢官令 15 (4) | chief of the park of the funerary temple 諸廟園官令 15 (4)
■ **garden**
chief commandant of the palace gardens 水衡都尉 40 (6) | chief of wooden materials at the Eastern Garden 東園主章令 37 (7)
■ **garment**
chief of royal garments 御府令 32 (6)
■ **garrison**
company commander of the Ch'ang-shui garrison 長水校尉 47 (8) | company commander of the gate for the northern garrison 中壘校尉 46 (8)
■ **gate**
chief marshal of the palace gates 公車司馬令 19 (2) | chief of the gatekeepers in the household of the heir apparent 太子衛率 39 (7) | city gate scout 城門候 46 (8) | commander of gatekeepers in the household of the princess 諸公主門尉 25 (2) | company commander of the city gate 城門校尉 46 (8) | company commander of the gate for the northern garrison 中壘校尉 46 (8) | counselor to the keeper of the palace gate*光祿大夫 16 (2) | keeper of the palace gate*光祿勳 16 (2) | lord of the gate to the heir apparent 太子門大夫 37 (6) | senior officer of watch gates 戶將 17 (3)
■ **gatekeeper**
chief of the gatekeepers in the household of the heir apparent 太子衛率 39 (7) | commander of gatekeepers in the household of the princess 諸公主門尉 25

(2)

■ **gentleman**
palace gentleman*中郎 16 (3)

■ **goods**
head of the office of iron goods 鉄官長 44 (7); 45 (7)

■ **government**
chief of the government artisans 考工室令 29 (4)

■ **government**
master of government 大司徒 10 (1) | secretary of government 大司空 10 (1)

■ **grain**
chief commandant for requisitioning grain*搜粟都尉 27 (4) | chief of grain offerings and animal sacrifices 廩犧令 44 (6) | chief of the grain selectors 導官令 28 (3) | secretary in charge of grain*治粟內史 26 (2)

■ **granaries**
chief of granaries in the capital 都內令 26 (2)

■ **granary**
chief of the central granary 太倉令 26 (2)

■ **guard**
chief of the night guard in the household of the heir apparent 太子率更 39 (6) | chief of the palace guard 衛士令 19 (2) | colonel of the guard*衛尉 18 (2) | company commander of the guard of the Imperial Forest Park 步兵校尉 47 (8) | marshal of the palace guard 衛司馬 19 (2) | mounted guard to the heir apparent*太子先馬 37 (7)

■ **guest**
chief master of guests 謁者僕射 17 (3) | director of foreign guests 典客 23 (2) | master of documents and guests 中書謁者令 31 (5) | master of guests 謁者 17 (3)

■ **hall**
chief of the Long Halls Palace 永巷令 33 (6) | chief of the Long Halls Palace 永巷令 40 (7)

■ **harem**
supervisor of the harem*大長秋 40 (6)

■ head of water control of the left at the imperial parks 左都水長 44 (7)

■ **historian**
grand historian*太史令 13 (2)

■ **horse**
chief commandant of the imperial horses 駙馬都尉 47 (8) | chief of carriage and horses for the Eternal Palace 未央令 20 (2) | chief of cavalry horses 騎馬令 22 (3) | chief of the emperor's horses 挏馬令 20 (2) | chief of the heir apparent's horses 太子僕 39 (7) | chief of the imperial household's horses 家馬令 20 (2) | company commander of nomadic horsemen 胡騎校尉 47 (8) | horseman of the Feather and Forest Guard*羽林郎 18 (4)

■ **horseman**
horseman of the Feather and Forest Guard*羽林郎 18 (4)

■ **household**
chief of patrol in the household of the heir apparent 太子中盾 39 (7) | chief of the fields of the imperial household 禁圃令 42 (7) | chief of the gatekeepers in the household of the heir apparent 太子衛率 39 (7) | chief of the imperial household's horses 家馬令 20 (2) | chief of the kitchen and stables in the household of the heir apparent 太子廚廄 39 (7) | chief of the night guard in the household of the heir apparent 太子率更 39 (6) | commander of gatekeepers in the household of the

336

princess 諸公主門尉 25 (2) | grand butler of the imperial household 太官令 27 (2) | grand physician for the imperial household 太医令 27 (2) | retainer in the household of the heir apparent*太子舍人 37 (7) | steward in the household of the empress 中長秋 39 (7) | steward in the household of the heir apparent*太子家令 39 (7) | steward in the household of the princess 諸公主家令 25 (2)

■ hunting
chief of hunting archery for the emperor 佽飛令 29 (4) | chief of light hunting chariots 路軨令 21 (3) | chief of the emperor's hunting assistants 左弋令 29 (4)

■ husbandry
chief of animal husbandry 掌畜令 45 (6)

■ imperial
chief commandant of the imperial carriage 奉車都尉 47 (8) | chief commandant of the imperial horses 駙馬都尉 47 (8) | chief of criminal affairs in the imperial family 都司空令 24 (2) | chief of the control of the imperial parks 鉤盾令 31 (6) | chief of the craftsmen of the imperial tombs 東園匠令 30 (5) | chief of the fields of the imperial household 禁圃令 42 (7) | chief of the imperial credentials 符節令 27 (2) | chief of the imperial farm of curio offerings 御羞令 41 (7) | chief of the imperial household's horses 家馬令 20 (2) | chief of the imperial stables 大廄令 19 (2) | head of water control at the imperial parks 都水長 14 (4); 30 (5); 45 (7) | director of the imperial clan*宗正 24 (2) | grand butler of the imperial household 太官令 27 (2) | grand physician for the imperial household 太医令 27 (2) | head of the office of imperial burial places 均官長 13 (3) | head of the office of imperial burial places 均官長 30 (5) | head of water control of the left at the imperial parks 左都水長 44 (7) | imperial inquisitor in brocade robe 繡衣直指 11 (1) | imperial master of ritual 奉常 12 (2) | imperial secretary*御史大夫 10 (1) | master of the imperial clan 宗伯 24 (2)

■ implement
chief of ritual implements 私府令 40 (7)

■ inner
attendant in the inner palace*侍郎 16 (3) | chief of the inner chamber of the funerary temple 諸廟寢官令 15 (4)

■ inquisitor
imperial inquisitor in brocade robe 繡衣直指 11 (1)

■ interior
chief of the palace interior 內者令 33 (6)

■ interoffice
chief of interoffice liaison 寺互令 35 (2)

■ interpreter
chief of interpreters 訳官令 23 (2)

■ invocator
grand invocator*太祝令 12 (2)

■ iron
head of the office of iron goods 鉄官長 44 (7); 45 (7) | head of the control of iron monopoly 鉄市長 27 (3) | head of the office of salt, iron, and liquor taxes 斡官長 26 (3)

■ judge
judge of the left 左平 22 (2) | judge of the right 右平 23 (2)

■ junior
junior officer of the picked troops 期門 18 (4) | junior officer of the picked troops 虎賁郎 18 (4)

■ **justice**
commandant of justice*廷尉 22 (2)
■ **keeper**
chief of the gatekeepers in the household of the heir apparent 太子衛率 39 (7) | commander of gatekeepers in the household of the princess 諸公主門尉 25 (2) | counselor to the keeper of the palace gate*光禄大夫 16 (2) | keeper of the palace gate*光禄勳 16 (2)
■ **kitchen**
chief of the kitchen and stables in the household of the heir apparent 太子廚廄 39 (7)
■ **labour**
chief of compulsory labour of the left 左司空令 30 (4) | chief of compulsory labour of the right 右司空令 30 (4) | commander of the front over compulsory labour 前校令 38 (7) | commander of the left over compulsory labour 左校令 37 (7) | commander of the middle over compulsory labour 中校令 38 (7) | commander of the rear over compulsory labour 後校令 38 (7) | commander of the right over compulsory labour 右校令 38 (7)
■ **language**
chief of foreign languages 九訳令 40 (6)
■ **lead**
captain of the lead bannermen 式道候 35 (3)
■ **lesser**
lesser tutor to the heir apparent*太子少傅 37 (6)
■ **liaison**
chief of interoffice liaison 寺互令 35 (2)
■ **light**
chief of light hunting chariots 路軨令 21 (3)
■ **liquor**
head of the office of salt, iron, and liquor taxes 斡官長 26 (3)
■ **long**
chief of the Long Halls Palace 永巷令 33 (6) | chief of the Long Halls Palace 永巷令 40 (7)
■ **lord**
lord of the gate to the heir apparent 太子門大夫 37 (6)
■ **maintenance**
chief of the maintenance of the sacred fire 別火令 23 (2) | supervisor of the maintenance of ponds at the Imperial Forest Park 上林十池監 31 (5)
■ **marketplace**
head of the Chang'an four marketplaces 長安四市長 44 (7)
■ **marshal**
chief marshal of the palace gates 公車司馬令 19 (2) | grand marshal*大司馬 10 (1) | marshal of scouts 候司馬 19 (2) | marshal of the palace guard 衛司馬 19 (2) | marshal of the stationed unit 屯司馬 19 (2) | marshal*司馬 34 (2), 46 (8)
■ **material**
chief of stone materials 石庫令 37 (6) | chief of wooden materials at the Eastern Garden 東園主章令 37 (7)
■ **measure**
head of the office of weights and measures 內官長 24 (2)
■ **messenger**
chief of messengers 行人令 23 (2) | grand messenger*大行令 23 (2)
■ **metal**
chief of metal casting 鍾官令 43 (7)
■ **middle**

commander of the middle over compulsory labour 中校令 38 (7) | middle aide*中丞 11 (1) | officials of the middle two thousand picul class*中二千石 12 (1)

■ military

master of titles military commander 主爵中尉 45 (6) | military commander of the capital*中尉 34 (2)

■ minister

minister of revenue 大司農 26 (2) | nine highest ministers*九卿 11 (1) | three highest ministers*三公 10 (1)

■ monopoly

head of the control of iron monopoly 鉄市長 27 (3)

■ mounted

mounted guard to the heir apparent*太子先馬 37 (7)

■ musician

grand musician 太楽令 12 (2)

■ night

chief of the night guard in the household of the heir apparent 太子率更令 39 (6)

■ nomadic

company commander of nomadic horsemen 胡騎校尉 47 (8)

■ northern

company commander of the gate for the northern garrison 中塁校尉 46 (8)

■ offering

chief of food offerings at the funerary temple 諸廟食官令 15 (4) | chief of grain offerings and animal sacrifices 廩犧令 44 (6) | chief of the imperial farm of curio offerings 御羞令 41 (7)

■ office

chief of interoffice liaison 寺互令 35 (2) | chief of the office for the balanced standard 平準令 26 (2) | chief of the office of carriage 車府令 20 (2) | chief of the transport office for equalizing prices 均輸令 26 (2) | chief of the transport office for equalizing prices 均輸令 41 (7) | head of the office of imperial burial places 均官長 13 (3) | head of the office of imperial burial places 均官長 30 (5) | head of the office of iron goods 鉄官長 44 (7); 45 (7) | head of the office of salt, iron, and liquor taxes 斡官長 26 (3) | head of the office of weights and measures 内官長 24 (2) | head of the provincial offices in the capital 郡邸長 23 (2)

■ officer

junior officer of the picked troops 期門 18 (4) | junior officer of the picked troops 虎賁郎 18 (4) | senior officer of carriage 車将 17 (3) | senior officer of cavalry 騎将 17 (3) | senior officer of palace corridor attendants at the "Five Bureaus"五官中郎将 16 (2) | senior officer of palace corridor attendants for the Feather and Forest Guard 羽林中郎将 18 (4) | senior officer of palace corridor attendants for the picked troops 虎賁中郎将 17 (4) | senior officer of palace corridor attendants of the left 左中郎将 16 (3) | senior officer of palace corridor attendants of the right 右中郎将 16 (3) | senior officer of watch gates 戸将 17 (3)

■ official

official of the two thousand picul or over rank 比二千石 47 (8) | official of the two thousand picul rank*二千石 36 (3) | officials of the middle two thousand picul class*中二千石 12 (1)

■ palace

attendant in the inner palace*侍郎 16 (3) | chief commandant of the palace gardens 水衡都尉 40 (6) | chief marshal of the palace gates 公車司馬令 19 (2) | chief of palace corridor attendants 郎中令 16 (2) | chief of palace writers*中書令 31 (5) | chief of the detention room in the palace 居室令 30 (4) | chief of the palace guard 衛士令 19 (2) | chief of the palace interior 内者令 33 (6) | chief of the sacred field in the palace 籍田令 26 (3) | counselor to the keeper of the palace gate* 光禄大夫 16 (2) | keeper of the palace gate*光禄勳 16 (2) | marshal of the palace guard 衛司馬 19 (2) | master of palace writers 尚書令 27 (2) | palace corridor attendant 郎中 17 (3) | palace counselor*中大夫 16 (2) | palace gentleman*中郎 16 (3) | senior officer of palace corridor attendants at the "Five Bureaus"五官中郎将 16 (2) | senior officer of palace corridor attendants for the Feather and Forest Guard 羽林中郎将 18 (4) | senior officer of palace corridor attendants for the picked troops 虎賁中郎将 17 (4) | senior officer of palace corridor attendants of the left 左中郎将 16 (3) | senior officer of palace corridor attendants of the right 右中郎将 16 (3)

■ **park**
chief of the control of the imperial parks 鉤盾令 31 (6) | chief of the park of the funerary temple 諸廟園官令 15 (4) | head of water control at the imperial parks 都水長 14 (4); 30 (5); 45 (7) | head of water control of the left at the imperial parks 左都水長 44 (7)

■ **patisserie**
chief of the emperor's patisserie 湯官令 28 (3)

■ **patrol**

chief of patrol in the household of the heir apparent 太子中盾 39 (7)

■ **physician**
grand physician for the imperial household 太医令 27 (2) | grand physician*太医令 13 (3)

■ **picked**
company commander of the picked troops 虎賁校尉 47 (8) | junior officer of the picked troops 期門 18 (4) | junior officer of the picked troops 虎賁郎 18 (4) | senior officer of palace corridor attendants for the picked troops 虎賁中郎将 17 (4)

■ **pond**
supervisor of the maintenance of ponds at the Imperial Forest Park 上林十池監 31 (5)

■ **prefect**
left prefect of the capital*左馮翊 43 (6) | prefect in charge of the eastern area of the capital*左内史 43 (6) | prefect in charge of the western area of the capital*右内史 44 (6) | prefect of the capital*京兆尹 44 (6) | right prefect of the capital*右扶風 45 (6)

■ **price**
chief of the transport office for equalizing prices 均輸令 26 (2), 41 (7)

■ **princess**
commander of gatekeepers in the household of the princess 諸公主門尉 25 (2) | steward in the household of the princess 諸公主家令 25 (2)

■ **privy**
privy treasurer*少府 27 (2)

■ **provincial**
head of the provincial offices in the capital 郡邸長 23 (2)

■ **public**

340

職官名キーワード索引

master of construction works | master of public works 将作大匠 37 (6)
■ quarters
chief of the women's quarters 掖庭令 33 (6)
■ rank
official of the two thousand picul or over rank 比二千石 47 (8) | official of the two thousand picul rank*二千石 36 (3)
■ rear
commander of the rear over compulsory labour 後校令 38 (7)
■ rectitude
director of rectitude*司直 10 (1)
■ rendezvous
archery captain at the Rendezvous Gate 期門僕射 17 (4)
■ requisition
chief commandant for requisitioning grain*搜粟都尉 27 (4)
■ retainer
retainer in the household of the heir apparent*太子舎人 37 (7)
■ revenue
minister of revenue 大司農 26 (2)
■ ritual
chief of ritual implements 私府令 40 (7) | imperial master of ritual 奉常 12 (2) | master of ritual*太常 12 (2)
■ robe
imperial inquisitor in brocade robe 繡衣直指 11 (1)
■ room
chief of the Kuntai detention room 昆台令 30 (4) | chief of the detention room in the Palace of Sweet Springs 甘泉居室令 30 (4) | chief of the detention room in the palace 居室令 30 (4) | chief of the eastern weaving room 東織令 30 (5) | chief of the western weaving room 西織令 30 (5) | supervisor of the detention room 保宮令 30 (4)
■ royal
chief of royal garments 御府令 32 (6) | chief of the royal craftsmen 尚方令 31 (6)
■ sacred
chief of the maintenance of the sacred fire 別火令 23 (2) | chief of the sacred field in the palace 籍田令 26 (3)
■ sacrifice
chief of grain offerings and animal sacrifices 廩犧令 44 (6) | chief of performing sacrifices 祠祀令 40 (8)
■ salt
head of the office of salt, iron, and liquor taxes 斡官長 26 (3)
■ scout
city gate scout 城門候 46 (8) | marshal of scouts 候司馬 19 (2) | scout*候 34 (2), 40 (6)
■ secretary
chief secretary*長史 10 (1) | chief secretary*長史 10 (1) | imperial secretary*御史大夫 10 (1) | secretary in charge of grain*治粟内史 26 (2) | secretary of the censorate*侍御史 11 (1) | secretary to the heir apparent 太子庶子 37 (7)
■ security
commander of the security force 中壘令 34 (2)
■ selector
chief of the grain selectors 導官令 28 (3)
■ senior
senior officer of carriage 車将 17 (3) | senior officer of cavalry 騎将 17 (3) | senior officer of palace corridor attendants at the "Five Bureaus" 五官中郎将 16 (2)

| senior officer of palace corridor attendants for the Feather and Forest Guard 羽林中郎将 18 (4) | senior officer of palace corridor attendants for the picked troops 虎賁中郎将 17 (4) | senior officer of palace corridor attendants of the left 左中郎将 16 (3) | senior officer of palace corridor attendants of the right 右中郎将 16 (3) | senior officer of watch gates 戸将 17 (3)

■ **servant**
grand servant 太宰令 13 (2)

■ **spring**
chief of the detention room in the Palace of Sweet Springs 甘泉居室令 30 (4)

■ **stable**
chief of the imperial stables 大廄令 19 (2) | chief of the kitchen and stables in the household of the heir apparent 太子廚廄 39 (7) | head of stables 廄長 45 (7)

■ **standard**
chief of the office for the balanced standard 平準令 26 (2)

■ **state**
director of dependent states*典属国 40 (6)

■ **stationed**
company commander of the stationed cavalry 屯騎校尉 46 (8) | marshal of the stationed unit 屯司馬 19 (2)

■ **steed**
chief of famous steed 駿馬令 22 (3)

■ **steward**
steward in the household of the empress 中長秋 39 (7) | steward in the household of the heir apparent*太子家令 39 (7) | steward in the household of the princess 諸公主家令 25 (2)

■ **stone**
chief of stone materials 石庫令 37 (6)

■ **superintendent**
superintendent of the center 正監 22 (2) | superintendent of the left 左監 22 (2) | superintendent of the right 右監 23 (2) | superintendent-general of the capital 司隷校尉 45 (8)

■ **superintendent-general**
superintendent-general of the capital 司隷校尉 45 (8)

■ **supervisor**
supervisor of the detention room 保宮令 30 (4) | supervisor of the harem*大長秋 40 (6) | supervisor of the maintenance of ponds at the Imperial Forest Park 上林十池監 31 (5)

■ **sweet**
chief of the detention room in the Palace of Sweet Springs 甘泉居室令 30 (4)

■ **tax**
head of the office of salt, iron, and liquor taxes 斡官長 26 (3)

■ **temple**
chief of food offerings at the funerary temple 諸廟食官令 15 (4) | chief of the inner chamber of the funerary temple 諸廟寝官令 15 (4) | chief of the park of the funerary temple 諸廟園官令 15 (4)

■ **thousand**
official of the two thousand picul or over rank 比二千石 47 (8) | official of the two thousand picul rank*二千石 36 (3) | officials of the middle two thousand picul class*中二千石 12 (1)

■ **title**
master of titles chief commandant*]主爵都尉 45 (6) | master of titles military commander 主爵中尉 45 (6)

■ **tomb**
chief of the craftsmen of the imperial

tombs 東園匠令 30 (5)

■ **transport**
chief of the transport office for equalizing prices 均輸令 26 (2), 41 (7)

■ **treasurer**
privy treasurer*少府 27 (2)

■ **tribe**
company commander of cavalrymen of the Yueh tribe 越騎校尉 47 (8)

■ **troop**
company commander of the picked troops 虎賁校尉 47 (8) ｜ junior officer of the picked troops 期門 18 (4) ｜ junior officer of the picked troops 虎賁郎 18 (4) ｜ senior officer of palace corridor attendants for the picked troops 虎賁中郎将 17 (4)

■ **tutor**
grand tutor to the heir apparent*太子太傅 36 (6) ｜ lesser tutor to the heir apparent*太子少傅 37 (6)

■ **unit**
marshal of the stationed unit 屯司馬 19 (2)

■ **vassal**
director of foreign vassals*大鴻臚 23 (2)

■ **warehouse**
chief of the warehouses 倉廐令 40 (7)

■ **watch**
senior officer of watch gates 戸将 17 (3)

■ **water**
chief of the water police 都船令 35 (2) ｜ head of water control at the imperial parks 都水長 45 (7), 14 (4), 30 (5)

■ **weaving**
chief of the eastern weaving room 東織令 30 (5) ｜ chief of the western weaving room 西織令 30 (5)

■ **weight**
head of the office of weights and measures 内官長 24 (2)

■ **west**
chief of the western weaving room 西織令 30 (5) ｜ prefect in charge of the western area of the capital*右内史 44 (6)

■ **western**
chief of the western weaving room 西織令 30 (5) ｜ prefect in charge of the western area of the capital*右内史 44 (6)

■ **women's**
chief of the women's quarters 掖庭令 33 (6)

■ **wooden**
chief of wooden materials at the Eastern Garden 東園主章令 37 (7)

■ **works**
master of construction works ｜ master of public works 将作大匠 37 (6)

■ **writer**
chief of palace writers*中書令 31 (5) ｜ master of palace writers 尚書令 27 (2)

■ **yellow**
chief the Yellow Gate 黄門令 31 (5)

# 職官名関連和英表現集英和索引

## 凡例

この索引は英和対訳ではない。左列の英語に対し、右列の日本語で職官名関連和英表現集を引くと用例が見つかることを示している。

[例] alters of the soil and grain の意味を調べたいとき、本索引には alters of the soil and grain という項目がないが、alter, soil, grain のいずれかを職官名関連和英表現集で引くと「社稷」に行き着く。

abide 基づいて 86
abolish やめる 73
accomplish 功遂りて 102
accomplishment 官爵功名 83
accord 心を合わせて 129
account 外戚伝 82
accuse 讒言する 110
accused of 罪に坐し 108
accused of 罪を得る 108
acting 守 119
action 義務 88｜故事 97｜行事 105
actor 幸倡 103
actual 実 117
adamantly 固辞 97
adjudicator 黄帝李法 80
administration 裁判 108
administration 執法 117
admit 罪に伏し 108
admit 承服 125
admonish 諫める 85
admonisher 諫言の官 85
advance 遷任 135
advantage 乗じる 127
advice 従う 121

advisory 議曹 88
affluence 驕奢放縦 91
afoot いつわりのあること 70｜姦詐がある 83
age 後世に 98｜治道 116｜まっとうした 73
aide 守丞 119｜丞 127
airs 気 86
alert 機敏 86
allegiance 臣 130
alley 遊侠 172
allow ほしいままにし 72
altar 社稷 117
amnesty 恩赦 80｜赦令 117
amuse 戯れる 87
ancestral 高廟 105｜宗廟 120
anger 心が解け 128
annihilation 滅ぶ 170
announcement 告令 105
antiquity いにしえ 70
antiquity 古の 97
apartment 殿中 155
apology 謝す 117
appoint 為す 75
appraisal 賛に言う 110

appropriate 時の宜しき 116
approval 可 81
approval 制日可 132
armies 師旅 113
arms 股肱 97
around 左右の者 107
arrogance 驕兵 91
arrogant 驕慢放恣 91
arrogate ほしいままにして 72
arrogate もっぱらにし 73
arts 術 122
aside しりぞけ 71
aside 親に忍びない 130
ask 言上 97
assigned to 至った 113
associate 交われば 100
associate 一族 75
astronomer 羲和の官 88
astuteness 聡明 137
atone 贖う 128
attend 侍して 114
attendance 左右に 106
attendance 貴人 87
attendant 官属 84
attendant 従官 121

344

attendant 従史 121
attendant 掾 79
attention 好み 103
audacious 諫官 85
audience 謁見 78
audience 参朝 109
audience 朝見した 150
authorities 有司 171
authority 権勢 95
authority 権力 95
authority 生殺の大権 133
authority ほしいままに 72
authority 女主 123
avoidance 過つことなく 81
await 侍詔の 114
award 賜与 114
awe 威を示し 74
awe 威力 74
awe 仰ぎみるところ 91
awe 畏れた 75
awesome 威名 74
bait ばかにしてからかい 72
ban 禁錮 91
bandit 逆賊 88
banish 流され 174
banter ばかにしてからかい 72
barbarian 夷狄 74
barbarian 胡児 97
barbarian 胡人 97
be なる〈廷尉と～〉72
be made なる 72
bear 執り〈武器を～〉116
bear 怨みなく 79
Beautiful Companion 倢

仔 126
behavior 驕奢放縦 91
belittle 軽視 94
bell 鐘をつき 126
bellow 呼号して 97
belong 所有 122
benefit 国益 105
benevolence 仁恩 131
benevolence 義 88
benevolence 仁義 131
benevolent 仁人 131
benign 寛やか 84
berate 責める 134
best よいではないか 73
best よろしく…する 73
bewilderment わけがわからない 73
blame 咎 92
blame 罪 108
blame 罪を帰し 108
blame 罪 109
blessing ご恩 71
blessing 幸甚 103
blind 暗く 74
block 遮る 118
blood 骨肉 106
blow 回 81
bodily 形骸 93
bond 繋がれた 94
bowman 強弩将軍 90
brand 汚名を負わせ 80
breach 礼を責め 175
Bright Companion 昭儀 125
bring against 罪を得た 108
brocade 繡衣 121
brotherly 孝弟 103

build 城旦 127
bureau 諸官署 123
bureaus 官署 83
buzz さわぎ 71
by way of かかわる 70
byway 邑里 172
call 引見 75
campaign 義兵 88
campaign 応兵 80
campaign of zxarrogance 驕兵 91
cap 冠 83
capability 器の大きい 86
capital 京師中大夫 89
careful 察す 109
carpenter 将作 123
case 事案 114
case 冤獄 79
case 獄 106
cast 親に忍びない 130
castration 宮刑 88
casual 親疎 130
catty 黄金二十斤 80
catty 斤 91
cautious 謹む 91
cautious 事を謹む 114
censure 権をもっぱらにする 95
centuries 近くは 91
centuries 近古 91
chaos 混乱させ 106
chaos 傾け混乱させる 93
character 賢良 96
charge 罪 108
charge 執法 117
charge 罪を得た 108
charge 劾せられる 82
chariot 軽車 94

charity 恩恵 80
chivalrous 義俠 88
chosen 挙げられ 89
circuit 刺史 111
circumspect 慎み深さ 129
circumspection 自重する 116
circumstance みだりに 73
citizen 民〈吏～〉169
city gate 城門 127
civil 国容 106
claim 空名 92
clan 姓 132
classical 経術の士 94
clear 申す 129
clearing かかわり 70
clerk 掾 79｜左曹 107｜史 111｜侍曹 114｜諸曹 123｜主吏 119｜掌故の職 125｜少史 124
close 近習 91
coachman 御者 99
coat 珠襦 120
cold 寒心して 83
collateral zxline 支宗 113
come from 下す 81
Comely Person 美人 160
comings 進退 130
command 侍詔 114
command 詔して 125
command 親政 130
command 制詔して〈御史に〉132
command 詔 125
commentary 経伝 94
commercial 商利 123

commissary 軍市令 93
common 衆人 121
common 庶民 123
commoner 庶人 123
Companion 健伃 126
company 校王 104
competent 愚臣などには 92
competent 任える〈職責に〉158
compile 箇条書き 81
comply 具え 92
concern 憂慮 171
concubine 妾 123
condemn 譏る 87
condemn 処せられ 122
condemn 刑余の人 93
condemn 罪に当てる 108
condescend 心を留め 129
conduct 案内謁者 74
conduct 行い 104
conduct 行義 104
conduct 汚穢 80
conduct 孝行 103
confession 誣告 163
confinement 拘束 103
Confucian 儒生 120
Confucianism 儒術 120
confusion 乱し 173
consider 謹んで思いますに 91
considerable time 久しくして 88
constant 常道 128
consult 参与させ 109
contempt 辱め 128

contentment 安楽 74
contrive 人事 130
control 権力 95
convict 城旦 127
cord 印綬 75
corporal 刑余の人 93
corpse 屍体 113
correct 匡す 90
corrupt 軽薄 94
cottage 田も家も 155
council 枢機 131
course 間に 85
court 宮中 88
court 権力 95
court 謁見 78
court 召されて 123
courteous 礼譲 175
courtesy 礼意 175
courtier 群臣 92
courtier 舍人 117
courtier 臣〈群～〉130
craving 欲望 172
credential 璽〈符～〉116
credit 美徳 160
criminal 罪に当てる 108
criminal 獄 106
criminal 決曹 94
criticize 悪む 73
criticize 譖言する 110
crossbowman 彊弩都尉 90
crowd 衆人 121
crown prince 皇太子 104
crucial 枢機 131
curtain 幃幄 75
custom 故事 97
customary 故事 97
cut 腰斬 106

cut 処せられ 122
cut 斬して 110
danger 危うく 86
danger 傾け 93
danger 傾け混乱させる 93
dare あえて 70
dare 考えもしない 104
daring 勇 171
daring 義侠 88
dart 鉤弋 105
dead 死傷者 113
deal with 執行〈法を〉 117
death 死罪 113
death 死生 113
deceased 大行 142
decision 決裁 94
decline 固辞 97
decline 頽廃 146
deed 善行 136
deed 功遂りて 102
defense 固め 97
defiant 正視 133
defile 羞[はず]かしめ 121
defile 誣告し 163
deliberate 議す 88
deliberation 議郎 88
demerit 適[せ]められ 153
demerit 百適 161
demote 左遷 107
desert 去る 89
design 邪心 118
desire 欲望 172
devise 制定 132
devotion 節〈忠孝の〉

135
dictate 基づいて 86
dictate 礼 175
dictatorial 権をもっぱらにする 95
die 死罪 113
diligence 怠ることがない 141
diligent 謹み 91
director 刺史 110
disaster 災い 108
disaster 災患 108
disaster 災変 108
discharge やめさせる 73
discipline 修める 120
disgust 悪んで 73
disloyal 不臣 162
dismiss 退けて: 141
disorder 乱し 173
disorder 救う〈乱を〜〉 89
disorderly 乱脈 173
dispatch つかわし 72
dispatch 遣わし 96
disreputable 汚穢 80
distinguished 格別の 82
doff 冠を脱ぎ 83
dole out 財を散じて 109
don 着 147
draw up 上奏 126
drill 閲兵 79
driver 御者 99
drought 旱魃 85
duke 公侯 101
duly 上聞 127
duty 官職 84
duty 職掌 128
duty 職責 128
earn 号される 105

easygoing 寛容 84
edict 詔書 126
edict 遺詔 75
effect 実行にうつし 117
effect 匡正 90
embroidered 繍衣 121
eminence 尊貴の 138
eminent 名儒 169
emperor 主上 119
emperor 詔記 125
empty 空名 92
en masse 遮る 118
end 際限がなく 108
endanger 危うい 86
endeavor 心を尽くして 129
endless 往来の頻繁な 80
enfeoff 封ぜられ 164
enjoy 幸甚 103
enlightened 英明 77
enlist ひきい用いて 72
ennoble 爵位 119
enrage 恐れ憚り 90
enter 元服する 96
entrust 委任して 74
entrust 信任され 128
entrust 重用される 122
envoy 使者 110
envy 怨みの 79
epithet 号される 105
errand ほしいままに 73
error 過つことなく 81
error 過失 81
esteem 貴ぶ 86
estimation はかりしれない 72
etiquette 礼を責め 175
evil 悪 73

347

evil 姦をなす 83
evil 姦史 83
evil 姦邪 83
evil 悪吏 74
evildoer 悪を誅して 73
evildoer 悪人 73
exacting 威厳をつくろう 74
examination 省察する 125
examine 監察する 85
examine 観る 85
exceed すぎない侍郎 71
excess 盛ん 133
execute 斬った 110
expedition 出兵 122
expedition 微行 160
expose あばきたて 70
extravagance 奢侈 118
face 讒言する 110
failure 過失 81
fall 亡国 167
fall away 瓦解し 83
fame 官爵功名 83
family 氏 113
family 一族 75
family 家属 81
family 私家 113
far-sighted 遠見の明 79
fashion 孝弟 103
fashion 謙遜して 96
fault 罪に陥る 108
fault 匡す 90
fault 過を益す 81
favor 貴幸少府 86
favor 寵愛され 150
favoritism 驕奢放縦 91
fear 疑われる 87

fearful 恐れ憚り 90
felicitous 善祥 136
feudal 郡国 93
fief 国君 105
filial 孝弟 103
filial 孝行 103
filial 孝行 103
fill 具備され 92
fine りっぱな 73
firewood 鬼薪の刑 87
first これによる 71
fit 称う 125
flagrant 驕奢放縦 91
flesh 骨肉 106
flock 盛大で 133
flourish 盛ん 133
flow 酒肉の宴 120
foil 摧か[くじき] 108
folkway 風俗 164
follow 従います 121
follower 家属 81
follower 一味 75
follower 群臣 93
follower 従官 121
force 出兵 122
foreign 四夷 111
forge 矯[いつわり] 90
form 形骸 93
found 建て 94
four seas 海内 82
friend 故旧 97
friendship 交わって 99
frivolous 軽薄 94
from … on down はじめとして 72
from … on down 以下 74
frustrate 逆らい 88

fund きわまりなく 70
fundamental 道理 157
funerary 園邑 79
gain 商利 123
garrison 護軍 99
gate 郭門城門 82
gather 招致 125
gather 謁見 78
gather 遮る 118
gather ほしいままに 72
generous 深厚 129
gentle 温柔 80
gentleman 士 111
gentleman 諸公 123
gentleman 士大夫 112
gentleman 志士 113
gentleman 処士 122
gentleman 賢人 96
gentleman 公子 102
get along with 意見が合わず 75
ghosts 鬼神 87
gift 賜与 114
gift 賜い 113
give all … to 帰す 86
glance 気色 86
glance 正視 133
glib-tongued 便嬖の 165
gods 鬼神 87
goings 進退 130
good 恭謙で 90
good 治まった 116
good 安治 74
good 綱紀 104
good 賢良 96
good at 書を善くする 123
goodness 賢良の科 96
government 国益 105

government 権力 95
government 官 83
government 県官 95
government 公府 102
government 宮人 88
government 安治 74
government 治乱 116
government 国容 106
government 郡 93
government service 骸骨 82
governor 郡守 93
governor 州牧 120
graciously 幸いに 103
grain 社稷 117
grain 穀物 106
grandmother's 外戚家 82
grandson 子孫 112
grant 更生 103
grave 重大な 122
gravity and zxrespect 敬重 94
great-grandson 皇曾孫 104
grudge 怨みなく 79
guard 戸衛 97
guard 宿衛 122
guilt 罪に伏し 108
guilty 遺漏のない 75
hand ほしいままに 72
hand ゆだねられず 73
hand 手書 120
happen たまたま 71
happening 異聞 75
happy 敬んで 94
hardly 十死一生の大事 121
harm よいではないか 73

harmony 和を得る 177
harmony 和合し 177
harmony 和睦 177
harmony 治平 116
haste すみやかに[…し ない] 71
head 右に出ようとする九卿 76
heart 寒心して 83
heart 好み 103
heartless 残酷 110
heavens 三光 109
heed 前向きに 136
heed 従う 121
heir 子孫 112
heir apparent 皇太子 104
hemp-robed 布衣のやから 162
higher 上 126
highest 至尊 113
highly 称賛する 125
hold 執り 116
home 国内 106
honesty 清廉潔白 133
honor 気節を好む 86
honor 尊ぶ 138
hoodwink 欺 87
hoodwink 誣欺 153
hook 鉤弋 105
hope 考えもしない 104
hope 国君の後継者 106
horseman 騎士 87
hound 排斥 159
house 宗室 120
household 王室 80
humbled くじき 71
humiliate 誣欺 153
humility 謙譲の心 96

humility 不遜 162
humility 礼譲 175
ideal 義 88
ideal 志を損ない 113
ignorant 愚かにも 92
impeccable 清廉潔白 133
imperial 詔 125
imperial 詔獄 125
imperil 危うくし 86
imperturbable 偶儻大節 153
impose upon 課す 81
improvement 匡正 90
in attendance 侍った〈左右に〜〉114
in charge of 守校尉 119
in person 自ら公主 116
incite 扇動した 135
incognito 微行 160
indict 劾せられる 82
indictment 詔獄 125
indirectly 遠回しに 79
indiscretion 過失 81
inferior 下の者 81
inferior 上下 126
inflexible 剛毅 105
influential 豪強 105
injured 死傷者 113
injustice 冤獄 79
injustice 冤罪 79
inmate 繋がれている者 94
inner 枢機 131
inner 宮門内 88
inner wall 城門 127
insolence 傲慢 105
inspection 閲兵 79

349

| | | |
|---|---|---|
| inspection 巡狩 122 | knight 徒〈任侠の〉 155 | life 寿命 120 |
| inspector 刺史 111 | labour 城旦 127 | light 鑑みる 85 |
| instruction 遺詔 75 | lack 遺漏のない 75 | light 軽重 94 |
| insult 辱め 128 | lady 官女 84 | lightly 軽んじ 94 |
| insult 侵害侮辱長公主 128 | lady 宮女 88 | liking 見初めて 95 |
| | lady 貴人 87 | line 支宗 113 |
| insure 安んじ 74 | lance-bearer 執戟 116 | list 箇条書き 81 |
| integrity 清廉 133 | lane 邑里 172 | listen to 従う 121 |
| intent 大切にする 145 | lane 街里 82 | literary 経典 94 |
| intercede 取りなす 119 | lascivious 淫楽 75 | live まっとうした 73 |
| interested 嗜む 114 | late もとの 73 | lodge 郡邸 93 |
| interview 謁見 78 | later その後 71 | lodge 若舎 119 |
| interview 引見 75 | laudable 美わしい 160 | lofty 偶儻大節 153 |
| intimidating させない 71 | law 執法 117 | long 久しく 88 |
| invariably 必ず 160 | law 綱紀・法度 104 | longevity 寿命 120 |
| investigate 獄を治める 106 | law 制度 132 | look 気色 86 |
| investigate 取り調べた 119 | law 禁令法網 91 | look 軽んじ 94 |
| | law 厳刑峻法 96 | look after 監督保護 85 |
| investigation 案験 74 | lawlessness 姦邪 83 | look after 保護～ 165 |
| invite 呼び戻す 97 | lead 従え 121 | look over 観る 85 |
| irreverence 不敬 161 | league 気脈を通じる 86 | look up to 仰ぎみるところ 91 |
| issue 告令 105 | lean 春 122 | |
| item by item 箇条書き 81 | learn 探知して 146 | lord 君侯 92 |
| jail 獄丞 106 | learning 学識 83 | lord 子大夫たち 112 |
| joy 苦楽を共にする 92 | learning 経術の士 94 | lord 国君 105 |
| judge 決曹 94 | lease 更生 103 | love 好み 103 |
| justice 裁判 108 | legs 股肱 97 | love 信愛 128 |
| keeper 嗇夫 128 | lesser 群臣 93 | lower 下 80 |
| killer 刺客 110 | lesson 経術 94 | loyal 心をつかんで 129 |
| kind 罪不道 109 | letter 尺牘 119 | loyalty 節〈忠孝の〉 135 |
| kindness 恩恵 80 | letter 書付け 123 | luminary 三光 109 |
| kindness 仁恩 131 | letter 書嚢 123 | luxury 奢侈 118 |
| kindness 陰徳 75 | letter 璽書 116 | magistrate 県令 95 |
| king 校王 104 | letter 上書 126 | magnified 過りを益す 81 |
| kingdom 郡国 93 | levy 課税 81 | Majesty 皇帝 104 |
| knight 遊侠 172 | licentious 淫乱 75 | make use of 因りて〈これに～〉 75 |
| knight 豪侠 105 | life 生殺の大権 133 | |
| | life 死生 113 | malefaction 邪 118 |

man 士 111
man 衣冠の士 75
manhood 元服する 96
manners 恭謙で 90
mark 王たり 80
marquis 侯 100
marquise 王侯 80
marquise 公侯 101
marriage 外家 82
masses 元々 96
maternal 外戚 82
maternal 外祖父 82
matter 諮問 113
matter 下して 81
matter 案験 74
mealymouthed 佞臣 158
mean 浅薄 135
meat 酒肉の宴 120
mediocrity 中人 148
meet with たまたま 71
meet with 謁見 78
memorial 諸曹 123
memorial 詔書 126
memorial 奏上 136
memorial 章奏 125
memorial 上疏して言った 126
mentor 師傅 113
mercy 恵む 93
mercy 聖徳仁恩 134
mere およそ［･･･で］70
mere 幼弱 172
merit 功 102
merit 功徳 103
meritorious 功臣 102
message 詔記 125
message 書類袋 123
messenger 使者 110

messenger 従史 121
metropolitan area 京師 89
military 史 111
minister 諫官 85
minister 郡臣 93
minister 臣 129
minister 卿人夫 90
minister 卿の身分 90
minister 君臣 92
ministry 公府 102
misstep 蹉跌 107
mistreat 侵害侮辱長公主 128
model 治まった 116
modest 謙遜して 96
modest 謙遜恭謹 96
money 財を散じて 109
mother's 外戚家 82
mourn 服喪 164
moved 好み 103
mumble 暗誦 74
nation 国家の大綱 105
nature 人がら 130
nature 人となり 130
nature 人情 130
nature 剛毅 105
nature 資質 113
net 禁令法網 91
never-ending zxfund きわまりなく 70
no more than すぎない 71
nobility 諸公 123
noble 貴人 87
notation 署名 123
notch 刻 105
numerous 盛大 133

observe 察す 109
occasion 賜る 114
occurrence 小変事 124
ode 詩経 113
offender 姦人 83
office 位におり 74
office 官を失い 83
office 郡府 93
office 仕官 110
office 卿の身分 90
office 官名大司馬 84
office-holder 位にある者 74
officer 士卒 112
official 悪吏 74
official 史 111
official 卿大夫 90
official 掾 79
official 下僚 81
official 官吏 84
official 群臣 92
official 守丞 119
official 諸吏 123
official 有司 171
official 士人 112
official 小臣 123
official 小役人 124
officials 士大夫 112
old まっとうした 73
on any zxerrand ほしいままに 73
opinion 謹んで思いますに 91
oppose 諫める 85
order 治まった 116
order 匡正 90
orderly 嗇夫 128
ordinary 士人 112

351

originally であった 72
outer 郭門城門 82
outing 外出し 82
overall zxstrategy 策 109
overbearing 驕慢 91
overseer 家令∷81
overseer 監 84
oversight 過失 81
oversight 遺漏のない 75
overstep 越えず 79
overstep 踰える 171
pacify 平定 165
palace 宮門内 88
palace 後宮 97
paragon 風格がある 164
pardon 赦し 117
pardon 赦令 117
park 園邑 79
pass 関吏 85
pass away 薨じる 105
past 今年の 106
past 古今の 97
paternal 外戚の 82
patron 手厚い 119
peace 治道 116
peace 安んじる 74
peace 安治 74
peace 和睦 177
peace 治平 116
pearl-sewn 珠襦 120
people 庶民 123
performance 実 117
permanent 真令 129
persecute 賊殺 138
personally ひそかに 72
personnel 主吏 119
perspicacity 聡明 137
persuade 暁す 91

pervert 天性を変え 154
petition 上書 126
petty 少史 124
petty 小臣 123
petty 小役人 124
petty 小故 123
petty 小変事 124
physician 侍医 114
picul 官二千石 84
piety 孝行 103
pity 何と不幸な 81
plane 上 126
plane 下 80
platform 堂皇 156
plea 愬え[うったえ] 136
please ほしいままに 73
please 驕盛 90
please 御意にかなう 98
plot はかる 72
point できなくなる 72
policy 儒術 120
polite 字 116
populace 群衆 92
populace 大衆 144
portent 善祥 136
portent 咎[とが] 92
portent 祥 125
portent 天変 154
position 至尊 113
position 衣冠の士 75
position 位 74
position なる 72
position 爵位 119
post なる典属国 72
post 位 74
post 官 83
post 官属 84
post 職を辞す 128

posthumous 諡された 114
pouch 書嚢 123
pouch 書類袋 123
pour forth 往来の頻繁な 80
poverty and zxwant 困苦欠乏 106
power 権をもっぱらにする 95
power ほしいままに 72
power 権勢 95
power 権柄の臣 95
power 権力 95
powerful 貴人 86
powerful 豪強 105
practice 故事 97
practiced 習熟し 121
praise 名声 169
precedent 掌故の職 125
precedent 綱紀・法度 104
precedent 故事先例 97
precedent 故事 97
prefecture 郡県 93
premature 夭折 172
presence 引見 75
present 古今の 97
present 謁す胞人胞人 78
present 賞賜 126
present 賜い 113
prime minister 宰相 107
prime minister 守相 119
princess 公主 102
principle 志士 113
principle 清廉潔白 133
principle 治乱 116
principle 国家の大綱

352

105
private 私家 113
privy 厠 114
procedures 国容 106
professional 刺客 110
prominent 長者 151
promote 右に出ようとする
九卿 76
pronouncement 賛文 110
proper 遇する 92
proportion 小変事 124
propriety 匡正 90
prosperity 治道 116
province 郡県 93
province 郡国 93
province 郡国 93
provincial 郡 93
provincial 州牧 120
provincial zxdirector 刺史 110
public 仕官 110
public 仕官して 110
public service 骸骨 82
punishment 刑余の人 93
punishment 厳刑峻法 96
punishment 処断する 122
pursue 敬慕し 94
pursuit 本業 168
quarter 官署にいる 83
quarter 四方 111
quarter 宿衛 122
quarters 後宮 98
quarters 後庭 98
question 正視 133
quirk みだりに 73
rank 官 83
rank 高爵のもの 105

reach できなくなる 72
reach なる 72
read と述べ 72
read 観る 85
read 言う 96
realize 察知 109
rebel 逆賊 88
rebellious 傲慢不遜 105
recent 近くは 91
recent 近古 91
recite 暗誦 74
record 治績 116
rectify 身を正し 130
rectify 救う〈乱を〜〉 89
rectitude 匡し 90
reduced to 削られ 109
refer 号する 105
refer 下して 81
refer 案験 74
refer to 下す御史 81
refer to 諮問 113
reform 匡正 90
refused しようとしない 71
regicide 主上殺し 119
regulation 故事 97
regulation 制度 132
reign 上にあり 126
rein 綱紀 104
relation 交渉 100
relative 外戚 82
relative 宗族 120
release 骸骨 82
relief 救う 88
remark 言う 96
remonstrance 諫めて 85
repair 城旦 127
report 上奏 126
report 上聞 127

reprimand 諫めた 85
reprimand 諫争 85
resign 職を辞す 128
respect 敬重 94
respect 敬われ 93
respect 重んじ 121
respect 崇ぶ 131
respect 遇する 92
respectfully 謹んで 91
respite 時節をはずれ 116
response 応兵 80
responsibility 重用される 122
responsible せい 71
restore 匡正 90
retainer 客 88
retainer 舎人 117
retainer 食客 128
retirement 処士 122
retiring 謙遜して 96
review 考査 104
rewarded 授かり 120
rider 騎士 87
right もっとも 73
right 義 87
righteousness 義 88
righteousness 仁義 131
rightful 嫡嗣として 147
ripe まっとうした 73
rise にまでなり 72
rise 掌握 125
robe 繍衣 121
robe 衣〜 75
robe 祭服 108
rule 常道 128
rule 綱紀 104
rule 軍法 93

rule 郡治 93
ruler 下す 81
ruler 君 92
ruler 主 119
ruler 少主 124
ruler 君臣 92
ruling 宗室 120
sacred 賢聖 96
sacrifice 祭服 108
sad 頽廃 146
safety 安んじ 74
safety 安楽 74
sage 聖主 134
sage 聖人 134
sages 賢聖 96
salute 拝謁 159
say 言は 96
scheme 図む 131
scheme 陰謀 75
scholar 士〈経術の〉 112
scholar 儒生 120
scholar 経術の士 94
scold 譴責 96
seal 璽〈符〜〉 116
seal 璽書 116
seal 印綬 75
secret 枢機 131
secret 陰謀 75
secretary 史 111
secretary 主簿 119
select 挙げられ 89
self-effacing 礼譲 175
sense 前後をとりちがえ 136
sentiment 親疎 130
sentiment 心ばせ 128
serious 罪不道 109
serious 軽重 94

servant 臣[偃] 130
serve 侍って 114
serve 従事 121
serve 宿衛 122
serve 徇う[したがう] 122
service 仕官して 110
service 功徳 103
service 願う 85
set out 酒宴を催し 120
severe 厳刑峻法 96
shabby 末流 168
shallow 浅薄 135
shine 光輝の少ない 100
shortcoming 過失 81
shout 呼号して 97
sickroom 暴室 167
side 左右に 106
sinister 邪心 118
size 九市之宮 92
skin 身を全う 130
slander 誣告し 163
slanderer 讒言する者を 110
slandering そしり 71
slanderously 讒言する 110
slaughter 殺戮 109
slave 宮人 88
slave 家婢 81
slave 奴 156
slight 些細ではない 106
soil 社稷 117
solace 安撫する 74
soldiers 士卒 112
sometime その後 71
sometimes 遠くは・・・近くは・・・ 79
son 子孫 112

sorrow 苦楽を共にする 92
spare 減じて 96
speak 称賛する 125
speak out 直言諫争 151
speculation 怪しんで 81
spell 風雨 164
spirits 鬼薪の刑 87
spirits 鬼神 87
spite 小故 123
splendid 盛徳 133
squeeze 銭を貪り 136
state 郡国 93
state とある〈司馬法に〜〉・・・ 72
state 自然の勢い 116
state 治平 116
statute 制度 132
stern 厳格 96
stern 威厳をつくろう 74
steward 舎人 117
stood in zxawe 畏れた 75
stop 禁止 91
strait-laced 法度をまもる 167
strategy 策 109
stream 往来の頻繁な 80
street 遊侠 172
street 街里 82
strike 鐘をつき 126
strike down 斬って 110
strong 豪 105
strong 豪傑 105
strong man 豪侠 105
study 師事した 113
stupid 愚臣は 92
subject 不臣 162
subject 処断する 122

submit 章奏 125
submit 上書する 126
submit 上疏して言った 126
subordinate 属官 138
subside 心が解け 128
subtle 機微 86
subversion 傾け混乱させる 93
succeed 継いだ 94
succeed 後を嗣ぐ
succeed 襲す 121
successor 少主 124
suddenness にわかに 72
suggestion 献策 95
sullen むすっとして 73
summarily ついに 72
summon 出頭する公車 122
summon 召されて 123
summon 引見 75
superior 上 126
supervision つかさどらせる 72
supply 穀物 106
supporting 護軍 99
surmount 救う 89
surround 親近 130
survive 十死一生の大事 121
suspicion 怪しんで 81
swaggering 傲慢 105
sycophantic 邪詔 118
symbolic 象徴 126
take after 似ている 114
talent 器量 86
talent 賢材 96
tarnish 志を損ない 113

task 職責 128
teachings 経術 94
team 四頭立て 111
temple 高廟 105
temple 宗廟 120
temporarily 試守して 113
ten 十死一生の大事 121
testamentary 遺詔 75
text 経書 94
text 経伝 94
text 師法 113
text 賛文 110
the throne 上書 126
think 意志 75
third year 三年 109
thought 思い 113
thought 急[うなが]す 88
throne 漢室 84
throne 皇位 104
bewilderment わけがわからない 73
tile 瓦解し 83
title 官爵功名 83
title 官名大司馬 84
title 爵位 119
titled 位に列なって 74
topped 高蓋 105
tour 巡狩 122
train 教えさとす 90
transfer 遷り 135
travel 巡行 122
treason 大逆 142
treasonable 大逆無道の 142
treasury 御府 99
treat 重んじる 121
treat 遇する 92

trial 議 88
tribe 四夷 111
tribute 朝賀 150
troop 精兵 134
trouble 危うい 86
trouble 擾乱 128
true facts 実情 117
trust 信愛 128
try 試守して 113
turn over to 下る 81
tutor 師傅 113
two 斬して 110
two 腰斬 106
unassuming 謙遜恭謹 96
unassuming 恭謹 90
unbending 剛 105
unbending 剛毅 105
underlying 大局 142
understanding 機微 86
understanding 感知する 84
unknown 陰徳 75
unprincipled 大逆無道の 142
unrestrained 放縦 167
unruly 驕慢放恣 91
unruly 驕奢放縦 91
unruly 淫乱 75
unruly 放恣 167
unusual 小変事 124
unwilling しようとしない 71
unworthy 資格がなく 113
uphold 奉じる 166
upright 正直 133
upright 方正の科 167
upset 困って 106

355

| | | |
|---|---|---|
| urgent 急[うなが]す 88 | way 王道 80 | 124 |
| usurp 簒奪 110 | wealth 厚い 103 | youthful 少主 124 |
| vagrancy 流離 174 | wealth 財多ければ 109 | |
| venture 謹んで 91 | welfare 大策 143 | |
| venture 存じます 138 | well along 春秋が高い 122 | |
| vermilion 徤朱く 156 | | |
| versed in 精通した 133 | well-spoken 話がじょうず 177 | |
| vest 権力をもって 95 | | |
| vestment 衣服 75 | western 右方の地 76 | |
| vestment 衣服の制 75 | wholesome 資質 113 | |
| vestment 所服 122 | wild みだりに 73 | |
| vicious 邪諂 118 | wine 酒宴を催し 120 | |
| vie 争うて 137 | wine and meat 酒肉の宴 120 | |
| vile 便嬖の 165 | | |
| village 園邑 79 | wisdom 承服 125 | |
| villainous 悪吏 74 | wisdom 遠見の明 79 | |
| villainous 姦臣 83 | woman 女主 123 | |
| virtue 空名 92 | women 後宮 97 | |
| virtue 功徳 103 | women's 後宮 98 | |
| virtue 盛徳 133 | women's 後庭 98 | |
| virtuous 賢大夫 96 | works 経典 94 | |
| visit 行幸 104 | worship 尊ぶ 138 | |
| visit 行幸 104 | worth 賢士 96 | |
| volunteer 願う 85 | worth 賢良の科 96 | |
| vying 争うて 137 | worth 賢良 96 | |
| waggery 滑稽 83 | worth 賢材 96 | |
| waist 腰斬 106 | worthies 賢聖 96 | |
| wait 左右にいて | worthless 軽薄な 94 | |
| wall 城旦 127 | worthless 徒〈任侠の〉155 | |
| wall 郭門城門 82 | | |
| wandering 遊侠 172 | worthy 賢 96 | |
| want 困苦欠乏 106 | worthy 賢者 96 | |
| warm 深厚 129 | worthy 賢人 96 | |
| warm 温柔 80 | wrangling 小故 123 | |
| warning 徇う[したがう] 122 | wrongdoing 罪不道 109 |
| | you 卿 90 | |
| warning 戒め 82 | young 公子 102 | |
| watch 監察 84 | Young Attendant 少使 | |

■編者紹介

藤田　敏正（ふじた・としまさ）
　翻訳家
　1952年生　京都大学大学院農学研究科修了

冨谷　至（とみや・いたる）
　京都大学人文科学研究所　教授
　1952年生　京都大学大学院文学研究科修了

中国古代官制和英用語集
2011年7月25日　初版第1刷発行

　　　　　編　者　藤田　敏正
　　　　　　　　　冨谷　　至
　　　　　発行者　齊藤万壽子
　　〒606-8224 京都市左京区北白川京大農学部前
　　　　　発行所　株式会社　昭和堂
　　　　　　　　振込口座　01060-5-9347
　　　　　TEL(075)706-8818／FAX(075)706-8878
　　ホームページ http://www.kyoto-gakujutsu.co.jp/showado/

　　　　　　　　　　　　　　　印刷　亜細亜印刷
　©藤田敏正・冨谷至　2011
　　　　ISBN 978-4-8122-1111-3
　　　＊落丁本・乱丁本はお取り替え致します。
　　　　　　　Printed in Japan

本書のコピー、スキャン、デジタル化等の無断複製は著作権法上での例外を除き禁じられています。本書を代行業者等の第三者に依頼してスキャンやデジタル化することは、たとえ個人や家庭内での利用でも著作権法違反です。